T3-BPX-805

Foundations of Decision Theory

DISCARDED

University of Winnipeg, 515 Portage Ave., Winnipeg, MB R3B 2E9 Canada

DISCARDED

HD
30.23
F72
1994

Foundations of Decision Theory

Issues and Advances

Edited by
Michael Bacharach
and
Susan Hurley

BLACKWELL
Cambridge MA & Oxford UK

Copyright © Michael Bacharach and Susan Hurley, 1991

First published 1991
Paperback edition 1994
Reprinted 1994

Blackwell Publishers
108 Cowley Road, Oxford, OX4 1JF, UK

238 Main Street
Cambridge, Massachusetts 02142, USA

All rights reserved. Except for the quotation of short passages for the purposes
of criticism and review, no part of this publication may be reproduced, stored in
a retrieval system, or transmitted, in any form or by any means, electronic,
mechanical, photocopying, recording or otherwise, without the prior permission
of the publisher.

Except in the United States of America, this book is sold subject to the
condition that it shall not, by way of trade or otherwise, be lent, re-sold, hired
out, or otherwise circulated without the publisher's prior consent in any form of
binding or cover other than that in which it is published and without a similar
condition including this condition being imposed on the subsequent purchaser.

British Library Cataloguing in Publication Data

A CIP catalogue record for this book is available from the British Library.

Library of Congress Cataloging in Publication Data

Foundations of decision theory: issues and advances/edited by
Michael Bacharach and Susan Hurley.
p.   cm.
Includes bibliographical references and index.
ISBN 0-631-17236-X (hardback)
0-631-19063-5 (paperback)
1. Decision-making.   2. Social sciences—Decision making.
I. Bacharach, Michael.   II. Hurley, S. L. (Susan L.)
HD30.23.F72   1991
003'56-dc20   90-38493
                                                        CIP

Typeset in 10 on 12 pt English Times
by Colset Private Limited, Singapore
Pinted in Great Britain by Athenæum Press Ltd, Newcastle upon Tyne.

This book is printed on acid-free paper

Contents

Introduction

Issues and Advances in the Foundations of Decision Theory

Michael Bacharach and Susan Hurley

1 FIVE ISSUES IN THE FOUNDATIONS OF DECISION THEORY

Decision theory, in the broad sense here employed, includes the study of individual decision-making, the theory of games, social choice theory, and certain philosophical approaches to the study of rational action. It is about the ways in which decisions are related to the decision-maker's aims and to her beliefs about how her options serve her aims. It has two special features. First, its subject is the rational agent. Second, it aspires to produce abstract theories of rational agency: systematic constructions in which all is explicit, deduced from axioms that are valid independently of the topic of the decision-making. The most famous of these theories are expected utility theory and the theory of games.

Decision theory is unfinished. Indeed, despite its brilliant achievements, it finds itself today in a state of turbulence, far from agreed solutions; some even doubt that there are solutions to be found to many problems of rational choice. And so it is inevitable that attention is turned increasingly toward the foundations of decision theory. These include its methodological commitments, the possible limitations of formalization, the meanings of its primitive terms, its basic assumptions, and its ultimate goals.

It may be useful to distinguish five broad headings under which issues raised in this volume fall: the structure of attitudes; deliberation; humanity; individualism; and determinacy.

The first of these topics, the *structure of attitudes*, includes questions about the restrictions on the attitudes of the decision-maker – her beliefs and preferences, subjective probabilities and utilities – that rationality imposes. One such question is whether, for the agent to be rational, her preferences must be exclusively focused on the *consequences* of her options, and this immediately raises the further question of how much it is proper to include in the description of the consequences as distinct from, say, the paths which lead to them. A second question, which is closely related to the first, concerns whether the agent's preferences have the important property of *separability*, relatively to one or another way of describing the consequences. When what makes a prospect desirable has several components, its desirability is said to be separable over those components if the way that it varies with one is independent of the levels of the others. Separable preferences are "componentwise-independent" preferences. They are in this sense *context-independent* preferences: preferences about any one component are independent of the context set by the levels of the other components. A third major question of attitudinal structure, which pervades the theory of games, is how decision-makers' knowledge of one another should be treated. How, for instance, should we model the idea that in games players set out with beliefs about each other's tendencies to make mistakes? Are there things that rational players believe that one another believe, and so on to higher degrees? What should be assumed to be "common knowledge"? A fourth question of attitudinal structure is whether there is warrant for the (increasingly popular) Bayesian assumption that rational players have probability distributions over all matters of concern, including one another's decisions.

One way, at least, in which a rational decision is related to the decision-maker's beliefs and preferences is that she must *deliberate* her way to it from (initial values of) them. The question of what these deliberations are actually like has until recently been conspicuous by its neglect in decision theory. Bringing deliberation in has a potential to resolve problem cases. For example, in some cases the process of deliberation throws up new information for the deliberator, and this information can steer her toward what seems to our intuitions the right conclusion or resolve an otherwise indeterminate problem.

The *humanity* of the decision-maker has at least two aspects: her *boundedness* and her *culture*. Thinking about the real-time process of deliberation reminds us of the bounded nature of the intellectual capacities of mere human beings: the finiteness of their powers of inference, of the time at their disposal, and of their inventories of beliefs. This human boundedness forces on our attention a methodological question: whether decision theory, notwithstanding these human bounds, will progress best by assuming away some or all of them because it will thereby gain in tractability what it loses in realism. Recent work in which deliberation is modeled explicitly suggests that even an extreme idealization of inferential powers fails to deliver the goods in the shape of determinate solutions to games. It has turned out that there cannot be game-playing Turing machines which in general complete their computations (see for example Binmore, 1987, 1988). Such discoveries seriously undermine the methodological case for idealization. They suggest too that, if we are to avoid the conclusion that rational action in games is impossible, it may be necessary to move away from the conception of rationality of traditional decision theory toward a more naturalistic conception in which "ought" implies "can."

Decision theory studies precisely stated *decision problems*, the specification of which includes ascriptions to the decision-maker of definite beliefs and preferences: the *attitude data* of the decision problems. These conventionally exclude many aspects of cultural common sense. For example, in games as traditionally specified the attitude data are limited to preferences over the game's outcomes, plus knowledge of the rules of the game and of the other players' rationality, preferences, and similar knowledge. The problem is to show that it follows from the attitude data that a rational agent decides so and so. It is not regarded as solved if, in identifying the correct decision, appeal is made to attitudes not included in the attitude data, even if the further attitudes are quite consistent with these. So we may not use the fact that every real player has the general knowledge her culture gives her, such as knowledge of which arrangements are salient or traditional in that culture and so provide foci of coordination. The limitation to attitude data which omit such knowledge dehumanizes the decision-maker in the opposite direction to the traditional idealization of her powers: instead of exaggerating her resources, it understates them.

Decision theory began with the individual and expected utility theory, and it has continued to treat the expected utility maximizing individual as a basic normative reference point. However, a number of questions arise about the relationship between individual rationality and game-theoretic rationality. We usually think of individual decision theory as in a sense prior to game theory, but at several points in the present volume we are led to question whether games may be embedded within supposedly individual decision problems. Moreover, there may be doubt about the determinacy of individual rationality of the traditional sort in the interactive setting of games. In a game, the decision-maker knows that the extents to which her options serve her aims depend on the choices of other players who are similarly placed with respect to her. So the attempt to decide what to do by applying principles of individual rational choice seems only to lead to an endless regress of mutual prediction.

Von Neumann and Morgenstern (1944), however deeply conscious they were that games are decision problems *sui generis*, nevertheless set out to derive a theory of rational play in games from one of rational individual decision-making. Their successors have not deviated from the faith that this can be done, which we may call *individualism* in game theory. One way in which individualism figures in foundational discussion is that it leads game theorists to look to new developments in individual theory, such as "causal decision theory" and the notion of "ratifiability," for clues to the resolution of deep problems in game theory. Among such problems, the most discussed of the last decade has been the "refinement problem," the problem of formulating a concept of equilibrium in games that refines out intuitively irrational solutions admitted by less stringent equilibrium concepts.

A *solution* of a decision problem is a decision of the agent that is related to the attitude data in a way that is rational in some interestingly defined sense. The general topic of the *determinacy* of decision theory – the fifth foundational theme in decision theory distinguished here – concerns the size of the set of solutions. A small but growing number believe that the problem of games, as traditionally posed, is indeterminate: for the typical game there are many solutions in this sense. Some even regard the project of individualism in game theory as a mistake, responsible for such indeterminacy: game-theoretic rationality is a silk purse, expected utility maximization a sow's ear. But the blame for indeterminacy may also lie elsewhere: the traditional attitude data may misspecify the attitudes of real decision-makers, underendowing them with information. Recent years have seen the rise of a radically different, Bayesian way of specifying a game, which attributes to the players prior probability distributions over all relevant matters, not excluding the decisions of the other players. One effect of this move is to shift the place where indeterminacy shows from the solution of the game to the specification of attitudinal structure, since we have little idea how to select appropriate prior distributions.

The papers which make up this volume concern these five interlocking topics in the foundations of decision theory, in varying combinations. In the rest of this chapter we shall briefly describe their contents and discuss some of the issues that, singly or when juxtaposed, they raise. The papers are written by economists and philosophers, and are addressed to all those interested in the foundations of decision theory, whatever their home disciplines. They illustrate our conviction that the study of rationality has much to gain by triangulation from different disciplines – by efforts to overcome barriers of jargon and style between disciplines, to ponder the interpretation and significance of formal arguments, and to conduct informal argument in the light of formal results. All the same, some contributions willy-nilly involve technicalities of particular disciplines;

another purpose of this chapter is therefore to provide some introduction to these more technical matters.

The varying approaches of the papers by Broome, Levi, Machina, and Pettit to two issues about attitudinal structure – consequentialism and the description of consequences – are described in the next section. This leads into the discussion of the notion of context-dependent evaluation and its relation to the various senses of "consequentialism" in section 3. Section 4 concerns aspects of attitudinal structure which figure in Roemer's paper on the problem of a benevolent planner with imperfect knowledge of individuals' preferences. Section 5 turns to deliberation: Smith focuses on its necessary boundedness, and Skyrms uses a deliberational model as a way of embedding game theory in individual decision theory. A number of interrelated ideas in contemporary game theory, including the new "refined" equilibria, are described in section 6. Ratifiability and causal decision theory – further needed background to the papers of Shin and Harper – are explained in section 7. These papers take up the individualist baton, setting out to show that refined equilibria have a basis in principles of rationality and causal decision theory. The theme of Sugden's paper – the role of culture in making rational decision-making determinate in games – is discussed in section 8.

2 CONSEQUENTIALISM, SEPARABILITY, AND DESCRIPTION

In problems involving dynamic or sequential choice, the decision-maker cannot make irrevocable decisions before uncertainty is resolved, that is, before Nature makes her moves. Because of this, sequential choice problems allow us to distinguish between an individual's planned choices and her actual choices when she arrives at a point of decision after the resolution of some uncertainty by Nature. Now, it is known that, on certain assumptions, an agent is an expected utility maximizer if and only if her preferences respect the Independence Axiom, which requires that one prefers A to B if and only if one prefers a probability p of A plus a probability $1 - p$ of C to a probability p of B plus a probability $1 - p$ of C. In Machina's framework, obeying the Independence Axiom is equivalent to having preferences with a certain *separability* property with respect to mutually exclusive possible states of the world. Loosely speaking, preferences are separable with respect to two "locations," such as two persons, two time periods, two possible states of the world, two types of good, etc., if preferences relating to what happens at one location do not depend on what happens at the other; that is, what happens at one location can be evaluated independently of what happens at the other. Thus they are separable with respect to mutually exclusive states if what would happen in one state (e.g. in the case of a Head) can be evaluated independently of what would happen in another (e.g. in the case of a Tail).[1] It is often argued that an agent who does not maximize expected utility because her preferences violate Independence and hence are not separable in this way will, in problems involving sequential choice, be dynamically inconsistent in her choices in a manner that permits a bookmaker to make a "Dutch book" against her, that is, to get her to accept a set of bets that would guarantee that he won money at her expense.

Mark **Machina** explains the way in which such arguments implicitly assume one of the features of *consequentialism* in Peter Hammond's sense, which has the effect (at least with respect to traditional descriptions of consequences) of requiring decision-makers to ignore risks that they have already borne in deciding what to do next. A consequentialist decision-maker, finding herself at a choice node in a decision tree, "snips off" and ignores the part of the tree preceding the current choice node, which represents risk already borne, what would have been the case had Nature chosen differently. She assesses her options at the node by considering the alternative possible continuations, apart from the context of these continuations in the structure of the entire decision tree, for her assessments of the options are a function only of her evaluation of terminal consequences. Machina explains that such snipping off essentially involves a dynamic version of the very separability of preferences that non-expected utility maximizers reject; it is hardly surprising that if separability is imposed in this way *ex post* on decision-makers who start out with nonseparable preferences, inconsistency results. Machina demonstrates that when non-expected utility preferences over uncertain prospects are treated in dynamic choice settings in the same manner that economists treat sure-prospect preferences that are nonseparable across time, commodities, or any other dimension, dynamically inconsistent behavior does not result; so dynamic consistency does not entail snipping off.

Machina admits that consequentialism in Hammond's sense would apply to decision-makers with dynamically nonseparable preferences if we redescribed consequences to incorporate distinctions concerning already borne risk. However, he points out that unrestricted redefinition of consequences would render the expected utility model and the Independence Axiom irrefutable. He concludes by suggesting an emerging consensus in the separability literature on three points: (a) issues about separability must be relativized to given descriptions of consequences; (b) separability may be required by rationality given an inclusive enough description of consequences; (c) however, such inclusive descriptions may not be those economists typically deal with or are able to observe.

Isaac **Levi** presents a complex view of various senses of "consequentialism" and their implications. Both Independence and the principle that the preference relation over acts is an *ordering* (that is, transitive and complete) are disputed in the rational choice literature. Levi notes Hammond's claim to settle these disputes in favor of both principles by showing that they are implied by "consequentialism," which Hammond regards as a principle almost beyond question in modern normative decision theory (though certainly not in ethics). But Hammond's claim depends on the way he defines consequentialism: *Hammond consequentialism* amounts to the reduction principle that a rational agent in a sequential choice problem pursues a given course of action, as represented in *extensive form* (that is, with the sequential aspects of the problem, the order of choice and chance nodes, and the probabilistic structure of the various possible paths to various possible outcomes explicitly represented as in a decision tree) if and only if the corresponding course of action in the associated *normal form* (which abstracts from the sequential aspects of the problem) is rational. Hence problems with the same normal form must have the same solution, though their extensive forms, and so the paths through them to the outcomes, may differ. Thus the reduction principle amounts to this: an agent should choose her next act as if she had control over her whole path. Now this principle implies that, in sequential decision problems, the rational agent's preferences satisfy two principles: they form an ordering, and they are separable in the way that Machina characterizes in terms of snipping off. On Hammond's account, therefore, it is impossible for a consequentialist to deny either Ordering or Independence.

Levi sets out to show here that Hammond's impossibility conclusion is false with respect to Ordering, for it depends on his particular, and particularly strong, conception of consequentialism. He explains the difficulties that arise when an agent attempts to integrate predictions of how she will decide between her current options into her deliberations about those options; these difficulties cut against the reduction of extensive to normal form. He proceeds to distinguish various types of consequentialism from Hammond consequentialism, and considers their interrelationships. *Weak consequentialism* requires that the evaluation of options is determined by the evaluation of consequences and their conditional probabilities given that the options are implemented; whatever is an object of value qualifies as a consequence, and no substantive restrictions are placed on the description of consequences, which may include descriptions of acts themselves. This sense of consequentialism is so weak as to be unavoidable; any decision problem can be given at least one weak-consequentialist representation.

A stricter, and in Levi's view overly restrictive, sense of consequentialism – *strict consequentialism* – enforces a sharp distinction between descriptions of acts and of consequences, and requires that the value of a consequence does not depend on which act brings it about; rather, the value of acts is dependent only on that of their consequences. Savage's well-known system is strictly consequentialist. It is also "state functional": it requires that there be some fixed partition of states such that all acts can be described as functions from the state-descriptions of this partition to strict consequence-descriptions. While the state-functional requirement is disputed, strict consequentialism is widely accepted in decision theory; in Levi's view this is the strongest version of consequentialism that can be regarded as almost unquestioned in decision theory (whether rightly is another matter).[2] Thus Levi proceeds to compare the implications for decision theory of strict consequentialism and of Hammond consequentialism.

Levi argues by reference to the example of a potential addict, who will be unable to abstain once she has tried the drug and so does not have control over her whole path, that Hammond consequentialism is stronger than strict consequentialism. Strict consequentialism would recommend that the addict abstain initially, but this would seem to violate consequentialism in Hammond's sense, unless the potential addict regards herself as in effect playing a game with another agent, her later self. But Levi considers that the latter tack would undermine the applicability of Hammond consequentialism to sequential choice in general. Levi also argues, by reference to another example involving a decision-maker with conflicting reasons for choice, that strict consequentialism, as distinct from Hammond consequentialism, does not imply Ordering. In both cases the argument turns on issues about what factors are under the deliberating decision-maker's control and what acts she ought therefore to recognize as options in sequential choice problems, which Levi regards as having been unduly neglected.

Strict consequentialism distinguishes act- and consequence-descriptions, and insists that the value of consequences should not depend on the act associated with them; in this way it restricts the acceptable descriptions of consequences. Levi indicates that strict consequentialism supports the Independence Axiom.[3] Machina, on the other hand, suggests that unrestricted redescription of consequences could be used to defend a form of Independence, dynamic separability (though with the danger of rendering it irrefutable).

In fact the two points are consistent. To clarify this we should distinguish *formal* from *substantive* separability; arguments for the former are not necessarily arguments for the latter (as Hammond certainly recognizes). Unrestricted description of consequences would allow us to preserve the form imposed by the Independence axiom on the agent's preferences, at the expense not only of empirical unrefutability but also of the substantive principle of dynamic separability. The latter implies that one's preferences ought not to be sensitive to a specific sort of thing, namely risks already borne. This substantive principle is sacrificed if consequences may be described without restriction, because distinctions with respect to risks already borne can be represented in the refined description of consequences in such a way that there is no formal violation of snipping off. If such refined descriptions of consequences are prohibited, then formal violations of snipping off will re-emerge as part of the theory's *description* of agents with dynamically nonseparable preferences (relative to "naive" descriptions of consequences). But when the prohibition on redescribing consequences is combined with the adoption of snipping off as a normative formal principle, it expresses a *normative* commitment to substantive dynamic separability. In brief, unrestricted description of consequences may protect formal separability, as Machina suggests, but restrictions on the description of the consequences, excluding the description of path and risks borne *en route* to them, as in strict consequentialism in dynamic contexts, are needed to give practical force to the formal principle and guarantee substantive separability.

Hammond's understanding of consequentialism in terms of the reduction of extensive to normal form, which leads to both snipping off and separability over mutually exclusive states of the world for sequential choice problems, has been salient in recent decision-theoretic literature. The question naturally arises what the relationship is of Hammond's sense of consequentialism, and issues about separability, to the various senses of consequentialism current in ethics. No simple answer to this question is immediately forthcoming, since decision theory assumes *agent-relative* evaluation of consequences – evaluations that differ from agent to agent – and so requires a sense of consequentialism compatible with agent relativity; one begins to wonder what, if anything, justifies the use of the same term in decision theory and ethics.

John **Broome**'s discussion contributes to the identification and classification of the different senses of consequentialism used in ethics. He distinguishes issues about the teleological character of ethical theories from both issues about the intrinsic value of acts as opposed to their consequences and issues about agent neutrality as opposed to agent relativity. He understands "teleological" ethics as (a) taking the right act to be the best act and (b) judging the goodness of an act by combining its various good and bad features in some way that involves a notion of good with certain structural features, such as the transitivity of "is better than."

Broome elaborates a three-dimensional grid of locations of goodness: at persons, at different times, and at possible states of nature. Overall goodness is obtained by combining the goodness at locations first within and then across these three dimensions. Parallel structural questions arise in each dimension about (a) separability, whether the goodness of what happens at any one location (to one person, at one time, in one state of nature) can be evaluated independently of what happens at other locations, and (b) distribution, whether there is value in more equal distributions of goodness across locations. It can be shown that if the answer to (a) is the same for two dimensions, the answer to (b) must be the same for them as well. The justification of teleological ethics, Broome suggests, should proceed not by simply identifying an externally given good to be promoted, but by identifying and justifying the structural features imposed by the notion of goodness.

He considers the relationship between practical rationality and goodness, and their relative priority, arguing that while the structure of goodness follows that of rationality – for example, in the transitivity feature – the structure of rationality in turn depends on the content of goodness. (Related claims about decision-theoretic rationality are elaborated in the contribution by Philip Pettit, while Robert Sugden's argument prompts the question whether the classical conception of rationality in games as neutral with respect to ethical issues is adequate.)

The tangle of issues discussed in these articles and elsewhere under the heading of consequentialism prompts further questions. Is there merely a series of family resemblances linking the issues, or is there some deep unifying issue standing behind them? What, if anything, do issues about dynamic separability and the snipping off of decision trees, about the reduction of extensive to normal form, about the distinction between act- and consequence-descriptions, about agent relativity versus agent neutrality, and about teleology and the relationship between the good and the right have in common? Why have these issues often been run together under the head of "consequentialism"? If they cut across each other, what is the diagnosis of the running together? The papers by Machina, Levi, and Broome expound various senses and some of their limitations and relationships, but it remains to find a single perspective from which all these issues fall into a clear pattern of relationships with one another. We shall return to this matter below.

Pettit addresses the question of the extent to which Bayesian decision theory explicates the central sound core of commonsense psychology, with utility and subjective probability as the idealized representations of desire and belief. Pettit argues that in fact decision theory neglects and abstracts away from some important features of commonsense psychology. In particular, it ignores (though it does not rule out) the "desiderative structure" of commonsense psychology: the way in which the desires that we have for various prospects are determined by the properties we think those prospects have – the friendly atmosphere that we think a certain job has, the moral quality that we think a certain act has – and our desires for properties. Decision theory tends to take prospect desires as given and to concentrate on their consistency while neglecting the way in which they are determined by the agent's values – the properties she cherishes in prospects.

In fact, Pettit argues, desiderative structure offers the best explanation of a variety of phenomena: internal conflict in desires, the distinction between simple desire and desire *prima facie* (that is, desire for something that has some property in so far as it has that property); the "non-extensionality" of sentences ascribing desires (the fact that the truth or falsity of statements about what is desired may depend on the way the object of desire is described); the way in which reasons for people's desires are often demanded of them. Moreover, the result of decision theory's neglect of desiderative structure is that it is incomplete, it is not autonomous, and it is not practical. Pettit highlights the way in which property desires may help in specifying prospects in a way that enables decision theory to apply determinately to the problem a decision-maker faces. His discussion is in harmony with suggestions made by Broome, Machina, and others about the need for sensible restrictions on admissible descriptions of consequences; issues about formal principles of rationality are only defined with respect to given descriptions. Pettit also argues that decision theory provides at most a *test* for the rightness of decisions rather than a *guide* to the right decision, since its use as the latter would involve a fundamental departure from the normal basis of decision-making provided by desiderative structure. When someone comes to prefer one option to alternatives, she often prefers it for an evaluative property other than that of merely answering in a certain way to her prospect desires; this is revealed by the different ways that prospect and property desires fare under certain challenges.

3 CONTEXT DEPENDENCE AND THE PROTO-CONSEQUENTIALIST ASSUMPTION

All the above contributors touch on the way in which formal questions in decision theory, such as those about the normative status of principles of separability or transitivity, depend on substantive questions about what counts as an acceptable way of specifying consequences. Now these substantive questions often (though by no means always) seem to have a particular character: they often contrast seemingly intrinsic character-izations of objects of preference with characterizations that are in various ways nonintrinsic. A nonintrinsic characterization of a good might be one in terms of the feelings it is associated with in combinations with other goods (disgust at lemon juice in coffee, in Machina's example), or in terms of what the alternatives to it happen to be, or in terms of counterfactuals about what goods (or bads) one might have ended up with instead if Nature had taken a different course (that is, risks borne *en route* to getting this good), or in terms of the character of the act which led to this good, or in terms of whether the agent is oneself or someone else. Preferences are often sensitive not just to the intrinsic characteristics of a good but also, in these various ways, to the context in which the intrinsically characterized good is located.

The theorist has a choice of whether to represent this sensitivity formally, relatively to intrinsic characterizations of the goods, or instead by means of context-involving characterizations of the goods. We have seen, for example, how there may be violations of the Independence Axiom with respect to austere intrinsic characterizations of consequences but not with respect to richer, context-involving characterizations of them; the violations disappear because the context dependence that produces them under the austere description is absorbed into the richer description. Context dependence is relative: what counts as context relative to an intrinsic characterization of outcomes may be absorbed into context-involving characterizations of outcomes, so that with respect to the latter no context dependence obtains. So an important class of these substantive questions is that of questions about the acceptability of context-involving characterizations of various kinds: can what happens at one "location," characterized intrinsically, properly be evaluated atomistically, independently of its context?

The notion of context dependence may be helpful in ferreting out answers to the questions posed earlier about what, if anything, may unify and motivate the various senses of consequentialism. Now decision-theorists may wish to avoid imposing substantive restrictions to the effect that only intrinsic features of goods should be of concern to a rational person, and for this reason may, in order to preserve formal properties like separability and transitivity, tolerate various types of context-laden characterization of consequences. However, there is a tendency, and not just among decision-theorists, to assume that there must be some level of description of decision problems at which all acceptable distinctions of context relative to naive characterizations of goods have been captured, and such that no context dependence of evaluation relative to it can be rational. At some level of description, it is assumed, a level which reflects all possibly relevant distinctions as to context, the atomistic form of evaluation, which is overly restrictive when applied to naive characterizations, must become appropriate.

We shall refer to this as the *proto-consequentialist* assumption. It seems to lie behind many of the positions that have been labeled consequentialist, and different types of consequentialism seem to reflect different positions about what forms of context-dependent evaluation are acceptable and hence what the favored level of description is. A hypothesis is that various senses of "consequentialism" can be regarded as implicitly specifying the favored level of description in different ways, thus ruling in or out various types of context dependence. Agent neutrality, for example, rules out evaluations of consequences that depend on who the agent is, in particular whether the agent is oneself or not; snipping off rules out evaluations of consequences that depend on the probabilistic structure of paths to them through decision trees; and so on. But the difference senses, on this hypothesis, have in common the higher-order proto-consequentialist assumption that there is some such level of description, even if they disagree about what it is.

Note the way in which this assumption quantifies over levels of description and relevant distinctions: there is some level of description of decision problems that captures all possible relevant distinctions. This is a strong claim, which does not follow from the weaker claim that for each possible relevant distinction there is some level of description that captures it. It does not follow because it might be that, for any level of description, further context dependence relative to that level might arise in a new case. (For this reason it is not clear whether the hypothesis of the previous paragraph would apply to Levi's "weak consequentialism," since Levi claims this to be unavoidable, whereas the proto-consequentialist assumption might be false.)

Consider a version of Diamond's well-known example, discussed by Machina and Pettit in this volume. The decision-maker in this case prefers a situation in which each of two children has a 50 percent chance of getting the only piece of candy to either child getting the candy for sure, on the grounds that the first situation is fairer. She thus may seem to have preferences that violate the Independence Axiom. But since the decision-maker has these preferences because she cares about the fairness of the procedure that leads to one of the children's getting the candy, we can avoid the violation by incorporating distinctions of fairness into our descriptions of the consequences and so reflecting this contextual concern explicitly.

So far so good. But now consider the possibility of a decision problem involving higher-level context dependence, that is, context dependence relative to a level of description of consequences that reflects not naive goods like children getting candy but goods like fairness, which are themselves context-laden goods in relation to naive goods. What is to prevent second-order context-dependence of various possible types from arising at this level of description for a reflective agent, an agent who is aware that fairness is of value to her, perhaps even of more value to her than other more concrete goods? For example, she might choose, out of relief at having avoided a possible serious Diamond-style unfairness, to celebrate by seeing a film rather than working, whereas she would have chosen work in the absence of the possible unfairness.[4] The unfairness itself is, as in Diamond's case, a matter of what might have happened in relation to more intrinsic goods; the relief is a matter of what might have happened in relation to what might have happened.

Higher-order context dependence of one type may embed first-order context dependence of other types in various ways. These complicated formal structures need not be understood by the decision-maker in order for her to be intuitively sensitive to the distinctions they represent, any more than the formal structure of Diamond's example needs to be understood by a decision-maker in order for her to be sensitive to the value of fairness. Perhaps some of these forms of higher-order context dependence can be rejected as unacceptable, as corresponding to no intuitively accessible distinction. However, we seem to have no guarantee that there must be some level of description at which no intuitively accessible form of still higher-level context dependence can arise. It is at least logically possible that, for any level of description, intuitive sense can be made of some cases of context-dependent evaluation relative to that level. Thus proto-consequentialism is a substantive assumption.

Consider the way in which the proto-consequentialist assumption implicitly features in the following argument in favor of the Independence Axiom as a principle of rationality (a version of an argument suggested by Broome in conversation with the editors):

1 When someone seems to violate the Independence Axiom, she is

drawing a distinction with respect to already borne risk, or, more generally, with respect to the probabilistic contexts of outcomes. Outcomes located in one probabilistic context are being distinguished from outcomes intrinsically the same but located in a different probabilistic context.

2 Either this distinction is rational to make and be sensitive to or it is not.

3 If it is, then it should be reflected in the description of the consequences; all contextual distinctions with respect to outcomes that it is rational to draw should be incorporated in the individuating descriptions of the consequences.

4 With respect to this full description of the consequences, no further rational violations of Independence can occur, since violations reflect distinctions between consequences and all those rational to make have already been reflected in the individuation of consequences.

5 If the distinction is not rational, then *ex hypothesi* the person is being irrational.

The proto-consequentialist assumption seems to lurk behind steps of this argument. Having identified its role in the argument, we can ask several questions.

(a) Suppose that the assumption is true, and that the level of description that fully captures context dependence in the specification of consequences does preserve some formal principle of evaluation, such as separability. What reason is there, nevertheless, to favor that level? If we have a choice between different ways of describing the same thing, that is, a choice as to whether to represent context dependence formally or via description of consequences, why choose the latter method of description? What is the advantage of preserving an atomistic form of evaluation if its substance is nonatomistic or context-involving? If people are in fact sensitive to risks already borne or probabilistic contexts, why not let the form of decision theory explicitly model this instead of insisting that this sensitivity belongs strictly to the description of consequences? Why should the probabilistic structure which accounts for the distinction being drawn by someone who seems to violate Independence be collapsed into the terminal characterization of consequences in order to preserve expected utility theory, rather than left explicitly represented by the formal structure of a non-expected utility theory? Are there general methodological principles that require this? Is there some fundamental normative appeal to formal context independence such that the burden of proof is on the other side? Is the burden to be placed pragmatically, as a matter of theoretical investments already made, as in expected utility theory? Is it that the form imposed by Independence is theoretically more fruitful, leads to more results, than any alternative would?

(b)   Do the answers to the questions under (a) vary with the type of context sensitivity in question? Take the analogies between separability in different dimensions discussed by Broome: how should we decide the appropriateness of representing separability or its absence formally rather than via redescription of consequences, in the cases of separability across possible states of the world, times, and persons respectively?

(c)   What argument can be given for the truth of the proto-consequentialist assumption in the first place? Is there any reason to think that at some level of description all intuitively sensible context dependence will or must be captured, and none will arise with respect to that level of description in a new decision problem? Or might the possibility of reflection on values always give rise to new possibilities of context dependence? What are the sources of failures of atomistic evaluation at naive levels of description, and what reason is there to think that they are avoidable at higher levels? If in fact context dependence results in part from contextual sensitivity of an essentially formal character, then (unless reflectiveness can at some point be ruled out) at no level will redescription avoid it for all cases.

Note that the admission that there must be constraints on what count as acceptable distinctions between consequences in order to avoid empty, irrefutable theories does not entail the truth of the proto-consequentialist assumption, for at any given level of description such constraints could rule some distinctions out but leave others in play. Note too that the falsity of the proto-consequentialist assumption would not make for a vicious regress or for radical indeterminacy in practical decision-making, since for any given decision problem there could be some definite level of description adequate to represent it and all forms of context dependence relevant to it, even though there were no one level adequate for all decision problems.

(d)   Lastly, what substantive arguments are there for or against context sensitivity of various types? On what basis can it ever be correct to refuse to individuate consequences with respect to contextual features of some kind? This question, about what distinctions it is rational to draw, should be distinguished from the question raised under (a) above, about what is the right way to represent the rational agent's sensitivity to these distinctions, whatever they may be.

An issue underlying the above clusters of issues at several points is this. Much of decision theory and game theory presupposes a sharp distinction between the agent's choices at a time and all else: between choice nodes and chance nodes, or between decisions by a person at one time and at later times, or between decisions by one person and by other persons she is interacting with. Take the first distinction and consider its relation to the question of context dependence. It is a characteristic feature of deliberation about conflicting values that how one trades one value off against another in the choice one faces may depend, via rational deliberation, on consistency with how one would trade them off against one another in different choice situations, hypothetical as well as actual: what one should here and now decide may depend on what one *would do* if one were in a different state of nature (see Hurley, 1989, part III). This is a sort of context dependence of choices within a network of actual and hypothetical choices. Compare this with cases of nonseparability across mutually exclusive states of nature, where what one should do here and now may seem to depend on what *would happen* in a different state of nature. The relationship between these two kinds of context dependence, and indeed the very distinction between them, depend in turn on the distinction between what one may do, should the occasion arise, and what may happen to one, because of what others or Nature may do. How is this distinction to be drawn? In the background are thorny issues about free will, which cannot be pursued here. But the answer may in part be a matter of how far one identifies oneself with events "in the world": if what would "happen" in a different state of nature is a matter of what someone else does, for example, and that someone else is one's spouse, or oneself at another point in time, the here-and-now decision may inherit, because of one's identification with the "other" decision-maker, the context dependence characteristic of rational deliberation, namely, of choice within a network of choices.

4 INDIVIDUAL AND GROUP RATIONALITY

We often take groups of individuals, such as nations or football teams, to have interests and to be better or worse off. The interests of the group we relate in varying ways to the interests of its members, and thus, if we think the members' interests consist in satisfying the members' preferences, to the levels of these satisfactions. Very often, the group welfare is taken to be increasing in the latter, that is, it is described by a social welfare function which satisfies the Pareto principle. But this is far from meaning that there is perfect agreement, as in the case of the idealized team.

The question arises whether the individuals' behavior conduces to the group interest. If the individuals are supposed rational in the sense of decision theory – say, they maximize expected utility – what we are asking is whether individually rational behavior is "rational for the group." The answer depends crucially on the institutions within which the individuals pursue their aims. When the group is the population of a market economy, and the preferences are over states of that economy, we have the central question of welfare economics.

A special and important class of decision problems is that of designing institutions in such a way that the answer is "Yes." The designer's problem is to choose institutions rationally with respect to the group interest: that is, to choose them to be such that individuals' actions rational with respect to their several interests will, as "no part of their intention," serve the group interest. A classic example is the design of taxes. Generally, the designer proceeds by using her available instruments to modify the way that the individuals' acts affect outcomes and, since the effects of any one individual's act vary with the other individuals' acts, this amounts to making them play a new n-person game among themselves.

The problem facing a socialist planner is a case in point. Typically, the planner sees the group interest as a matter of satisfying individuals' preferences, and she would have the means to promote it if only she knew these preferences. She does not, but their owners do: there is, in the jargon, "asymmetric information." In these circumstances the heart of the planner's problem is to elicit their preferences from the individuals themselves. However, because the planner's aim does not perfectly agree with all individuals' preferences, the individuals have a motive to misrepresent their preferences; indeed if they are classical expected utility maximizers they will in general do so. True, they might have a preference for telling the truth about their (first-order) preferences, but this only ensures that they do so if it infinitely outweighs the motive to misrepresent.

This situation creates a conflict for the planner. For one thing, measures she might take to encourage truthful reporting, as well as being needed if she is to pursue the group interest effectively, also in general damage it, because they are costly. But, in addition, the planner may think that it is in the group interest that arrangements be just, and so feel obliged to penalize duplicity even if condoning some duplicity and so saving resources would do "first-order" good.

John **Roemer**'s general topic is how to decentralize economic activity effectively under socialism, that is, without a market, when the planner knows only the distribution of individual agents' personal traits. One approach is that of the literature of allocative mechanism design stemming from Hurwicz (1973), Groves (1973), and others in which the decision-maker rationally chooses a game in order to bring about, as the outcome of players' individual choices, either a group optimum or the intermediate objective of true self-reports (when the mechanism is called "incentive compatible"). Note that this approach depends on having a correct theory of games!

In Roemer's own proposal there is no interaction among the members of the population, so that serious game-theoretic problems do not arise. He considers the situation of a planner who, in allocating goods, is able to inspect members of society for the traits that they have reported and penalize false reporting, and of individuals who take into account the probability that they will be inspected by the planner. Roemer highlights three desiderata in a democratic society.

1 "Horizontal equity": agents should not be penalized by inspection *per se*, in the sense that those who are inspected and have told the truth should receive the same allocation as those not inspected who report the same thing.
2 Welfare should be maximized: among those policies that satisfy horizontal equity the planner should announce the policy such that, if members of the population respond by reporting so as to maximize their expected utilities, expected social welfare will be maximized.
3 Duplicity should not be rational for the individuals: the policy the planner announces should be one to which the rational response of agents is to report their traits truthfully.

These three desiderata are consistent if there is only one good for allocation, for example, in the redistribution of income through taxation; that is, if there is one good, the welfare-maximizing policy ensuring horizontal equity is one that induces agents to report the truth. But Roemer shows that, if there is more than one good for allocation, insistence on horizontal equity may make the welfare-maximizing policy one that induces misrepresentation. We are left with a quandary for democratic government: which one of the three principles should be sacrificed?

Roemer's paper, and the mechanism design literature it belongs to, illustrate one way in which rational agents, hampered by having incomplete information about each others' attitudes, learn about them. Another is the now very active theory of extensive-form games of incomplete information stemming from Harsanyi (1967–8). Here the information-seeker does not get to choose a game whose outcome will reveal the unknown traits; instead players learn traits from observing choices as an exogenously given game unfolds. A third is exemplified by Brian Skyrms' work reported in this volume, in which the game is one-shot and the learning is not about traits but about how others will decide to act, and takes place in "deliberation time" through thought experiments. But these diverse models have one thing in common: their reliance on the Bayesian assumption that rational decision-makers begin with probability distributions for whatever it is that they do not know about each other.

5 THE DELIBERATIVE PROCESS

Holly **Smith** addresses the apparently infinite regress produced by the need to decide how far to deliberate about how to act before deciding how to act, to decide how far to deliberate about how far to deliberate about how to act before deciding how far to deliberate about how to act, etc. It seems as if, in order to stop the regress and enable ourselves actually to apply decision theory, we must at some level make an immediate decision not based on deliberation. But if that decision is thus not rationally based, how can any decision in turn based on it be rational?

Smith's dissolution of this problem begins with the assumption that "decision guides," usable principles for selecting an act, may be ordered in some way; she is not concerned with deliberation about this ordering but takes it as given with respect to particular decision problems. This means, among other things, that the agent with a decision problem and in a position to use either of two guides does not need to deliberate about which is the better one to use. The "higher" guides (such as expected utility maximization) may require richer beliefs (e.g. about utilities and probabilities) than a decision-maker has. According to Smith, it is rational for an agent to choose an action if and only if it is prescribed by the highest decision guide she is capable of using to make her decision (whether or not she believes it is so prescribed). To be able to use a decision guide a decision-maker must have beliefs of the kind required by the guide (such as the belief that a certain act would maximize expected utility) and so be able to infer in one step a recommendation as to action from these beliefs and the guide; the usability of a guide depends on an agent's stock of beliefs. But the rationality of a decision does not require the agent to believe that it is prescribed by a particular guide, only that she in fact decides in accordance with the highest usable guide. Employing this conception of rationality, Smith argues by means of a counter-example against the existence of an unavoidable infinite regress. (She considers separately at the end of her paper whether a regress threatens if, in addition, rationality requires that the enabling beliefs themselves be justified.)

Smith does not require for rational action that the agent believe (whether justifiably or not), concerning the guide that is in fact the highest guide she can use, that it is the highest guide she can use. If she were to require this, another regress might seem to be generated, as the question would arise as to how far to deliberate about what the highest decision guide one can use is (as opposed to whether to acquire the beliefs that would make higher guides usable). She says, in effect: Don't worry about whether to get more beliefs or not; just decide on the basis of the beliefs you have; decision in accord with the highest guide you can use given the beliefs you have is rational. By this means she aims to avert the threatened regress.

Smith's strategy raises many interesting questions about the roles of reflectiveness and luck in rationality, questions which may arise wherever Pettit's distinction between a test of rightness and a guide to rightness gets a grip. Suppose for the sake of argument that a significant range of relevant beliefs are "occurrent" states, immediately evident to their possessor, rather than dispositional states triggered by active reflection. Still, it will not be immediately evident to their possessor what the highest guide usable given these beliefs is. Even given a pre-ordered list of decision guides, it will take reflection to run down that list and determine that the highest guide one can use given certain beliefs is such and such. Therefore the question seems to arise as to how much such reflection to engage in; if it is allowed to arise, a regress may seem to start again in answer to it. But Smith deflects this line of thought by distinguishing "putative" rationality from rationality. Putative rationality concerns the decision guide that the agent believes to be highest, and may not always yield a recommendation, for example, when the agent has no such belief. Rationality *tout court*, on Smith's view, seems to be compatible with being merely lucky in various respects: lucky to perform the act that is in fact prescribed by a particular guide, even if one does not believe that it is, and lucky that that guide is one's highest usable guide, even if one does not believe this. (To be lucky in the sense meant here is not necessarily to benefit from mere accident. There may be a causal mechanism that accounts for beneficial results, but then one may be lucky that this mechanism operates.)

What makes the decision-maker who acts rationally on Smith's account lucky is not merely that she is not required to have justified beliefs (that the decision is prescribed by a certain guide, or that a certain guide is the highest usable), but also that she is not required to have any belief at all, justified or not, about these things. For rationality in Smith's sense, the decision-maker merely needs to decide in the way that is in fact prescribed by her highest usable decision guide. Another way of saying this is to say that the meta-principle of rationality, "decide in accord with your highest usable decision guide," does not have to be usable by the decision-maker in order to apply to her, for we have seen that she need not have any relevant beliefs about what her highest usable decision guide is or what it prescribes.

This may seem paradoxical, for in a sense this meta-principle is itself the highest decision guide; it embodies an overall conception of the rationality of decisions, which may be considered and endorsed by rational agents. It might, at any rate, be difficult to explain to a reflective agent who endorses it as the correct overall conception of rationality that it itself is not to be applied as a decision guide. Can a reflective rational agent prevent a valid test of rightness from being transformed by reflection into a guide to rightness? Why, moreover, does rationality (as opposed to putative rationality) not require that the meta-principle itself be usable in order for its recommendations to apply? What motivates the view that the demands of rationality are conditional on the usability of decision guides in the first place that does not by the same token motivate the view that the demands of rationality are conditional on the usability of the meta-principle? Is there some further meta-principle of rationality operating here to justify our taking the usability condition to have just this range of application?

"Deliberational dynamics" is the branch of decision theory in which one studies how the states of belief and intention of the decision-maker change during her deliberation. One way that this approach has been applied in one-agent decision theory is by supposing that she takes her own intentions as evidence relevant to the task of making the best decision. When the intentions are the definitive ones reached at the end of a deliberation, this taking of them as evidence yields the requirement on a rational decision that it be "ratifiable," to which we shall return in section 7. The dynamics of which Brian Skyrms has been a pioneer (see for example Skyrms, 1982) is concerned rather with ways in which a deliberator might "lean a little bit more this way or that" in response to evidence provided by her *interim* decisions. The leanings are modeled as probabilities that the decision-maker will finally do this or that act. Thus they are measures of decidedness: when an own-act probability reaches 1 the deliberation is over. But they are also assumed to be observable by the deliberator herself, and provide the evidence in question.

To see how they might work as evidence, consider Newcomb's Problem.[5] The deliberator, finding herself attaching a high probability to her choosing One Box, concludes that the conditional probability that there is a million in the first box given that she chooses Both Boxes is high. This leads her to look more favorably on Both Boxes, and it can be shown that "evidential decision theory" used in this dynamic way picks Both Boxes as the best act – but that is another story.

The use of such evidence in deliberation runs foul of the arguments of Spohn (1978) and of Levi in this volume against having the deliberator assign probabilities to her own acts, which go back to the view of Hart and Hampshire (1958) that "predicting undercuts deciding." Note that the objection is not to the agent's forecasting her act, but only to her doing so as a means for evaluating her acts. Again, there is no objection to forecasting others' acts as a means of evaluating your own. This gives Skyrms the opportunity, in applying deliberational dynamics to games, to use interim intention evidence without violating the Spohn–Levi embargo.

In his contribution **Skyrms** expands "deliberational dynamics" in games in two new directions. He considers a novel class of rules by which players adjust their beliefs during deliberation, "inductive rules," and he links deliberational theory with the theory of the new "refined" equilibria by showing conditions under which processes driven by these inductive rules lead to just such equilibria.

Skyrms' paper falls into two parts. In the first (sections 1–8) he reviews his earlier work and contrasts its "adaptive rules" with "inductive rules." An adaptive deliberator proceeds by "leaning" probabilistically toward whatever act of hers looks best (in expected utility terms) on the latest evidence she has. At each stage of a discrete process, an inductive deliberator retraces or "emulates" each fellow player's latest expected utility calculation, thus discovering his currently top act; she takes this to be an observation on an unknown statistical parameter θ – the vector of the probabilities with which he will finally choose one or another of his acts. Now she updates her current distribution for θ by some "inductive rule," that is, in accordance with the Bayesian theory of statistical inference. In this theory the investigator begins by having a prior distribution for the unknown statistical parameter and knowing the distribution of the observable variable for each possible value of that parameter.[6] Evidently, for this process to keep going there must be common knowledge between the players that they are proceeding in this way.

What allows Skyrms to manage without giving own-act probabilities an evidential role is that in ordinary games the only relevant evidence that a player has – and so the only sort that can emerge during deliberation – is evidence as to what others will do (contrast the extraordinary one-person problems exemplified by Newcomb's problem). For what they will do is the only unknown causally relevant feature of the world. Thus there is no point in looking at one's own (leanings to) decisions unless these give information about others' acts. Even if they do, there may be no need to look at them if there is another way of getting the latter information. In Skyrms' model (a) my leanings tell me nothing about your likely act that I cannot learn otherwise, for (b) I can learn about your likely act by thinking about your beliefs about my leanings; and the interposition of your beliefs here between my beliefs and my leanings means that I do not offend the Spohn–Levi embargo.

In the second part of the paper Skyrms shows that (given an independence assumption about the players' prior distributions) the process described above[7] converges to a Nash equilibrium. Moreover, in this limiting equilibrium *weakly dominated* acts have probability zero. An act α is weakly dominated by an act β if it is no better than β whatever other players do. Thus the Skyrms equilibria refine away some dross in the shape of equilibria which seem irrational to many intuitions.

It is to be noted that the process certainly does not describe ideally rational deliberation. In some cases a rational enough player *i* will realize that player *j*'s first-round "choice" is very far from what he will do (drawing Skyrms' diagrams would tell her this), and in that case she will not take this first-round choice at face value as sample evidence of what *j* will do. But the deliberators are partially rational. Like Harsanyi, with whose Tracing Procedure Skyrms' process has some affinity, Skyrms succeeds in the central enterprise for game theory of grounding equilibria in coherent inferences by players from a well-defined initial epistemic state. Better, the latter is one in which they know next to nothing of how each other will choose. But – a big but – the next to nothing that they do know is common knowledge! Thus Skyrms' success is dependent on a sizeable double departure from the rules of classical game-theoretic enquiry: less than full rationality, more than the minimal attitude data admitted in that enquiry.

6 NEW CONCEPTS OF EQUILIBRIUM IN GAMES

Two new and contrasting notions of equilibrium in noncooperative games – Aumann's (1974) *correlated equilibrium* and Selten's (1975) *perfect equilibrium* (or "trembling-hand perfect" equilibrium) – are advanced by their authors as "solution concepts" for games. That is, their authors claim that decisions of rational players make up equilibria of the respective kinds. Aumann's solution concept is laxer than Selten's; for example, it does not rule out the use of weakly dominated acts in two-person games. Whereas Selten's notion sternly "refines" Nash equilibrium, Aumann's complaisantly relaxes it.

6.1 Mixed acts and correlated equilibrium

Both equilibrium notions regard mixed acts. "Mixed acts" have two interpretations in game theory, which we may label the *mechanical* and the *personal*. How it is that Aumann's criterion relaxes the Nash criterion is most simply explained in terms of the former. Here a mixed act is a rule that the player uses to associate the act she will perform with the outcomes of a random experiment. An equilibrium in mixed acts is a pair (if there are two players) of these rules such that each is the best rule for its player to use given that the other uses his: each rule is a best reply to the other. "Best" means best in terms of expected utility: expected utility, that is, evaluated by using the posterior distribution after observing the outcome of the experiment.

A *Nash equilibrium* (in mixed acts) is an equilibrium in this sense, in the case in which the two players' random experiments are independent – say, spinnings of two physically unconnected wheels of chance. A *correlated equilibrium* is one in which this independence restriction is dropped. For example, the players might observe a single coin toss and tie their choices in a perfectly correlated way to its outcome, or they might observe, and tie their acts to, partly correlated features of the outcome of a more complex experiment. Allowing correlation makes more equilibria – for example, random alternation in Battle of the Sexes between going to the ballet and going to the boxing (see Luce and Raiffa, 1957, Ch. 5). In some cases (including this one) some of the extra equilibria are also better for all concerned than any of the Nash equilibria.

On the mechanical interpretation of mixed acts, however, a player who uses one consigns her decision, at a certain point, to chance. This makes for paradox in the shape of dynamic inconsistency in a theory that tells the agent to choose a mixed act: for such theories in general, there is nothing to ensure that the act that turns out to have been picked by the rule when the wheel comes to rest is the best act considered on its merits, nor therefore that the agent would be rational to keep to the rule that she has chosen. This and kindred difficulties have encouraged the move to the personal interpretation. Here there are no wheels, no abrogation: the probabilities in a "mixed act" of a player are merely probabilities in the mind of another (or indeed that) player. A mixed act is mixed with respect to a person's subjective probabilities. There is no choosing to mix.

This interpretation fits well with what we may call "universal Bayesianism," which modern game theory has taken from Jeffrey (1965) and others and now clasps to its breast. According to this doctrine, a rational decision-maker has probabilities for everything. More precisely, at the start of deliberation, she has a "prior distribution" over all propositions or events (expressible in the theory) – and so in particular for the decisions of herself and, in games, those of the other players. This is the framework of Aumann's (1987) paper and of those of Hyun Song Shin and Skyrms here. The doctrine that the agent has a universal prior distribution – one over all matters – must be distinguished from the assumption that there is a "common" prior – one that is the same for all agents. This further assumption is a staple one in contemporary game theory, and is also adopted by all of these authors.

It may be asked: "Isn't the idea that the players can correlate their acts out of place in a theory of *noncooperative* games?" Only on the mechanical interpretation and when, further, the experiment is the sort of thing the players would have to set up in collaboration. Aumann's (1974) metaphor of an "arbitrator" who makes "suggestions" to the players is misleading, suggesting as it does such collaboration. All that is in fact required for you and me to be able to correlate is that each of us has some random observable or signal and that the value of a signal tells its observer something about the probable value of the other's. Such signals might, and do, occur naturally. On the personal interpretation there is no question of collaboration. Whether mixed acts of ours are correlated is all down to our priors. Mixed acts (with respect to my personal beliefs) are correlated just if things like this are true of my prior: in it, the conditional probability of your finishing up doing β given that I finish up doing α depends on α. Such things may be true if, for instance, on my prior people with similar upbringings tend to choose the same acts and we two have similar upbringings.

What brings me to have the prior probabilities that I do for your deciding on one option and another is a question not answered (and rarely asked) by the Bayesian theory of games. The absence of an independent account of what is in the players' priors is a grave lacuna. There are many games for which, once the priors are given, the identities of the rational acts follow trivially, and then game theory itself is trivialized if it is merely assumed that the priors are such and such. To avoid this trivialization by Bayesianization, we must take the content of the priors in such cases to be the central unknowns of the theory, endogenous to it. And then methodological consistency demands that the priors be so treated also in the case of games in which the derivation of rational actions from the priors is a more complex task (such as extensive-form games in which players learn as the play unfolds).

6.2 Perfect equilibrium

Let α and β be pure acts for you and me. $\langle\alpha,\beta\rangle$ is a Nash equilibrium – in the original sense of that term – if α is best for me if you do β (and vice versa). In the Bayesian framework, it is one if our priors are such that I am certain you will do β and reckon α best for me, and you are certain I will do α and reckon β best for you – we may say, if the priors both *certify* and *rationalize* $\langle\alpha, \beta\rangle$.[8] $\langle\alpha, \beta\rangle$ is a *perfect equilibrium* if I still reckon α best though I am only almost certain that you will do β, but think it is just possible that you will do any old thing. For the equilibrium to be perfect, the optimality of α must be "robust with respect to" these probability traces of departures by you from your part in the equilibrium (and vice versa). Selten (1975) thinks of such departures as unintended, as when the hand of the player "trembles." He says that a rational player picks the best act in the light of both her belief about what the other intends to do and her appreciation of the faint possibility that he may fail.

The ideas of trembling and perfection, may be – and often are – generalized to the case of Nash equilibria in mixed acts. For instance, β might be the mixed act of yours in which your pure acts β_1 and β_2 have probability 0.5 each. Trembles of yours in the mixed case may be interpreted as probability traces in my mind of departures by you from your intended act, itself a random variable in my mind.

An equilibrium notion which rules out some pairs of acts that are ordinary Nash equilibria but which appear irrational to intuition is called a *refinement* of the Nash equilibrium criterion. The refinements literature is the story of a sequence of purges that have successively eliminated surviving pockets of intuitively irrational acts as they have surfaced in a series of counterexamples. The perfect equilibrium criterion is a powerful one: even the minute probability of trembling which it entertains derationalizes important tracts of intuitively irrational acts. For example, if α is weakly dominated for its player, the pair $\langle\alpha, \beta\rangle$ can be a Nash equilibrium, but perfect equilibrium eliminates it. That allowing a mere trace of uncertainty has such salutary effects on the solution set helps explain why the refinements literature has not gone further down the mistakes road: one "gets the right answers" without having seriously to psychologize game theory. But there is a tension which one day will have to be resolved between the idea that players are only human and the idea that they are an epsilon away from divinity.

Readers unfamiliar with the various refinements of the Nash equilibrium criterion will find helpful explanations of them in the papers of William Harper, Skyrms and Sugden. In addition to perfect equilibrium, the refinements known as *subgame-perfect* (weaker than perfect equilibrium) and *sequential* equilibrium (marginally weaker) have been much discussed and applied. Both these concern games in extensive form, and latch on to features of the dynamic unfolding of a game which seem to impose restrictions on rational choice. If a node and all that comes after it in a game tree themselves make up a game, this is called a *subgame* of the original game. The former criterion requires of a pair of *strategies* that it be a Nash equilibrium and in addition that, for any subgame of the game, the "tail" of the strategy pair which instructs players what to do in the subgame constitutes a Nash equilibrium in the subgame. Subgame perfection, the first of the refinements of Nash to arouse attention, eliminates the "bad equilibrium" of the One-round Chain Store game which we discuss below.

Sequential equilibrium is a more complicated animal, of Bayesian stock. A strategy pair is a sequential equilibrium if it is a Nash equilibrium in the Bayesian sense (each player's belief system certifies the other's and rationalizes her own part), and if in addition (a) it is so in a certain dynamic sense appropriate to extensive-form games and (b) it possesses a certain robustness to epistemic shocks. The dynamic gloss is this: as the equilibrium strategies are played out, and the players' beliefs are updated for what they see happen by the usual Bayesian conditioning rule, their beliefs continue to certify and rationalize. The robustness is in respect of possible observed deviations, along the way, of the players from their parts in the equilibrium: special rules are introduced by Kreps and Wilson for how the players would make sense of and update for choices "off the equilibrium path" – choices they were sure would not be made. They are forced into this. As we shall see in a moment, updating by Bayesian conditioning cannot be done when the evidence was thought impossible.

7 INDIVIDUAL RATIONALITY AND THE NEW EQUILIBRIA

7.1 Ratifiability

Shin's paper explicates the two notions of equilibrium in games just described in terms of an idea from individual decision theory: Jeffrey's "ratifiablity." When a decision-maker concludes her deliberation and decides for a certain act, she puts herself into a new information state. She now knows an extra thing – her own decision. And it cannot be ruled out that this is a piece of information that bears on the relative benefits of her different options! Now suppose that, in accordance with standard theory, the agent's measure of the benefit of an act α is her conditional expected utility given the event that she does α. Then it seems a reasonable requirement of the rationality of the decision to do α that α should come out top among acts in terms of conditional expected utility calculated using her probability distribution in her new information state – that is, using her posterior distribution given the decision to do α. Jeffrey (1983) calls the decision for α *ratifiable* if this is so. It is clear that whether α is ratifiable for me depends on how likely I think it that I might fail to carry out my decision. If, say, I think I might well, intending α, inadvertently do an act likely to have horrifying consequences, I might be better advised to decide on something safer than α. At the other extreme the notion of ratification runs into a difficulty. Suppose that I am certain of my steadiness; then in my posterior given my decision to do α, all acts other than α are null events (have zero probability). But then the conditional expected utility of α' is undefined for all acts α' but α, and this means that α is trivially ratifiable. So certainty of my steadiness means that the criterion of ratifiability is automatically met by whatever I decide to do, and so is useless.

Shin's paper displays both the correlated equilibrium criterion and the perfect equilibrium criterion as requirements that players' decisions be ratifiable: we get the stronger perfect equilibrium when the ratification test is stronger because the decision must hold up under a wider class of deviations of players' acts from their believed intentions. As to beliefs, Shin works in the usual framework of a prior both universal and common.

There is a snag in Aumann's own interpretation of correlated equilibrium (Aumann, 1987). He moves away from the "arbitrators" and "suggestions" of Aumann (1974), as he must for a general theory of noncooperative behavior. Instead he takes a player's "signal" to be her *act*. But the criterion of correlated equilibrium requires that the option tied to the signal be ranked top using the posterior given the signal. Here this criterion runs into the problem of undefined conditional expected utilities: using the posterior distribution given the information that I will do α, I cannot evaluate any act but α!

Shin proposes a reinterpretation: make the player's signal be her *decision*. This is an improvement, for one's decisions, unlike one's acts, are surely evident to one. Then the correlated equilibrium criterion says that, given my decision for α, the act α must have highest conditional expected utility. In other words, it says that decisions must be ratifiable! And now the correlated equilibrium criterion does purchase – provided, of course, that agents think that they may tremble, that is, provided that they are "modest," as Shin says. In sum, Shin explicates correlated equilibrium as a requirement of ratifiability on modest players.

Within this scheme of things perfect equilibrium also fits quite naturally. Suppose that our belief system has this feature: in any posterior, I have slight doubts not only about my own steadiness, but also about yours – I am "wary." Consider a Nash equilibrium, for simplicity a pure one, $\langle \alpha, \beta \rangle$ say. Then my decision to do α is ratifiable only if α comes out top in the face of the probabilities I ascribe to your strayings from β (where the probabilities are those of my posterior given my decision for α). This condition sounds mighty like that for α to be part of a perfect equilibrium. Shin shows that the criterion of perfect equilibrium is precisely a requirement of ratifiability on wary players. Both correlated equilibrium and perfect equilibrium, then, are criteria which require a form of retifiability, one Jeffreyan or "modest" and the other Seltenian or "wary."

In contrast with Skyrms, the neo-Bayesian authors of the notions of correlated and perfect equilibrium embrace wholeheartedly Jeffrey's attitude that self-observation by the decision-maker of her decision, and probability judgments concerning it, are legitimate inputs in rational deliberation. Whoever is right about this, it may be asked how it is that there is a role for such evidence in the Bayesian work when no Newcomb-like effects are in play. The answer is that it is exogenously assumed in the Bayesian approach that one's own decision is informative about others' actions. But what supports this assumption? The Bayesian universalist offers a grandiose defence: the rational agent has a joint prior probability distribution over all relevant matters, including therefore the decisions of herself and the other players; and there is no *a priori* reason to think that these random variables are independently distributed in this rational prior. But is there any reason to think that they are not? One possible reply is: "Yes – the analogy between one mind and another means that one player's decision is a significant indicator of others' decisions, when due allowances for differences are made." But this reply, in assimilating the minds of the players to each other, leads straight back to the Spohn–Levi objection.

7.2 Causalism

Shin's and Skyrms' papers are about one-shot games: the players make single simultaneous decisions. **Harper**'s paper is about games with a sequence of moves. Like Shin and Skyrms, Harper seeks to derive solutions from principles of rational individual choice. One is ratifiability, the other "causalism": that is, the principle that it is rational to choose an act only in virtue of its efficacy in causing desired consequences. Like Shin and Skyrms, Harper shows that his solutions give equilibria which are Nash equilibria refined in various ways. Like them too, Harper formally models his players in the Bayesian manner: they have probabilities for each other's acts and they update for information they get during deliberation. But Harper puts less weight on the probabilistic grain and the communality of their beliefs: fewer matters are the subject of common or indeed any probability judgments, and the probabilities that do the main work are 0 and 1.

A decision to do α is ratifiable if, with respect to the posterior given by this decision, it is precisely α that maximizes the conditional expected utility $E(u|\alpha')$ over all options α'. We have seen one trouble for this notion – the undefinedness of this conditional expected utility when the event α' is null. Another much chewed over trouble for it is that there are cases in which the conditional expected utility of an option α' seems to fail to measure what it is intended to: the benefits that doing α' is likely to *produce* for the agent. The most celebrated case of this kind is Newcomb's problem.

We can write the agent's conditional expected utility given that she does α' as $E(u|\alpha') = \text{pr}(O_1|\alpha')u(O_1) + \text{pr}(O_2|\alpha')u(O_2) + \ldots$, where O_1, $O_2, \ldots$ are the various possible outcomes.[9] The central tenet of *causal decision theory* is that the decision α' should be evaluated not by $E(u|\alpha')$ but by the magnitude we get if (for each outcome O_i) we replace the conditional probability $\text{pr}(O_i|\alpha')$ in it by the probability of the causal propensity of α' to produce O_i. If we do, we get the answers usually regarded as right on the basis of considerations of dominance in Newcomb's problem and its ilk. In Gibbard and Harper's (1978) well-known version of this theory the latter probability is taken to be $\text{pr}(\alpha' \,\square\!\!\rightarrow O_i)$, the probability of the counterfactual event *if α' were done*, O_i *would occur*; so that the act α' is evaluated by the weighted utility expression $\text{pr}(\alpha' \,\square\!\!\rightarrow O_1)u(O_1) + \text{pr}(\alpha' \,\square\!\!\rightarrow O_2)u(O_2) + \ldots$, which we shall call here the *causal expected utility* of α'. Causal decision theory reveals that the troublesome cases for the decision theory built on conditional expected utility are cases in which an event of the form $\alpha' \,\square\!\!\rightarrow O_i$ is *statistically dependent* on the event α', that is, in which the information that the agent is going to do α' bears on the probable effectiveness of α'.

Using causal expected utilities not only deals with Newcomb cases, it also deals with the undefinedness trouble. The probability of the event $\alpha' \,\square\!\!\rightarrow O_i$ is assuredly *not* undefined just because $\text{pr}(\alpha') = 0$. After all, if α' *were done*, O_i *would occur* is a *counter*factual proposition; just as its truth is independent of the truth of α', so is its probability. This is easily seen in terms of the Lewis–Stalnaker theory of counterfactuals (see for example Stalnaker, 1968): $\alpha' \,\square\!\!\rightarrow O_i$ is true (in our world) if (roughly) O_i is true in the nearest α'-world to ours; $pr(\alpha' \,\square\!\!\rightarrow O_i) = \pi$ if (roughly) in a proportion π of all worlds the nearest α'-world has O_i true.[10]

Harper formulates ratifiability using the posterior causal expected utilities of acts instead of their posterior conditional expected utilities. This formulation avoids the undefinedness problem, which explains why Harper can invoke ratifiability to identify solutions without having his players believe in trembling. It also allows the explicit treatment of a feature of games which has been neglected in formal game theory: the causal links among the events within them. Such links are undoubtedly present in extensive-form games under their intended interpretation: by my choice at my move I *put* you at a certain information set. Harper's main claim is that, when causal decision theory is used in assessing ratifiability, the causal structure of an extensive-form game makes "bad" equilibria come out unratifiable; thus "causal ratifiability" is a way of explicating the refinement proposals in the literature.

Harper's criterion for the ratifiability of an act in a game combines the principle of ratifiability itself with the idea of Transparency of Reason (see Bacharach, 1987). Transparency is central in the Indirect Argument of von Neumann and Morgenstern (1944) that rational actions in games must make up Nash equilibria. It is argued, first, that if reason dictates what to do, then players, each of whom knows the other's initial epistemic state and that he decides rationally, can discover each other's decisions; for all that is needed is to emulate their reasoning, and this is common to them and so is "transparent." Now say what reason dictates is α for me and β for you. Then I know that you will do β. But if I know that you will do β then reason dictates that I choose a *best reply* to β. Hence α must be a best reply to β, and, by a symmetric argument, β to α.

Harper's "best-reply ratifiability" is a necessary condition for the rationality of a choice which follows from a latter-day version of the Indirect Argument. Imagine player 1 trying to identify her rational strategy. Harper suggests that she does so by successive elimination. Say she begins by hypothesizing that it is s; now she argues that, if it is, then since 2 is rational he will see that it is, and so he will see that 1, being rational, will do it; it is certain, then, that the rational 2 will choose a best reply to s. Thus having adopted the s hypothesis, 1 is constrained by reason to set $pr(t|s) = 0$ for all non-best replies t to s. Armed with this constraint on 1's prior – call it the "transparency constraint" – Harper can now determine the counterfactual probabilities with which 1 assesses s for ratifiability. If s fails the test of ratifiability, 1 must discard the s hypothesis and (one supposes) try again.

Determining the counterfactual probabilities exploits certain theorems about such probabilities, notably (a) $\text{pr}(A \,\square\!\!\rightarrow B \,|\, A) = \text{pr}(B \,|\, A)$ for any events A, B, and (b) if B is causally independent of whether A or A' occurs, $\text{pr}(A' \,\square\!\!\rightarrow B \,|\, A) = \text{pr}(A \,\square\!\!\rightarrow B \,|\, A)$.

To see how all this works out, and how causal dependence undermines bad equilibria, consider an example, the celebrated One-round Chain Store game.[11] A Store (player 2) is sitting pretty on its monopoly profits when an Invader (player 1) considers entering the market in competition. If 1 does enter (E), 2 will know it; 2's strategies are either to fight (F) or "accommodate" (A) player 1 in this event, and the payoffs pairs are then $(-20, -20)$ and $(10, 0)$ respectively. If 1 withdraws (W), 1's payoff is 0. There are two Nash equilibria – (E, A) and (W, F) – but the latter is intuitively a bad'un, since even though F is (equal) best against W (since in the case of W it does not matter what 2's plan is), it would make no sense for 2 to carry through F if 1 did not do W. This counterexample to the alleged rationality of Nash equilibria has been seminal in the refinement programme.

The suspect strategy W for player 1 fails Harper's "best-reply ratifiability" test. 1, hypothesizing that W is rational, must compare the following two causal expected utilities (note that these are conditional causal expected utilities, because the hypothesis that W transpires is given):

$$v(E\,|\,W) = \text{pr}(E \,\square\!\!\rightarrow F \,|\, W)u(E,\ F) + \text{pr}(E \,\square\!\!\rightarrow A \,|\, W)u(E,\ A)$$

$$v(W\,|\,W) = \text{pr}(W \,\square\!\!\rightarrow F \,|\, W)u(W,\ F) + \text{pr}(W \,\square\!\!\rightarrow A \,|\, W)u(W,\ A)$$

that is,

$$v(E\,|\,W) = -20\text{pr}(E \,\square\!\!\rightarrow F \,|\, W) + 10\text{pr}(E \,\square\!\!\rightarrow A \,|\, W)$$

$$v(W\,|\,W) = 0\text{pr}(W \,\square\!\!\rightarrow F \,|\, W) + 0\text{pr}(W \,\square\!\!\rightarrow A \,|\, W) = 0$$

Suppose that F were causally independent of whether 1 adopts E or W (as is its counterpart in a simultaneous-play game with the same normal form); then we would have $\text{pr}(E \,\square\!\!\rightarrow F \,|\, W) = \text{pr}(W \,\square\!\!\rightarrow F \,|\, W) = \text{pr}(F\,|\,W)$. Since F is a best reply to W, 1 may without irrationality have 1 for this conditional probability, and in this case we get $v(E\,|\,W) = -20$, which is less than $v(W\,|\,W) = 0 \times 1 + 0 \times 0 = 0$, and W is ratified. However, Harper argues that in our game F is causally dependent on whether 1 adopts E or W, since the strategy F can only be enacted in case of E. So even if she has $\text{pr}(F\,|\,W) = 1$ she may have $\text{pr}(E \,\square\!\!\rightarrow F \,|\, W) = 0$. Indeed, if she is rational she will do, Harper says, for she knows that if she did choose E then 2, being rational, would reject F and choose A since A strictly dominates F. Here, it would seem, Harper is extending the application of the transparency constraint from strategies in the original game to strategies in subgames that may arise. On this very reasonable assumption we get $v(E|W) = 0 \times - 20 + 1 \times 10 = 10$, greater than $v(W|W)$, and W is unratifiable.

The study of ratifiability has made us aware of the delicate distinction between decision and act, and it may be asked what becomes of this distinction when, as in Harper's paper, games are analyzed in terms of strategies. A strategy is defined in terms of conditionals, which specify such and such acts in such and such contingencies. The most natural interpretation of a strategy is as a decision to do the specified act if and when each of the contingencies arises. However, if "F", for example, stands for a strategy in this sense, it does not seem that F is causally dependent on whether 1 adopts E or W, as Harper's argument requires. What is the enactment that stands to a strategy (so interpreted) as act stands to decision in one-off cases? Can we say that a strategy is enacted just if what happens is in accordance with it? This is perhaps too lax: we may want to add that the player would have followed it if other contingencies had arisen. However this may be, the "F" in Harper's argument from causal dependence seems not to stand for the enactment of a strategy in the sense suggested here, but rather for the event that, in the particular situation caused by entry, 2 performs a certain act (fighting) (or, what is much the same, perhaps for the strategy of fighting in the subgame which arises in this contingency).

In the last part of his paper Harper investigates the answers that his best-reply ratifiability criterion gives in some currently controversial games. In one of these,[12] a "backward induction" argument of Harsanyi and Selten (1988) purports to identify the solution by a process of elimination which is our old friend snipping off transferred to games! At one point this process keeps in contention a certain strategy ("BC") for player 1, even though this is strictly dominated in the normal form, on the grounds that its tail is rational. Kohlberg and Mertens (1986) defend a different strategy ("BD") by a so-called "forward induction" argument, according to which a player may rationally use her first act B to signal that she will do D in a later subgame. In effect, the Kohlberg–Mertens argument makes out B to be a Gricean "utterance" by 1 with the "S-meaning" that she will do D: that is, roughly, 1 intends her doing B to produce in 2 the belief that 1 will do D by means of 2's recognizing this intention (see Grice, 1957). Harper's criterion backs BD for different, non-Gricean, reasons, but it has in common with the Kohlberg–Mertens argument that strategies are ratified or not at the start, as wholes, rather than in truncated form as in backward induction approaches to game-theoretic rationality.

Ratifiability and trembling move game theory away from the realm of pure reason in which von Neumann and Morgenstern (1944) set it down, toward the study of imperfect creatures, endowed with commonsense theory and general knowledge. The Kohlberg–Mertens argument is a further step in the direction of acculturation; for it can be rational of 1 to do B as a signal of what she intends to do later only if she thinks that 2 will interpret her act (of moving a token or whatever) as a message (about how she will act later). And, for this prediction to be sensible, 1 must attribute to 2 the general semantical belief that people use items of one kind to symbolize items of another.

8 IS DECISION THEORY DETERMINATE?

Both Smith and Sugden are interested in the limitations to the deliberative capacities of human beings. But while Smith pursues this question in the context of skepticism about the determinacy of individual higher-order or reflective rationality, Sugden pursues it in the context of skepticism about the determinacy of individual rationality in games – interactive situations in which agents are trying to arrive at predictions about, *inter alia*, other agents who are trying to arrive at predictions about them. Moreover, as we saw, Smith wishes to defend determinacy against skepticism, while Sugden presses skepticism.

Harper, Shin, and Skyrms, in varying ways, presume that equilibria of individuals' reasonings (including reasonings about each other), as long as they are robust enough, give the answer to the question: "How is it rational to act in noncooperative games?" **Sugden** addresses the same question, but he does not make the presumption, and his conclusion sharply opposes it. Sugden argues that the question may have no answer (or, at least, in many games no univocal answer that we can discover), and that this lacuna undermines the solutions to games that are given in the literature.

Sugden considers the question for a special but important class of games: bargaining games. The solution concepts that the literature offers for these are of two sorts: those, sometimes called "axiomatic," based on axioms for bargaining outcomes with ethical content, descending from Nash's (1950) paper; and those yielded by the so-called "Nash program." This is the research program whose manifesto proclaims, reductively, that despite appearances bargaining games are noncooperative games whose solutions are mere instances of general solution concepts for noncooperative games; focuses on the tasks of modeling various bargaining situations as noncooperative games and finding their solutions; and employs the leading noncooperative solution concepts of our day – Nash equilibrium and its refinements.

Sugden claims that both sorts of solution concept for bargaining games presuppose the following Principle of Rational Determinacy:[13] given the formal specification of the game, reason dictates unique decisions. No warrant, Sugden claims, is to be found for this presupposition in the literature; it is made arbitrarily. The main thrust of the paper is the explanation of this claim in respect of Nash equilibrium and its refinements, and hence of the solution concepts for bargains to which the Nash program subscribes.

One might wish to protest that when there is a unique equilibrium (of some suitably refined kind) there is nothing arbitrary about the supposition. But this is mistaken, for the identification of being an equilibrium with being a solution is ultimately grounded only in the Indirect Argument, and this shows only the necessity of the Nash equilibrium property.

It does not help to insist on refinements, for adding necessary conditions, however plausible, to the Nash equilibrium condition does not ensure that the conjunctive condition is sufficient. Moreover, as Sugden notes for the case of perfect equilibrium, arguments for strengthenings often appeal to a premise that in some associated game (a subgame, or a perturbation of the original game) rational players play a Nash equilibrium. And this appeal is arbitrary, unless there is warrant for a Principle of Rational Determinacy.

Nor does it help to go Bayesian, putting a player's beliefs about what others will do first and deriving propositions about what she should do. In this way Aumann defends correlated equilibrium, but, as Sugden argues, only by assuming a common prior. And this assumption presupposes that there is a uniquely rational set of beliefs about actions in games given the shared information about the game situation.

Nothing has been said yet of the clause in the Principle of Rational Determinacy which describes the informational input which determines, via reason, what to do. This consists, according to the Principle, of no more than the formal specification of the game: in general, the extensive form; in the case of bargaining games, the set of feasible payoff pairs and the reference point. (In effect, the Principle asserts the solubility of games in which the "attitude data" consist of knowledge of these things, and no more.) In the last part of his paper Sugden argues, against the Principle, that there are games in which there is a rational thing to do which, however, is fixed by information which is not part of the formal specification. In so-called "tacit bargaining" it is sometimes rational to play one's part in a "focal point" in the sense of Schelling. A focal point is a Nash equilibrium whose salience or prominence is iterated knowledge between the players, such as the Nash equilibrium of the game of Rendezvous in which two tourists, accidentally separated in Paris, both proceed to the Eiffel Tower.

Like the commonsense belief in human error, and the basic semantical beliefs to which we have referred, the salience of actions is a cultural datum. Its role in determining what it is rational to do, like the roles of those beliefs, undermines the Principle of Rational Determinacy with its restricted domain of admissible information, and impels us toward a more cultural theory of rational play in which we allow players to make use in deciding what to do of some more of the things that all of us believe and know each other to believe.

The fundamental problem of classical game theory is to show that individual deliberators of unbounded powers but limited initial information (iterated knowledge of the specification of the game, and each other's rationality) reach conclusions. Skyrms displays a sophisticated deliberation which converges. Does he then crack this problem? No, for his ingenious and elegant theory is a theory of how equilibrium is reached by a boundedly rational reasoning process, one moreover in which the players start out with some nonclassical information, in the shape of common knowledge of each other's procedures. The process is boundedly rational for the same reason that adaptive expectations are in other contexts: the players plod along mechanically updating in response to the latest clash of incoming information with their beliefs, and never see the emerging pattern, let alone try, on seeing it, to understand where it will finally lead. If they did, and took each other to do so, everything would become unfixed again: they would face again the destiny of the ideal spirits we began with, hovering in gravitationless space in search of grounds for beliefs and finding only each other hovering in space in the same unending search.

NOTES

The editors would like to thank Derek Parfit, Samuel Scheffler, and contributors to the present volume for valuable comments on drafts of this Introduction.
  1 The essence of the connection of such separability with Independence is that Independence implies it if the agent has probabilities for all states, and it implies Independence if in addition the states are "ethically neutral."
  2 In ethics, at least one dominant sense of the term consequentialism involves the impersonal agent-neutral evaluation of consequences (see Scheffler, 1988),

as opposed to "strict consequentialism" in Levi's sense. Though both are controversial in ethics, what Levi calls "strict consequentialism" is even more widely questioned than agent neutrality; in fact, defences of agent neutrality sometimes take the form of demonstrating that it does not require a sharp act–consequence distinction or a denial of the intrinsic value or disvalue of certain types of acts.

3 See Seidenfeld (1988a), whose argument for the Independence Axiom employs a "strict" understanding of payoffs but does not depend on the reduction of extensive to normal form.

4 The example adapts one from Sen (1986).

5 There are two boxes, B1 and B2. The agent can have the contents of B1 or of B1 *and* B2. She knows that B2 contains £1,000, that a Demon has put £1 million or nothing in B1, and that the conditional probabilities that he has put in the million given that she chooses One Box and given that she chooses Both Boxes are 0.9 and 0.1 respectively. In consequence, One Box has higher conditional expected utility given her act (which she knows once she has decided) and so is recommended by standard expected utility theory. But Both Boxes dominates One Box! See Nozick (1969) and Eells (1982).

6 The specific rule Skyrms considers (for the case of two alternative acts) is Bayesian updating with θ beta-distributed and the observation process Bernoulli.

7 Specifically, the process involving the beta–Bernoulli rule suitably generalized to the many-act case.

8 Notice that, on the second definition, there can be at most one Nash equilibrium once a prior is given; a game can have many Nash equilibria only in the sense that there are many pairs such that there are priors that make them be Nash equilibria.

9 And harmlessly substituting $u(O_1)$ for $u(O_1 \cap \alpha')$, etc.

10 These advantages of causal expected utilities are unaffected if we condition the probabilities of counterfactuals in them on some background hypothesis H, obtaining "conditional causal expected utilities" of the form $pr(\alpha' \,\square\!\!\rightarrow O_1 \,|\, H)$ $u(O_1) + pr(\alpha' \,\square\!\!\rightarrow O_2 \,|\, H)u(O_2) + \dots$.

11 See Selten (1978). Harper himself uses a picturesque isomorph of this example which we owe to the librettist of *Gianni Schicchi*.

12 Harsanyi and Selten's (1988) Subgame Game.

13 A close cousin of what Bacharach (1987) and Selten (personal communication) call the Existence Postulate.

University of Winnipeg, 515 Portage Ave.. Winnipeg, MB. R3B 2E9 Canada

1

Dynamic Consistency and Non-expected Utility

Mark J. Machina

1 INTRODUCTION

In the last decade, the economic theory of choice under uncertainty has gone from one of the most settled branches of economics to one of the most unsettled. Although the debate encompasses several topics, it revolves around a single issue: the supremacy of the classical "expected utility" model of choice under uncertainty in light of a growing body of evidence that individuals do *not* maximize expected utility, and the development of a number of alternative "non-expected utility" models of decision-making.[1]

Before these alternative models will be adopted by economists, however, researchers in this area will have to accomplish three goals. The first, which can be termed the *empirical goal*, is to show that non-expected utility models fit the data better than the standard expected utility model. Since these models are typically generalizations (that is, weakenings) of the expected utility model, it is not enough that they simply be compatible with more observations. To be successful, they must weaken the expected utility hypothesis in a manner which captures the types of systematic violations of expected utility that *have* been cataloged, while retaining those of its empirical properties that *have not* been refuted. The second objective can be termed the *theoretical goal*. This is to show that non-expected utility models of decision-making can be used to conduct analyses of standard economic decisions under uncertainty, such as insurance, gambling, or investment, in a manner that at least approximates the elegance and power of expected utility analysis.

Researchers have come a long way toward attaining each of these two goals. The data on expected utility's key empirical property of "linearity in the probabilities" has been very uniform, exhibiting a systematic form of departure from this property which has been captured by several non-expected utility models and which continues to be observed in experimental investigations.[2] Although it has not been as extensive as the empirical work in the area, the theoretical application of non-expected utility models, both to standard economic questions as well as to theoretical issues which *cannot* be handled by the classical model, is also proceeding apace (e.g. Selden, 1978; Machina, 1982a, b, 1984; Chew, 1983; Fishburn, 1984a; Dekel, 1986, 1989; Karni, 1987; Segal, 1987; Green and Jullien, 1988).

However, there remains one more objective which must be attained prior to the general acceptance of non-expected utility models, which can be termed the *normative goal*. This is to counter the widely held belief that non-expected utility maximizers will behave in a dynamically inconsistent manner that is particularly subject to systematic manipulation and exploitation. This last objective forms the topic of this paper.

Given attainment of the empirical goal and the theoretical goal, why would a descriptive economist ever worry about the normative goal? Descriptive psychologists, for example, would never reject an empirically well-grounded and theoretically fruitful theory of decision-making (or perception, or belief formation, or memory,. . .) on the grounds that it was not "rational" – that, after all, is what distinguishes psychologists as behavioral scientists from, say, statisticians or philosophers.

Economists, on the other hand, do exhibit a considerable affinity for the property of "rationality," and we have been severely criticized for this in light of an onslaught of laboratory evidence. But there is a good reason for this attitude, which derives from the additional responsibility that economists as *social* scientists must bear. Whereas experimental psychologists can be satisfied as long as their models of individual behavior perform properly in the laboratory, economists are responsible for the logical implications of their behavioral models when embedded in social settings.

To take a related example, there is a lot of laboratory evidence indicating that individuals' preferences can be systematically intransitive in certain situations. Why have economists not responded by simply dropping the assumption of transitivity from their standard model of the consumer? Because if you take such a naive model of intransitive preferences and put it in a cage with a classical economic agent, it will be eaten alive by a simple "money pump" argument. Unless and until economists observe such explicit money-pumping in the real world, they will not adopt models that imply it must exist.

In other words, economists will not, and *should* not, employ behavioral models that imply economically self-destructive behavior in the presence of other (greedy) economic agents. This is not to say that we cannot allow the individual to exhibit such tendencies to some extent, or some of the time. Models in which the form of advertising or packaging has an effect on consumers' utility of a product constitute perfectly good economic models, and we can be sure that they are being fruitfully used by real-world marketing and packaging departments. But any model which is so unsophisticated as to imply that the agent can be invariably and repeatedly bilked out of cash will be rejected by any positive economist aware of the fact that such continual bilking simply does not take place.

Herein lies the importance of the normative goal to the general acceptance of non-expected utility models. There is a widespread belief that, just as intransitive preferences allow you to be "money pumped," non-expected utility preferences make you susceptible to a similar form of ruinous exploitation, namely, that someone can persuade you willingly to "make book against yourself." If this were true, economists would be right to reject these models regardless of their laboratory performance or theoretical properties. The objective of this paper is to dispel this impression, and to demonstrate that non-expected utility models are capable of generating behavior which is dynamically consistent and is not "manipulable" in any sense that is not also exhibited by preferences under certainty.

In the following section I develop the framework for these arguments by discussing the key distinction between expected utility and non-expected utility preferences, namely the property of *separability across mutually exclusive events*. In section 3, I review the two classes of arguments purporting to be able to trick non-expected utility maximizers into "making book against themselves." The first class of arguments – those involving "static choice" – can be dismissed quite easily, while the second class – involving "dynamic choice" – are seemingly more formidable. In section 4, I offer a critique of this latter group of arguments. In particular, I show that each of them relies upon a hidden assumption concerning how decision-makers behave in dynamic choice situations, namely *consequentialism* in the sense of Hammond (1988a, b, 1989). However, the property of consequentialism, though automatically satisfied by expected utility maximizers, is essentially a dynamic version of the very separability that non-expected utility maximizers reject, and is accordingly inappropriate to impose on such agents. In section 5, I show that when the assumption of consequentialism is dropped and non-expected utility preferences are extended to dynamic choice settings in the same manner that economists would extend nonseparable preferences across time, commodities or any other economic dimension, non-expected utility maximizers will be dynamically consistent and are not "manipulable" in any sense not shared by nonseparable preferences over commodities. Section 6 contains a discussion of several aspects of the process of modeling nonseparable (that is, non-expected utility) preferences under uncertainty.

2.1 Lotteries, preferences, and preference functions

An individual making a one-shot or "static" decision under uncertainty can be viewed as having to choose out of a set of alternative risky prospects or *lotteries*. Algebraically, we can represent a single-stage or simple lottery by the notation $\tilde{X} = (x_1, p_1; \ldots; x_n, p_n)$, where p_i denotes the probability of obtaining the outcome x_i. Depending upon the setting, the outcomes $\{x_1, \ldots, x_n\}$ could represent alternative final wealth levels, alternative changes from the individual's current wealth level, or alternative nonmonetary outcomes. We adopt the convention that the probabilities $\{p_1, \ldots, p_n\}$ in any lottery $\tilde{X} = (x_1, p_1; \ldots; x_n, p_n)$ are all positive and sum to unity. We do not require the outcomes $\{x_1, \ldots, x_n\}$ to be distinct, since different events could lead to the same outcome, although we shall identify $(\ldots; x, p; x, q; \ldots)$ and $(\ldots; x, p + q; \ldots)$ as the same lottery. Graphically, we can represent such lotteries as in figure 1.1, where the circle is known as a *chance node*.

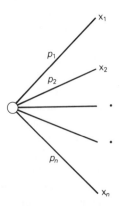

Figure 1.1   Graphical representation of a single-stage lottery.

As in standard consumer theory, we assume that the individual has a preference ordering over this set of lotteries, so that if $\tilde{X} = (x_1, p_1; \ldots; x_n, p_n)$ and $\tilde{Y} = (y_1, q_1; \ldots; y_m, q_m)$ are two lotteries, we have

$$\tilde{X} \sim \tilde{Y} \qquad (\tilde{X} \text{ is indifferent to } \tilde{Y})$$

or $\qquad \tilde{X} > \tilde{Y} \qquad (\tilde{X} \text{ is strictly preferred to } \tilde{Y})$

or $\qquad \tilde{X} < Y \qquad (\tilde{X} \text{ is strictly } less \text{ preferred than } \tilde{Y})$

Provided that it satisfies the appropriate notion of continuity, this preference ordering can be represented by a *preference function* $V(\cdot)$, in the sense that

$$\tilde{X} \sim \tilde{Y} \qquad \text{if and only if} \qquad V(\tilde{X}) = V(\tilde{Y})$$

$$\tilde{X} > \tilde{Y} \qquad \text{if and only if} \qquad V(\tilde{X}) > V(\tilde{Y})$$

$$\tilde{X} < \tilde{Y} \qquad \text{if and only if} \qquad V(\tilde{X}) < V(\tilde{Y})$$

The left-hand lottery in figure 1.2 represents a two-stage or compound lottery of the general form $(\tilde{X}_1, p_1; \ldots; \tilde{X}_n, p_n)$, that is, a lottery whose "outcomes" are themselves lotteries (termed *sublotteries*). Although the successive chance nodes in a compound lottery are resolved sequentially rather than simultaneously, we assume that this process does not require a significant amount of time, so that individuals have no reason to prefer single-stage over compound lotteries on grounds of impatience and/or planning benefits alone.[3]

Since the two-stage lottery in figure 1.2 yields a probability $p_1 q_1$ of obtaining the outcome x_1, a probability $p_1 q_2$ of the outcome x_2, etc., we say that it is *probabilistically equivalent* to the right-hand, single-stage lottery in the figure. Given the timing assumptions of the previous paragraph, we shall assume that the individual is always indifferent between any compound lottery and its probabilistically equivalent single-stage

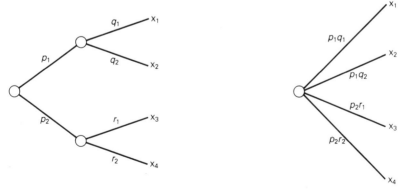

Figure 1.2   A compound lottery and its probabilistically equivalent single-stage lottery.

lottery, an assumption known as the Reduction of Compound Lotteries Axiom. By determining the probabilistically equivalent single-stage counterpart of each compound lottery, we can accordingly extend the individual's preference ranking and preference function from the set of all single-stage lotteries to the set of all compound lotteries.

Under these assumptions, behavior in a one-shot choice situation is fully determined: given an opportunity set of simple and/or compound lotteries, the individual will choose the lottery that is the most preferred or, equivalently, that yields the maximum value of the preference function $V(\cdot)$. Nature then determines the outcome that the individual will receive, according to the probabilities specified in the chosen lottery.

2.2 Expected utility preferences over lotteries

In regular consumer theory, we often make assumptions regarding the functional form of preference functions over commodity bundles (e.g. Cobb–Douglas, constant elasticiy of substitution, etc.). In choice under uncertainty, the *expected utility hypothesis* is the assumption that the preference function over lotteries takes, or can be monotonically transformed to take, the form

$$V(\tilde{X}) = V(x_1, p_1; \ldots; x_n, p_n) \equiv \sum_{i=1}^{n} U(x_i)p_i \equiv U(x_1)p_1 + \ldots + U(x_n)p_n$$

$$(1.1)$$

where $U(\cdot)$ is termed the individual's *von Neumann–Morgenstern utility function*. Under the Reduction of Compound Lotteries Axiom, the expected utility of both the single-stage and the compound lottery of figure 1.2 is $U(x_1)p_1 q_1 + U(x_2)p_1 q_2 + U(x_3)p_2 r_1 + U(x_4)p_2 r_2$. As alluded to above, economists have accumulated a considerable body of elegant and powerful theorems linking properties of an expected utility maximizer's von Neumann–Morgenstern utility function to his attitudes, and hence behavior, toward risk.

Separability across mutually exclusive events   The characteristic feature of the expected utility preference function (1.1) is that it is "linear in the probabilities," which implies that expected utility preferences exhibit what can be termed *separability across mutually exclusive events*. This general attribute can be broken down into two specific properties: *replacement separability* and *mixture separability*. Replacement separability follows from the additive structure of the expected utility preference function $\sum_{i=1}^{n} U(x_i)p_i$ and the fact that the contribution of each out-

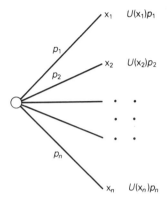

Figure 1.3   Contribution of each outcome-probability pair to the expected utility of a single-stage lottery.

come-probability pair (x_i, p_i) to this sum is independent of the other outcome-probability pairs, as seen in figure 1.3. Thus, if an individual would prefer to replace the pair (x_1, p_1) by (y_1, p_1) in the figure, or in other words if the lottery $(y_1, p_1; x_2, p_2; \ldots; x_n, p_n)$ were preferred to $(x_1, p_1; x_2, p_2; \ldots; x_n, p_n)$, then he would also prefer to replace (x_1, p_1) by (y_1, p_1) in any *other* lottery of the form $(x_1, p_1; x_2^*, p_2^*; \ldots; x_m^*, p_m^*)$.[4]

The property of mixture separability follows from the fact that the contribution of each outcome-probability pair to expected utility can be interpreted as the utility of its outcome $U(x_i)$ times its probability p_i. Since the conditions $U(y_1)p_1 > U(x_1)p_1$ and $U(y_1) > U(x_1)$ are equivalent, an expected utility maximizer will prefer $(y_1, p_1; x_2, p_2; \ldots; x_n, p_n)$ over $(x_1, p_1; x_2, p_2; \ldots; x_n, p_n)$ – that is, prefer a probability mixture of y_1 with $\{x_2, \ldots, x_n\}$ over the same probability mixture of x_1 with $\{x_2, \ldots, x_n\}$ – if and only if y_1 would be preferred to x_1 in an *outright* choice over these two sure outcomes.[5]

These two separability properties also extend to mutually exclusive sublotteries in a compound lottery. From figure 1.4 it is clear that the contribution of each sublottery to the expected utility of a compound lottery is independent of the other sublottery (or sublotteries) in the compound lottery. Thus, if an expected utility maximizer preferred replacing the upper sublottery in this figure by some other sublottery, for example, if the lottery in figure 1.5(a) were preferred to the lottery in figure 1.5(b), then this replacement would be preferred for any other configuration of the lower sublottery in the figure, which is replacement separability over sublotteries. It is also clear from figure 1.4 that

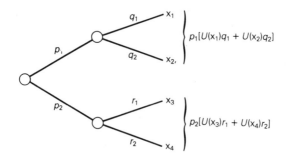

Figure 1.4   Contribution of each sublottery to the expected utility of a compound lottery.

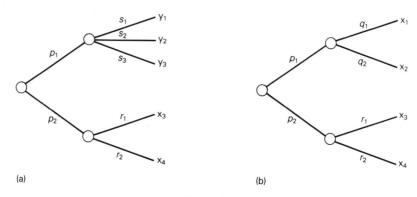

(a)   (b)

Figure 1.5

the contribution of each sublottery to expected utility can be interpreted as the expected utility of the sublottery itself (displayed in square brackets) times its probability of occurrence (p_1 or p_2). Since the condition $[U(y_1)s_1 + U(y_2)s_2 + U(y_3)s_3]p_1 > [U(x_1)q_1 + U(x_2)q_2]p_1$ is again equivalent to $[U(y_1)s_1 + U(y_2)s_2 + U(y_3)s_3] > [U(x_1)q_1 + U(x_2)q_2]$, an expected utility maximizer will exhibit the previously displayed preferences over compound lotteries if and only if

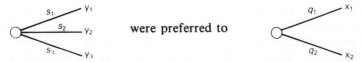

in an outright choice between these two single-stage lotteries, which is precisely mixture separability over sublotteries.

The properties of replacement and mixture separability across mutually exclusive outcomes and/or sublotteries can be combined and summarized in the following principle, known as the *Independence Axiom*:

The lottery $\tilde{X}$ is preferred (indifferent) to $\tilde{Y}$ if and only if $(\tilde{X}, p; \tilde{Z}, 1 - p)$ is preferred (indifferent) to $(\tilde{Y}, p; \tilde{Z}, 1 - p)$ for all lotteries $\tilde{Z}$ and all positive probabilities p.

This axiom implies mixture separability directly as stated. A double application yields

$$(\tilde{X}, p; \tilde{Z}, 1 - p) > (\sim)(\tilde{Y}, p; \tilde{Z}, 1 - p) \Leftrightarrow \tilde{X} > (\sim)\tilde{Y}$$
$$\Leftrightarrow (\tilde{X}, p; \tilde{Z}^*, 1 - p) > (\sim)(\tilde{Y}, p; \tilde{Z}^*, 1 - p)$$

which is replacement separability. As several researchers have shown, the Independence Axiom, and hence the above pair of separability properties, is equivalent to the property that the individual preference function (provided that it exists) takes the expected utility form $V(x_1, p_1; \ldots; x_n, p_n) \equiv \Sigma_{i=1}^{n} U(x_i)p_i$.[6]

The normative appeal of separability   Given the observed evidence against expected utility and the development of alternative models of non-expected utility preferences alluded to in section 1,[7] why do such a large number of researchers continue to cling to the expected utility model?

One reason that the expected utility model commands so much loyalty is its combination of theoretical simplicity and analytical power. After all, it involves nothing more than the familiar concepts of utility functions and mathematical expectation, and we have numerous theorems linking properties of the utility function $U(\cdot)$ with properties of risk preferences.

However, the main reason is the normative appeal of the property of separability over mutually exclusive events (or branches in a decision tree). To see this, recall that the Independence Axiom, which captures both forms of separability and is essentially equivalent to the property that the individual's preference function takes the expected utility form, states that for any lotteries $\tilde{X}$, $\tilde{Y}$, and $\tilde{Z}$ and positive probability p, we have

$$\tilde{X} > (\sim)\tilde{Y} \Leftrightarrow (\tilde{X}, p; \tilde{Z}, (1 - p)) > (\sim)(\tilde{Y}, p; \tilde{Z},(1 - p))$$

Consider a coin with probability $1 - p$ of landing tails, in which case you will win the lottery $\tilde{Z}$, and imagine being asked *before the flip* whether you would rather have $\tilde{X}$ or $\tilde{Y}$ in the event of a head. Such a choice is of course equivalent to determining your preferences between the right-hand prospects $(\tilde{X}, p; \tilde{Z}, (1 - p))$ and $(\tilde{Y}, p; \tilde{Z}, (1 - p))$. Now, either the coin will land tails, in which case your choice "won't have mattered," or else it will land heads, in which case you are "back to" precisely the left-hand choice between X̃ and Ỹ; so whichever lottery you would prefer in this outright choice should be the lottery you specify in the event of a head in the coin flip scenario.

It is important to note that this argument does *not* take the form "if you prefer X̃ to Ỹ you should prefer the combination of X̃ *and* Z̃ to the combination of Ỹ *and* Z̃." After all, cross-effects between X̃ and Z̃ or between Ỹ and Z̃ could well lead to a switch from the individual's preferences for X̃ alone versus Ỹ alone. Since the alternative events (in this case, heads versus tails) are *mutually exclusive*, the second choice is more properly described as being between X̃ *or* Z̃ and Ỹ *or* Z̃, so there "ought to" be no cross-effects.

Why have I placed the phrases "won't have mattered," "back to," and "ought to" in quotation marks? Because the point of this paper is that there may well be situations where rational individuals might exhibit such cross-effects between mutually exclusive outcomes, and that such cross-effects, if they exist, must be respected when modeling how agents behave in dynamic choice settings. But before doing so, let me turn from the normative issue of whether individuals *should* necessarily follow the precepts of expected utility maximization to the empirical issue of whether in fact they *do*.

2.3 Non-expected utility preferences over lotteries

Observed violations of separability   When the outcomes x_1, y_1, etc. represent wealth levels, replacing any outcome x_1 by a greater value y_1 always leads to a first-order stochastically dominating distribution, and the properties of replacement separability and mixture separability *over individual outcomes* are implications of the widely accepted property of first-order stochastic dominance preference over monetary lotteries.[8] However, it is crucial to note that the properties of replacement and mixture separability *over sublotteries* are strictly *stronger* properties, and *do not* logically follow from first-order stochastic dominance preference.[9]

As noted above, there is a growing body of evidence demonstrating that individuals' preferences over lotteries *do not* exhibit separability over sublotteries. An early example is the well-known Allais Paradox, which consists of the typical responses to the following two decision problems:

a_1:{1.00 chance of \$1,000,000   versus a_2:$\begin{cases} 0.10 \text{ chance of } \$5,000,000 \\ 0.89 \text{ chance of } \$1,000,000 \\ 0.01 \text{ chance of } \$0 \end{cases}$

and

$$a_3: \begin{cases} 0.10 \text{ chance of } \$5,000,000 \\ 0.90 \text{ chance of } \$0 \end{cases} \quad \text{versus} \quad a_4: \begin{cases} 0.11 \text{ chance of } \$5,000,000 \\ 0.89 \text{ chance of } \$0 \end{cases}$$

Researchers such as Allais (1953a), Morrison (1967), Raiffa (1968), Slovic and Tversky (1974), and others have given this problem to hundreds of subjects, and the modal if not majority choice has invariably been for a_1 over a_2 and for a_3 over a_4.

To see that the typical choices of a_1 and a_3 violate the expected utility hypothesis, we can invoke the Reduction of Compound Lotteries Axiom to rewrite these four prospects as

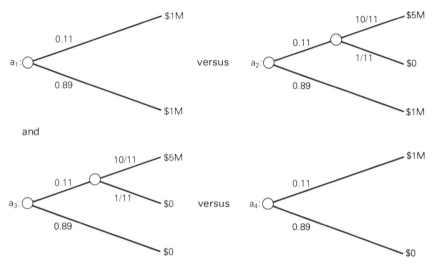

where $\$1M = \$1,000,000$. Viewed in this manner, the typical preferences in the Allais Paradox are seen to violate replacement separability over sublotteries, since a choice of a_1 over a_2 indicates a preference for replacing the upper sublottery in a_2 by a sure $\$1M$ when the lower branch yields $\$1M$, but a choice of a_3 over a_4 indicates an unwillingness to make this same replacement when the lower branch yields $\$0$.

The Allais Paradox is not an isolated example, but rather a member of a whole class of violations of replacement separability known as the "common consequence effect." This effect has been observed by MacCrimmon (1968), Moskowitz (1974), Kahneman and Tversky (1979), MacCrimmon and Larsson (1979), Chew and Waller (1986), and others. In each of these studies, the predominant form of departure from replacement separability corresponded to that of the Allais Paradox, namely a swing in preference from more risky to less risky sublotteries in one branch of a compound lottery as the sublottery in the *other* branch improves in the sense of first-order stochastic dominance.

A class of systematic violations of *mixture* separability involves pairs of the form

$$b_1:\begin{cases} p & \text{chance of } \$X \\ 1-p & \text{chance of } \$0 \end{cases} \quad \text{versus} \quad b_2:\begin{cases} q & \text{chance of } \$Y \\ 1-q & \text{chance of } \$0 \end{cases}$$

and

$$b_3:\begin{cases} rp & \text{chance of } \$X \\ 1-rp & \text{chance of } \$0 \end{cases} \quad \text{versus} \quad b_4:\begin{cases} rq & \text{chance of } \$Y \\ 1-rq & \text{chance of } \$0 \end{cases}$$

where $p > q$, $0 < X < Y$, and $0 < r < 1$. Invoking the Reduction of Compound Lotteries Axiom to write these four prospects as

and

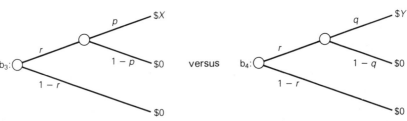

we see that mixture separability implies choices of either b_1 in the first pair and b_3 in the second pair, or else b_2 in the first pair and b_4 in the second pair. However, studies by Allais (1953a), Hagen (1979), Kahneman and Tversky (1979), MacCrimmon and Larsson (1979), and Chew and Waller (1986) have found a tendency for choices to depart from these predictions in the direction of preferring b_1 and b_4, a phenomenon known as the "common ratio effect." The reader is referred to the references in note 1 for discussions of these and other systematic violations of the expected utility property of linearity in the probabilities or, in other words, violations of separability across mutually exclusive events.

Non-expected utility models of preferences   Researchers have responded to this growing body of evidence by developing, analyzing, and testing nonlinear ("non-expected utility") functional forms for individual preference functions over lotteries, the most prominent of which are listed in table 1.1. Many (though not all) of these forms are flexible enough to exhibit the properties of stochastic dominance preference, risk aversion, and the types of observed violations of separability mentioned above, and have proven to be highly useful both theoretically and empirically.[10]

Table 1.1 Examples of non-expected utility preference functions

Subjective expected utility/prospect theory

$$\sum_{i=1}^{n} \nu(x_i)\,\pi(p_i)$$

Edwards (1955, 1962)
Kahneman and Tversky (1979)

Subjectively weighted utility

$$\left[\sum_{i=1}^{n} \nu(x_i)\,\pi(p_i)\right] \Big/ \left[\sum_{i=1}^{n} \pi(p_i)\right]$$

Karmarkar (1978, 1979)

Weighted utility

$$\left[\sum_{i=1}^{n} \nu(x_i)\,\tau(x_i)p_i\right] \Big/ \left[\sum_{i=1}^{n} \tau(x_i)\,p_i\right]$$

Chew and MacCrimmon (1979)
Chew (1983), Fishburn (1983)

Anticipated utility

$$\sum_{i=1}^{n} \nu(x_i)\left[g\left(\sum_{j=1}^{i} p_j\right) - g\left(\sum_{j=1}^{i-1} p_j\right)\right]$$

Quiggin (1982)

General quadratic

$$\sum_{i=1}^{n}\sum_{j=1}^{n} T(x_i,x_j)p_i p_j$$

Chew et al. (1988)

Optimism/pessimism

$$\sum_{i=1}^{n} \nu(x_i)g(p_i; x_1...,x_n)$$

Hey (1984)

Ordinal independence

$$\sum_{i=1}^{n} h\left(x_i, \sum_{j=1}^{i} p_j\right)\left[g\left(\sum_{j=1}^{i} p_j\right) - g\left(\sum_{j=1}^{i-1} p_j\right)\right]$$

Segal (1984)
Green and Jullien (1988)

3 STATIC AND DYNAMIC ARGUMENTS AGAINST
NON-EXPECTED UTILITY PREFERENCES

As noted above, two classes of "making book" arguments have been made against non-expected utility maximizers: those involving "static choice" and those involving "dynamic choice." Accordingly, it is useful to review the distinction between these two concepts.

3.1 Static versus dynamic choice situations

An uncertain situation is said to involve *static choice* if the individual's final decision or decisions must be made (in the sense of *irrevocably* made) before any of the alternative lotteries (or stages of compound lotteries) are resolved. In other words, Nature does not make any moves until the decision-maker has irrevocably made all his own moves.

On the other hand, a situation involves *dynamic choice* if it involves decisions which are made *after* the resolution of some uncertainty. This could be because the individual does not have to commit to a decision until after some uncertainty is resolved, or because the set of available choices depends upon the outcome of the uncertainty. In any event, a dynamic choice setting includes at least some choices which the individual can (or must) postpone until after Nature has made at least some of her "moves."

It is convenient to represent the sequencing of choice and chance stages in a dynamic choice problem by the standard decision tree diagram. In figure 1.6 the individual begins at the left end or *root* of the tree, where the initial round chance node indicates that Nature makes the first move with the displayed probabilities. Each branch leads to a square *choice node*, where the individual must make a decision which will lead to either another chance node, another choice node, or a final outcome. Although the individual learns the outcome of each chance node before having to make any subsequent decisions, we again assume that this process does not involve a significant amount of time, and hence continue to assume the Reduction of Compound Lotteries Axiom, so that the individual has no preference for few-staged versus many-staged trees *per se*.

Of course, we can also represent static problems with decision trees, as in figure 1.7 which represents the two static choice problems of the Allais Paradox. Given these definitions, it follows that a decision tree represents a static choice problem if and only if no chance node is ever followed by a choice node, and represents a dynamic choice problem if and only if at least one chance node *is* followed by a choice node.

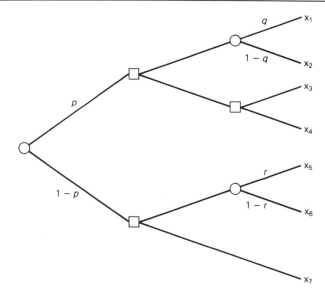

Figure 1.6   Example of a decision tree representing a dynamic choice problem.

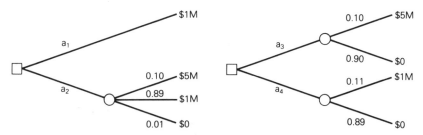

Figure 1.7   Decision tree representation of the two static choice problems of the Allais paradox.

The relevance of the distinction between static and dynamic choice is that, while static choice situations imply that all decisions are irrevocably made before the resolution of any uncertainty, dynamic choice situations allow us to distinguish between an individual's *planned* choices for each choice node at the beginning of the decision problem (that is, at the root of the tree) and his *actual* choices upon arriving at a given choice node. It is this distinction which lies at the heart of the dynamic consistency issue.

3.2 Static arguments against non-expected utility maximizers

Before treating the issue of dynamic consistency, however, it is useful to examine the classic static arguments against non-expected utility maximizers, if only to demonstrate how a properly designed non-expected utility model will be immune to each of them.

Intransitive preferences over lotteries The simplest of these arguments is against someone whose preferences over lotteries (or for that matter, any other objects) are intransitive (see for example Davidson et al., 1955; Raiffa, 1968, pp. 77–9; Yaari, 1985; Schick,1986; Anand, 1987). Say the individual exhibits the triple of strict preference rankings

$$\tilde{Z} > \tilde{Y} \qquad \tilde{Y} > \tilde{X} \qquad \tilde{X} > \tilde{Z}$$

and say that he currently owns the (not yet resolved) lottery $\tilde{X}$. By continuity of preferences, there will exist some small positive ϵ such that $\tilde{X} - \epsilon > \tilde{Z}$, where $\tilde{X} - \epsilon$ denotes the lottery $\tilde{X}$ with the amount ϵ subtracted from each possible payoff (including zero, if it were a possible payoff). To 'make book' against such an individual, begin by offering him $\tilde{Y}$ in exchange for $\tilde{X}$. Given his preferences, he will accept it. Next, and before allowing any of the lotteries to be resolved, offer $\tilde{Z}$ in exchange for $\tilde{Y}$ (once again, it will be accepted). Finally, offer $\tilde{X} - \epsilon$ in exchange for $\tilde{Z}$ (again, it will be accepted). Thus, an individual who started out owning $\tilde{X}$ has ended up owning $\tilde{X} - \epsilon$ or, in other words, has been bilked out of the sure amount ϵ.

It is often argued that you could continue this process and turn the individual into a "money pump" which gushes out ϵ dollars at each push of the handle (each cycle) until he has delivered his entire net worth over to you. However, since the first cycle leaves him with $\tilde{X} - \epsilon$ rather than $\tilde{X}$, continuing this process requires that his preferences contain an intransitive cycle involving $\tilde{X} - \epsilon$, another cycle involving $\tilde{X} - 2\epsilon,\ldots$, which does not necessarily follow from the existence of the original cycle. However, this argument does claim to show that, *to the extent* that preferences are intransitive, the individual can be exploited.

However, since each of the non-expected utility models of table 1.1 represents preferences by a real-valued maximand $V(\cdot)$, and since it is impossible for three real numbers to satisfy $V(\tilde{Z}) > V(\tilde{Y}) > V(\tilde{X}) > V(\tilde{Z})$, these models will never exhibit intransitive cycles. Thus they cannot be subjected to this form of making book.

Violations of first-order stochastic dominance preference A second type of static making book argument does apply to some (though not all) of the non-expected utility preference functions in table 1.1. Take the "subjective expected utility" form $V(x_1, p_1; \ldots; x_n, p_n) \equiv \sum_{i=1}^{n} \nu(x_i)\, \pi(p_i)$. If the function $\pi(\cdot)$ is not linear, there will exist probabilities $p_1, \ldots, p_m$, summing to unity, such that $\Sigma_{i=1}^m \pi(p_i) \neq \pi(1)$. Say that $\Sigma_{i=1}^m \pi(p_i) > \pi(1)$. In this case, there will exist outcome levels $x_1 < x_2 < \ldots < x_m < x^*$ such that

$$\sum_{i=1}^m \nu(x_i) \, \pi(p_i) > \nu(x^*) \, \pi(1)$$

Since this implies that the individual prefers the lottery $(x_1, p_1; \ldots; x_m, p_m)$ to a sure x^*, we could accomplish in a single trade that which in the previous argument took three trades, namely bilking an individual holding x^* out of a strictly positive amount of money – at the very least $x^* - x_m$, and perhaps more (the case where $\Sigma_{i=1}^m \pi(p_i) < \pi(1)$ follows similarly).

Of course, the property of this preference function that allows this is its violation of first-order stochastic dominance preference. Since the subjective expected utility form $\Sigma_{i=1}^n \nu(x_i) \pi(p_i)$ was for several years the most prominent example of a non-expected utility model in the literature (e.g. Edwards, 1955, 1962; Tversky, 1967a, b; Wallsten, 1971), this feature contributed to the general impression that *all* departures from linearity in the probabilities implied violations of first-order stochastic dominance preference.[11] However, as noted in section 2.3 (especially note 9), violations of separability across mutually exclusive events and violations of first-order stochastic dominance preference are distinct concepts, and the last five forms in table 1.1 will all exhibit first-order stochastic dominance preference provided that their component functions $\nu(\cdot), \tau(\cdot), g(\cdot), \ldots$ satisfy the proper monotonicity conditions.[12] This fact, along with the transitivity of these forms, ensures that it is impossible to make book against them via any sequence of (well-specified) probability distributions in any static choice situation.

Incoherent subjective probabilities A third type of static making book argument is against someone whose probabilistic beliefs are not *coherent*, that is, do not satisfy the standard laws of probability theory (e.g. that the probability of the union of disjoint events is the sum of their probabilities). First set forth by Ramsey (1926) and de Finetti (1937), these arguments show that if the agent possesses event probabilities that are not coherent, and is willing to accept betting odds based on these "probabilities," then he can be induced to accept a set of bets which jointly imply that he cannot win money and has a positive probability of losing money (see also Kyburg and Smokler, 1980, pp. 3–22; Schick, 1986; Yaari, 1985).

Do violations of linearity in the probabilities *per se* expose the non-expected utility preference functions of table 1.1 to such arguments?

No – these arguments involve the construction of event probabilities and their use in the evaluation of functions from events to payoffs ("acts" or "bets"), whereas the preference functions in table 1.1 are defined over well-specified coherent probability distributions, such as the type presented in the Allais Paradox and similar examples. To make an analogy with consumer theory, it is clearly possible to "make book" against someone who cannot correctly add different amounts of the same good, or who cannot correctly multiply quantities by prices. But if an individual with monotonic preferences *can* perform such operations correctly, it is not possible to make book against him just because these totals enter nonlinearly into his utility function.

3.3 Dynamic arguments against non-expected utility maximizers

We have seen that a properly designed non-expected utility model will be immune to each of the above static notions of making book. However, the following class of arguments, involving dynamic choice, seem to pose a more formidable challenge.

Argument for the dynamic inconsistency of non-expected utility maximizers   The best known of these arguments (see for example Markowitz, 1959, pp. 218–24; Raiffa, 1968, pp. 82–3) can be illustrated using the typical non-expected utility preferences expressed in the Allais Paradox, namely a preference for lottery a_1 over a_2, and for a_3 over a_4. The first step consists of obtaining (and, for good measure, writing down) the individual's preferences over the pair of options.

The second step consists in presenting him with the dynamic choice problems of figure 1.8.

Consider the opportunity set of lotteries implied by the left-hand tree in this figure. A planned choice of the upper branch at the choice node, when combined with the probabilities at the initial chance node, would imply overall probabilities {0.10, 0.89, 0.01} of receiving the outcomes {$5M, $1M, $0}, which is precisely lottery a_2 of the Allais Paradox. A planned choice of the lower branch at the choice node would yield a sure chance of $1M, which is, of course, prospect a_1.[13] Thus an individual with the typical Allais Paradox preferences of a_1 over a_2, if he had to

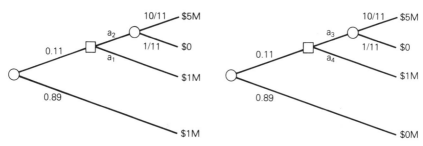

Figure 1.8 Dynamic choice problems which generate the same opportunity sets as the Allais paradox problem.

make this decision in advance, would plan to choose *down* at the choice node in the left-hand tree. A similar calculation shows that the opportunity set for the right-hand tree consists of the Allais Paradox prospects $\{a_3, a_4\}$, so that an individual who preferred a_3 over a_4 would plan to choose *up* at the choice node in the right-hand tree.

At this point (goes the argument), an individual with Allais-type preferences will be in trouble. Say that his first-step preference had been for $\tilde{W}$ over the sure $1M. If Nature were to choose *up* at the initial chance node in the left-hand tree, he would be facing precisely this choice and would accordingly reverse his original plan of choosing *down* (to obtain the $1M) in favor of choosing *up* (to obtain $\tilde{W}$). On the other hand, say his first-step choice had been for the sure $1M over $\tilde{W}$. In that case, he would undertake a similar volte-face should he arrive at the choice node in the right tree. In other words, his behavior in one of these two trees will be dynamically inconsistent, in the sense that his actual choice upon arriving at a choice node will differ from his planned choice for that node.

It is important to note that this argument does not depend upon the specific lotteries in the Allais Paradox, but can be constructed out of any violation of replacement separability, mixture separability, or the Independence Axiom, that is, any departure from expected utility preferences.[14] Thus, unlike the static arguments of the previous section – which we have seen do not apply to "properly designed" non-expected utility models – this argument seems to demonstrate that non-expected utility maximizers are *generically* incapable of behaving consistently in even the simplest of planning situations.

Classical argument for making book against non-expected utility maximizers Several researchers have shown how the above dynamic inconsistency argument can be adopted to explicitly make book against (that is, extract a sure payment from) a non-expected utility maximizer.[15] As observed in note 14, any non-expected utility maximizer will exhibit the preferences

$$\tilde{X} > \tilde{Y} \quad \text{but} \quad (\tilde{Y}, p; \tilde{Z}, (1 - p)) > (\tilde{X}, p; \tilde{Z}, (1 - p))$$

for at least some lotteries $\tilde{X}$, $\tilde{Y}$, $\tilde{Z}$, and probability p. By continuity of preferences, there will exist some small positive ϵ such that

$$\tilde{X} - \epsilon > \tilde{Y} \quad \text{but} \quad (\tilde{Y}, p; \tilde{Z} - \epsilon, (1 - p)) > (\tilde{X}, p; \tilde{Z}, (1 - p)).$$

Say that there is some event E with probability p and that the individual currently owns the prospect ($\tilde{X}$ if E; $\tilde{Z}$ if $\sim$ E), which implies that he owns a compound lottery of the form ($\tilde{X}, p; \tilde{Z}, (1 - p)$). In exchange for this initial holding, offer him the prospect ($\tilde{Y}$ if E; $\tilde{Z} - \epsilon$ if $\sim$ E). Since this prospect implies the lottery ($\tilde{Y}, p; \tilde{Z} - \epsilon, (1 - p)$), which is preferred to ($\tilde{X}, p; \tilde{Z}, (1 - p)$), the offer will be accepted. Now let the first stage of uncertainty be resolved. If $\sim$ E occurs, the terms of your exchange imply that you receive the lottery $\tilde{Z}$ and must pay the individual $\tilde{Z} - \epsilon$, and so you have made a gain of ϵ. If E occurs, you receive the lottery $\tilde{X}$ and must pay him $\tilde{Y}$. However, from the ranking displayed above it follows that he would be happy to accept the lottery $\tilde{X} - \epsilon$ instead of $\tilde{Y}$, and so you again make a gain of ϵ. When the dust clears, the individual who initially held the prospect ($\tilde{X}$ if E; $\tilde{Z}$ if $\sim$ E) has come out of this process as if he held ($\tilde{X} - \epsilon$ if E; $\tilde{Z} - \epsilon$ if $\sim$ E), and you (who entered the story with no resources at all) have come out with (ϵ if E; ϵ if $\sim$ E). In other words, you have found a way to bilk a generic non-expected utility maximizer out of a sure ϵ.

Argument that non-expected utility maximizers could be averse to information   It is almost a truism that advanced resolution of uncertainty in a dynamic choice problem, that is, prior knowledge of what Nature's "moves" will be, could never make an individual worse off *ex ante*, and in general will be strictly preferred. However, a final argument, put forth by Wakker (1988) and Hilton (1989) (see also Keasey, 1984; Loomes and Sugden, 1984b) purports to demonstrate that "sophisticated" non-expected utility maximizers can actually be made *worse off* by receipt of this type of information in dynamic choice settings. Although we shall illustrate this argument using the lotteries and preferences in the Allais Paradox, it is important to note that, once again, such an example can be constructed out of any departure from expected utility preferences.

Take an individual with the typical Allais preferences $a_1 > a_2$ and $a_3 > a_4$, who prefers

Let E be an event with probability 0.11 and consider the four event-contingent prospects, shown in table 1.2, which generate the four correspondingly named lotteries from the Allais Paradox. If the individual must choose one of these four prospects before learning whether E has or has not occurred, he will choose a_1, since a_1 first-order stochastically dominates a_4, a_2 stochastically dominates a_3, and a_1 is preferred to a_2. Thus, in the "no information" case the individual will choose a_1, or, in other words, the bundle ($1M if E, $1M if ~ E).

But say the individual was told that he would be given knowledge of whether E or ~ E occurs *before* having to choose. If he were to learn that E occurred, he could obtain either $\tilde{W}$ (by choosing a_2 or a_3) or else a sure $1M (by choosing a_1 or a_4), and, by the preferences displayed above, he knows that he would choose $\tilde{W}$. On the other hand, if he were to learn that ~ E occurred, he would clearly choose to obtain $1M rather than $0.

Thus (alleges the argument), a "sophisticated" non-expected utility maximizer will realize that, if given prior information as to the occurrence/nonoccurrence of E, he would end up consuming the state-contingent prospect ($\tilde{W}$ if E, $1M if ~ E), which reduces to lottery a_2 from the Allais Paradox. If not given this information, he would consume $1M with certainty (the lottery a_1). But since a_1 is preferred to a_2, the individual would therefore *rather not* have the information![16]

4 CRITIQUE OF THE DYNAMIC ARGUMENTS

We have seen that while each of the static arguments against non-expected utility maximizers can be deflected by a properly designed non-expected

Table 1.2

	E (0.11 chance)	~E (0.89 chance)
a_1	$1M	$1M
a_2	$\tilde{W}$	$1M
a_3	$\tilde{W}$	$0
a_4	$1M	$0

utility model, the class of dynamic arguments is apparently more formidable. In this section we shall take a closer, more rigorous look at
these arguments, discover that they each rely upon a hidden assumption concerning behavior in dynamic choice situations, and argue that
this assumption is inappropriate to impose on non-expected utility
maximizers.

4.1 The hidden assumption in these arguments: consequentialism

Consider an individual at the root of the dynamic decision problem
illustrated in figure 1.9. How would he act in such a situation? The
classical economic model of choice assumes that, as in any decision
problem, he would (a) determine the opportunity set implied by the
situation, (b) identify the most preferred element of this set, and (c) adopt
the strategy which leads to this most preferred element.

We have already noted that, since such situations involve uncertainty,
the elements of the opportunity set are not the alternative outcomes, but
rather probability distributions over these outcomes. The opportunity set
of distributions implied by this tree, and the strategies that generate each

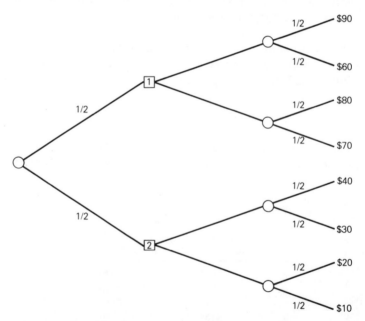

Figure 1.9   Example of a decision tree representing a dynamic choice problem.

Table 1.3 Opportunity set of probability distributions for figure 1.9

Strategy	Probability distribution	Preference function value
(U, U)	($90, $\frac{1}{4}$; $60, $\frac{1}{4}$; $40, $\frac{1}{4}$; $30, $\frac{1}{4}$)	V($90, $\frac{1}{4}$; $60, $\frac{1}{4}$; $40, $\frac{1}{4}$; $30, $\frac{1}{4}$)
(L, U)	($80, $\frac{1}{4}$; $70, $\frac{1}{4}$; $40, $\frac{1}{4}$; $30, $\frac{1}{4}$)	V($80, $\frac{1}{4}$; $70, $\frac{1}{4}$; $40, $\frac{1}{4}$; $30, $\frac{1}{4}$)
(U, L)	($90, $\frac{1}{4}$; $60, $\frac{1}{4}$; $20, $\frac{1}{4}$; $10, $\frac{1}{4}$)	V($90, $\frac{1}{4}$; $60, $\frac{1}{4}$; $20, $\frac{1}{4}$; $10, $\frac{1}{4}$)
(L, L)	($80, $\frac{1}{4}$; $70, $\frac{1}{4}$; $20, $\frac{1}{4}$; $10, $\frac{1}{4}$)	V($80, $\frac{1}{4}$; $70, $\frac{1}{4}$; $20, $\frac{1}{4}$; $10, $\frac{1}{4}$)

of them, are listed in table 1.3. In the table, strategies are denoted by ordered pairs of the form (U, U), (U, L) . . ., which specify how the agent would act at each of the two choice nodes, where U or L denote a choice of the upper or lower branch.

Since the third and fourth distributions in the table are stochastically dominated by the first and second, neither is optimal, and so the individual must choose which of the lotteries

$$($90, \tfrac{1}{4}; $60, \tfrac{1}{4}; $40, \tfrac{1}{4}; $30, \tfrac{1}{4}) \quad \text{or} \quad ($80, \tfrac{1}{4}; $70, \tfrac{1}{4}; $40, \tfrac{1}{4}; $30, \tfrac{1}{4})$$

is the most preferred. Say the former is most preferred; in other words, say that

$$V($90, \tfrac{1}{4}; $60, \tfrac{1}{4}; $40, \tfrac{1}{4}; $30, \tfrac{1}{4}) > V($80, \tfrac{1}{4}; $70, \tfrac{1}{4}; $40, \tfrac{1}{4}; $30, \tfrac{1}{4})$$

Therefore he would plan on choosing up at either choice node, which is the strategy (U, U).

So much for his *initial* choice of probability distribution and associated strategy. How should the individual act if given the chance to *reconsider* his plans in the middle of a decision tree? Say he adopted the strategy (U, U) and that Nature chose up at the initial chance node, so that he is now at choice node 1. Should a recalculation of his strategy lead to any revision in his original plans? On the one hand, he has received new information – Nature's choice at the initial node – and new information is often a cause for revision in plans. On the other hand, since his plans at choice node 1 were *conditional on precisely this circumstance* (on Nature choosing up), we might feel that a recalculation of his optimal strategy at this point should yield the same result. The key to the dynamic consistency issue lies in the manner in which such recalculations are assumed to be undertaken.

Like the individual's initial calculation, any recalculation in the middle of a decision tree must involve specifying an opportunity set of alternatives and a maximand or preference function over this set. It seems obvious that, whatever the opportunity set is, it now consists of only two elements. But there are two different approaches to specifying just what

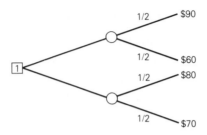

Figure 1.10   Decision tree resulting from the consequentialist procedure of "snipping off" just before choice node 1 in figure 1.9.

these two elements, and the individual's ranking of them, are.

Roughly speaking, the consequentialist approach to this decision consists of "snipping" the decision tree at (that is, just before) the current choice node, throwing the rest of the tree away, and recalculating by applying his *original* preference ordering (or original preference function) to alternative possible continuations of the tree. In other words, the individual would act as if he had *started out* with the tree in figure 1.10, or equivalently the opportunity set of table 1.4, and make a choice based on his preferences over the lotteries

$$(\$90, \tfrac{1}{2}; \$60, \tfrac{1}{2}) \qquad \text{versus} \qquad (\$80, \tfrac{1}{2}; \$70, \tfrac{1}{2})$$

that is, make the comparison

$$V(\$90, \tfrac{1}{2}; \$60, \tfrac{1}{2}) \gtreqless V(\$80, \tfrac{1}{2}; \$70, \tfrac{1}{2})$$

where $V(\cdot)$ is his original preference function. The philosophy behind this approach is that the uncertainty involved in the rest of the tree, as implied by the probabilities and planned choices at the snipped-off nodes, is now irrelevant and should be treated as if it never existed.[17] In other words, the only determinants of how decisions should be made in the continuation of a decision tree are the *original* preference ordering over probability distributions and the attributes of the *continuation* of the tree.

What would it mean *not* to be consequentialist? Roughly speaking, it means that the individual would not snip off the rest of the tree, but would

Table 1.4 Opportunity set at choice node 1 of figure 1.9 under the assumption of consequentialism

Strategy	Probability distribution	Preference function value
(U)	$(\$90, \tfrac{1}{2}; \$60, \tfrac{1}{2})$	$V(\$90, \tfrac{1}{2}; \$60, \tfrac{1}{2})$
(L)	$(\$80, \tfrac{1}{2}; \$70, \tfrac{1}{2})$	$V(\$80, \tfrac{1}{2}; \$70, \tfrac{1}{2})$

instead take this past uncertainty (that is, the risks that he has borne) into account in a manner consistent with his original preferences. But before formally presenting this alternative approach and arguing that it is more appropriate than consequentialism in the case of non-expected utility preferences, it is useful to go back and demonstrate how each of the three dynamic arguments against non-expected utility maximizers implicitly relies upon consequentialism to achieve its conclusion.

Consequentialism in the dynamic inconsistency argument   The assumption of consequentialism is implicitly invoked in the dynamic consistency argument at the point where we asked how a non-expected utility maximizer would behave if nature were to lead him to the choice nodes in either of the decision trees in figure 1.8. The argument maintained that, at this point, he would basically snip off the unrealized lower branch, ignore what its probability had been as well as what outcome it would have led to, and choose exactly as he would have in the first-step decision problem, that is, as if he were starting out with a choice between the lotteries

In other words, the argument has assumed that the individual's behavior at the choice node in each of the trees is fully determined by his answer to the first-step question.

Consequentialism in the classical making book argument   Consequentialism is invoked in the classical making book argument in its assertion of how a non-expected utility maximizer owning the event-contingent prospect ($\tilde{Y}$ if E; $\tilde{Z} - \epsilon$ if $\sim$ E) would behave if the event E should occur and he were then offered the lottery $\tilde{X} - \epsilon$ in exchange for his holding of $\tilde{Y}$. Once again, the argument asserts that his choice in this case would be determined by the original displayed preference ranking $\tilde{X} - \epsilon > \tilde{Y}$, that is, as if he were to snip off the "$\sim$ E–branch" of the prospect and choose as if he had started out with a decision between the lottery $\tilde{Y}$ and the offer of $\tilde{X} - \epsilon$.

Consequentialism in the aversion to information argument   This argument invokes consequentialism when asserting how a "sophisticated" non-expected utility maximizer would predict his own behavior should the event E occur. In this case (goes the argument), the individual would ignore ("snip off") what would have happened in the event $\sim$ E, consider himself back to a *de novo* choice between the lottery $\tilde{W}$ and a sure \$1M, and choose on the basis of his original ranking of these two prospects.

4.2 Consequentialism is inappropriate when preferences are nonseparable

There is no question that, given their implicit or explicit assumption of consequentialism, these three dynamic arguments succeed in making individuals with non-expected utility preferences look rather foolish. However, the thrust of my critique of these arguments is that is it inappropriate to impose the property of consequentialism on non-expected utility maximizers. I want to argue that consequentialism is essentially a dynamic version of the very separability that non-expected utility maximizers reject, and that assuming it in this context is much like assuming, say, that an agent with intertemporally nonseparable preferences would neglect his consumption history when making subsequent decisions.

Parental example   Let me motivate this critique by an example involving the ultimate normative authority: one's Mom.[18] In this case, Mom has a single indivisible item – a "treat" – which she can give to either daughter Abigail or son Benjamin. Assume that she is indifferent between Abigail getting the treat and Benjamin getting the treat, and strongly prefers either of these outcomes to the case where neither child gets it. However, in a violation of the precepts of expected utility theory, Mom *strictly prefers* a coin flip over either of these sure outcomes, and in particular, strictly prefers $\frac{1}{2}:\frac{1}{2}$ to any other pair of probabilities.

This random allocation procedure would be straightforward, except that Benjie, who cut his teeth on Raiffa's classic *Decision Analysis*, behaves as follows:

> Before the coin is flipped, he requests a confirmation from Mom that, yes, she does strictly prefer a 50:50 lottery over giving the treat to Abigail. He gets her to put this in writing.

> Had he won the flip, he would have claimed the treat.

> As it turns out, he loses the flip. But as Mom is about to give the treat to Abigail, he reminds Mom of her "preference" for flipping a coin over giving it to Abigail (producing her signed statement), and demands that she flip again.

What would *your* Mom do if you tried to pull a stunt like this? She would clearly say "You had your chance!" and refuse to flip again. This is precisely what Mom does.

What is happening in this example? The set of possible outcomes is given by

{A, B} = {Abigail receives the treat, Benjamin receives the treat}[19]

Since Mom strictly prefers a 50:50 lottery to either A or B, she has the non-expected utility (that is, nonseparable) preference ordering

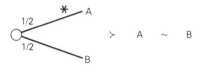

and so chooses the first of these (the lottery) over either sure outcome. The coin having landed in favor of Abigail (that is, Nature having chosen the upper branch), Benjamin has tried to impose consequentialism on Mom by snipping the tree at the point *, throwing the rest of the tree away, and applying her *original* preference ranking to the continuation of the tree, thereby trying to get her to replace

By replying "You had your chance," Mom is reminding Benjamin of the existence of the snipped-off branch (the original $\frac{1}{2}$ probability of B) and that her preferences are not separable, so the fact that Nature *could* have gone down that branch *still matters*. Mom is rejecting the property of consequentialism – and, in my opinion, rightly so.

What is Mom (or any other nonseparable agent) telling us? Mom's original preference for {A, $\frac{1}{2}$; B, $\frac{1}{2}$} over (among other lotteries) {A, $\frac{1}{4}$; B, $\frac{3}{4}$}, that is (under the Reduction of Compound Lotteries Axiom), her preference for the prospect

tells us that conditional on having borne, but not realized, a $\frac{1}{2}$ probability of B (that is, conditional on being at the point ∗), she strictly prefers the outcome A to the lottery {A, $\frac{1}{2}$; B, $\frac{1}{2}$}. Since this is her attitude *ex ante*, Mom is only being dynamically consistent in maintaining the same attitude *ex post* by refusing to flip the coin again at the point ∗.

This, in a nutshell, is why it is inappropriate to impose consequentialism on non-expected utility maximizers. We have seen in section 2 that such agents have nonseparable preferences across alternative events (or decision tree branches), and so their *ex ante* attitudes toward what happens along one branch may well depend upon what would have happened along the other branches. By forcing them to "snip" the rest of the tree once they are halfway down a branch and then act as if these other branches had not existed (that is, act as if they were *starting out* with what remains of the tree), consequentialism is essentially imposing separability upon them *ex post*, and it is no surprise that doing so would make their behavior look inconsistent (or worse) or that a non-expected utility maximizer like Mom would reject the validity of this procedure.

Analogy with nonseparable intertemporal preferences   In order to best exploit our intuition in this regard, it is useful to consider how the notions of nonseparability, consequentialism, and dynamic inconsistency appear in the framework of choice over intertemporal consumption streams rather than uncertain prospects. The reader has my promise that, at the end of this excursion, I will be quite explicit about what I feel this analogy *does* and *does not* imply about the case of choice under uncertainty.

Consider the following preferences over consumption streams:

$$(Star\ Wars\ I) > (Star\ Wars\ II)$$

$$(Star\ Wars\ I,\ Star\ Wars\ I) < (Star\ Wars\ I,\ Star\ Wars\ II)$$

where "(*Star Wars I*)" denotes seeing that film once this evening, "(*Star Wars I, Star Wars I*)" denotes seeing it twice in succession, etc. Since this individual's preferences for seeing *Star Wars I* versus *Star Wars II* depends upon whether or not he has just seen the former movie, his preferences over consumption streams are not intertemporally separable. The analog of "consequentialism" in such a context would be the property that, if given a chance to revise at some point in time, the individual would snip the consumption stream at (that is, just before) the current point in time, throw the earlier part away, and recalculate by applying his *original* preference ranking to the alternative possible continuations of his consumption stream.

Given this, the analog of the dynamic inconsistency argument in section 3.3 would run as follows: "I note from your displayed preferences that, if given a choice between seeing *Star Wars I* and *Star Wars II*, you would choose the former – let's just jot that fact down and see it aside for a moment. Now, let me offer you a different choice: We could either go to the Bijou Theater and see the double feature of *Star Wars I* and *Star Wars II*, or we could go to the Paradise Cinema, which is only showing *Star Wars I*, but we could sit through it twice. The showings are at 7.00 pm and 9.00 pm at each theater."

Given your displayed preferences, you reply that we should go to the Bijou and see the pair of movies. But at the 8.45 intermission, I say "Ah, but *now* we are back to a choice between seeing *Star Wars II* (by staying here) or else seeing *Star Wars I* (by going across town to the Paradise). Since I see from this piece of paper that you would rather see *Star Wars I* than *Star Wars II*, it follows that you would want to change theaters at this point" (or "that you would be willing to pay me ϵ in order to change theaters," etc.).

Your response in this situation would be the analog of Mom's, namely that the preferences written on the paper were for an outright choice, and that your displayed preferences made it clear from the start that, *conditional on having already seen Star Wars I*, you would rather see *Star Wars II* than see *Star Wars I* again. Put more formally, "the intertemporal analog of consequentialism, which states that an agent would neglect his consumption history when recalculating in the middle of an intertemporal choice situation, is clearly inappropriate to impose on someone who has intertemporally nonseparable preferences. For such an agent, the fact that past consumption is gone in the sense of *consumed* does not mean it is gone in the sense of *irrelevant*."[20]

As noted above, it is important to be explicit about what this analogy does and does not have to say about nonseparable preferences over alternative events. It does not show that since it can be reasonable to have nonseparable preferences over time, it must, *ipso facto*, be reasonable to have nonseparable preferences over events. Rather, it seeks to highlight the point that *if an individual informs you from the start that his preferences are nonseparable* (over time, events, or any other dimension), then it is inappropriate to impose separability *ex post* by explicitly or implicitly invoking consequentialism, and it is hardly surprising that doing so would lead to predictions of nonsensical behavior.

5 DYNAMICALLY CONSISTENT NON-EXPECTED UTILITY MAXIMIZERS

The analogy with intertemporal choice can fulfill an additional purpose, namely to motivate the manner in which nonseparable (that is, non-expected utility) preferences are *appropriately* extended to dynamic choice settings, and how such an extension will lead to dynamically consistent choice behavior.

5.1 Extending nonseparable intertemporal preferences to dynamic choice situations

Consider an individual with the nonseparable preference ranking

$$\text{(pizza, pizza, salad, salad)} > \text{(pizza, pizza, pizza, pizza)}$$
$$> \text{(pizza, pizza)} > \text{(salad, salad)}$$

or equivalently

$$V\text{(pizza, pizza, salad, salad)} > V\text{(pizza, pizza, pizza, pizza)}$$
$$> V\text{(pizza, pizza)} > V\text{(salad, salad)}$$

where "(pizza, pizza)" denotes eating two (small) pizzas sequentially this evening, "(pizza, pizza, salad, salad)" denotes eating the two pizzas and then eating two salads, etc. If such an individual could choose one of these four streams, he would clearly choose the upper left-hand one, and start eating pizza.

Now say he has finished his two pizzas and was asked to reconsider his choice between a pair of salads at this point versus a third and fourth pizza. How would we properly represent the mathematics of his recalculation? The key point is to keep in mind that, while the first two pizzas are gone in the sense of having been consumed, they are not gone in the sense of irrelevant. Accordingly, we could either plug each of the *entire* time streams into the individual's *original* preference function $V(\cdot)$ (using bars to indicate the items that have already been consumed), so that the recalculation consisted of the comparison

$$V(\overline{\text{pizza}}, \overline{\text{pizza}}, \text{salad, salad}) \quad \text{versus} \quad V(\overline{\text{pizza}}, \overline{\text{pizza}}, \text{pizza, pizza})$$

or, equivalently, plug the *continuation* of each time stream into the individual's *conditional* preference function $V_{\text{pizza, pizza}}(\cdot)$, so that the recalculation consisted of the comparison

$$V_{\text{pizza, pizza}}\text{(salad, salad)} \quad \text{versus} \quad V_{\text{pizza, pizza}}\text{(pizza, pizza)}$$

where we define

$$V_{\text{pizza, pizza}}(x, y) \underset{x,y}{\equiv} V\text{(pizza, pizza, x, y)}.$$

Of course, these alternative notational procedures are equivalent, and both will imply that this nonseparable agent will stick with his original plan of moving on to the two salads rather than eating two more pizzas (that is, he will be "dynamically consistent"). In either case, the rest of the original displayed preference ranking, that is, the ordering

$$\text{(pizza, pizza)} > \text{(salad, salad)} \qquad \text{or equivalently}$$
$$V\text{(pizza, pizza)} > V\text{(salad, salad)}$$

is quite irrelevant, given that at this point in the problem the individual has already eaten two pizzas. I feel that the above procedure is the natural way to extend the individual's original nonseparable preferences over time streams to the dynamic choice problem generated by giving him the opportunity to reconsider halfway through the problem.

5.2 Extending non-expected utility preferences to dynamic choice situations

The proper way to extend non-expected utility preferences to dynamic choice settings is analogous. Consider for example an agent with the non-expected utility preferences

$$\left(x_1, \tfrac{1}{4}; x_2, \tfrac{1}{4}; x_3, \tfrac{1}{4}; x_4, \tfrac{1}{4}\right) > \left(x_1, \tfrac{1}{4}; x_2, \tfrac{1}{4}; y_3, \tfrac{1}{4}; y_4, \tfrac{1}{4}\right)$$
$$> \left(y_3, \tfrac{1}{2}; y_4, \tfrac{1}{2}\right)$$
$$> \left(x_3, \tfrac{1}{2}; x_4, \tfrac{1}{2}\right)$$

or equivalently.

$$V\left(x_1, \tfrac{1}{4}; x_2, \tfrac{1}{4}; x_3, \tfrac{1}{4}; x_4, \tfrac{1}{4}\right) > V\left(x_1, \tfrac{1}{4}; x_2, \tfrac{1}{4}; y_3, \tfrac{1}{4}; y_4, \tfrac{1}{4}\right)$$
$$> V\left(y_3, \tfrac{1}{2}; y_4, \tfrac{1}{2}\right)$$
$$> V\left(x_3, \tfrac{1}{2}; x_4, \tfrac{1}{2}\right)$$

who faces the decision tree in figure 1.11. From the top line of his displayed preferences, he will clearly make plans to choose up should he reach the choice node.

Say that Nature chooses down at the initial chance node. What is the appropriate way to represent the agent's recalculation? As with intertemporal nonseparability, the key point is to remember that an agent with non-expected utility/nonseparable preferences feels (both *ex ante* and *ex post*) that risk which is borne but not realized, that is, the $\tfrac{1}{4}$ probabilities of having obtained x_1 or x_2, is gone in the sense of having been *consumed* (or "borne") rather than gone in the sense of *irrelevant*. Accordingly, we could either plug each of the entire probability distributions into the original preference function $V(\cdot)$ (using bars to indicate risk that has already been borne) and compare

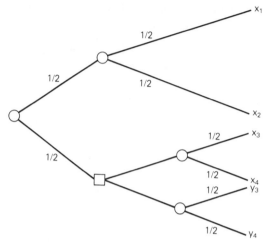

Figure 1.11 Decision tree illustrating a dynamic choice situation.

$$V(\overline{x}_1, \tfrac{1}{4}; \overline{x}_2, \tfrac{1}{4}; x_3, \tfrac{1}{4}; x_4, \tfrac{1}{4}) \qquad \text{versus} \qquad V(\overline{x}_1, \tfrac{1}{4}; \overline{x}_2, \tfrac{1}{4}; y_3, \tfrac{1}{4}; y_4, \tfrac{1}{4})$$

or equivalently plug the continuation of each branch into the conditional preference function $V_{x_1, \frac{1}{4}; x_2, \frac{1}{4}}(\cdot)$ and compare

$$V_{x_1, \frac{1}{4}; x_2, \frac{1}{4}}(x_3, \tfrac{1}{2}; x_4, \tfrac{1}{2}) \qquad \text{versus} \qquad V_{x_1, \frac{1}{4}; x_2, \frac{1}{4}}(y_3, \tfrac{1}{2}; y_4, \tfrac{1}{2})$$

where we define

$$V_{x_1, p_1; x_2, p_2}(\tilde{Z}) \equiv V(x_1, p_1; x_2, p_2; \tilde{Z}, (1 - p_1 - p_2)).$$

As in the intertemporal case, these alternative notational procedures are equivalent, and both imply that the agent will stick with his original plan of choosing up at the choice node. Again, the rest of the original displayed preference ranking, that is, the ordering

$$(y_3, \tfrac{1}{2}; y_4, \tfrac{1}{2}) > (x_3, \tfrac{1}{2}; x_4, \tfrac{1}{2}) \qquad \text{or equivalently}$$

$$V(y_3, \tfrac{1}{2}; y_4, \tfrac{1}{2}) > V(x_3, \tfrac{1}{2}; x_4, \tfrac{1}{2})$$

is irrelevant, since by the time that the individual is at the choice node he has already "consumed" (that is, has already borne) some risk.

Going back to our "test example" of figure 1.9, what does this approach imply about the opportunity set, preference function values, and *ex post* choice of an individual sitting at choice node 1 in that figure? Since he would clearly have planned on choosing up at choice node 2, we know that by the time he is at node 1 he will have borne a $\frac{1}{4}$ chance of receiving \$40 and a $\frac{1}{4}$ chance of receiving \$30. The remaining oppor-

Table 1.5 *Opportunity set at choice node 1 of figure 1.9 without the assumption of consequentialism*

Strategy	Probability distribution	Preference function value
(U, $\overline{U}$)	($90, $\frac{1}{4}$; $60, $\frac{1}{4}$; $\overline{\$40}$, $\overline{\frac{1}{4}}$; $\overline{\$30}$, $\overline{\frac{1}{4}}$)	V($90, $\frac{1}{4}$; $60, $\frac{1}{4}$; $\overline{\$40}$, $\overline{\frac{1}{4}}$; $\overline{\$30}$, $\overline{\frac{1}{4}}$)
(L, $\overline{U}$)	($80, $\frac{1}{4}$; $70, $\frac{1}{4}$; $\overline{\$40}$, $\overline{\frac{1}{4}}$; $\overline{\$30}$, $\overline{\frac{1}{4}}$)	V($80, $\frac{1}{4}$; $70, $\frac{1}{4}$; $\overline{\$40}$, $\overline{\frac{1}{4}}$; $\overline{\$30}$, $\overline{\frac{1}{4}}$)

tunity set and its associated preference function values under this approach are accordingly not as given in table 1.4, but rather the first two elements of the *original* opportunity set and original preference function values from table 1.3, using bars to indicate the risk that has already been borne (see table 1.5). Under our original assumption that

$$V(\$90, \tfrac{1}{4}; \$60, \tfrac{1}{4}; \$40, \tfrac{1}{4}; \$30, \tfrac{1}{4}) > V(\$80, \tfrac{1}{4}; \$70, \tfrac{1}{4}; \$40, \tfrac{1}{4}; \$30, \tfrac{1}{4})$$

(displayed at the beginning of section 4.1), it follows that the individual will indeed choose the upper branch upon arriving at choice node 1, just as originally planned.[21]

Immunity to the dynamic inconsistency argument Besides corresponding more closely to our treatment of nonseparable preferences in other settings, this manner of extending non-expected utility preferences to dynamic choice situations is immune to each of the dynamic arguments against non-expected utility maximizers presented in section 3.3. As illustrated in the previous paragraph, the resolution of uncertainty which takes such an agent to a particular choice node does not lead to a new opportunity set of probability distributions and associated preference function values, but rather to that subset of the original opportunity set (and preference function values) that corresponds to the choices still available, with bars used to denote those risks that have already been borne. No matter what moves Nature has made, the element of the original opportunity set that was most preferred (and hence corresponded to the *ex ante* plan)[22] will *always remain* in this subset.[23] Since it will continue to have a preference function value higher than any of the remaining elements, the agent will always stick with his original plans. In other words, such agents will be dynamically consistent.

Immunity to the classical making book argument Unlike the dynamic consistency argument, the classical making book argument involves introducing a new opportunity halfway through a choice problem. This consists of the offer to swap $\tilde{X} - \epsilon$ for $\tilde{Y}$ after the agent has borne a

$1 - p$ chance of the prospect $\tilde{Z} - \epsilon$. Under our approach, the agent would evaluate this offer by comparing the distributions

$$(\tilde{X} - \epsilon, p; \overline{\tilde{Z} - \epsilon, 1 - p}) \qquad \text{versus} \qquad (\tilde{Y}, p; \overline{\tilde{Z} - \epsilon, 1 - p})$$

or equivalently the preference function levels

$$V(\tilde{X} - \epsilon, p; \overline{\tilde{Z} - \epsilon, 1 - p}) \qquad \text{versus} \qquad V(\tilde{Y}, p; \overline{\tilde{Z} - \epsilon, 1 - p}).$$

But since we know that he has the ranking

$$(\tilde{Y}, p; \tilde{Z} - \epsilon, 1 - p) > (\tilde{X}, p; \tilde{Z}, 1 - p)$$

we obtain

$$V(\tilde{Y}, p; \overline{\tilde{Z} - \epsilon, 1 - p}) > V(\tilde{X}, p; \overline{\tilde{Z}, 1 - p}) > V(\tilde{X} - \epsilon, p; \overline{\tilde{Z} - \epsilon, 1 - p})$$

and so he will refuse this offer, and the argument cannot proceed beyond this point. More generally, an individual would only accept a new offer in the middle of a decision problem if, when combined with the risk that he has already borne, it yields a higher preference function value than his original optimal distribution (and, *a fortiori*, than his original holding).

Immunity to the aversion to information argument   The point at which the aversion to information argument fails against this approach is in its prediction that the individual in the example would foresee himself choosing the lottery $\tilde{W}$ should he learn that the event E has occurred. Such a choice would indeed follow from the ranking $\tilde{W} > \$1M$ if he were consequentialist. But since he would have borne a 0.89 chance of obtaining $1M by the time he learns that E has occurred, the appropriate comparison is not between $\tilde{W}$ and $1M but rather between the prospects

$$(0.11, \tilde{W}; \overline{0.89, \$1M}) \qquad \text{versus} \qquad (0.11, \$1M; \overline{0.89, \$1M})$$

or equivalently the preference function values

$$V(0.11, \tilde{W}; \overline{0.89, \$1M}) \qquad \text{versus} \qquad V(0.11, \$1M; \overline{0.89, \$1M}).$$

Since these distributions are the same as the Allais choices a_2 and a_1 respectively, it follows that our individual would prefer the latter prospect and hence stick with his planned choice of the $1M should E occur. Given this, information on whether or not E occurs will not cause him to depart from his original choice of $a_1 = (\$1M \text{ if } E, \$1M \text{ if } \sim E)$, and hence would not have a negative value.

   On the other hand, since he would choose a_1 whether or not he knew whether E occurred, advance information will not have any *positive* value in this example either. Does this mean that our approach assigns "too small" a value to information?

No. For one thing, an individual with expected utility preferences will *also* assign zero value to advance knowledge in this example. The reason is that, given the opportunity set {$1M, $\tilde{W}$} should E occur and the opportunity set {$1M, $0} should ~ E occur, the set of event-contingent prospects {a_1, a_2, a_3, a_4} forms a *complete event-contingent opportunity set*, in the sense that it allows for all combinations of choices from the available sets {$1M, $\tilde{W}$} under E and {$1M, $0} under ~ E. In such a case, advance information concerning the event ought to have exactly zero value for either expected utility maximizers or (nonconsequentialist) non-expected utility maximizers.

Say, however, that an expected utility maximizer and a nonconsequentialist non-expected utility maximizer agreed that a_1 was preferred over the other choices, and consider what would happen if it were eliminated, so that the set {a_2, a_3, a_4} no longer formed a complete event-contingent opportunity set. Since a_2 stochastically dominates a_3, which is in turn preferred to a_4, both individuals would pick a_2 if forced to make a choice before learning which event occurred. However, both would assign a *positive* value to information regarding the occurrence or nonoccurrence of E in this case, since it would allow them an alternative way of attaining the preferred event-contingent option ($1M if E, $1M if ~ E), namely by choosing a_4 should E occur and a_2 should ~ E occur.

In other words, expected utility maximizers and nonconsequentialist non-expected utility maximizers share the features that they never assign a negative value to information, assign a zero value to information when they face complete event-contingent opportunity sets, and assign a positive (or at least nonnegative) value to information in the absence of a complete event-contingent opportunity set.

A three-way classification of decision-makers We can summarize the above discussion with the following classification of decision-makers in terms of their underlying preferences over lotteries and the manner in which they behave in dynamic choice situations:

α-people: expected utility maximizers. Since their underlying preferences are separable anyway, their behavior in the middle of a decision tree will be the same whether or not they snip off the unrealized branches. Such individuals are therefore *de facto* consequentialist as well as dynamically consistent.

β-people: non-expected utility maximizers who are consequen-

tialist. These are the type of non-expected utility maximizers portrayed in the dynamic arguments of section
3.3. Such individuals are *not* dynamically consistent.

γ-people: non-expected utility maximizers who are not consequentialist. These are the type of non-expected utility maximizers described in this section. Such individuals *are*
dynamically consistent.

6 MODELING NONSEPARABLE PREFERENCES UNDER UNCERTAINTY

The thoughtful reader will have undoubtedly anticipated several potential
difficulties with and/or objections to the approach presented in the
previous section. The purpose of this section is to address and respond
to these. Although the specific issues vary widely, the unifying theme
behind my responses will be that the modeling of such agents involves
no problems beyond those implied by the modeling of nonseparable
preferences across time, commodities, or any other economic dimensions.

6.1 When do you start the process and what if you cannot observe the past?

According to our approach, if the risk that an individual bears in some
event E affects his *ex ante* ranking of lotteries under some alternative
event E*, then it will have the same effect on his *ex post* ranking of these
lotteries should the event E* in fact occur. In the limit, this means that
preferences over today's choice of lotteries are affected by what would
have occurred in each of the alternative unfoldings of an individual's life.
Doesn't this make the modeling of non-expected utility maximizers
analytically intractable?

 Not if we remind ourselves of the manner in which this is handled in
the case of nonseparable preferences over consumption streams. In the
intertemporally nonseparable case, what the individual consumed in the
past does indeed affect his preferences over today's consumption choices.
However, this is handled by simply subsuming past consumption into his
current preferences, so that what we refer to as his preference ranking
over consumption streams beginning with the current period are really his
conditional preferences for such streams, given his past consumption. It
is true that without specific knowledge of this past stream we cannot
know his exact preferences from now on, but most useful features of
intertemporal preferences, such as diminishing marginal rates of substitution across time-dated commodities, will be inherited by these condi-

tional preferences. The only caveat about subsuming past consumption into current preferences in this manner is that it must be done only *once*, and at the *start* of the problem at hand.

The case of nonseparable preferences over events is identical. The effect of risk that has already been borne can be subsumed into the individual's preferences (or preference function) over today's lotteries. Economically meaningful properties of preferences, such as risk aversion, will be inherited by these conditional preferences. Again, the only restriction is that this be done only once, and at the start of the decision problem.

6.2 How far do you drag along unrealized outcomes?

Of course, having subsumed all previously borne risk into preferences at the outset, all risk borne during the remainder of a choice problem must be explicitly represented. In the simple examples of section 5.2, this was not very hard. But say the individual faces a complicated decision tree with dozens of choice and chance nodes. Are we supposed to carry the influence of each of these alternative branches throughout the whole problem?

In principle, yes. But, in principle, this must also be done in any long intertemporal decision problem, or for that matter in any static multi-commodity consumption problem. After all, since there is no normative justification for separability across commodities, the individual's demand for (say) peaches can in general depend upon the prices of pencils, shoelaces, etc. However, we live with this fact in the same manner in each of these settings – by assuming (or hoping) that such cross-effects, while theoretically present, at least approach zero as the commodities become "farther and farther away" in some appropriate sense. Thus we assume that the effect of consumption sufficiently far in the past, or of a commodity which is sufficiently unrelated, or of an unrealized event that branched off sufficiently long ago, has an effect which for all practical purposes can be neglected. Lest this sound as if I am trying to invoke consequentialism implicitly myself, recall that we would not want to invoke this argument for consumption in the very recent past, for commodities (substitutes or complements) which are closely related, or for significant (e.g. large probability or extreme outcome) risks that have recently been borne.

6.3 What about the sunk cost fallacy?

"What's spent is spent, and should have no effect on optimal plans from this point on." This maxim, which is often termed the "sunk cost theorem," is taught in every course on the principles of economics. But if funds that actually *were* spent are irrelevant, does it not logically follow that outcomes that *did not even occur* should also be irrelevant?

No, it does not logically follow. Like so many of the other arguments in this literature, this argument is an example of taking a property which is a logical implication of separability and assuming that it must be true for the nonseparable case as well.

To see this, consider what an example of the sunk cost principle looks like when it is actually formulated as a theorem (that is, as a formal statement capable of mathematical proof). Say a firm's maximization problem is given by

$$\max_{L} R(L) - wL - wL_0$$

where $R(\cdot)$ is revenue (sales value of output) as a function of the input level L, w is the wage, and L_0 is some amount of labor that has already been contracted and paid for, but whose services were put to waste (the sunk cost of this problem), and hence does not enter into the revenue function. It is clear that the optimal value of L (call it L^*) will solve

$$R'(L^*) = w$$

and thus it will not depend on L_0.

But say the firm is a monopsonist for labor, so that its maximization problem is

$$\max_{L} R(L) - C(L + L_0)$$

where $C(L) \equiv LS^{-1}(L)$ is the total cost of inputs, given that the firm must raise its offered wage and move up the labor supply curve $S(\cdot)$ in order to obtain additional labor. In this case, the optimal value of L solves

$$R'(L^*) = C'(L^* + L_0)$$

which certainly does depend upon the "sunk cost" L_0.

The lesson, of course, is that sunk costs are only irrelevant when one's objective function is separable in the sunk cost variable – in this case L_0 – as with the first maximization problem but not the second. Thus claiming that an agent with nonseparable (that is, non-expected utility) preferences is committing the "sunk cost fallacy" reflects a misunderstanding of the mathematics of sunk costs.

6.4 What about "folding back"?

Besides α-people, β-people, and γ-people, there is another class of dynamically consistent non-expected utility maximizers – δ-people – who determine their optimal strategies in decision trees by a recursive process known in the decision theory literature as "folding back." Under this procedure, the individual begins by considering the terminal choice nodes of a decision tree (that is, those choice nodes not followed by any other choice node), determines the opportunity set of lotteries following from each such node, and uses his *original* preference function to determine the optimal choice out of that node. He then considers those choice nodes that are only followed by terminal choice nodes (or chance nodes) and repeats the process, subject to the previously determined path out of each terminal choice node. This procedure of "folding back" then continues to earlier and earlier choice nodes, until the path out of each choice node in the tree has been determined. In the decision tree of figure 1.6, for example, the individual would determine his optimal choice at the right-most choice node on the basis of the comparison

$$V(x_3, 1) \lesseqgtr V(x_4, 1)$$

and would determine his optimal choice at the lower choice node on the basis of

$$V(x_5, r; x_6, 1 - r) \lesseqgtr V(x_7, 1)$$

In the event (say) that the left-hand quantity is greater in each of these cases, he would then determine his choice at the upper left choice node on the basis of the comparison

$$V(x_1, q; x_2, 1 - q) \lesseqgtr V(x_3, 1)$$

Such a model has been analyzed by Bell (1985), Karni and Safra (1986, 1988), Hazen (1987), and Seidenfeld (1988a), who have applied it to various economic problems.

It is clear that δ-people will be dynamically consistent whether or not their preference functions are linear in the probabilities, since a repetition of this procedure halfway through any tree would produce the same optimal choice at each subsequent choice node. Since they are also consequentialist to boot,[24] why not adopt δ-people rather than γ-people as our model of dynamically consistent non-expected utility maximizers?

One reason is that such a procedure implies some undesirable properties of behavior. One implication, noted by Keeney and Winkler (1985), LaValle and Wapman (1986), and Hammond (1988c), is that it can lead to different choices in strategically equivalent decision trees (that is, trees which imply the same opportunity sets of lotteries), which can in turn lead to nonindiffference between such trees. To see this, take a δ-person with the typical Allais Paradox preferences of

$$a_1 > a_2 \quad \text{and} \quad a_3 > a_4$$

who also happens to prefer

a sure $1M   to $\bar{W}$: (10/11) $5M / (1/11) $0

and consider the decision tree of figure 1.12.

Such an individual would act as follows. Since a_3 is strictly preferred to a_4, he would choose up in the event that he arrives at the upper choice node in the figure. Since a sure $1M is strictly preferred to $\bar{W}$, he would choose down should he arrive at the lower choice node. This implies that his choice at the initial choice node is between a_3 if he chooses up or $a_4 = ($1M, 0.11; $0, 0.89)$ if he chooses down. Since we know that $a_3 > a_4$, such an individual would strictly prefer to choose up at the initial choice node in the figure. But since the upper and lower subtrees in this figure each imply an opportunity set of $\{a_3, a_4\} = \{(\bar{W}, 0.11; $0, 0.89), ($1M, 0.11; $0, 0.89)\}$, they are strategically equivalent, so that an individual who was indifferent between strategically equivalent trees (or subtrees) ought to be *indifferent* at the initial choice node. In fact, if we replace the payoffs $\bar{W}$ and 0 in the topmost sublottery by $\bar{W} - \epsilon$ and $-\epsilon$ for some small enough ϵ, we obtain an example in which the individual

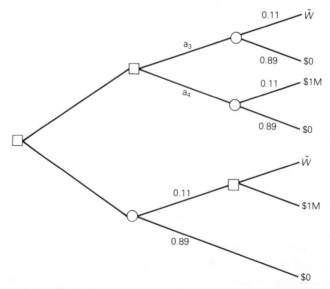

Figure 1.12 Choice between a pair of strategically equivalent subtrees.

would actually forgo the lottery ($\tilde{W}$, 0.11; \$0, 0.89) (obtainable by choosing down at the initial and bottom choice nodes) in order to receive the *stochastically dominated* lottery ($\tilde{W} - \epsilon$, 0.11; $- \epsilon$, 0.89) (by choosing up at the initial and top choice nodes).[25]

A second undesirable implication is that such individuals can exhibit aversion to costless information in decision trees. Indeed, a re-examination of the aversion to information argument of section 3.3 reveals that its notion of a "sophisticated" decision-maker, that is, a consequentialist who anticipates his future decisions and takes them into account at earlier stages, is precisely what we have defined to be a δ-person.

However, the more fundamental objection to this approach is that, as a formal optimization tool, folding back is *only appropriate* when the objective function is *separable* across the various subdecisions of a problem, and this is simply not true for an individual with nonseparable (that is, non-expected utility) preferences in a dynamic choice situation.

To see this in the context of nonseparable intertemporal preferences, say that my preferences over restaurant meals (written as consumption streams) are

(steak, sherbet) > (fish, banana split) > (pizza, sherbet) > {all other meals}

and say that I "fold back" – that is, I work backwards by choosing my dessert first (ignoring information about the entrées) and then choose the entrée subject to my choice of dessert. If my choice for dessert is sherbet, this procedure will lead me to a suboptimal choice of pizza should the evening's selection of entrées turn out to be {fish, pizza}. But if my dessert choice is a banana split, this procedure will lead me to a suboptimal choice of fish should the selection of entrées turn out to be {steak, fish}.

The problem of course is that my preferred dessert cannot be determined independently of the rest of my meal or, in other words, that my preferences over desserts and entrées are not separable. If we consider the structure of objective functions in decision problems where folding back can legitimately be applied, such as intertemporal maximization of discounted profits or discounted utility, we see that they are each separable across the different stages of the problem (that is, different time periods), which implies that the optimal continuation from a given point is independent of the particular path that led up to that point. In other words, folding back, like consequentialism, is *inherently inappropriate* to apply to nonseparable preferences, be they over many-commodity consumption bundles, time streams of consumption, or lotteries.

6.5 Hidden nodes and branches: coordination in the face of zero probability events

We have seen how the model of non-expected utility preferences developed in section 5 is immune to the classical making book argument. However, this approach is subject to a different type of procedure, which would appear to be another form of making book.[26]

Consider, for example, a non-expected utility maximizer with the preferences

$$(\tilde{X}, \tfrac{1}{2}; \tilde{X}, \tfrac{1}{2}) \sim (\tilde{Y}, \tfrac{1}{2}; \tilde{Y}, \tfrac{1}{2}) > (\tilde{Y}, \tfrac{1}{2}; \tilde{X}, \tfrac{1}{2})$$

for some pair of lotteries $\tilde{X}$ and $\tilde{Y}$. By continuity, it follows that

$$(\tilde{X} - \epsilon, \tfrac{1}{2}; \tilde{X}, \tfrac{1}{2}) > (\tilde{Y}, \tfrac{1}{2}; \tilde{X}, \tfrac{1}{2}) \quad \text{and} \quad (\tilde{Y}, \tfrac{1}{2}; \tilde{Y} - \epsilon, \tfrac{1}{2}) > (\tilde{Y}, \tfrac{1}{2}; \tilde{X}, \tfrac{1}{2})$$

for some small positive ϵ. Say the individual is currently endowed with the event-contingent prospect ($\tilde{X}$ if heads; $\tilde{Y}$ if tails) for some fair coin. Since he would be indifferent between this and the reversed prospect ($\tilde{Y}$ if heads; $\tilde{X}$ if tails), a "manipulator" who owned the latter prospect could presumably convince the individual to swap his original endowment for this new one. Say the two of them make this exchange.

Now flip the coin. If it lands heads, the individual receives the lottery $\tilde{Y}$, having borne a 50 percent chance of having received the lottery $\tilde{X}$. But the ranking $(\tilde{X} - \epsilon, \tfrac{1}{2}; \tilde{X}, \tfrac{1}{2}) > (\tilde{Y}, \tfrac{1}{2}; \tilde{X}, \tfrac{1}{2})$ implies that under these circumstances (that is, having borne a 50 percent chance of $\tilde{X}$) he would rather possess $\tilde{X} - \epsilon$ than $\tilde{Y}$. In other words, should heads come up, he would be willing to trade his holding of $\tilde{Y}$ for the lottery $\tilde{X} - \epsilon$. A similar argument shows that in the event of a tail he would be willing to trade his holding of $\tilde{X}$ for the lottery $\tilde{Y} - \epsilon$. Thus, a γ-person who began with the endowment ($\tilde{X}$ if heads; $\tilde{Y}$ if tails) ends up as if having the prospect ($\tilde{X} - \epsilon$ if heads; $\tilde{Y} - \epsilon$ if tails).

Have we finally succeeded in making book? To understand this example, consider its decision tree representation in figure 1.13. The initial choice node represents the pre-flip offer, where the individual may either stick with his endowment ($\tilde{X}$ if heads; $\tilde{Y}$ if tails) by choosing down, or else accept the pre-flip offer of ($\tilde{Y}$ if heads; $\tilde{X}$ if tails) by choosing up. As indicated by the unstarred arrow out of the initial choice node, he accepts the pre-flip offer and awaits the flip of the coin at the upper chance node under the impression that he will now receive $\tilde{Y}$ if it lands heads and $\tilde{X}$ if it lands tails.

Each of the broken squares and lines in figure 1.13 indicates a "hidden" node or branch, that is, a post-flip trade opportunity which is not revealed

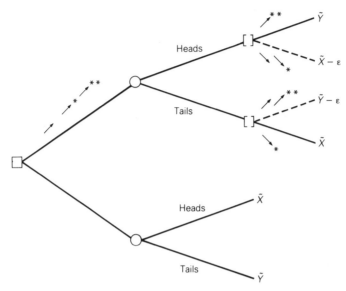

Figure 1.13   Decision tree representing a dynamic choice situation.

unless and until the individual actually reaches that particular point. Say the coin in the upper chance node lands heads, so that the individual, expecting to receive $\tilde{Y}$ having borne a 50 percent chance of $\tilde{X}$, is suddenly offered $\tilde{X} - \epsilon$ (that is, the upper hidden choice node is revealed). Since he is not (and at this point, never will be) aware of the other hidden choice node, he is under the impression that he really would have received $\tilde{X}$ had the coin landed tails, and on this basis opts for the post-flip swap to $\tilde{X} - \epsilon$, as indicated by the unstarred arrow out of this choice node. A corresponding situation would occur if the coin had landed tails.

To see that this procedure depends upon the manipulator's keeping these nodes hidden, consider how the individual would have acted had he been aware of these nodes from the start, that is, if the broken nodes and branches had been solid. Given his original displayed preferences, the individual would have either chosen the strategy indicated by the single-starred arrows, which would yield the distribution $(\tilde{X} - \epsilon, \frac{1}{2}; \tilde{X}, \frac{1}{2})$, or chosen the strategy indicated by the double-starred arrows, which would yield the distribution $(\tilde{Y}, \frac{1}{2}; \tilde{Y} - \epsilon, \frac{1}{2})$. If, for example, he adopted the single-starred strategy, he would plan on making the post-flip exchange if heads comes up, but not if tails comes up.

In other words, given full knowledge of the set of nodes and branches in the tree, the individual would willingly forgo ϵ to make exactly one of the post-flip swaps (that is, would pay $\epsilon/2$ in expected value terms). The reason that the manipulator can get him to pay ϵ no matter which way the coin lands is by hiding the fact that such an offer would have been available to the individual even if the flip had turned out the other way.

This leads to the question of precisely which comparison should be used in judging whether the individual has acted irrationally. Do we compare the outcomes under the individual's endowment ($\tilde{X}$ if heads, $\tilde{Y}$ if tails) with the outcomes that would actually arise from the procedure (that is, $\tilde{X} - \epsilon$ if heads and $\tilde{Y} - \epsilon$ if tails)? Or do we make a separate comparison for each state of nature, taking into account the different information that the individual has in each state? In the latter case, this would mean the following separate comparisons.

For heads: choosing $\tilde{X} - \epsilon$ over $\tilde{Y}$ having (so he thought) borne a 50 percent chance of $\tilde{X}$.
For tails: choosing $\tilde{Y} - \epsilon$ over $\tilde{X}$ having (so he thought) borne a 50 percent chance of $\tilde{Y}$.

Given the individual's original preference rankings ($\tilde{X} - \epsilon$, $\frac{1}{2}$; $\tilde{X}$, $\frac{1}{2}$) > ($\tilde{Y}$, $\frac{1}{2}$; $\tilde{X}$, $\frac{1}{2}$) and ($\tilde{Y}$, $\frac{1}{2}$; $\tilde{Y} - \epsilon$, $\frac{1}{2}$) > ($\tilde{Y}$, $\frac{1}{2}$; $\tilde{X}$, $\frac{1}{2}$) and given the information he has in each event, each of these decisions seems to be fully rational.

As with the other issues considered in this section, the problem of coordination in the light of unforeseen events is an inherent feature of nonseparable preferences under uncertainty or certainty. To see this, consider the following example: You are throwing a dinner party and you want the wine and food to match, so that your preferences are

{beef, red wine} ~ {fish, white wine} > {beef, white wine} ~ {fish, red wine}

Say you call the local butcher, who says that there is no chance of getting any fish today, although they do have beef. You also call the local wine shop, and are told that there is no chance of getting any red wine today, although they do have some nice whites. While beef with white wine is not your favorite dinner, it is better than nothing. Accordingly, you send your cook to the butcher and your butler to the wine shop. Both are aware of your preferences, as well as the information that you have received from the two shops. Upon arriving at the butcher, your cook finds that there has been an unexpected shipment of fish. Given his knowledge of your preferences and the fact that the wine shop only had white wine, your cook would be willing to pay an additional ϵ to purchase the fish. But in the meantime, your butler has arrived at the wine shop, to find (you guessed it) that a surprise shipment of red wine has come in, and acts similarly. By trying to respect your nonseparable commodity preferences in response to these unforeseen events, and unaware that there was an unforeseen event in *each* store, your agents have between themselves made you worse off.

The problem, of course, is that decision-makers with nonseparable preferences under uncertainty *or* certainty require full knowledge of the opportunities available in each component of the problem (for both heads and tails, or both the entrée and the wine) in order to make the proper choice in any one component. When this information is not known, or is incorrectly known, suboptimal and even dominated choices can be made.

How to handle this problem? Perhaps the best approach is simply to recognize the interdependence of component-wise decisions under non-separable preferences, and to remain mindful of its stronger informational requirements. In other words, when the manipulator offered the original pre-flip swap, the individual should have asked, "Do you have any *other* offers in store for me?" We have seen that a truthful answer to this question would prevent the manipulator from being able to make book. A lie would have the same effect as a lie would in an exchange under certainty, namely that the individual could end up being exploited. An answer of "maybe" ought to lead the individual to incorporate the possibility of these other offers formally by the addition of chance nodes with branches leading out to these possible choice nodes.

The upshot, as mentioned above, is that making decisions with non-separable preferences under uncertainty has greater informational requirements than it does with separable preferences, just as it does under certainty (would you think of ordering the wine at a restaurant before looking at the list of entrées?). As with the other issues discussed in this section, the way we should live with this fact is the same as the way we live with it under certainty, namely by restricting the interaction effects we consider to the ones that we feel are the most important, but then explicitly taking them into account in the manner outlined in section 5.

6.6 The operational definition of consequences

A final objection to this approach, and in some sense to the formal modeling of non-expected utility preferences in general, is the allegation that observed "violations" of the expected utility hypothesis are in fact not violations at all, but merely examples of improper definition of the basic outcomes or consequences. We can motivate this discussion by means of a simple example, based upon the ideas and examples of Samuelson (1952a), Drèze (1974), Machina (1981), and Sen (1985).

Say I face the four event-contingent prospects shown in table 1.6. In this example, "movie" means seeing a new romance film featuring my

Table 1.6

	0.03 chance	0.97 chance
c_1	Hamburger	Bicycle
c_2	Movie	Bicycle
c_3	Hamburger	WK
c_4	Movie	WK

favorite movie star, with whom I am deeply in love, "bicycle" is a new 10-speed bicycle, and "hamburger" is a gourmet hamburger at a local restaurant. If I had to choose between c_1 and c_2, I would certainly hope that I win the bicycle (and given the odds, I probably will), but if I do not, let us assume that I would rather see the movie, so that I prefer c_2 over c_1.

How should I rank the options c_3 versus c_4? I hope that no reader who claims to subscribe to the precepts of expected utility theory feels that he or she needs to know what WK stands for, since by replacement separability (or the Independence Axiom) I ought to prefer c_4 over c_3 *regardless* of the nature of this outcome.

In fact, WK stands for "week on a secluded tropical island with the self-same movie star." Given this, I reason as follows. I have a 97 percent chance of bliss. On the other hand, what would I feel like doing in the unlikely and unlucky event that I do *not* win that week on the island? Do I really want to be sitting (alone) in a (cold) movie theater watching the object of my affection sail off into the sunset with *somebody else*? No, I would rather be eating a hamburger in that event, and accordingly I would prefer c_3 over c_4.

Such preferences do not seem irrational. Do they violate the Independence Axiom or, equivalently, separability? To me, the answer is "Yes – in fact, by definition." However, defenders of expected utility might argue as follows:

A preference of c_1 over c_2 and c_4 over c_3 in this example does not violate separability across alternative outcomes, since what we call "movie" in prospect c_4 is in fact a different outcome from "movie" in c_2. Specifically, "movie" in c_2 can be described as "seeing the movie," but "movie" in c_4 is "seeing the movie while disappointed." Since these are clearly different outcomes, let us call the latter "movie*" to distinguish it from the former, in which case a preference for c_1 over c_2 and c_4 over c_3 in this example is completely consistent with expected utility.

I certainly agree that my *attitude* toward seeing the movie is different in c_2 from that in c_4. But is it legitimate to claim that I have not violated expected utility on the grounds that they are *different outcomes*? As alluded to in note 19, a similar objection might be made that A = "Abigail getting the treat outright" and A* = "Abigail getting the treat when Benjamin also had a fair chance at it" are different outcomes in the "Mom" example.

Once again, consider how this kind of argument would sound in the context of standard consumer theory. In table 1.7 the options d_1 through d_4 are not event-contingent prospects, but rather standard commodity bundles involving the simultaneous consumption of a beverage and a condiment. Since I happen to like lemon with my tea but milk with my coffee, I prefer d_2 over d_1 but prefer d_3 over d_4.

Personally, I would simply describe my preferences as nonseparable and be done with it. But say someone tried to make the following argument:

> Your preference for d_2 over d_1 and d_3 over d_4 in this example does not really violate separability between beverage and condiment, since what we call "lemon" in bundle d_4 is in fact a different commodity from "lemon" in d_2. Specifically, "lemon" in d_2 can be described as "drinking lemon with your beverage," but it is clear that "lemon" in d_4 means "drinking lemon while disgusted." We should accordingly call the latter "lemon*" to distinguish it from the former, in which case your preference for d_1 over d_2 and d_4 over d_3 is completely consistent with separability.

Once again, I agree that my attitude toward adding lemon, even the sign of its marginal utility, is different in the bundle d_2 than in the bundle d_4. But the key question is, *why* is my attitude different? Is it really because it is a different commodity in these two bundles, or is it because it is combined with different commodities in these two bundles? I think that most economists would say the latter, and pronounce a verdict of nonseparability. After all, classical consumer theory presumes that we can define each "commodity" (such as milk or lemon juice) on the basis of

Table 1.7

d_1	Milk	Tea
d_2	Lemon	Tea
d_3	Milk	Coffee
d_4	Lemon	Coffee

its attributes alone, independent of which other items one consumer or another happens to like (or dislike) mixing it with. On the other hand, perhaps the maxim *de gustibus non disputandum est* compels us to respect the wishes (including the definitions) of any consumer who feels that "lemon juice that is put in tea" and "lemon juice that is put in coffee" really are two different commodities.

The situation is similar for choice under uncertainty. Ideally, a fair application of the expected utility model should proceed as follows.

1 We begin by agreeing upon a set of "consequences" $\{x_1, x_2, \ldots\}$.
2 The axioms then imply that we can assign individual utility levels $U(x_1)$, $U(x_2)$, etc., to each of these consequences, with the following property:
3 The expectation of these utility levels can be used to evaluate the relative desirability of any probability distribution over these consequences.

If a proponent of expected utility should decide in retrospect that receiving the amount x_1 in some lottery $\tilde{Y}$ is in fact a different consequence from receiving x_1 in some other lottery $\tilde{Z}$ (or that "movie" in the prospect b_2 is a different consequence from "movie" in the prospect b_4), then perhaps we really should grant him the right to go back to step 1 and start over. However, it is important to realize that invoking such a right is tantamount to defending the expected utility model by rendering it irrefutable, since, for example, an individual with the typical preferences in the Allais Paradox could also prove his "consistency" with expected utility by claiming that the \$0 prize in the prospect a_2 is really a different "consequence" from the \$0 prize in a_3 etc., and the arguments against non-expected utility in section 3.3 would be helpless against this defense.[27]

I have engaged in the above "definition of a consequence" argument with several proponents of expected utility whom I greatly respect. Experience shows that the only mutually acceptable way out of it is to adopt the following three-part compromise.

1 The properties of separability/nonseparability must always be discussed with reference to a *given* set of consequences (that is, with respect to a particular level of description of the consequences).
2 For my part, I will grant that separability may well be rational provided that the descriptions of the consequences are sufficiently deep to incorporate any relevant emotional states,

such as disappointment (e.g. at having won $0 when you might have won $5,000,000), regret (at having forgone a sure chance of $1,000,000 and then landing a 1 percent chance of $0), jealousy (over your favorite movie star), feelings of unfairness (that Benjamin won the treat in an unfair flip), etc.

3 However, for their part, proponents of expected utility must grant that this level of description may be below the usual level at which economists typically operate or can observe, and that preferences over regular economic variables may well be nonseparable. The values of monetary outcomes, which child ends up receiving the treat, etc. are examples of consequences at the ordinary economic level of description. In particular, the various non-expected utility models of table 1.1 could legitimately represent risk preference consequences at this description level.

These ideas are not new. As Samuelson noted some time ago, separability across alternative consequences

must always be applied to a definite set of entities – e.g., (1) single-event money prizes, (2) single-event vectors of goods, (3) single-event money prizes *cum* gaming and suspense feelings . . . . [Separability] then has implications and restrictions upon choices among such entities; but, strictly speaking, it need not impose restrictions upon some different (and perhaps simpler) set of entities.

In what dimensional space are we "really" operating? If every time you find my axiom falsified, I tell you to go to a space of still higher dimensions, you can legitimately regard my theories as irrefutable and meaningless . . . . From my own direct and indirect observations, I am satisfied that a large fraction of the sociology of gambling and risk taking will never significantly be discernible in terms of money prizes alone, as distinct from elements of suspense . . . . Samuelson (1952a, pp. 676–7)

The above compromise tries simultaneously to acknowledge (a) the normative appeal of separability at some deep enough level of consequence description, (b) normative reasons why preferences might be nonseparable at the level of description typically used by economists, and accordingly (c) the potential value of non-expected utility models for descriptive economists who can only observe (or only work in terms of) the usual economic variables. Along with the critique of section 4 and the dynamic model of section 5, it is offered as a contribution to what I have termed the "normative goal" in the campaign for the general acceptance and use of non-expected utility models.

NOTES

Adapted from *Journal of Economic Literature*, December 1989, ©1989 American Economic Association, but entirely rewritten for this volume. I am grateful to Michael Bacharach, John Conlisk, Vincent Crawford, Eddie Dekel, Mark Durst, Larry Epstein, Peter Fishburn, Jerry Green, Ted Groves, Faruk Gul, Susan Hurley, Edi Karni, Robin Keller, David Kreps, R. Duncan Luce, Edward McClennen, Frank Milne, Louis Narens, Michael Rothschild, Uzi Segal, Teddy Seidenfeld, Max Stinchcombe, Robert Sugden, Amos Tversky, Peter Wakker, and especially Peter Hammond and Joel Sobel for helpful discussions on this material, and to the Alfred P. Sloan Foundation and the Center for Advanced Study in the Behavioral Sciences for financial support. Responsibility for errors and opinions is my own.

 1 For surveys of these empirical findings and theoretical developments, see Machina (1983a, b, 1987), Sugden (1986), and Weber and Camerer (1987).
 2 Again, see the references in note 1.
 3 For discussions of the applicability of expected utility theory when delays in the resolution of uncertainty *are* significant, see Mossin (1969), Spence and Zeckhauser (1972), Kreps and Porteus (1979), and Machina (1984).
 4 It is important to note that this applies even when one or more of the outcomes $\{x_2, \ldots, x_n\}$ or $\{x_2^*, \ldots, x_m^*\}$ take on the same value as x_1 or y_1.
 5 Again, this applies even if some outcomes in $\{x_2, \ldots, x_n\}$ take the same value as x_1 or y_1.
 6 See Marschak (1950), Samuelson (1952b), or Herstein and Milnor (1953), as well as the expository treatments in Luce and Raiffa (1957), Fishburn (1982a), or Kreps (1988).
 7 These empirical findings and alternative models will be described in detail in section 2.3.
 8 One probability distribution is said to *first-order stochastically dominate* another if it can be obtained from the latter by shifting probability from lower to higher outcome levels. Thus, for example, the distributions (\$100, $\frac{2}{3}$; \$20, $\frac{1}{3}$) and (\$100, $\frac{1}{2}$; \$30, $\frac{1}{2}$) both first-order stochastically dominate (\$100, $\frac{1}{2}$; \$20, $\frac{1}{2}$). *First-order stochastic dominance preference* means that such dominating distributions are always preferred.
 9 To make an analogy with regular consumer theory, consider commodity bundles of the form (a, b, c, d). In this context, "dominance" (preference for vector-dominating bundles) implies that if (a^*, b, c, d) is preferred to (a, b, c, d) then (a^*, b', c', d') will be preferred to (a, b', c', d') for any other b', c', and d', which is replacement separability *over individual commodities*. Dominance does *not* imply that if (a^*, b^*, c, d) is preferred to (a, b, c, d) then (a^*, b^*, c', d') will be preferred to (a, b, c', d') for any other c and d, which would be replacement separability over *subbundles*. For more on the distinction between dominance and separability in choice under uncertainty, see Marschak (1986).
10 Additional analyses of these and related forms can be found in Fishburn

(1982b, 1984a, b, 1988), Loomes and Sugden (1982, 1986), Chew et al. (1987), Röell (1987), Segal (1987), Yaari (1987), and Rubinstein (1988).

11 The issue of stochastic dominance preference in Kahneman and Tversky's "prospect theory," which combines the subjective expected utility form $\Sigma\nu(x_i)\,\pi(p_i)$ with psychologically based "editing stages," is less straightforward. Kahneman and Tversky (1979, pp. 275, 284) stated that "dominated alternatives are detected and eliminated prior to the evaluation of prospects." Tversky and Kahneman (1986) suggest that elimination might be limited to cases where dominace is "transparent," and that violations of dominance in nontransparent cases are consistent with the theory.

12 A general condition for a (differentiable) non-expected utility preference function to satisfy first-order stochastic dominance preference is given by Machina (1982a, thm 1).

13 Since it offers the same opportunity set of lotteries, this tree is said to be *strategically equivalent* to the left-hand tree in figure 1.7 (e.g. LaValle and Fishburn, 1987).

14 Any violation of replacement separability, mixture separability, or the Independence axiom implies that the individual will exhibit preferences of the form $\tilde{X} > \tilde{Y}$, yet $(\tilde{Y}, p; \tilde{Z}, 1 - p) > (\tilde{X}, p; \tilde{Z}, 1 - p)$ for some lotteries $\tilde{X}, \tilde{Y}, \tilde{Z}$ and probability p. Construct a decision tree whose initial chance node leads down with probability $1 - p$ to $\tilde{Z}$, and up with probability p to a decision node offering a choice of $\tilde{X}$ or $\tilde{Y}$. According to the argument, the individual would *plan* on choosing $\tilde{Y}$ at the choice node but would *in fact* choose $\tilde{X}$ should he actually arrive there.

15 For example, Raiffa (1968, pp. 83–5), Yaari (1985), Shafer (1986), Border (1987), Green (1987), and Seidenfeld (1988a). We refer to this as the "classical" making book argument to distinguish it from the one discussed in section 6.5.

16 Once again, as the authors cited above have shown, it is possible to base such an argument upon any departure from expected utility preferences.

17 In this case, the uncertainty involved in the snipped-off part of the tree was the $\frac{1}{4}$ chance of receiving \$40 and the $\frac{1}{4}$ chance of receiving \$30 which, having chosen the strategy (U, U), the individual bore at the time that the initial chance node was resolved.

18 This example is based on several discussions and examples in the literature on interpersonal fairness or equity under uncertainty, in particular Harsanyi (1955, 1975, 1978), Strotz (1958, 1961), Fisher and Rothenberg (1961, 1962), Diamond (1967), Keeney (1980), Broome (1982), Hammond (1983), Fishburn (1984b), Keeney and Winkler (1985), and Sen (1985), and especially Broome (1984) and Binmore (1988).

19 The claim that this is *not* the set of appropriate outcomes is discussed in section 6.6.

20 The analog of the making book argument in section 3.3 would be similar. Start with someone who owns tickets to (*Star Wars I, Star Wars I*) at the Paradise. By the second line of the preferences displayed above, he would pay you ϵ for tickets to (*Star Wars I, Star Wars II*) at the Bijou. Then, at the intermission, invoke the first line of his displayed preferences to get him to pay you ϵ to

switch back to the Paradise and see *Star Wars I*. He has ended up seeing *Star Wars I* twice, which was his original holding, but has paid you 2ϵ in the process. Of course, my objection to the dynamic inconsistency argument applies to this one as well.

21 Antecedents of the formal approach presented here can be found in Donaldson and Selden (1981, p. 213), Machina (1981, p. 173), Loomes and Sugden (1984a, 1986), Johnson and Donáldson (1985, p. 1453) who reject it, Yaari (1985), Anand (1987, pp. 209-10), and McClennen (1988a, b, 1989) who terms it "resolute choice."

22 In the previous example, this was the distribution (\$90, $\frac{1}{4}$; \$60, $\frac{1}{4}$; $\overline{\$40}$, $\overline{\frac{1}{4}}$; $\overline{\$30}$, $\overline{\frac{1}{4}}$), which corresponded to the plan (U, $\overline{\text{U}}$).

23 Why is this true? Let $\tilde{X}^*$ be the optimal distribution in the original opportunity set. As seen in the previous paragraph, the distributions still available at a given choice node consist of the set of possible strategies following from that node, combined with the risk that has been borne by this point, where that risk is determined by the original optimal strategy along each of the unresolved branches. Since $\tilde{X}^*$ is precisely the distribution that corresponds to having followed the optimal strategy along these unrealized branches, combined with making the optimal choices from this point on, it will be an element of this remaining subset of distributions.

24 This follows since the individual's action at each choice node depends only on his original preference ordering and the continuation of the tree from that point on.

25 In the opposite case when the individual prefers $\tilde{W}$ to a sure \$1M, replace each occurrence of \$0 in figure 1.12 by \$1M, replace a_3 and a_4 by a_2 and a_1, and then apply essentially the same argument as above.

26 This procedure is based on examples by Uzi Segal and Eddie Dekel.

27 Formally, saving the expected utility property by expanding the definition of a consequence implies that the individual maximizes $\Sigma p_i U(x_i, f_i)$, where x_i is the original observable component of the "expanded consequence" (x_i, f_i), and f_i is his "feeling" about receiving x_i: elation, disappointment, relief, inequity, etc. Since f_i can depend on how x_i compares with what otherwise might have happened and how likely these other outcomes were, we have $f_i = f(x_i | x_1, p_1; \ldots; x_{i-1}, p_{i-1}; x_{i+1}, p_{i+1}; \ldots; x_n, y_n)$, so that this formula becomes

$$\sum_{i=1}^{n} p_i U\big(x_i, f(x_i | x_1, p_1; \ldots; x_{i-1}, p_{i-1}; x_{i+1}, p_{i+1}; \ldots; x_n, y_n)\big)$$

To see that this approach is irrefutable in the sense that it is consistent with any preference function, pick an arbitrary preference function $V(x_1, p_1; \ldots; x_n, p_n)$, define

$$f\big(\xi | x_1, p_1; \ldots; x_{i-1}, p_{i-1}; x_{i+1}, p_{i+1}; \ldots; x_n, y_n\big)$$

$$\equiv V\bigg(x_1, p_1; \ldots; x_{i-1}, p_{i-1}; \xi, 1 - \sum_{j \neq i} p_j; x_{i+1}, p_{i+1}; \ldots; x_n, p_n\bigg)$$

and define $U(x_i, \zeta) \equiv \zeta$, which together imply the identity

$$\sum_{i=1}^{n} p_i U\big(x_i, f\big(x_i \,|\, x_1, p_1; \ldots; x_{i-1}, p_{i-1}; x_{i+1}, p_{i+1}; \ldots; x_n, y_n\big)\big)$$

$$\equiv V\big(x_1, p_1; \ldots; x_n, p_n\big)$$

In other words, *any* non-expected utility preference function over the observables (the x_i and the p_i) can be represented as "expected utility" with a suitably expanded definition of the consequences.

2

Consequentialism and Sequential Choice

Isaac Levi

1 EXTENSIVE AND NORMAL FORM

P.J Hammond opens his important 1988 paper by writing:

An almost unquestioned hypothesis of modern normative decision theory is that acts are valued by their consequences. Indeed, Savage (1954) *defines* an act as a function mapping uncertain states of the world into a domain of conceivable consequences, thus identifying an act with the state-contingent consequence function which it generates. (Hammond, 1988b, p. 25)

Hammond thinks that much of the controversy concerning acceptable principles of rational behavior (such as, for example, the status of the requirement that preferences should be weakly ordered[1] and should satisfy the "independence postulate"[2]) could be resolved if we appreciated the implications of the "almost unquestioned" consequentialism lying at the core of modern normative decision theory for sequential decision-making.

When an agent faces a choice among a set of available options, some or all of them may present him with fresh opportunities for choice among options which, in turn, may yield new opportunities for choice and so on. The decision problem is representable in a "tree form" or "extensive form" illustrated by figure 2.1.

At stage 1, the agent has a pair of options A and B. Option A has as a sure outcome that the agent confronts a choice between 1 and 2. Option B has as a sure outcome that the agent confronts a choice between 3 and 4. In more sophisticated examples, the sequences of stages with opportunities for choice can ramify. In addition, considerations of uncertainty and risk can be added. The c_is are the consequences.

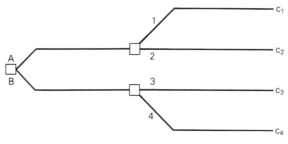

Figure 2.1

When the decision problem characterized by figure 2.1 abstractly is recast in normal or strategic form, it is assumed that at the initial stage the agent does more than choose between the options A and B. He also forms a plan or strategy as to how to choose at subsequent stages. A plan will specify for each choice node which option at that choice node the agent takes and, in this sense, identifies a path in the "decision tree." The normal-form representation of the agent's decision problem glosses over the sequential aspects of the agent's predicament and views him as if he were making a single choice at the initial stage. Thus, the normal-form representation corresponding to figure 2.1 is given in figure 2.2.

The normal-form version of the predicament abstracts away from the sequential features of the decision problem revealed in figure 2.1. The options such as A1 in figure 2.2 could be available for the agent to choose at the initial node without opportunity to renege at some later stage. Alternatively, however, Al could represent a strategy or a program for sequential choice endorsed at the initial node but open for reconsideration with the option of reneging at a later stage. These situations are quite different. Figure 2.1 disambiguates in favor of the second reading.

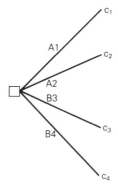

Figure 2.2

Hammond contends that a consequentialist who ignores the sequential aspects of the agent's decision problem revealed in the extensive-form representation and pictures the predicament as in figure 2.2 will understand the problem as one of choosing among the available consequences. The options admissible for choice will be precisely those determining admissible consequences. This is not big news.

Hammond thinks that, in those situations where a figure 2.2 representation is an alternative to a figure 2.1 representation abstracting away from the details of sequential choice, consequentialism yields more substantial results. It tells us that the decision-maker is rationally entitled to pursue a course of action (sequence of choices) if and only if it corresponds to an option in the normal-form representation yielding an admissible choice of a consequence. The criteria for choice in the extensive-form sequential decision problem are thereby derived from consequentialist criteria for a single-choice normal-form decision problem. Hammond argues that, given this reduction of extensive to normal form, rational preference should induce a weak ordering among options and should satisfy independence. Consequentialism is thereby seen as supporting two pillars on which advocates of the injunction to maximize expected utility have often rested their position.

My aim is to call into question the contention that consequentialism has the implications Hammond claims it has. I am not suggesting any reason to doubt the cogency of Hammond's proofs. Furthermore, I am inclined to agree with Hammond that not only is consequentialism a widely endorsed assumption of modern normative decision theory but so is the reduction of extensive to normal form. I object to Hammond's assumption that consequentialism in the sense in which it is endorsed by Savage and others presupposes the reduction of extensive to normal form and to the implication which Hammond correctly derives from this assumption that consequentialism entails ordinality.

The matter is of some importance. Although both consequentialism and the thesis of the reducibility of extensive to normal form are widely endorsed among contemporary decision theorists, the consequentialism invoked by "modern normative decision theory" is less controversial than the reducibility of extensive to normal form.[3] Those who reject the latter need not reject the former. Those who accept the former need not accept the latter. I, for one, have gone on record as rejecting the ordering conditions on preferences favored by Savage and others (Levi, 1974, 1980, 1986a). At the same time, I am in favor of adhering to the independence postulate (Levi, 1986a, b) given the satisfaction of certain structural conditions and am convinced by Seidenfeld's argument that consequentialism does sustain this conclusion (Seidenfeld, 1988a). If Hammond is right, this position is untenable. Ordering and independence are indivisible. I think that Hammond is wrong.

2 ACT, STATE, CONSEQUENCE

According to the procedure that Savage (1954) adopted as canonical for representing decision problems, three notions are deployed in the representation: the notions of an act, a state, and a consequence. Many philosophers have followed the lead of R.C. Jeffrey in complaining about a wrong-headed ontology which insists on trinitarianism where monotheism should do. Jeffrey (1965) suggests that acts, states, and consequences are all events or propositions.

I do not want to quarrel with Jeffrey's suggestion. To me, something rather like it should turn out right. But I do not see why it should be supposed, as Jeffrey does intimate, that Savage would disagree or, for that matter, that Ramsey (1926) would disagree. Perhaps, Ramsey and Savage may be convicted of what now seems like loose talk, but it is loose talk that is easily repaired without damage to the substance of their views. Instead of speaking of acts, states, and consequences, Savage could have spoken of act-descriptions, state-descriptions, and consequence-descriptions.

There are, to be sure, important differences in a Savage framework in the attitudes that the decision-maker has towards act-descriptions, state-descriptions, and consequence-descriptions. State-descriptions are objects of personal probability judgments (I prefer calling them "credal" probability judgments), consequence-descriptions are objects of utility judgment, and act-descriptions are objects of expected utility judgment. There is nothing in the Savage system to prevent assigning utilities to state-descriptions or probabilities to consequence-descriptions. Indeed, it seems clear that Savage intended the state-descriptions to be evaluated with respect to utility in a certain way although, as is well known, his axioms do not capture his intent. However, the utility assigned to a state must be conditional on the act chosen. That is, given that act a_i is chosen and state s_j is true, the utility assigned to s_j conditional on a_i is equal to the unconditional utility of the consequence c_{ij}. Unless the consequences of all available options in a given state bear equal utility, the only way to derive an unconditional utility for the state is to compute the expectation of the conditional utilities of the state (unconditional utilities of the consequences) utilitizing unconditional probabilities for acts. Similarly, credal probabilities are assignable to consequences, but are conditional on the option chosen. Unless consequences are identical for all options in a given state, the only way to compute unconditional probabilities for consequences is with the aid of unconditional probabilities for those options which yield them in some state or other.

These restrictions derive from the fact that, in Savage's formalism, unconditional credal probabilities are not assigned to acts – that is, the agent's options. According to the Savage approach, one begins with a preference or value ranking of acts or options which satisfy the axioms he proposes. From this ranking, one may derive a unique unconditional credal probability distribution over the states and an unconditional utility function unique up to a positive affine transformation over the consequences which is state independent. Utilizing this information, it is possible to derive a probability distribution over consequences conditional on acts and a utility function for states conditional on acts (the utility of state s_j conditional on act a_i is the utility of consequence c_{ij}). However, the Savage theory fails to determine an unconditional credal probability distribution over acts and, as a consequence, an unconditional utility function for states and an unconditional probability distribution over consequences.

To be sure, the Savage axioms, even when construed prescriptively as norms of rationality, are designed so that one might elicit from information about an agent's preferences among acts information about his probabilities and utilities. The fact that information about preferences among acts unsupplemented with other information fails to yield information about unconditional probabilities of acts need not imply that the agent fails to make such probability judgments. Nonetheless, even if it did have this implication, the further thesis that acts, states, and consequences are distinct types of entities would not follow. By replacing talk of acts, states, and consequences by talk of act-descriptions (act-propositions), state-descriptions (state-propositions), and consequence-descriptions (state-propositions), the differences between acts, states, and consequences are seen to be differences between propositions or descriptions deriving from differences in the propositional attitudes which the decision-maker may have towards act-descriptions, state-descriptions, and consequence-descriptions.[4] The same sentence or proposition may qualify as a state-description relative to one network of propositional attitudes and as a consequence-description or, indeed, even an act-description relative to another. We may therefore endorse Jeffrey's insistence on regarding acts, states, and consequences propositionally without accepting his contention that the decision-maker should assign "desirabilities" (utilities or expected utilities) and probabilities over propositions of these three kinds.

As Spohn (1977, 1978) has rightly recognized, we should resist Jeffrey on this last point. Decision-makers should not assign credal probabilities to the acts which are available to them.

Spohn notes that such probabilities are irrelevant to the ranking of the options to be used in identifying optimal or admissible options. This correct observation does not entail a prohibition against the deliberating agent assigning credal probabilities to hypotheses predicting his decision. But it serves notice on those who insist that such probability assignments may be made, and perhaps ought to be made, that they should identify some function that such probability assignments can serve other than in guiding a choice among the options under consideration. Spohn reminds us that assigning such probabilities is not crucial in applications of the prescription to maximize expected utility or, for that matter, to my preferred recommendation that choice be restricted to E-admissible options (Levi, 1974, 1980).

I think, however, that there is an additional argument for insisting that the deliberating agent avoid assigning credal probabilities to predictions as to what he will choose.

The aim of a normative theory of rational choice is to provide criteria for identifying a set of options which are optimal or, at least, "admissible" in the sense that they are not ruled out by the principles of choice given his beliefs and his values. If the deliberating agent is to reach a stage in deliberation where he can use such principles to identify a set of admissible options, he must identify a set A of available options or option-descriptions from which the set $C(A)$ of admissible options is selected. No option can be admissible unless it is available. If the agent changes his mind as to what is available, then the set of admissible options can change even if everything else relevant remains the same.

If agent X recognizes a as an available option (description), X is certain of the following: (a) that he has the ability to choose that a be true given that he deliberates at time t, (b) that he is deliberating at time t, and (c) that if he chooses that a be true on the deliberation at time t, a is true. (If this condition were violated, choosing that a be true would be inefficacious and a's truth would not be under X's control.)

There is a fourth availability condition stipulating claims about which X should not be certain:[5] (d) if X is certain that he lacks the ability to choose that a be true given that he deliberates at time t and given also that his deliberation meets some other conditions C, X must not be certain that his deliberation meets the conditions C. If he were certain, then he would also be certain that he does not choose a. This is so even though he satisfies conditions (a), (b), and (c).[6]

In addition to identifying a set A of available options and hence of making assumptions satisfying the availability conditions (a)–(d), in order to identify an admissible subset $C(A)$, X must know enough about his values and his beliefs (both full beliefs and probability judgments) and have enough logical omniscience and computational capacity to use his principles of choice to determine the set $C(A)$. That is, his state of full belief must meet a self-knowledge condition and a logical omniscience condition. We do not need perfect self-knowledge or perfect logical omniscience but just enough so that, if X has identified a set A of available options, he uses his principles of choice to identify the admissible set.

Suppose that X's cognitive state meets the availability, self-knowledge, and logical omniscience conditions. In that case, he is certain what the elements of the admissible set $C(A)$ are.

Suppose, in addition, that X's cognitive state meets an additional condition – a condition of smugness about rational virtue. This smugness condition states that X is certain that, on the deliberation at time t, X will choose an admissible option. ˙

Assuming that X's logical omniscience enables him to identify elementary logical consequences of adding this assumption to those satisfying the availability, self-knowledge, and logical omniscience conditions, C must be certain that he will not choose an inadmissible option.

By the availability conditions (c) and (d), it follows that no inadmissible option is an available one. The set of admissible options must coincide with the set of available ones: $C(A) = A$. Though this result is not contradictory it implies the vacuity of deploying principles of rational choice. Such principles are supposed to offer criteria for reducing a set of options recognized to be feasible to a set of admissible options. Sometimes such criteria fail to furnish a reduction. If they always fail, one might as well drop the criteria. For this reason, I reject the equanimity with which Schick (1979) has accepted this untoward result.

Thus, at least one of the assumptions which leads to the trivialization of principles of rational choice as criteria for self-criticism needs to be abandoned if trivialization is to be avoided. We cannot abandon the availability conditions, the omniscience conditions, or the self-knowledge condition without precluding the use of the principles of rational choice by the deliberating agent to identify the admissible options given his state of belief.[7] For *this* purpose, however, we can abandon the smugness about rational virtue. X should not be sure that he will choose an admissible option (that is, choose rationally by his own lights) in the current deliberation (Levi, 1986a, ch. 4).

I am not suggesting that the agent should be certain that he will choose an inadmissible option. When X of this opinion, no admissible option would be recognized to be feasible and this result is at least as objectionable as the previous one.

I wish to go further than this and support Spohn's view that the decision-maker should not assign either determinate or indeterminate credal probabilities to hypotheses as to how he will choose.

As Spohn pointed out, such credal probabilities have no bearing whatsoever on which option X ought to choose. Perhaps, however, X might be offered a bet on one of the options a that he recognizes to be available to him. X's credal probabilities as to which option he will choose might be germane to determining whether he ought to accept the bet. That would be so to the extent that X's probabilities reflect predictions as to how he will choose in the original decision problem which should guide his decision about the bet. It can be argued that such degrees of belief should be zero if the option is inadmissible.[8] By the previous argument the option would then be unavailable.

All this is predicated on the assumption that we are concerned with the degree of credal probability that X should or should not have and not the degree of credal probability that X does or will have. X might be concerned to predict his own choices, but when he does so, he is not functioning as deliberating agent concerned to identify which of these options he is not rationally prohibited from making. Oblomov-like he takes the posture of a spectator concerning his own performances. To the extent that he does so, he ceases to be an autonomous agent.

X might very well take such a predictive or explanatory attitude toward the choices of other agents or toward his own choices at future times.

Thus, in the sequential choice problem represented by the extensive form of figure 2.1, X at the initial stage might very well assign credal probabilities concerning how he will choose at stage 2 if he chooses A at stage 1 or if he chooses B at stage 2. But at stage 1, X does not regard his options at stage 2 as available to him at stage 1. His choice at stage 1 is between A and B.

In this respect, there is a significant difference between the sequential decision problem represented in figure 2.1 and the decision problem cast in normal form in figure 2.2 when this is understood not as a skimpier description of the same sequential decision problem but as a non-sequential single-choice node decision problem. According to the figure 2.2 representation, X has four options available at stage 1 and none at stage 2. The question of predicting how he will choose at stage 2 given, let us say, that he chose A1 at stage 1 does not arise. Given that he chose A1 at stage 1, it is certain that he will implement A1. Perhaps he will implement only A at stage 1 and the implementation of 1 will be delayed to stage 2. But from X's perspective at stage 1, it is certain that 1 will be implemented later given the choice of A1 at stage 1. If X did not judge choosing A1 to be efficacious, he would not regard choosing A1 as an option available to him. From his stage 1 perspective, his future self has no say in the matter.

The situation is different when X's predicament is represented by figure 2.1. In that case, at stage 1, X has control over whether A or B is true but not over whether A1, A2, B3, or B4 is true. He can make a prediction, however, as to how he will choose at stage 2 and guide his choice of A or B accordingly.

Thus there is a sense in which credal probabilities may be assigned to acts or options, but these credal probabilities have no meaningful role at the stage of deliberation when a choice is to be made between these options. If X does assign such credal probabilities to his acts, he does not, while doing so, regard his acts as options between which the choice is under his control, and the question of exploring which of these acts he ought to perform becomes irrelevant.[9]

Someone may object that by refusing to take into account X's views about whether he will choose rationally, relevant information is suppressed. That, however, is not so. The only information that X is entitled to suppress, and indeed should suppress as a deliberating agent, concerns whether X will choose rationally. X should not be certain that he will choose in conformity with his principles of rational choice and he should not be certain that he will violate them. He should make no assumptions as to the chances or statistical probabilities of his choosing rationally or irrationally. Descriptions of X as choosing rationally or irrationally in the decision problem under consideration are irrelevant information in the context of X's deliberation.

Nonetheless, even if X removes hypotheses about the rationality of his current choices from the algebra of propositions to which he assigns probabilities, he may still have information in his corpus *K* of certainties, evidence, or knowledge (the set of propositions X takes for granted at time *t*) which entails that he will or will not choose a given option or which assigns a chance or statistical probability to his choosing (or not choosing) a given option. Such information obligates X via direct inference to assign credal probability to his choosing (not choosing) that option. As such, it precludes X's considering that option as one which is available in the context of deliberation.

As long as X does not have any knowledge entailing that he will (will not) choose true a given act-description or specifying chances of his choosing (not choosing) true such an act-description, he is not committed to assigning credal probabilities to hypotheses as to what he will choose and as a deliberating agent should not do so.

This view has profound ramifications for many topics. It seems that the so-called "common knowledge" assumptions often considered in game-theoretic contexts imply that X is certain that he will choose rationally or assigns probabilities to his doing so. On the view that I am advocating, this is incompatible with his having available to him options other than admissible ones – the implication which is fatal to decision theory in general and game theory in particular at least when these theories are used prescriptively.[10]

Of more immediate concern, however, is the relevance of all of this to consequentialism and sequential choice. In this connection, the first point that I am belaboring is that (*pace* Jeffrey) Savage is surely right in contrasting act-descriptions with consequence-descriptions and state-descriptions. Act-descriptions, in so far as by this we mean propositions representing available options, are not to be assigned unconditional probabilities. Hence, any proposition whose truth is probabilistically dependent on which option is exercised is not to be assigned unconditional probability. Moreover, no proposition whose truth is probabilistically independent of the option chosen should be assigned unconditional utility unless every available option bears the same value when that proposition is true.

More crucial to the concerns of this essay, moreover, the view of availability just sketched suggests that the options available to the agent at the initial node in a sequential decision problem in the extensive form of the sort illustrated by figure 2.1 do not correspond to the options available in the nonsequential normal-form version illustrated by figure 2.2.

Advocates of the reduction of extensive to normal form might concede this point and still insist that, to be rational, the path that the agent should follow in the figure 2.1 predicament ought to correspond to the option he should choose in the figure 2.2 predicament. But the argument for this view cannot rest on the assumption that precommitment to following any one of the paths in the figure 2.1 decision tree is an available option to the decision-maker at the initial node. The question before us is whether a version of consequentialism presupposed by "modern normative decision theory" can be deployed to make an alternative case for the conclusion.

To explore this matter further, we shall turn our attention to consequence-descriptions, state-descriptions, and consequentialism.

3 WEAK AND STRICT CONSEQUENTIALISM

Loosely speaking, consequentialism as it is relevant to "modern normative decision theory" holds that the evaluation of options by a decision-maker in a given context of choice should be determined by the values the agent assigns to the consequences of the several options and the probabilities of these consequences being realized given the implementation of these options. Different kinds of consequentialism may be distinguished, however, depending on how we understand what is to count as a consequence of an option. I have already argued that the set A of propositions representing options availabe to the decision-maker depends on the agent's corpus K of certainties or full beliefs. Given K and any option description a_i in A, let O_i be a set of propositions such that K and a_i (K/a_i) entail that exactly one element of O_i is true and such that each element of O_i is consistent with K/a_i. Let O be the union of the O_i.

Any representation of X's decision problem in terms of the set A and for each a_i a set O_i such that each element of O is assigned an unconditional utility is a *weakly consequentialist* representation and the elements of O_i are consequence (-descriptions) in the weak sense of a_i.[11]

Every decision problem is representable in weakly consequentialist form, for every available option bears an unconditional utility and by identifying the elements of O with the elements of A a weakly consequentialist representation is available.

A representation of X's decision problem is *nontrivially weakly consequentialist* if and only if, for some a_i, a_i is not the sole element of O_i. The expected utility $Eu(a_i)$ of a_i is $\Sigma p(o_{ij}/a_i)u(o_{ij})$.

Observe that if there is a nontrivial weakly consequentialist representation of a given decision problem, then, for every a_i in A, the unconditional utility u of a_i should equal $Eu(a_i$ and this should be so for every nontrivial weakly consequentialist representation.

For every act-description a_i in A, one can always construct a set O_i by taking any set Q_i of sentences such that K/a_i entails exactly one element of Q_i and each element is consistent with K/a_i and by letting O_i be the set of sentences of the form $a_i \& q_{ij} = o_{ij}$ where the o_{ij} are assigned unconditional utility. This representation is the weak consequentialist representation generated by the set of descriptions Q. Every decision problem, therefore, is representable in a nontrivial weakly consequentialist form as long as the conceptual framework is sufficiently rich to allow for the construction of sets Q_i.

Weak consequentialism (the idea that every decision problem should be representable in weakly consequentialist form so that the evaluation of available option-descriptions is determined by the evaluation of the consequence-descriptions and the probabilities of their occurrence given the implementation of the options) ought not to be a focus of controversy. Critics of consequentialism in moral theory cannot be complaining about weak consequentialism since it is sufficiently flexible to accommodate any mode of nonconsequentialist evaluation that they care to consider. Moreover, strict Bayesians advocating the principle of expected utility maximization need not presuppose any stronger version of consequentialism than weak consequentialism.

Is weak consequentialism so understood what Hammond has in mind? Hammond writes:

As a normative principle, however, consequentialism requires everything which should be allowed to affect decisions to count as a relevant consequence – behaviour is evaluated by its consequences, and nothing else. (Hammond, 1988b, p. 26)

Hammond seems to be saying that whatever is an object of value in the context of deliberation qualifies as a consequence. Moreover, he seems to think that such consequentialism is neutral with respect to disputes over "practical" (substantive?) normative principles. These demands are met by weak consequentialism. Weak consequentialism does not state in advance which descriptions are in the domain of consequence-descriptions. That is a matter for practical or substantive values – as Hammond says.[12]

The neutrality of weak consequentialism is greater, however, than Hammond may be prepared to require of consequentialism. For any decision problem whatsoever, there is at least one weak consequentialist representation. No one can avoid being a weak consequentialist – not even Kant and Bernard Williams. I am not sure that Hammond intends his version of consequentialism to be as weak as all that.

It is not clear, for example, whether Hammond means to allow option-descriptions to be consequence-descriptions as well. Nor is it obvious that he means to allow as consequence-descriptions weak consequence-descriptions which are conjunctions of option-descriptions with other sentences. In any case, Savage seems to have endorsed versions of consequentialism imposing stronger demands than weak consequentialism entails.

A representation of a decision problem is in *strict consequentialist* form if and only if (a) it is nontrivially weak consequentialist and (b) it is generated by a set of descriptions Q in the value domain where, for every pair of options a_i and $a_{i'}$, if q_{ij} is the same description (sentence, proposition) as $q_{i'j'}$, $a_i \& q_{ij}$ is equivalued with $a_{i'} \& q_{i'j'}$. In this case, the elements of Q are *strict consequence descriptions*.

Strict consequentialism is the view that for every decision problem there should be a representation in strict consequentialist form. Unlike weak consequence-descriptions, strict consequence-descriptions never have act-descriptions as conjuncts. In such representations, there is a sharp separation between act-descriptions and consequence-descriptions. The value of a consequence-description does not depend upon which act determines it to be true. What "affects" decisions are the values of the strict consequence-descriptions. Act-descriptions have value, and indeed unconditional value, but their unconditional value is supposed to be "dependent" on the unconditional value of their strict consequence-descriptions. At the level of generality at which this discussion is being carried on, the notion of "dependence" cannot be explained precisely because such an explanation will appeal to principles of rational choice determining which options are admissible from a set of available options. We have been avoiding the assumption of such principles. But, if one is an advocate of the expected utility principle, strict consequentialism may be construed as saying that the value of an option-description must be represented as an expected utility derived from information about the utilities of strict consequence-descriptions and probabilities assigned to them conditional on the option-description's being true.

Savage was committed to some form of strict consequentialism. This is a far more substantive thesis than weak consequentialism and, indeed, has value implications which I find far too restrictive (although Savage seemed to think that the restrictions could be finessed somehow).

Strict consequentialism does not imply that strict consequence-descriptions represent "possible" effects of the events described by act-descriptions. On the contrary, there is nothing to prevent a consequence-description, when true, from describing the same event as an act-description. If George has forgotten whether he borrowed the $10 from Ron or from Nancy but is sure that he borrowed from one of them, he may face a choice of paying Ron or paying Nancy. Given his corpus, it is a serious possibility that if George pays Ron the $10, the event-description "the paying of his debt" refers to the same event as "the paying to Ron of the $10." Causality on almost nobody's account enters into the matter. Yet, "George pays his debt" is a possibly true consequence-description for the act-description "George pays Ron $10."

We could envisage a version of consequentialism which, in addition to requiring representation of decision problems in strict consequentialist form, insisted that the applicability of strict consequence-descriptions be causally dependent on the option chosen. Fortunately, we do not have to worry about this version of consequentialism or the vexing problems of clarifying the notion of causal dependency it deploys. Savage does not seem to have presupposed such causal versions of consequentialism. Nor, as far as I can see, do other students of decision theory including advocates of so-called causal decision theories.[13]

Savage's motive for adopting a stronger version of consequentialism is his interest in deriving an agent's belief probabilities and utilities from information about his preferences for the "acts" or options that he faces or, more accurately, for his preferences for a hypothetically available set of options in which the options that the agent actually faces are embedded. The axioms that he imposed on such preferences presupposed that the hypothetically available set of options could be represented in strict consequentialist form and not merely in weak consequentialist form.

To achieve his purpose, Savage endorsed a still stronger form of consequentialism. As Hammond pointed out in the passage cited initially, Savage required that options be representable in what I shall call "state-functional form," so that each option-description is equivalent to a representation of an option as a function from a system of "state-descriptions" to a system of strict consequence-descriptions.[14]

As just noted, the chief motivation for the additional restrictions imposed by Savage appears to be that they facilitate derivation of numerical probabilities and utilities from preferences over act-descriptions when suitable axioms are adopted constraining the preferences. But we ought not to impose conditions which support such derivation as requirements of rationality merely for this reason. I would regard strict consequentialism as excessively restrictive as a condition of rationality. *A fortiori*, state-functional strict consequentialism ought not to be accorded that status.[15]

Students of the foundations of Bayesian decision theory as well as non-Bayesian decision-theorists have registered reservations to the state-functional strict consequentialism of Savage and have sought to mitigate the severity of its demands. Whatever tinkering they do, however, seems to leave unsullied the strict consequentialist requirement. The thesis that "acts are valued by their consequences" which is "almost unquestioned" by "modern normative decision theory" seems to me to be best captured by strict consequentialism. Weak consequentialism is, indeed, unquestioned and rightly so. But students of decision theory have tended to assume that the stronger strict consequentialist condition is in place in their work. I fail to see that anything relevantly stronger than strict consequentialism has been "almost unquestioned." Even critics of utilitarianism and utilitarian-like moral theories may be willing to concede that in some contexts the conditions for representing a decision problem in strict consequentialist and, indeed, even in strict consequentialist state-functional form may be satisfied. Hence, in spite of its excessively restricted character, it will be useful to compare the assumptions of strict consequentialism with the version of consequentialism that Hammond investigates.

4 HAMMOND'S CONSEQUENTIALISM

Hammond introduces a conception of consequentialism and claims that it does entail ordinality. Consequentialism as he understands it is a constraint on "behavior norms." Our next task, therefore, is to explain the notion of a behavior norm and to state what a consequentialist behavior norm amounts to. With this understood, we shall then be in a position to state the relation between Hammond's consequentialism, strict consequentialism, and ordinality.

For the present purpose, we can focus on decision problems in extensive form, where every node except a final node is a decision node. There are finitely many terminal nodes each of which is represented by propositions in the value domain Y generated by a set Q of consequence-descriptions.[16] We are assuming that the elements of Y are strict consequence-descriptions as well as "terminal" in the sense indicated. Hence the value of any option available to a decision-maker at a decision node in the decision tree is determined by the values of the elements of Y and the probability of realizing such elements conditional on choosing the option.

Consider any such decision tree. A *behavior norm* specifies, for any such tree and any decision node in the tree, the admissible set of options (that is, "branches") from the set available at that node. It can be represented by a function $\beta(T, n)$ where T is a decision tree and n is a node in the tree. Given any such tree T, let T(n) be that subtree obtained by considering the paths emanating from node n in T. T(n) is a tree and hence the behavior norm should be defined when it is an argument. In particular, $\beta(T(n), n)$ should have a value. Hammond insists that in order for the behavior norm to be an "accurate description" of behavior, $\beta(T(n),n)$ should equal $\beta(T, n)$. Since, by hypothesis, there are no features of the situation relevant to evaluating value other than those packed into the consequence-descriptions at the terminal nodes, if the agent, in tree T at node n, recognizes a certain subset of available options as admissible, he should do the same even if the tree began at node n as long as he is wedded to the same behavior norm. This seems to be Hammond's position.

Now Hammond claims that if the agent chooses in conformity with a given set of principles of rational choice (whatever they may be) and is consequentialist, his behavior norm for all trees in the domain will meet a certain condition which I shall now explain.

Let $F(T, n)$ be the set of consequence-descriptions which are terminal nodes of the subtree $T(n)$ of T. $C_\beta(F(T, n))$ is the set of consequence-descriptions, the choice of which the agent would regard as admissible if the agent were to have available to him at a single-choice node the choice between the elements of $F(T, n)$. The subscript β serves to remind us that a single-shot choice between consequence-descriptions is itself a tree with a single decision node, that the behavior norm is defined for that tree, and that the "choice function" C_β is the one determined by the given behavior norm.

Suppose then that the agent is at node n in tree T or at node n in subtree $T(n)$. In general, the agent will not have available at that stage a direct choice between consequences but the behavior norm will specify the set of admissible options $\beta(T, n)$ at that node and, assuming that the agent obeys the behavior norm at every subsequent stage in the tree leading from an admissible option, will determine a set of admissible subsequent paths in the decision tree. The set of consequence-descriptions which are terminal nodes in this set of admissible subsequent paths is the set $\Phi_\beta(T, n)$. In effect, taking n to be the initial node in subtree $T(n)$, $\Phi_\beta(T, n)$ is the set of possible consequences of following the behavior norm in the agent's extensive-form sequential decision problem and $C_\beta(F(T, n))$ is the set of possible consequences of following the behavior norm in the corresponding nonsequential strategic or normal-form decision problem when the agent's evaluation of the consequences is held fixed.

According to Hammond's version of consequentialism, the set of admissible option sequences in the extensive-form sequential decision problem should have as terminal nodes the same set of consequences as the corresponding nonsequential normal-form decision problem. *Hammond's consequentialism* can thus be expressed as

$$\Phi_\beta(T, n) = C_\beta(F(T, n))$$

Return to the schematic example of an extensive-form decision problem represented by figure 2.1 and the corresponding normal-form decision problem represented by figure 2.2. If the agent prefers c_1 over c_2 over c_3 over c_4, then it is clear that as long as the figure 2.2 predicament is in strict consequentialist form (that is, as long as the c_i are strict consequence-descriptions), the agent should choose A1. In the figure 2.1 predicament, at the second stage, if the agent had already chosen A he should choose option 1, and if he had already chosen B he should choose 3. Hence, at the first stage, he should choose option A, for in that event, if he follows the behavior norm, he will end up with c_1. Thus, under the hypothesis that the consequences are weakly ordered, the verdict of strict consequentialism and Hammond's consequentialism coincide.

Consider, however, Hammond's well-known treatment of the potential addict which he discusses afresh in Hammond (1988b). At the initial time t_1 the potential addict faces a choice whether to try out some addictive substance. He does not want to become permanently damaged by addiction but he wants to enjoy briefly the pleasures of the substance without damage. Thus he prefers Pleasure without damage to Complete abstinence to Damage. If he chooses to partake of the substance, at t_2 he has a choice of refraining from further use with the result of Pleasure without damage or continuing with the result of Permanent addiction and damage. We suppose that, at t_2, he has already become addicted. The decision tree is represented in figure 2.3.

Consider, at least as a thought experiment, the corresponding single-choice predicament where the potential addict has three options: Pleasure without damage, Complete abstinence, and Permanent damage. Given the preferences that we identified, we suppose that the behavior norm specifies a uniquely admissible option for this case: Pleasure without damage. This is the value for the choice function C_β for this case. The only kind of behavior norm covering the extensive-form problem as well which meets Hammond's consequentialist requirement is the one which recommends partaking at the first stage and stopping at the second stage. But, by hypothesis, the potential addict is incapable of conforming to the behavior norm. He might even know this at the initial choice node. What behavior norm should he live by which is compatible with the behavior norm specified for the normal-form problem? Hammond singles out two

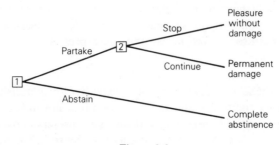

Figure 2.3

Table 2.1

	Tree	Node	Admissible set
Naive β_1	T(1)	1	Partake
	T(1)	2	Continue
	T(2)	2	Continue
Sophisticated β_2	T(1)	1	Abstain
	T(1)	2	Continue
	T(2)	2	Continue

candidates (table 2.1). Both these behavior norms are consistent in Hammond's sense. Neither of them satisfies the condition of Hammond's consequentialism, as Hammond himself emphasizes.

The naive behavior norm violates the precepts of strict consequentialism. At the first stage, the agent knows that, assuming he partakes, he will end up with permanent addiction. He also knows that if he does not partake he will end up with total abstention. By hypothesis, at the first stage he would prefer the latter consequence over the former. If only the consequences matter to him, then as a good strict consequentialist, he should choose to abstain. Naiveté leads to abandonment of strict consequentialism as well as Hammond's consequentialism.

The sophisticated behavior norm also violates Hammond's consequentialism; but strict consequentialism is satisfied. Hammond's consequentialism requires that the results of applying the norm lead to consequences that would be chosen in a normal-form version of the problem – that is, to pleasure without damage. It recommends that the agent partake at the first stage and then stop. But the agent cannot do that. The sequence of choices just specified is not feasible. The sophisticated decision-maker realizes this. His behavior norm is implementable, as is the norm of the naive decision-maker, but, more crucially, yields the best consequences from those accessible to the decision-maker.

By requiring that a sequence of choices yield the same consequences as would be chosen in a normal-form version of the decision problem, Hammond's consequentialism insists on the agent's making sequences of choices that determine those consequence-descriptions at terminal nodes which would be chosen by the agent initially if choosing these descriptions to be true were available options to him at the initial node. If the agent had his druthers, he would have the temporary pleasure of partaking without lasting addiction and damage. The sophisticated potential addict takes into account only those elements of Y which he can be certain will be true given his initial choice. These are the elements of Y which are initially directly accessible to the potential addict.

Hammond's consequentialism is a much more demanding prescriptive standard than strict consequentialism. If the potential addict is certain that he will not stop at the second stage, he is certain that partaking will lead to permanent addiction. That is the strict consequence of his partaking from his point of view. Abstaining coheres with strict consequentialism.[17]

Hammond's consequentialism requires the decision-maker at the initial stage to proceed as if he had available to him at the initial stage the option of obtaining any element of Y – that is, a consequence-description at a terminal node of his decision tree. The example of the potential addict illustrates one of several ways in which this condition can break down. It is presumed to be false in the case of the potential addict that the agent is able to choose the strategy of first partaking and then stopping. At the initial stage, the potential addict has control over whether he partakes or not. He has no control over what he will choose at the second stage. Hence the consequence of partaking and then stopping is not available to him.

Suppose, for example, that our strict consequentialist potential addict were a strict Bayesian like Savage and were deciding whether to partake or abstain on the basis of expected utility. The expected utility of partaking is determined by the utilities of the elements of Y accessible from the second choice node and the probabilities of the potential addict's stopping or continuing to take the drug at the second stage. This procedure violates Hammond's consequentialism. But it does not betray the strict Bayesianism of Savage, Ramsey, De Finetti, and others. Strict Bayesianism may entail consequentialism in some sense or other but not in Hammond's sense.

Hammond himself admits that, given the potential addict's predicament, "sophisticated behavior seems clearly the best, despite its violation of consequentialism" (Hammond, 1988b, p. 36). Hammond immediately goes on to say:

This does not imply, however, that consequentialism is irrational. Rather the potential addict is really two (potential) persons, before and after addiction, and the decision problem has to be analysed as a "game" between two "rational players".

Thus, for Hammond, the fact that the best thing for the potential addict to do is to behave according to the nonconsequentialist sophisticated behavior norm does not undermine the rationality of consequentialism as he understands it. He claims to be restricting his discussion to "single-person decision-theory." Multi-person decision theory is to be left for future consideration. The predicament of the potential addict belongs to multi-person decision theory. Hammond does not explain why he thinks that the potential addict is really two persons before and after addiction. Is it because the potential addict has different preferences or values after addiction than before or is it because the change in preferences is not the product of well-reasoned reflection?

Suppose that we heed the entirely sensible attitude favored by Kadane and Larkey (1982) that when an individual faces a choice in a game against another individual or set of individuals he should regard hypotheses about the choices of the other players as objects of probability judgment. In a similar vein, at the initial choice node, the potential addict should treat hypotheses as to his future choices as objects of probability judgment. In this respect, the predicament of the potential addict does indeed resemble that of a participant in a game. The other player is the potential addict himself at the second choice node.[18]

However, in this sense, every sequential decision problem is a game between the decision-maker at the initial node and the decision-maker at subsequent nodes. It does not matter whether the agent has or has not altered his values at the several nodes and, if he has, whether he has done so in a reasonable fashion or under the grip of an addiction. If Hammond thinks that the predicament of the potential addict is a multi-person decision problem not covered by his discussion, then all sequential decision-making is multi-person decision-making. Hammond's account of consequential behavior norms then has application only to trees with single choice nodes – counter to his intention.

Hammond must have in mind a different view of multi-person decision-making from the one that I have just mentioned. He owes us an explanation of what it is. Regardless of the answer, Hammond's consequentialism is stronger than strict consequentialism in two respects: (a) it prohibits recognition of opportunities for choice as uncertain prospects counting as consequences, and (b) it demands that a behavior norm in a decision tree yield the same terminal consequences as the corresponding normal-form decision problem does.

It is now time to consider whether strict consequentialism entails ordinality. We shall address a predicament where the decision-maker is to choose autonomously at several stages without changing her preferences or values from one decision node to another. Phillippa has had the good fortune to be offered beginning teaching positions at three philosophy departments at universities A, B, and C. Phillippa judges the teaching conditions and intellectual environment at A to be vastly superior to those at B, which are in turn negligibly superior to those at C. C offers much better salary and tenure prospects than B which in turn is slightly better in these respects than A. University B has never hired a woman to its faculty. C has hired a woman but does not have one now. A has several women on its faculty. Phillippa is concerned primarily with teaching conditions and intellectual environment on the one hand and salary and tenure prospects on the other. The record of the university in hiring women would matter to her only if she could not make up her mind on the basis of the primary considerations.

On the basis of the primary considerations, Phillippa is clear that she will not choose B. It is nearly as bad as the worst of the three according to both dimensions of value that she recognizes as primary. If she countenances potential resolutions of the conflict between these two dimensions, no compromise rates B on a par or better than the other two alternatives. So she rules B out as inadmissible on primary considerations. But she cannot make up her mind between A and C. In this case, however, she appeals to the desirability of the presence of a woman at university C and chooses in its favor.

Observe, however, that if her choice had been between B and C without the opportunity to choose A, professional considerations would not have enabled her to decide. B would have been better with respect to teaching conditions and intellectual environment but would have paid less and had poorer prospects of tenure. As a feminist, she would do better to break the ice at university B rather than to be the second woman on the staff at C. So she chooses B.

This is an example of a violation of an important condition on choice functions (Sen's property α (Sen, 1970)). C is uniquely admissible in the three-way choice, but B is admissible and C inadmissible in the two-way choice. Violation of this choice-consistency principle either indicates that Phillippa has changed her values when facing the pair of options from the values she endorsed when facing three or does not have an evaluation of her options representable as a weak ordering. As I have portrayed her predicament, her behavior is not a manifestation of a change in values but derives from the fact that her primary values are in unresolved conflict (Levi, 1986a) and cannot induce a weak ordering on her options. This portrait seems consistent and, more crucially, there is nothing in it to suggest that Phillippa's values are incoherent or irrational.

Phillippa's decision problem was nonsequential. She faced a choice between three options. But suppose that her choice is sequential. Suppose that university A requires a "yes" or "no" response tomorrow whereas universities B and C call for a response within a week of tomorrow. In a three-way choice, I have suggested that Phillippa would choose C. If Hammond's consequentialism were to obtain, the behavior norm would have to recommend refusing university A at the first stage and choosing

C at the second. But that behavior norm does not conform to the vision of her values that I have suggested. If she does refuse A at the first stage, Phillippa has a choice between B and C, and so I have suggested that she should choose B. If, at the first stage, Phillippa is certain that she will choose B at the second stage, she sees her first-stage options as choosing A and refusing A followed by choosing B. If her values are as I have specified, she should refuse A and choose B. However, in the normal-form version of Phillippa's predicament, she should choose C. Hammond's consequentialist condition is clearly violated.

Phillippa, I submit, has been a loyal strict consequentialist. Given her conviction that she will choose B at the second stage, the only "consequence-descriptions" accessible to her from her initial point of view are A and B. C is not accessible. The reason is that Phillippa recognizes at the initial stage that, should she refuse A at the outset, she will face another choice. The second choice is autonomous. From her initial point of view, how Phillippa will choose subsequently is no more under her control at the initial stage than what someone else would choose if the decision as to whether Phillippa goes to B or C when A is rejected were left in the hands of a third party. Phillippa can at best predict what her second-stage self will choose. From the vantage point of the first choice node, Phillippa regards her second-stage opportunity for choice between B and C as a strict consequence of refusing A. That is, in point of fact, the consequence accessible to her. If she is sure that she will choose B, then B is an accessible consequence as well. If she is uncertain, neither B nor C is accessible. Only if she is certain that, upon refusing A, C will be chosen is C accessible. In the situation we are envisaging, C is inaccessible. This is not because at the second stage Phillippa is crazed by addiction. On the contrary, it is because Phillippa has nonarbitrarily and resolutely stuck by her values and principles. She is not of two minds. Her second-stage self endorses the same values as her initial-stage self. At both stages, Phillippa is in unresolved conflict. Yet Phillippa behaves like a good strict consequentialist.

Phillippa's predicament illustrates why the strict consequentialism presupposed by Savage and other students of "modern normative decision theory" does not imply ordinality. As mentioned earlier, Seidenfeld has shown that when decision trees terminate in strict consequence-descriptions the independence postulate should be satisfied whether or not reduction of extensive to normal form obtains. I have argued elsewhere (Levi, 1987) that the principle of revising probabilities by temporal conditionalization can be justified by betting arguments along the lines of Teller (1973) only if the reduction of extensive to normal form is presupposed. It would be a mistake to conclude from Hammond's argument that conditionalization, independence, and ordering are all underwritten by strict consequentialism. Only independence is.

The idea that individual decision-makers facing a sequence of decision problems ought to make sequences of choices in their extensive-form decision problem constituting a path corresponding to an admissible option in the associated normal-form or strategic decision problem is shared by a great many economists, statisticians, philosophers, and decision-theorists interested in rational choice.[19] Arguments defending choice consistency and ordinality, the independence postulate, temporal conditionalization, and other facets of Bayesianism have been based on some version of the reduction of extensive to normal form. For quite some time Hammond has been both an advocate of this idea and an insightful investigator into its ramifications (see for example, Hammond, 1976, 1977).

The philosophical novelty introduced in his recent paper on this theme (Hammond, 1988b) is the claim that consequentialism, as presupposed by a wide variety of decision-theorists including Savage, assumes the reduction of extensive to normal form. I have argued that this claim is incorrect. Consequentialism claims that only consequences matter. Of course, consequentialists need to qualify this claim by taking into account the probabilities of consequences ensuring the implementation of options and quite crucially what is to count as an available option. There remains, of course, the widespread skepticism about the merits of consequentialism both in ethical theory and as a condition of rational choice. I share that skepticism regarding strict consequentialism.[20] Even so, there are many contexts where the conditions of strict consequentialism seem to be satisfied fairly well. The burden of this paper has been to argue that, when planning future choices in a strict consequentialist setting, the question of what the decision-maker ought to recognize as an available option presents a stumbling block to those who, like Hammond, seek to reduce sequential decision problems to nonsequential decision problems and derive strong conclusions about rational choice in strict consequentialist settings. The question of recognized availability has suffered uncritical neglect in studies of modern decision theory. The neglect is undeserved.

NOTES

Thanks are due to Michael Bacharach and Susan Hurley for extensive and helpful comments. I wish to thank the Fellows of All Souls College for providing me with the leisure to work on the materials from which this paper emerged.

1 "Preference" is to be understood as a propositional attitude comparing

propositions as better or worse according to the agent's value commitments. Such comparisons may take into account political, economic, prudential, moral, cognitive, or personal concerns. The requirement that the propositions in the domain under comparison be weakly ordered implies that for every pair of propositions in the domain either one of them is ranked above (is strictly preferred to) the other or they are ranked together (are equipreferred or equivalued). The requirement of weak ordering rules out cases of noncomparability.

2 By speaking of "the independence postulate" I mean to allude to a family of related assumptions such as Savage's (1954) "sure-thing principle" or the monotonicity and substitutibility axioms of Luce and Raiffa (1957, pp. 27–8) which impose a constraint on preferences over propositions describing options available to the decision-maker. The technical details will not be required in this discussion, but roughly speaking it is a variant on principles prohibiting the choice of an option when there is another available which dominates it. a dominates b if it is better than b in all possible situations according to at least one way of identifying a set of exclusive and exhaustive possible situations. Alternatively, we may be given a stock of prizes which the agent weakly orders with respect to his preferences and say that a "stochastically dominates" b if and only if the probability of obtaining a prize no better than x is less if a is chosen than if b is chosen for some x and is no greater for every x. Among the several technical issues which complicate the formulation of a simple, neutral, and accurate version of this principle is the circumstance that, given the same pair of options a and b, a may (stochastically), dominate b relative to one way of partitioning into possible situations (possible prizes) but not relative to another. Advocates of the independence postulate insist that if there is at least one way of partitioning relative to which a (stochastically) dominates b, a should be preferred to b. Critics of the independence postulate like Allais (1953b) and Machina (1982a), in effect, relativize dominance requirements to privileged partitions into possible situations (prizes). For a survey of some of the formal variants of the independence postulate, see MacCrimmon and Larsson (1979).

3 Although the consequentialism endorsed by "modern normative decision theory" is less controversial than the reduction of extensive to normal form, consequentialism has been a focal point of objections to utilitarian and utilitarian-like ethical theories. In this paper, I shall not be addressing the issues raised in this debate. However, by identifying the sense in which consequentalism is presupposed by "modern normative decision theory," we may obtain as a by-product a juster appreciation of the extent to which contemporary decision theory is or is not caught up in this controversy.

4 A whiff of causality may seem to be introduced into our discussion by the recognition of the distinction between act-descriptions and consequence- and state-descriptions. Act-descriptions are sentences or propositions whose truth values are subject to the agent's control. By his choice, their truth values are settled. Or, more strictly speaking, propositions which are act-descriptions according to agent X are propositions whose truth values are subject to X's

control according to X's corpus of certainties K. However, no matter what a deeper analysis of the concept of control might reveal, as far as decision theory is concerned, the epistemic condition that X satisfies when we say that the truth of act-descriptions is under X's control is this: the "expansion" $K/$"X chooses a_i" of X's corpus K by adding the information that X chooses a_i contains a_i, that is, entails the truth of a_i, while K does not. We may also say that the truth value of a proposition which is not an act-description is under X's control according to K if and only if there is some a_i such that K/a_i entails h and an $a_{i'}$ such that $K/a_{i'}$, entails ~ h. The truth of h is under X's control according to K if and only if there is an a_i such that K/a_i entails h and another a* such that $K/$a* entails neither h nor ~ h. This characterization of control of truth values proceeds along entirely epistemic lines once we are given a list of option-descriptions. Causality does not enter into the picture. In this sense, agents are in control of which of their options they choose and which of the "sure" consequences of their options will be realized. They are not in control of unsure consequences or of states.

5 The availability conditions (a)–(d) do not explicate the concept of feasibility or availability of options. They furnish some conditions on X's state of full belief or conviction which should be satisfied if X recognizes elements of a set A are options available to him. Y may disagree with X's representation of the situation. X himself may change his mind about what was available to him at t at some other time. The conditions characterize X's state of full belief at time t and do not comment on whether his state does or does not contain error.

6 If the agent is certain that he will choose an admissible option from among those available, the inadmissible options must be unavailable from his point of view. This is not to deny that the agent is certain that he is able to choose the option through his deliberation. But that conviction is consistent with his full belief that he is not being able to do so through his deliberation subject to the constraint. If the agent is also certain that his deliberation is subject to the constraint, the option is not available in the relevant sense. Just as a coin is capable of landing heads on a toss while at the same time it is incapable of landing heads on a toss which situates the coin in a mechanical state constraining its trajectory so that it lands tails, so too an agent may be able to perform some action through deliberation but not be able to perform that action through deliberation of some more specific kind. In the case of the coin, we may say that the coin has a 50 percent chance of landing heads on a toss but has a 0 percent chance of landing heads on a toss which situates the coin in the tails-inducing mechanical state. When we consider a bet on the outcome of a toss, if we are certain that the coin is tossed, we may assign a 0.5 belief probability to the hypothesis that the coin lands heads provided we are ignorant as to whether the coin is so situated. But if we have extra information about the particular toss in question so that we are certain that the toss is of the tails-inducing variety, we should assign 0 belief probability to that hypothesis. The agent may remain certain that the coin has a 0.5 chance of landing heads on a toss. But the information available to him should preclude

his basing his subjective probability assessment on that chance. A similar observation applies to the deliberating agent. If the inquiring agent is certain that the deliberation in which he is engaged is one where he will not implement a given policy, then even though he knows that he is able to implement that policy through deliberation, given that he is also certain that he is not able to do so in a deliberation which terminates with his not choosing that alternative, he must base his judgments as to what is feasible to him on his information as to what he is able to do on deliberations where the option in question is not implemented. See Levi (1984, sections 4.1, 4.2) for an elaboration of this argument. Background discussion of relevant conceptions of possibility and ability can be found in Levi (1977, 1979, 1980, chs 1, 11, 12).

7 Perhaps the agent ought not to be sure that if he chooses A his choice will be implemented. That will not do because then his option is not choosing A but choosing to try to realize A and the inquirer will presuppose that he is efficacious in choosing to try. Perhaps, we should think of the predicament of the agent prior to his identifying his values and beliefs and making the calculations and deductions from his data requisite to determining which options are admissible. It may be argued that, until the deliberation is brought to a successful fruition, the agent is not sure which options are admissible and which are not and, hence, trivialization is avoided. Even so, prior to identifying the data requisite to applying the criteria of choice and prior to making the calculations required, the deliberating agent has not applied his criteria of choice to determine an admissible set of options. To avoid trivialization and retain applicability, we need to be able to apply the criteria when all the data are in and the computations made necessary to apply the principles and, given performance of this task, we need to be able to distinguish the admissible set from the feasible set relative to the information then available.

8 To see this, suppose that the original decision problem is one where X faces a choice between options a and b. Prior to making a choice, X is offered a bet on the proposition that he will choose a, where he wins a positive number W of utiles if he does choose a and loses a positive amount D if he chooses b. Now X's decision problem has been altered. He has four options, not two. He can choose a and accept the bet or–choose a and reject the bet, and he has two similar options through choosing b. It is clear immediately that X should not choose a and refuse the bet or choose b and accept it. Choosing a and accepting the bet dominates the first alternative and choosing b and rejecting the bet dominates the second. If we assume (as could be true and is the simplest case to discuss) that the utility of one of these conjunctive propositions is the sum of the utilities of the conjuncts, which of the remaining two options X should choose depends on $W + E(a)$ where $E(a)$ is the expected value of a as compared with $E(b) - L$. Under these conditions, as long as $E(a) > E(b)$, X should be prepared to accept the bet even when $W = 0$ so that the "fair betting rate" determining X's degree of belief that he will choose a should be 1. By similar reasoning, if $E(a) < E(b)$, the betting rate for the prediction that X chooses b should be 1. Thus, when one of the two options

is uniquely admissible, the agent is sure that he will choose it so that, by the previous argument, the alternative is not an available option. The only way that both options can be admissible is if they are both available. This is, of course, precisely the difficulty we have been seeking to avoid. We can, of course, avoid the problem just raised by denying that assigning probabilities to predictions about the option one will choose in the decision problem one currently faces is revealed by judgments concerning fair betting rates for these propositions. In that event, it becomes obscure what the point of such probability judgments is.

These considerations do not show that probabilities cannot formally be assigned by X to propositions predicting his choice in a manner consistent with the calculus of probabilities. They do show that X's credal probability judgments concerning what he will choose cannot be used to determine betting rates on hypotheses as to what he will decide. It is not clear that there is any other role that they can play in deliberation and inquiry. Spohn seems right in insisting that the agent X should not assign credal probabilities to act-descriptions representing the options that he is facing in a deliberation.

9 The issue of foreknowledge of one's choices is discussed by Shackle (1969), Jeffrey (1977) and Schick (1979). The suggestion that one should not be certain that one will choose an admissible option is proposed by Levi (1986a). T. Seidenfeld in discussion and W. Spohn in print (Spohn, 1977) prompted me to address the question of the relevance of probabilities of predictions of choice to determining betting rates and hence to link the question of probabilities of options with the response to the foreknowledge conundrum advocated by Levi (1986a).

10 Pettit and Sugden (1989) take notice of the fact that common knowledge conditions in game theory imply that the options available to players coincide with the options admissible for them but they distinguish that case from the case of common belief where they do not recognize such an implication. As Schick rightly notes, however, the puzzle that we are attending to is a puzzle about forebelief as much as about foreknowledge. The options available to the agent in a decision problem are the options the decision-maker recognizes as available to him. If the agent is certain that he will not choose a given course of action even though he is certain that he is able to do so through deliberation and his conviction is correct, that option is not available to him. Thus, if the option dominates alternatives which are available to him, the injunction against choosing a dominated option is not operative, for it applies (whenever it does) only when the dominated option is dominated by an available option. The notion of availability relevant in discussing criteria for rational choice intended for agents in deliberation is a notion of feasibility as recognized by the deliberating agent and not by a third party such as a court of law or God. It is entertainable that other notions of availability are appropriate when assessing moral or legal responsibility. Relative to such notions, the distinction between common knowledge and common belief might be relevant. I deny that it is relevant in either game theory or decision theory.

11 This formulation needs some modification in order to be adequate to our

purpose. As it stands, it presupposes that the consequence-descriptions in *0* are assigned numerical utilities unique up to a positive affine transformation. Our aim in this discussion is to explore the extent to which consequentialism entails that available options in *A* be weakly ordered with respect to value when sequential choice is taken into account. If we characterize consequentialism as weak consequentialism – that is, the thesis that every decision problem be representable in weakly consequentialist form – there is no need to invoke considerations of sequential choice to yield the result. Assuming that the expected utility of an option is its utility, the formulation that we have given insures that options representable in weak consequentialist form order the available options in *A* without any consideration of sequential choice.

To avoid such trivialization of Hammond's thesis, let us suppose that the agent X facing a decision problem assigns value to some propositions but not to others. The propositions assigned value belong in the *value domain*. Other propositions do not. We assume that all elements on *A* are in the value domain and that the conjunctions (consistent with *K*) of elements of *A* with any proposition are in the value domain (so that for every option-description in *A* every proposition has a value conditional on that option-description.) In addition, if, for every a_i and $a_{i'}$ in *A* such that h&a_i and h&$a_{i'}$ are consistent with *K*, h&a_i is equivalued with h&$a_{i'}$, h is in the value domain. No other propositions are in the value domain. The evaluation of the propositions in the value domain need not be representable by a utility function unique up to a positive affine transformation over the value domain. The evaluation may yield at most a weak ordering of the value domain. Perhaps only a quasi-ordering is obtainable. In any case, when we say that a proposition is asssigned unconditional utility, we mean only that it is in the value domain. If h&e is in the value domain and a utility function is defined over the value domain, the utility of h given e is equal to the utility of h&e.

12 I would supplement Hammond's observation by pointing out that the value domain of consequence-descriptions for agent X (see note 8) is relative to (a) the agent's corpus *K*, (b) the agent's values, and (c) the agent's credal probability judgments. Thus, whether h&a has the same value for every option a in *A* and hence is in the value domain depends on factors (a) and (c) as well as factor (b). h could be equivalent given *K* to a set of exclusive and exhaustive hypotheses. It may meet the requirements for belonging in the value domain in virtue not only of the agent's values but of the corpus and the credal probabilities over these alternatives. Still I agree with Hammond that consequentialism imposes a constraint on consequence-descriptions. Which systems of descriptions meet the constraints is a substantive issue.

13 Causal decision theorists insist that issues of causal dependence are relevant to determining which options are admissible, but they do not insist that there be at least one causal and strict consequentialist representation for every decision problem. Indeed, causal decision theorists need not be strict consequentialists.

14 Given X's corpus *K*, *S* is a set of *proto-state descriptions* if and only if (a) *K* entails that exactly one element of *S* is true and each element is consistent

with K and (b) the elements of S are not in the value domain. Proto-state-descriptions, like state-descriptions, are not objects of unconditional utility evaluation. We have not required, however, that proto-state-descriptions be assignable credal probabilities not conditioned on the option chosen. That is, we have not required proto-states to be probabilistically independent of the option chosen. In this respect, they resemble consequence-descriptions. Given X's corpus K and state of credal probability judgment, S is a set of state-descriptions if and only if (a) S is a set of proto-state-descriptions relative to K and (b) for every option-description a in A, the state of credal probability judgment for S given a is the same.

Savage assumed that every decision problem should be representable in a form which is at once strictly consequentialist and where there is a set S of state descriptions such that for every option a_i of A and every element s_j of S, there is an element q_{ij} of Q such that $K/a_i \& S_j$ entails q_{ij}. When this is the case, the corpus K and option-description a_i determine a function from the S to Q. Such a representation is state functional and strict consequentialist. If S is a set of proto-states but not states, the representation is proto-state functional. Two or more option-descriptions may determine the same function from proto-state-descriptions to consequence-descriptions. More-over, in general two such option-descriptions need not be equivalued. Savage, however, insists that if two acts have the same consequences in every state of the world "there would be no point in considering them different acts at all" (Savage, 1954, p. 14). That is, they would be equivalued. This is a very substantial value and probability assumption. For one thing, it presupposes strict consequentialism. For another, if the value of an option is supposed to be its expected utility, a proto-state-functional strict consequentialist represen-tation presupposes that the probability distribution over the proto-states is independent of which of the acts yielding the same consequences in the same states is chosen. This is not quite probabilistic independence of states from acts. It does not presuppose that the probability distribution over S is the same for all elements of A but only for those yielding the same consequences for the same states. Savage, who is not merely proto-state functionalist but state functionalist, endorses axioms which insure this probabilistic independence. It is useful to keep in mind, however, that assumptions about probability and utility are built into the requirements of even proto-state functionalist con-sequentialism which are not explicit in the axioms proposed by Savage or in alternative systems.

Savage and many others who are state-functional, strict consequentialists claim that acts are or are represented by functions from states to con-sequences. I do not deny that when decision problems are representable in state-functional strict consequentialist form, one can replace the option- or act-descriptions by characterizations as functions from states to conse-quences. However, in some situations it may be important to consider that there are two or more options which determine the same function. As long as the corpus, the state of credal probability judgment, and the state of utility judgment remain what they are, the several options are equivalued. But such judgments could change. As a consequence, the representation of the decision problem could cease being state functional of even strict consequentialist. There is nothing in the Savage axioms which make explicit the properties of the corpus, the state of credal probability judgment, and the state of value judgment which secure the state-functional representability of the elements of A.

Given a decision problem representable in strict consequentialist form, is it always possible to obtain another representation, which is equivalent given the corpus K, in proto-state-functional strict consequentialist form? If so, is it possible to obtain a representation which is in state-functional strict consequentialist form? Unless one invokes the use of conditionals (as is tacit in Fishburn (1970) and explicit in Gibbard and Harper (1978)) or, barring that, introduces other enlarged conceptual resources, the answer to the first question seems to be negative. As Gibbard and Harper appreciate, even if we indulge in the use of conditionals to construct proto-states, we cannot guarantee that the proto-states will qualify as states. I do not think that conditionals ought to be treated as truth-value-bearing propositions (Levi, 1977, 1979, 1988). For this reason, I agree with Spohn (1977) that neither proto-states nor states should be constructed as conjunctions of conditionals with elements of A in the "if" clause and elements of Q in the "then" clause. I am doubtful of the availability of acceptable modes of conceptual innovation which can be deployed to obtain the desired representations. Just as strict consequentialism is stronger than weak consequentialism, proto-state-functional strict consequentialism is more restrictive than strict consequentialism which, in turn, is weaker than state-functional strict consequentialism.

15 Causal decision theorists differ from strict Bayesians in how they treat decision problems representable in proto-state-functional strict consequentialist form. They insist that when the proto-state-descriptions are causally independent of the option chosen (in some sense or other), they should be treated as strict Bayesians would treat them if they were state-descriptions. That is, the value of an option is to be assessed by using expected utility calculated by assigning unconditional probabilities to the proto-states. Causal decision theorists, in effect, apply approaches like Savage's (who considers only decision problems in state-functional strict consequentialist form) to problems not countenanced by such approaches.

16 The elements of Y may belong to the set Q, they may be descriptions of lotteries on finitely many consequence-descriptions in Q, or they may be functions from proto-state-descriptions to consequence-descriptions in Q (or lottery-descriptions on Q) relative to the corpus at the last choice node and the information as to which option is chosen at that node. Whether we assume proto-state-functional or state-functional consequentialism, this must be possible.

17 Perhaps it will be objected that the potential addict is not certain that he will choose to continue at the second decision node. He may judge this highly probable but not certain. If he does that, he is in the position of predicting how he will choose at the second stage. As we pointed out, at the first stage

the agent may assign credal probabilities to hypotheses as to his future choices at later stages conditional on his initial choice. If the agent reaches the second stage and knows it, then these hypotheses become option-descriptions. Because the agent at the second stage regards himself as having a choice at that stage, he does not convert his erstwhile conditional probabilities as to how he will choose into unconditional probabilities as good Bayesians will do. For reasons that we have already explained, he should refrain from probability judgment concerning these propositions.

Consider now the hypothesis that the potential addict will reach the second-stage choice node – that is, will face the choice between stopping and continuing. That hypothesis is a strict consequence-description from the initial point of view. Its value (as assessed relative to the situation at the initial node) is determined by the values assigned to the hypotheses that the potential addict will stop or continue and the probabilities of these hypotheses conditional on his having taken the drug at the initial state. Thus the potential addict might assign a high probability at the initial stage to his continuing with the drug at the second stage, thereby sinking into abject addiction with permanent damage. His second-stage opportunity for choice is an uncertain prospect with an expected utility. Even if we do not assume that uncertain prospects are evaluated with respect to expected utility but with respect to some other sort of index, if the propositions at the nodes immediately following the choice node representing the current opportunity for choice are strict consequence-descriptions, relative to the options available at the initial node, so the description of the opportunity for choice – that is, the choice node.

Hence, for a strict consequentialist, the uncertain prospect is itself a strict consequence-description. But it is not the terminal set Y. However, unlike the elements of *Y* accessible from the second-stage choice node, it is accessible to the potential addict at the initial node. From the initial point of view, the two strict consequence-descriptions directly under the potential addict's control are the uncertain prospect describable by the opportunity for choice at the second node and the terminal consequence of complete abstinence. Strict consequentialists would recommend that the potential addict choose the admissible element from this pair without pretending to have available directly under his control all elements of *y*.

18 This claim implies nothing more about the addict's identity over time than that, at the initial choice node, the opportunities for further choice that he expects to realize through the decision he makes are uncertain prospects.

19 An important exception to this consensus among economists is Yaari (1987).

20 Weak consequentialism ought, however, to be noncontroversial, and within the framework of weak consequentialism it remains possible to be a strict Bayesian (or, as I would prefer, to be a "quasi-Bayesian" who abandons the requirements of ordering as well as the requirements of temporal conditionalization).

3

The Structure of Good: Decision Theory and Ethics

John Broome

1 TELEOLOGICAL ETHICS AND AGENT NEUTRALITY

John Rawls defined an ethical theory as teleological if "the good is defined independently from the right, and then the right is defined as that which maximizes the good" (Rawls, 1971, p. 24). This is a fine definition, but it needs some explaining. It relies on a contrast between the right and the good that is not perfectly transparent. In the first three sections of this paper I shall try to elucidate the definition. What, exactly, distinguishes teleological from nonteleological ethics?

The terms "consequential" and "nonconsequential" are nowadays commoner than "teleological" and "nonteleological." I prefer the older terms for reasons that will appear.[1] But it is the same distinction I am making.

Rawls is thinking of goodness as a property of states of affairs and rightness as a property of acts. So one might interpret his definition like this: teleological ethics first evaluates states of affairs, and then determines the value of an act by the goodness of the state of affairs it leads to (of its consequences, that is). A teleological value is a good or bad feature of a state of affairs. Nonteleological ethics, on the other hand, assigns intrinsic value to some acts, independently of their consequences. One nonteleological view, for instance, is that breaking a promise is wrong in itself, quite apart from its consequences.

The trouble with this interpretation is that it is not clear where an act leaves off and its consequences begin. If you break a promise, one consequence will be that you have broken a promise, and the wrongness of promise-breaking could be taken as a bad feature of this consequence. It could be taken as a teleological value, that is. So an evaluation of the consequences of promise-breaking could take account of the wrongness of promise-breaking itself. In this way, the intrinsic values of acts could be absorbed into teleology, leaving no room for a nonteleological ethics.

In any case, even if the intrinsic value of acts could be clearly separated from the value of their consequences, it would not give us the distinction we want. Suppose you have made a promise to visit St Andrews. Then the act of visiting St Andrews is both to make a pleasant trip and to keep a promise. The pleasantness, just as much as the fact that it is keeping a promise, is a feature of the act. Yet, on any account, the pleasantness is a teleological rather than a nonteleological value.

This, then, is not the right way to distinguish teleological and nonteleological. This fact is widely recognized. In all the recent debate between teleology and other ethical views, nothing has been made to depend on separating the value of an act from the value of its consequences. The fact that an act has been done is generally counted amongst the consequences of that act, and the intrinsic value of an act is counted as a teleological consideration in its favor (e.g. Williams, 1973, p. 24; Scheffler, 1982, pp. 1–2, n. 2). I shall follow this practice. I shall not try to distinguish between the value of an act and the value of its consequences. I shall apply the notion of goodness to acts as well as to their consequences. I shall take both the goodness of an act and the goodness of its consequences to include any intrinsic value the act may have, as well as any good that may result from it. (This is one reason I use the term "teleological" instead of "consequential": whatever the distinguishing feature of teleological ethics may be, it is not that it values only consequences.)

But if "teleological" is given such a wide interpretation, how does that leave any room for nonteleological ethics? It may seem to make teleology true by definition. Certainly, many considerations that have traditionally been classed as nonteleological can be brought under the umbrella of teleology taken this way, provided one recognizes the existence of goods and bads other than the most conventional utilitarian ones. If, for instance, unfair treatment is taken as a bad thing in itself, whether or not the victim is made unhappy by it, then teleology can recognize the value of fairness (see Scanlon, 1978).

Nevertheless, there are views that are incompatible with even this widely conceived teleology. A famous example is this (see Williams, 1973, p. 26). Suppose that by breaking a promise I can bring it about that in the future five promises are kept that otherwise would have been broken. According to some ethical views, I ought to keep my promise nevertheless, unless the circumstances are exceptional. This opinion, however, seems inconsistent with teleological ethics. If breaking promises is bad, then the breaking of five promises must be worse than the breaking of one. Other things being equal, then, keeping my promise will have worse consequences than breaking it, even taking account of the intrinsic badness of promise-breaking. So, it seems, teleology must be in favor of breaking it.

How might one justify the view that I ought to keep my promise even at the expense of five broken promises? Here is one way. In this moral dilemma, the argument goes, it is wrong for me to take up a neutral impersonal standpoint, from which everybody's promise-keeping counts the same. My own special position makes a difference to what I ought to do. Keeping *my* promise has a special value for *me*. It may count for me more than the keeping of five other people's promises. My valuations should be "agent relative," as it is generally put. And why should that be? One possible answer (see Williams, 1973, pp. 30–1) is that I have a greater responsibility for my own acts than I do for the acts of others, even if they are brought about by me. In this case, the five people who break their promises bear the responsibility for this wrongdoing more than I do, even though it is brought about by my promise-keeping.

A lesson commonly drawn from this example, and others like it, is that nonteleological ethics must be agent relative. If it is right for me sometimes to do something that will not have the best possible consequences, that must be because of my particular position as an agent. Conversely, agent neutrality is often included within the *definition* of consequentialism.[2] (This is my second reason for using the term "teleology" instead: to free myself from this definition.) Thus teleological ethics has come to be distinguished by agent neutrality, and nonteleological ethics by agent relativity. Most of the recent discussion of teleology has really been a discussion of agent neutrality.[3]

I think, though, that it is a mistake to identify teleological ethics with agent neutrality and nonteleological ethics with agent relativity. The distinction between agent neutrality and agent relativity marks an important issue in ethics. But there is a different issue that is best marked by the distinction between teleological and nonteleological ethics. Conflating the two distinctions diverts attention from the second issue. The two issues cut across each other; as I am going to characterize teleology, there are nonteleological ethical theories that are agent neutral, and also teleological theories that are agent relative.

2 TELEOLOGICAL ETHICS AND GOOD

When there is a decision to be made, there may often be ethical considerations on both sides. Against breaking my promise in the example is that this would be a wrong act. In favor is that it will prevent five wrongs of promise-breaking. How do conflicting considerations come together to determine which act is right? I believe that teleological theories should be distinguished from nonteleological theories by the answer they give to this question.

The answer of teleology is that each consideration contributes to the goodness or badness of the alternative acts. All the considerations together determine how good or bad the acts are. Then the act that turns out to be the best is the one that ought to be done.[4] Goodness is determined first, and rightness follows. The nonteleological answer, on the other hand, is that ethical considerations do not always work in this particular way. They may determine what ought to be done, not by first determining goodness, but in some other way.

Teleology, then, is distinguished by a particular view about the way that ethical considerations work. The intrinsic wrongness of breaking a promise, for instance, is taken as a bad feature of the act of promise-breaking, which goes together with other good and bad features to determine the overall goodness of the act. The metaphor of weighing often fits teleological deliberation. Each consideration is a good or bad feature of the act in question. The overall goodness is determined by an aggregation of the goodness and badness of these features. This is analogous to weighing. Not all teleological deliberation need be much like weighing, though. It is consistent with teleology to think that some considerations dominate others lexically. You might think, for instance, that any unjust act is worse than any just act, whatever other features the acts possess. There is nothing in literal weighing analogous to this. Teleology can also accommodate complicated interactions amongst considerations, which would also strain the metaphor of weighing. Weighing is typical but not definitive of teleology.

I mentioned above one opinion about the promising example: I ought to keep my promise because my promise-breaking counts more for me than other people's. This is an agent-relative opinion. It may also be teleological, as I am distinguishing teleology. It weighs the badness of my promise-breaking against the badness of other people's, to determine the overall badness of the alternative acts. Because my promise-breaking weighs more for me than other people's does, breaking my promise comes out worse overall for me. Therefore I ought not to do it. This has the form of a teleological argument, but only if we take goodness and badness to be themselves agent relative. Provided that an agent-relative notion of good is acceptable, this particular agent-relative opinion is teleological. Not many authors have been willing to accept an agent-relative notion of good; Amartya Sen is an exception (Sen, 1982b). However, I shall explain in section 3 that there is a good reason to do so.

Now, here is an example of a nonteleological opinion. It is also in favor of my keeping my promise in the example, but for a different reason. It also takes breaking a promise to be intrinsically wrong. But it does not treat this intrinsic wrongness as a consideration to be weighed against others in determining the overall goodness of the alternative acts. Instead, the wrongness simply determines that I ought not to break my promise. It is what Robert Nozick (1974) calls a "side-constraint." The argument goes directly to what I ought to do, without first estimating the goodness of the alternatives.

Side-constraint theory is different from any recognized sort of teleology. For instance, the claim that promise-keeping is a side-constraint is not the same as the teleological claim that promise-keeping is a value that dominates others lexically. The latter claim would imply that I should break my promise in the example, since that would lead to five promise-keepings instead of one. Nor is it the same as the agent-relative teleological claim that my promise-keeping is a value that, for me, dominates others lexically. To see this, imagine that the five other promises are actually mine: by breaking a promise now I can bring it about that I shall, in the future, keep five promises that otherwise I would have broken. The agent-relative teleological claim would imply that I should break my promise now, since that would lead to five of my promise-keepings instead of one. Yet a true side-constraint theory about promises would say that I ought to keep my present promise.

One could imagine an agent-moment-relative teleological theory, according to which my present promise-keeping is a value that, for me now, lexically dominates all other values including my promise-keeping at other times. (I do not know how such a theory could be defended.) But side-constraint theory is not the same as agent-moment-relative lexical teleological theory either. In the case of promising, it might well lead to much the same conclusions in practice. But let us change the example. Consider the view that, whenever a miner is in mortal danger trapped in a mine, all resources should be devoted to rescuing him. This will reduce the resources available for safety measures in mines, and so lead to the deaths of more miners in the future. Nevertheless, it is what ought to be done. This is a side-constraint view. But it is agent neutral. It says that all of us, equally, should contribute to saving the miner as far as we can.

Side-constraint theory, then, is not intrinsically agent relative or agent moment relative. It might, perhaps, be called moment relative. At present we have a reason , dominating all others, to rescue the miner who is now trapped. When the next miner is trapped, we shall then have a reason to rescue him. That reason will then be just as dominating as the present reason is now. But at present it does not count at all; it gives us no reason to save resources for the future rescue. The reason, then, applies at one time but not at another. This might justify calling it a moment-relative reason. It even seems possible to me that the ethics of side-constraints might be identified with some sort of moment-relative teleology. Perhaps it might be brought within the fold of teleology that way. But for the moment it must be recognized as a nonteleological theory.

Here, then, is an agent-neutral nonteleological theory. I shall be mentioning others in section 3.

I propose, in summary, this simple definition of "teleological": a teleological theory is one that says, when there is a choice between alternative acts, that the right one to choose is the best. I take this definition to be the same as Rawls's.

3 THE STRUCTURE OF GOOD

What, I believe, drives other authors to more complicated definitions involving agent neutrality is the thought that this simple definition can exclude nothing. How could any ethical theory deny that, when faced with a choice between acts, you should choose the best? I have already offered the side-constraints theory as an example of a nonteleological theory, on the grounds that it does not work by assessing the goodness of the alternative acts. But whatever a theory says about the working of ethical considerations, once it has decided which act ought to be done, one might think that there is nothing to stop it just *calling* this act the best. So any theory could be made teleological in arrears. But actually, this cannot generally be done, because teleology is constrained by the structure of good.

A teleological theory, according to my definition, implies that between acts there is a betterness relation

$$\text{— is at least as good as —} \qquad (3.1)$$

(where the blanks are to be filled in with acts), and that this relation determines what is the right thing to do. When I speak of the structure of good, I mean more exactly the structure of the betterness relation.

I can immediately say one thing about the structure of this relation. It is an *ordering*. That is, it is transitive and reflexive.[5] If A is at least as good as B, and B at least as good as C, then A is at least as good as C. And, A is at least as good as A (for any act A). This is an instance of the general law of logic that for any property ϕ the comparative relation

$$— \text{ is at least as } \phi \text{ as } —$$

is transitive and reflexive. That is, things are ordered by their ϕness.[6] A teleological theory, then, claims that acts are ordered by their goodness and that one ought to choose an act that is as high up on this ordering as possible.

My definition identifies a teleological theory by its *structure*. It has a maximizing structure: a teleological theory is one that says that you should do the act that is ranked highest by an ordering relation. To be sure, a teleological theory is one that aims to maximize specifically *good* rather than something else, and this seems to be a matter of content as well as structure. But the reference to good in the definition is actually redundant. If an *ethical* theory aims to maximize anything, then what it aims to maximize must be what the theory takes to be good. Amongst ethical theories, the teleological ones can be picked out by their structure alone.

Look back to one of the views that I mentioned about the promising example: the view that my promise-keeping outweighs, for me, the promise-keeping of others. Although this is agent relative, I said that it could be considered teleological if an agent-relative notion of good was permitted. Now we have a reason for permitting it. Suppose that this theory has a structure consistent enough to imply the existence of an ordering relation amongst acts, in such a way that I ought to do the act that is ranked highest by this relation whenever I am faced with a choice. Then the theory defines something that I ought to maximize. This thing must be what the theory takes as good, even though it is agent relative.

The fact that the betterness relation is an ordering is a major constraint on teleological ethics. It rules out the side-constraints theory, and many other theories too.

It rules out "naive majoritarianism," for instance. A naive majoritarian believes that, when there is a choice between two alternative acts, the one that ought to be done is the one that the majority of people prefer. It is well known that there may be three acts A, B, and C such that the majority of people prefer A to B, and the majority prefer B to C, and the majority prefer C to A. About these three acts, our majoritarian will believe that, when there is a choice between A and B, A ought to be done, and when there is a choice between B and C, B ought to be done, and when there is a choice between C and A, C ought to be done. But it cannot be the case that A is better than B, B better than C, and C better than

A. Therefore our majoritarian's view is nonteleological. There is, though, nothing agent relative about it.

The majoritarian might be tempted to think, because the majority prefer A to B, that A is better than B, and similarly that B is better than C, and that C is better than A. But she must avoid logical inconsistency, so this is a temptation she must overcome. It is not really a very strong one. But some examples given by Derek Parfit (1984, part IV), involving changes in the world's population, create a much more powerful temptation of the same sort. Larry Temkin (1987) has used Parfit's examples to argue powerfully that betterness is an intransitive relation. But this is a conclusion that cannot logically be drawn. If there are intransitivities, they cannot be in the betterness relation. The situation must be described in other terms, however tempting it may be to use the terms of betterness. What these examples show, I think, is the hold that teleology has on us. We are drawn to organize our moral thinking around the concept of good. But using that concept imposes a structure – a transitive one – on our thinking. If our thinking does not fit the structure, we shall have to give up teleology. We must not slip into logical inconsistency.

The fact that the betterness relation is an ordering is a considerable constraint on teleology, and there is much more to the structure of good than just that. I call any ethical theory teleological if it has a maximizing structure. Any maximizing ethical theory implies a notion of good in what it aims to maximize, and it implies a betterness relation that is an ordering. But a teleological theory cannot be *correct* unless its notion of good conforms to all the other structural requirements on good. The purpose of this paper is to delve further into these requirements. It describes some of the questions that arise and some of the methods that can be used to answer them. It does not give many answers, but some more can be found in my book *Weighing Goods* (Broome, 1991c).

It is not just teleological ethics that is concerned with the structure of good, but any ethical theory that gives some role to teleological considerations – to good, that is. And this includes almost every theory.

I must also mention satisficing theories (e.g. Slote, 1989). Satisficing theories hold that, when there is a choice between alternative acts, what it is right to do is determined by the goodness of the alternatives. But they deny that it is necessarily only the best of the alternatives that is right; any action may be right if it is "good enough." These theories can fairly be called teleological, because they suppose that the way ethical considerations work is by determining the goodness of the alternatives. But they are not maximizing. In identifying teleological theories with maximizing theories, I have therefore been oversimplifying. I hope I may be forgiven for continuing to do so. To speak always of "maximizing or satisficing" rather than "maximizing" would complicate the wording of this paper without affecting the substance. Satisficing and maximizing theories have exactly the same view of goodness and its structure; they only hold different views about the derivation of rightness from goodness.

4 LOCATIONS OF GOOD

I am interested in one particular group of questions about the structure of good. They all have the same general form: good comes at many "locations" as I call them; how does the good occurring at all the different locations go together to make up overall good?

Here is an example of what I mean. Suppose we have to compare alternative economic policies that will lead to different distributions of welfare. One will make people's welfare higher on average, but leave it very unequally distributed. Another will promote equality, but at the cost of a lower average level. Which is better? Here we have a good – welfare – coming to many different *people*. A person is a location for good. The good of all the people taken together determines the overall goodness of the distribution. The question is: how, precisely? The goodness of the distribution depends on the good of the people, but in what way? The value of equality is one of the central issues here. One theory is that good is simply the total of people's good; the better of two distributions is the one that has the greater total. Another theory is that a smaller total may sometimes be better, if it is more equally distributed.

A second example is this. The different times in a person's life are good to a greater or lesser degree. A life may have ups and downs, or it may have an even tenor. Which is better? Here the locations of good are *times*. The question is: how does the good that comes to a person at different times go together to make up her overall good? In this case the value of temporal evenness is at issue.

Good, in fact, is strung out on a two-dimensional grid of locations; alternative acts will distribute good differently across the grid. One of the dimensions is people and the other time. Good occurring at all the locations goes together to make up general good. One can think of this as a two-stage aggregation. First, the good of each person at all the different times goes together to make up that person's good. Then all the different people's good goes together to make up general good. The structure of good has two layers. In the top layer general good is constructed from people's good. In the lower layer each person's good has a structure built out of the person's good at times. So each person's betterness relation

$$\text{— is at least as good for the person as —} \qquad (3.2)$$

is a component of the general betterness relation (3.1). In investigating the structure of the latter, therefore, we shall also need to investigate the structure of the individual relations.

I do not mean to insist that *all* good necessarily has a place on the grid. The following two principles claim it does.

> *The Principle of Personal Good.* If two alternatives are equally good for everyone, they are equally good. And if one alternative is better than another for someone, and at least as good for everyone, then it is better.
>
> *The Principle of Temporal Good.* If two alternatives are equally good for a person at all times, they are equally good for her. And if one alternative is better for a person at one time and at least as good for her at all times, then it is better for her.

Briefly, all good belongs to someone, and all good is dated. The truth of these principles needs to be investigated; that is part of my question about structure.

5 TELEOLOGICAL ETHICS AND UNCERTAINTY

Decision theory is an essential instrument for investigating the aggregation of good across locations. This may seem surprising. The special domain of decision theory is uncertainty, which I have not yet mentioned. Therefore in this section and the next I shall turn to the apparently unrelated question of how teleology should accommodate uncertainty. The connection with questions about the location of good will appear in section 7.

I said in section 1 that nothing useful was achieved by separating the value of an act from the value of its consequences. But at that point I was ignoring the fact that the consequences of an act will normally be uncertain. Now I want to ask what difference this uncertainty makes.

Uncertainty is generally thought to complicate the formulation of teleological ethics. Suppose that a choice has to be made amongst alternative acts whose consequences are uncertain. Which ought to be done? To answer, teleological ethics is generally thought to need a two-stage theory. It needs, first, to determine the goodness of each act's possible consequences. And, second, on this basis, it needs to provide a formula for determining which act ought to be done. Decision theory is thought to help at the second stage (see for example Jackson, forthcoming). The actual formula that is most often offered is this: the act that ought to be done is the one that leads to the greatest expectation of good; one ought to maximize expected good.[7] Derek Parfit says: "What we ought . . . to do is the act whose outcome has the greatest *expected* goodness" (Parfit, 1984, p. 25).

This formula, on the face of it at least, is most implausible. It is open to two serious objections. The first is that it presumes too much arithmetical precision in the notion of good. To form an expectation, good must be an arithmetic quantity.[8] I have said already that the betterness relation must be an ordering, but to operate on good arithmetically requires it to have much more structure than simply being an ordering. One might reasonably doubt that it has as much. But suppose for a moment that good *is* an arithmetic quantity, and consider an example. Suppose that a choice has to be made between an act that will lead, for sure, to 100 units of good, and one that will lead, with equal probability, to either no units or 201 units. The latter has the greater expectation of good. But one might reasonably doubt that it is the right one to choose. It is a risky choice, and playing safe might well be better. Maximizing expected good implies *risk neutrality* about good: only the expectation of good matters, and riskiness counts for nothing. But there seems to be no reason why teleological ethics should insist on risk neutrality. Indeed, on the face of it, it is quite implausible that it should. It seems perfectly reasonable for teleology to give value to safety. That is the second objection.

It is commonly thought that the formula of maximizing expected good is directly implied by conventional decision theory. But this is actually not so. The common opinion arises from a misunderstanding of the theory (which is explained briefly in section 6 below and in more detail in Broome, 1987, 1991a). It is definitely a mistake to commit teleology unnecessarily to risk neutrality about good. So this particular formula should definitely be dropped.

But then, what *should* we say that teleology requires in the face of uncertainty? We should not say it requires the maximizing of expected good. But within the two-stage scheme, it is hard to find the right alternative formula.

I think we should say, simply, that teleology requires one to do the best act. This is the formula I have been using all along, and uncertainty need make no difference to it. I do not think of teleology as a two-stage theory with separate accounts of the goodness of consequences and the rightness of acts. It has just an account of goodness, which includes the goodness of acts.

I suggest, then, that we should apply the notion of goodness to acts, even when the consequences of the acts are uncertain. (We should also apply to acts the notions of goodness for a person and goodness at a time.) This is only a way of speaking, but a useful one. Its major advantage is that it permits a simple and unified account of teleology: teleology is the view that one ought to do the best act. The right response to uncertainty becomes a matter of the internal structure of good: how is the goodness of an act related to the goodness of its possible consequences? This makes it parallel to other questions about the structure of good: how is general good related to the good of individuals? How is overall good related to good at times? All these questions turn out to be, not only analogous, but also logically connected, as I shall be explaining. Applying the notion of goodness to acts is the best way of bringing out the analogies and connections.

The most immediate advantage of my suggestion is that it easily frees teleology from a commitment to risk neutrality about good,[9] whereas it is hard to find a two-stage formula that avoids this commitment. The goodness of an act need not be the expected goodness of its consequences. It may depend on the act's riskiness as well. A risky act may be worse than a safe one that has the same expectation of good. The substantive question, though, still remains open: how, exactly, *is* the goodness of an act related to the goodness of its possible consequences? On investigation, it might yet turn out to be just their expected goodness. Risk neutrality might turn out to be right. I shall return to this question in section 7.

There are benefits to be had, then, from applying the notion of goodness to acts with uncertain consequences. There is a possible objection, however. Doing so makes goodness relative to probabilities: different judgments of probability will lead to different judgments about the goodness of an act. And this may seem wrong. Suppose that, at the moment, it seems likely that some act will lead to a good result. According to me this is a good act. But suppose it turns out that the result is actually bad. Then it seems that the act was not good after all. When I said it was good, I seem not to have been telling the truth. It seems I ought never to assert on the basis of probabilities that an act is actually good, because probabilities are not adequate grounds for judging goodness. Only the actual result can determine goodness.

This argument suggests that, of acts with uncertain results, we ought not to say that they are good or bad, but only that they are right or wrong (or that they ought or ought not to be done). Probabilities are adequate grounds for *these* judgments. If I do an act that seems likely to have good results, then I act rightly. Even if its results turn out bad, it will still be true that my act was right. After all, I could only act on the information that I had at the time, and so I did nothing wrong. Judgments of rightness are therefore not retrospectively falsifiable in the way that judgments of goodness are.

A part of this objection is a matter of the use of words, and that does not bother me. Look more closely at the use of "right." If I do an act that is likely to have good results, I shall say my act is right. But if the results turn out bad, I may very well say the act was not right after all: as it turns out, it was the wrong thing to do. But I shall certainly not say I was telling a falsehood in the first place. I shall say that in one sense my act was right, and in another sense wrong. Perhaps I shall say it was subjectively right and objectively wrong.[10] In one way or another I shall make sure that my original judgment is not made false by the later one. And whatever I say about rightness, I can say the same about goodness. I can say there are different senses of goodness, perhaps subjective and objective senses. Whenever an act that I judged to be good on the basis of probabilities turns out to be bad, I can make sure it does not follow that my original judgment was false. If, therefore, the notion of rightness can apply to acts, so can the notion of goodness.

Besides, virtually *all* our judgments of goodness are relative to probabilities. If someone is killed in an accident, that is bad. But it may turn out to have been a good thing because nuclear war may come the next week. So if judgments of goodness are illegitimate whenever they are relative to probabilities, virtually all judgments of goodness are illegitimate. And presumably they are not.

However, there is also a more substantive side to the objection. It points out that what ultimately *matters* is what actually happens. When the account of how well the world went is finally made up, it will be an account of the good that actually happens. Consequently, judgments of good based on what actually happens do at least supersede judgments based on probabilities, even if I am right to claim that they do not falsify them. The probability-relative goodness of an act is, at best, a sort of interim goodness, which must be corrected in the final account.

Consider this example. A government is faced with a choice between two alternative acts. One will be equally good for everyone; as a result of the act, everyone will end up better off by the same amount. The other gives everyone an equal *chance* of ending up better off, but it also gives everyone an equal chance of ending up worse off. Using "good" in the probability-relative way I am proposing, I would say that the second act is equally good for everyone. I would say, then, that the first and the second acts both distribute good equally. But this statement conceals a vital difference between them. The second act will lead to some people's ending up well off, and others' ending up badly off. So in the sense that reflects what actually happens – in the final audit – this second act is not equally good for everybody. The first, on the other hand, is. And, the objection goes, this is the sense that ultimately matters. Suppose we value equality in the distribution of good between people. Then on this value the first act scores high, and the second scores low. In the sense that matters, the second act simply is not equally good for everyone. This is not to deny that it may score high on other values: for instance, we may value equality in the distribution of *chances* of good, and on that it scores high. But this is a different (and more dubious) value. If equality in the distribution of good is really valuable, then the first act is definitely better than the second. According to my usage, though, the second act *does* distribute good equally. Therefore this usage is deceptive. Furthermore, there is a genuine risk of error here. Many economists favor what is known as the *ex ante* approach to evaluating acts of governments.[11] This means that they assess the goodness of the acts in my probability-relative manner, and then suppose that this assessment is all that there is to say about the acts' goodness. Therefore, of the second act in the example, they would say it distributes good equally, and suppose this is all there is to say about the way that it distributes good. They would conclude that it distributes good just as equally as the first act, and see no reason to prefer the first on grounds of equality. This is clearly an error.

I think there is a lot in this objection. But I think it points out a danger of error, rather than an actual error, in a probability-relative notion of good. To avoid error, we need to bear in mind that this is indeed an interim sort of good, and it is not all that there is to be said about the goodness of acts. The two acts in the example are not, indeed, equally equal in their distribution of good. For the benefits of the practice I recommend, it is worth the trouble of taking care not to step over the line into error.

6 DECISION THEORY AND THE STRUCTURE OF GOOD

Decision theory is the theory of right decision-making in the face of uncertainty. I see it, therefore, as a theory of good.

It is standardly interpreted, though, as a theory of *preferences*. Take a person and a range of things that she has preferences over. What these things are supposed to be varies from one version of decision theory to another. But it will do no harm to assume that they include both acts and the consequences of acts; I shall call them vaguely "prospects." Amongst prospects, then, there is a "preference relation"

the person prefers — to — or is indifferent between them

(3.3)

where each blank is to be filled in with one of the prospects. Decision theory describes the structure of this relation. It specifies a number of axioms to which, it claims, the preference relation will conform.

Different versions of decision theory have different axioms. I spoke earlier of "conventional" decision theory. What I meant was "expected utility theory," which is one variety of decision theory. There are some unconventional decision theories too (e.g. Machina, 1982a), but I shall concentrate on this one. Expected utility theory includes amongst its axioms transitivity and reflexivity, which imply that the preference relation is an ordering. There are many other axioms too (an important one is mentioned in section 7). The theory shows that, if a person's preferences conform to the axioms, they can be "represented" by "utilities." What this means is that each of the prospects can be assigned a number – its utility – in such a way that, of any pair of alternatives, the one that is preferred has a higher utility. Furthermore, these utilities are "expectational," by which I mean that the utility of an act is the expectation of the utilities of its possible consequences. Briefly, the utility of an act is its expected utility. Acts with higher expected utilities are preferred; the person is a maximizer of expected utility.

The evidence is that in practice people's preferences conform rather poorly to the axioms of expected utility theory (see Tversky and Kahneman, 1986). Therefore expected utility theory is now generally taken as a theory of rational preferences only: it describes the structure of the preferences that a person would have if she were rational. There are good arguments to show that rational preferences will indeed conform to expected utility theory.[12]

That is the standard interpretation of decision theory. But the theory can also be interpreted differently as a theory of the structure of good. First, it can be interpreted as a theory of the structure of an *individual's* good: the axioms, which are standardly applied to a preference relation (3.3), can be applied instead to an individual's betterness relation (3.2). Second, it can be interpreted as a theory of the structure of *general* good: the axioms can be applied to the general betterness relation (3.1). There is good reason to think that the individual and general betterness relations will indeed conform to the axioms of expected utility theory. The full argument for this point is too long to give here; I have set it out elsewhere

(Broome, 1991b). But I hope it will seem plausible anyway.

I can give a brief, rather peculiar, argument here. (I shall put it in a form that applies to an individual's betterness relation, but it is obvious how to modify it for the general betterness relation too.) Take any person. It would presumably be possible for her to possess a personal deity who is concerned for nothing except her good, but for her still to have the same betterness relation as she actually has, at least over mundane matters not directly connected with the existence of the deity. The preference relation of this deity would coincide with the person's betterness relation, and this preference relation would presumably be rational. Therefore, since a rational preference relation conforms to the axioms of decision theory, the person's betterness relation must also conform.

Whatever the merits of this argument, it does serve to illustrate one point. The fact that the betterness relation satisfies the axioms is a consequence of the fact that a rational preference relation satisfies them. The structure of good follows the structure of rationality, one might say. This is to be expected on my view of good. Clearly, first, good and rationality are closely connected: to say that one alternative is better than another is to make a statement about reasons. It is to say that there are stronger reasons of a particular sort for achieving the first alternative than the second. The "sort" of reasons I mean are reasons that work in the particular way described in section 2: teleological reasons as I described them there. Second, in the particular context of uncertainty, it is inevitable that goodness will follow rationality rather than the other way round. The goodness of an act with uncertain consequences is determined by the goodness of its possible consequences. Of two acts, what determines which is better? The possible good consequences of one act are teleological reasons in favor of that act; the possible bad consequences are teleological reasons against it. The possible good consequences of the other act are teleological reasons in favor of *it*, and so on. Putting all these reasons together determines which act it would be rational to do, if one were concerned with teleological reasons only. And that act, being the one favored by teleological reasons, is the better one. So the goodness of an act is determined by considerations of rationality: considerations of what it would be rational to do.

In summary, I conclude that expected utility theory describes the structure of good.

In follows that, just as a preference relation can be represented by expectational utilities, so can the betterness relation. That is, utilities can be assigned to each of the prospects in such a way that better prospects have higher utilities and, furthermore, the utility of an act is the expectation of the utilities of its possible consequences. The fact that utilities represent betterness in this way has led many people to assume that a prospect's utility is nothing more nor less than its goodness: the utility of a prospect measures how good it is. Now, we know by the definition of utility that, of any group of alternative acts, the best is the one with the highest utility, and also that its utility is the expectation of the utility of its consequences. So if utility were goodness, the best act would necessarily be the one whose outcome has the greatest expectation of good. This would give us Parfit's formula for teleology quoted in section 5. But all this is a mistake. It is certainly true that better prospects have higher utilities. Utilities represent the *order* of good. But nothing says they represent *amounts* of good.[13]

7 THREE DIMENSIONS FOR GOOD

Expected utility theory, then, does not insist that the goodness of an act is necessarily the expected goodness of its consequences. But then the question remains: how, exactly, *is* the goodness of an act related to the goodness of its consequences? This is a question about the value of risk. If risk is neither good nor bad, but neutral, then the goodness of an act is the expected goodness of its consequences. But if risk is either good or bad, this will not be the right formula. So what is right?

I want to cast this question in a particular form. I shall adopt the framework of Leonard Savage's decision theory (Savage, 1972). Savage models uncertainty as follows. He supposes that there are a number of "states of nature." Any one of them may occur, but the uncertainty is that we do not know which. An act determines, for each state of nature, a consequence; one might say that it locates a consequence in each state. For instance, the act of betting on Blue Mink locates the consequence of being $50 richer in the state where Blue Mink wins, and the consequence of being $5 poorer in the state where Blue Mink loses. On the other hand, the act of refraining from betting locates the consequence of being no richer or poorer in both states.

Each consequence is good to some degree. So an act locates some good in each state of nature. Our question is now: how does good located in the different states of nature go together to make up the overall goodness of the act?

It turns out, then, that this question about the value of risk has the general form that I introduced in section 4: how does good distributed across various locations go together to make up overall good? In section 4, I spoke of a two-dimensional grid of locations. We now have a three-dimensional grid. An act distributes good to each person, at each time, in each state of nature. Our general question is: how is good distributed across this grid aggregated to make up general good?

At the moment, we are dealing with the dimension of uncertainty: how is good aggregated across different states of nature? This is the central domain of decision theory. It is the place where decision theory can most directly help in answering our question. But the point of working with the three-dimensional grid is that there are connections between the dimensions that make it useful, indeed essential, to treat them together. The first thing to notice is some symmetries between the dimensions. I shall mention two.

We were investigating the value of risk. Let us continue formulating the question in our new terms. Take two acts whose consequences have the same expectation of good. But suppose that one of them is safer and the other more risky. Are they equally good, or is the safer one perhaps better? The two acts produce the same average level of good across states of nature; this is what it means for them to produce the same expectation of good. The difference between them is that the safer act distributes good more evenly across states of nature, so that whichever state occurs the result will be pretty much the same, and the more risky prospect distributes good less evenly. So our question is: for a given average level of good, is there a benefit in having it more evenly distributed across the dimension of states of nature? Between states of nature, is equality valuable? This way of putting it reveals a symmetry between this question about risk neutrality and the questions that I asked in section 4 about other dimensions. For a given average, I asked, is it better to have good equally distributed across people: is equality valuable between people? And for a given average, is it better to have good evenly distributed across times: is equality valuable between times?

A second symmetry is over an issue technically known as *separability*. One fundamental axiom of expected utility theory is the sure-thing principle or Strong Independence Axiom (Samuelson, 1952b; Savage, 1972, pp. 21–4). This is an axiom of separability. It says, roughly, that what happens in one state of nature can be evaluated independently of what happens in any other: when assessing the goodness of a act, it is only necessary to consider the consequences in each state one by one; there are no interactions between the states that need to be taken into account. There has been a great deal of controversy over the truth of this axiom. In the other dimensions also, there are difficult issues of separability. When assessing a distribution across people, can the good of one person be evaluated independently of what happens to anybody else? In judging the goodness of a life, can good at one time be evaluated independently of what happens at other times? It turns out that the Principle of Personal Good stated in section 4, when applied to uncertain acts, amounts to the claim that good is separable between people, and the Principle of Temporal Good amounts to a claim that it is separable across time. So these principles acquire a new significance in the context of uncertainty.

There is no reason to think that, just because there are analogous questions in different dimensions, the answers are likely to be the same. My own view about separability, for instance, is that, provided the formal setting-up is done appropriately, good is separable across states of nature and across people, but not across times. The point of mentioning the symmetries is not to show up mere similarities between the dimensions. The point is that there are mathematical theorems that build on the symmetries to make strict connections between the dimensions.[14]

The central theorem, described very roughly, is this. Take any pair of dimensions. Suppose good is separable in both. Then the way good is aggregated in one has to be in a certain respect the same as the way it is aggregated in the other. I shall not try to specify the "respect" exactly, but I can describe one implication. If equality of good has value in one dimension, then it has it in the other also. Take, for instance, the two dimensions of people and states of nature. Suppose that good is separable in both. Then if it is good to avoid risk to good (equality of good is valuable across states of nature), it is also good to avoid inequality of good between people. Conversely, if there is no value in avoiding risk to good, then there is no value in equality of good between people either.

Since I believe the premise that good is separable both across states of nature and between people, I think this is an important theorem. I believe that John Harsanyi was the first to make use of it (Harsanyi, 1955). Harsanyi believed there is no value in avoiding risk to good, and so he drew the conclusion that there is no value in equality of good between people. Indeed, he drew the utilitarian conclusion that good is simply the total of people's good. No doubt this is going too far. The formal arguments can scarcely take us as far as utilitarianism. Nevertheless, this type of argument is very powerful. Taking two and three dimensions together, the theorems tell us much more about the structure of good than we can find by considering the dimensions independently.[15] Indeed, to consider the dimensions independently is perilous, because it is easy to take up positions that the theorems show to be inconsistent. Discussions of inequality, of uncertainty, and of prudence are usually conducted in isolation from each other. I think this is a mistake.

So this is what decision theory can do for us in ethics.

8 DOES GOOD EXIST?

I have proposed the project of describing the structure of good. But at the beginning of her paper "Utilitarianism and the virtues," Philippa Foot (1985) denies there is such a thing as the goodness of a state of affairs. This is a serious challenge to the project of describing its structure. So I shall finish this paper by saying something about Foot's denial.

Later in her paper it turns out that Foot is happy with a notion of good that "appears *within* morality as the end of one of the virtues" (namely benevolence). What she really objects to is a notion of "the best outcome" that "stands *outside* morality as its foundation and arbiter" (Foot, 1985, p. 238). Teleological ethics, she believes, sees good like this. Is she right? Certainly, teleology aims at good, and that is its defining characteristic. But it need not necessarily take good to stand outside morality as an objective for morality to aim at. This paper suggests a different possibility. The pursuit of good may give to morality, not an objective, but a structure.

Compare decision theory, and specifically expected utility theory. If I understand him, Daniel Bernoulli, the first expected utility theorist, thought that a rational person would recognize what is good for her, and form her preferences on the basis of her recognized good (Bernoulli, 1954). She would always prefer, of two alternatives, the one that gives her the greater expectation of good. Rationality requires her to have these preferences, Bernoulli thought, because they best promote her good. Her good, then, constitutes an objective for her preferences. But I explained in section 6 that modern decision theory works differently. It sets up a number of axioms about the structure of preferences, and claims that a rational person will have preferences that satisfy them. The theory shows that, if a person's preferences do satisfy the axioms, then utilities can be defined in such a way that the person maximizes the expectation of utility. But the reason why rationality requires her to have preferences that satisfy the axioms is not that this best promotes utility; utility is only a formal construction, and there is no reason to pursue it in its own right. Instead the axioms are justified individually by arguing in some other way that a rational person must conform to them. Normally the argument is that it would be inconsistent for her not to. Modern "axiomatic" expected utility theory, then, is grounded in structural consistency rather than in the pursuit of an objective.

Perhaps the relationship between teleological ethics and good is like the relationship between rationality and utility in axiomatic expected utility theory. In sections 2 and 3 I did indeed argue that teleology is to be identified by its structure, rather than by the nature of its objective. Any ethical theory that has a particular – maximizing – structure is teleological. The structure determines something that the theory aims to maximize, and that thing is what the theory takes to be good.

But this is not enough to answer Foot. What is at issue is not the definition of teleology but its justification: what justifies a maximizing structure in ethics? A defender of teleology must argue that ethics (specifically, what one ought to do) does indeed have a maximizing structure. There are two sorts of justification she might offer. She might say that what one ought to do is determined by the objective of promoting good. Ethics has a maximizing structure because it aims to maximize good. This would be analogous to Bernoulli's justification of expected utility theory. It would imply a notion of good that stands outside ethics and gives it its object. It would be teleology as Foot conceives it. Alternatively, a defender of teleology might justify each of the structural requirements – transitivity, the strong independence axiom and so on – individually on some other grounds. She might use grounds of consistency, for instance. The notion of good would then be built out of this structure. This would be analogous to modern expected utility theory, and it would constitute an answer to Foot.

I have not said much about justification in this paper, and so I can only make a tentative remark now. In section 6, I made a particular claim about the structure of good: I said it conforms to the axioms of expected utility theory. (The connection with expected utility theory is more than just an analogy, therefore.) How did I justify this claim? I did not give a full argument. But I did argue that the justification must come from the direction of rationality. The structure of good follows the structure of rational preferences, I said. So if rational preferences can be shown to conform to the axioms of expected utility theory, the demonstration should also carry over to the structure of good. If rational preferences can be shown to conform without appealing to an external objective, that should also be possible for the structure of good. Modern axiomatic expected utility theory tries to give just that sort of a demonstration; it tries to justify the axioms, applied to rational preferences, on internal grounds of coherence, and not on grounds of an external objective. If it succeeds, the same strategy should work for the structure of good. Teleology, then, at least in the area of uncertainty, could be justified on internal grounds of coherence, without appealing to an external notion of good as its foundation and arbiter.

This is only one part of the structure of good – the part to do with uncertainty. Nevertheless, I hope it suggests how teleological ethics may be able to escape Foot's criticism. Teleology is best identified by means of its structure. And its structure might be justified without appealing to an external good. The notion of good would then be built out of the structure.

However, it is plain that actually the notion of good cannot be determined entirely by structural conditions. A complete description of the structure of good does not constitute a complete analysis of the meaning of "good." If an ethical theory has the right structure, it is teleological and it possesses a conception of good. But its conception may be wrong. Take, for instance, the theory that, when faced with a choice, one should always pick the act likely to produce the greatest total of pain. This is a teleological theory, with all the right structure, and its conception of the good is pain. But good does not actually consist in pain. Therefore this theory is incorrect.

It follows that external criteria must in some way be involved in justifying teleological ethics. Internal consistency cannot be all there is to it. Indeed, I have argued elsewhere (Broome, 1991b) that conditions of internal consistency actually require external criteria of goodness to fix their meaning. But it does not follow that teleology needs to appeal to a complete prior notion of good. I think that our notion of good is formed out of external and internal conditions woven together.

I think the notion of good provides, not an object for ethics to aim at, but a valuable organizing principle in ethical argument. It is an accommodating principle; many ethical views can be made consistent with it. It can accommodate the value of fairness. It can accommodate certain agent-relative views. It can accommodate the lexical domination of some values over others. But there are limits. Some limits are structural: there are ethical views that do not fit the structure of good; I have mentioned some. Some limits are substantive: the view that one should maximize pain is excluded by a substantive limit. There may be excellent ethical theories beyond the limits, which cannot be fitted within the structure of good. But even if there are, I think the organizing work done by the notion of good, and the discipline that it imposes on ethical argument, is valuable.

NOTES

Presented at the Conference on Contemporary Moral Theory at the University of St Andrews in September 1988. I am grateful to Nicholas Denyer for his excellent comments presented at the conference, to the other participants, and to Susan Hurley, Philip Pettit, and Larry Temkin for the very helpful comments I have received from them.
1 Susan Hurley recommended them to me. Rawls himself uses "deontological"

for "nonteleological." But I prefer "nonteleological" because "deontological" traditionally has a more specific meaning connected with obligation.

2 For instance by Scheffler (1988, Introduction) and Pettit (1988b). Scheffler therefore takes his own moral theory, which allows an agent to give special weight to her own concerns, to be a rejection of consequentialism (Scheffler, 1982).

3 See, for instance, the papers in the collection edited by Scheffler (1988).

4 This is an oversimplification because it ignores satisficing theories. See the comment at the end of section 3.

5 A relation R between acts is transitive if and only if a R b and b R c implies a R c for all acts a, b, and c. It is reflexive if and only if a R a for all acts a. Many authors call a transitive and reflexive relation a *quasi-ordering* rather than an ordering.

6 For an analysis of degrees of ϕness, see Morton (1987).

7 To find an act's expectation of good (expected good), take its possible consequences one by one. For each, multiply its goodness by the probability that it will occur. Then add all these products.

8 To be more precise, if the formula of maximizing expected good is to work properly, good must be a number defined uniquely up to an increasing linear transformation.

9 This point is made in more detail by Broome (1987).

10 See, for instance, Jackson (1986) and Parfit (1984, p. 25). Thomson (1985), following Moore (1966, pp. 99–101), takes the strong line that even rightness cannot be relative to probabilities. "Surely," she says, "what a person ought or ought not to do, what it is permissible or impermissible for him to do, does not turn on what he thinks is or will be the case, or even on what he with the best will in the world thinks is or will be the case, but instead on what *is* the case." She denies that there is a subjective sense of "ought." Her argument is this. "On those rare occassions on which someone conceives the idea of asking for my advice on a moral matter, I do not take my fieldwork to be limited to a study of what he believes is the case; I take it to be incumbent on me to find out what *is* the case." This is no doubt true. But it would be equally true if someone asked Thomson's advice on a matter of probability: is such and such an event likely? The answer to a question about probability, like a question about "ought", seems to call for an investigation beyond a person's beliefs. This is a problem for subjectivism about probability. Naturally the problem carries over to subjectivism about "ought," which depends on probability. It is a problem for probability theory, not ethics. To the extent that we are entitled to statements about probability, we are entitled to statements about "ought," subjective though they may be. And Thomson is happy to use statements about probability.

11 There has been a great deal of discussion about this. See, for instance, Kanbur (1987).

12 This has also been doubted, most notably by Allais (1979a). My defence is in Broome (1991b, c).

13 For a fuller explanation of this point, see Broome (1987, 1991a).

14 The most general theorem is in Gorman (1968). It is perhaps worth my explaining briefly how the theorems work. The question, remember, is how good at the different locations aggregates together to make up general good. Because there are three dimensions, the aggregation has three stages. Take a person and a time. An act gives to that person at that time some good in each of the states of nature. The good in all the states aggregates together to determine the good of the person at that time. That is the first stage. Then – the second stage – the good of the person at all times aggregates together to determine the good of the person. Finally – the third stage – the good of all the people aggregates together to determine general good. But we did not have to take the stages in that order. We might have started instead, say, with a given person in a given state of nature. The person's good in that state at all times aggregates together to determine her good in that state. Then all the people's goods in that state aggregate together to determine general good in that state. Finally, good in all the states aggregates together to determine general good. These are merely two different routes to determining overall good. Therefore they must give the same answer. This means that aggregation in one dimension cannot be independent of aggregation in another. That is the basis of the theorems.

15 I have examined the two dimensions of uncertainty and people, and particularly Harsanyi's argument, in Broome (1987). Broome (1991d) tries to take the third dimension into account too. Broome (1991c) is a fuller investigation.

4

Decision Theory and Folk Psychology

Philip Pettit

1 INTRODUCTION

The standard view of how Bayesian decision theory relates to folk psychology is that it provides an explication, under idealization, of the central sound core of that psychology. David Lewis gives expression to this explication thesis as follows.

Decision theory (at least if we omit the frills) is not esoteric science, however unfamiliar it may seem to an outsider. Rather it is a systematic exposition of the consequences of certain well-chosen platitudes about belief, desire, preference and choice. It is the very core of our common-sense theory of persons, dissected out and elegantly systematised. (Lewis, 1983a, p. 114)

But if decision theory explicates certain well-chosen platitudes of folk psychology, the alleged core of our commonsense theory of persons, does it ignore any others? In this paper I identify one neglected platitude and argue for its importance. I assume that the explication thesis is sound but I complement it with an abstraction thesis: a thesis that although decision theory explicates certain platitudes, it abstracts away from others.

The paper is in five sections. The second rehearses the main assumptions of Bayesian theory in its different versions. The third presents the explication thesis and the fourth argues for the abstraction thesis. Finally the fifth section looks at the significance of the abstraction alleged. I argue that the abstraction means that decision theory is incomplete, nonautonomous, and nonpractical. The nonautonomy result may be the most interesting for decision theorists, connecting with pressing concerns about the individuation of options.

There are a number of different versions of Bayesian decision theory but we need not concern ourselves with their distinguishing features. All that we need to appreciate is the hard core of propositions that those versions share. There are three subsidiary principles associated with the theory and one central principle of rationality. The principle of rationality has two sides to it, being first a principle of rational preference and second a principle of rational choice.

The first subsidiary principle is that for any chooser to whom the theory applies we can identify a suitable domain of items over which he can have preferences and a suitable domain of items to which he can attach probabilities. In some versions these domains are the same; in others they are different. One of the things that makes the domain of preferences suitable is that it includes items that can be equated with the options facing the agent in any situation of choice or can be used to construct something equivalent; an option is usually identified as an exhaustive and exclusive disjunction of outcomes and the domain of preferences will include such disjunctions or at least such outcomes. One of the things that makes the domain of probabilities suitable is that it ensures that there will be a suitable probability associated with any outcome.

The second subsidiary principle is that the choosers to whom the theory is intended to apply have an appropriate preference ordering over the items in the preference domain. The ordering must be complete in the sense that no item fails to be ranked. It must be consistent, in the sense that if A is preferred to B and B to C then C cannot be preferred to A. It must also satisfy one or more other conditions, of which the most common imposed is a form of continuity assumption.[1]

The third subsidiary principle is that the agents to whom the theory is intended to apply have an appropriate probability ordering over the items in the domain of probability. If that domain is suitable, then it will constitute a Boolean algebra; this means that if it includes two propositions A and B, for example, then it also includes not A, not B, A and B, A or B, and so on. The probability ordering will be appropriate if and only if it enables us to assign to every item X in the algebra a real number $P(X)$, such that it satisfies the Kolmogorov axioms and represents the agent's probability for that item. These stipulate the following (see Skyrms, 1975, ch. 6):

1   $P(X) \geq 0$ for every X;
2   $P(X) = 1$ if X is a tautology;
3   $P(X \text{ or } Y) = P(X) + P(Y)$ if X and Y are mutually exclusive.

That an agent satisfies these three subsidiary principles does not mean that he will be intuitively rational in his preferences. The principles allow this sort of irrationality, for example: that someone should prefer a disjunction of A and B both to A and to B. The principle of rationality for preference rules out such possibilities. Let the items in the domain of preference be ranked according to the agent's preferences on some scale, say from 0 to 10; its place on the scale determines what is known as an item's subjective utility. The principle of rationality for preference dictates the appropriate place on the scale, the appropriate subjective utility, for any disjunctive item such as A-or-B, where the alternatives are exclusive and exhaustive. It says that the place ought to be determined by the sum of the scale figures for A and B, each figure being discounted by a number which represents the appropriate probability, in the mind of the agent, of that item's being realized rather than the other. If A is scaled at 2 and B at 7, and if A has a probability of $\frac{3}{4}$ and B of $\frac{1}{4}$ – the numbers must add to 1 – then the appropriate place on the scale for A-or-B is $2 \times \frac{3}{4} + 7 \times \frac{1}{4} = 3\frac{1}{4}$. When subjective utility is so understood that it can be determined in this way as well as more directly, we speak of subjective expected utility (SEU).

Any theory which ascribes rational preferences makes for a decision theory, so far as each option in any situation of choice can be equated with an item in the domain of preference or with an exhaustive and exclusive disjunction of such items. The principle of rationality for choice says that the choice of an option will be rational as long as it maximizes subjective expected utility. The choice of an option O_1 over an option O_2 will be rational if and only if SEU $(O_1) >$ SEU(O_2). If O_1 and O_2 are simple items in the domain of preference, then O_1 must be ranked above O_2. If they are disjunctions the appropriate sum for O_1 must be higher than that for O_2.

Different versions of Bayesian decision theory differ in a number of ways.[2] They differ in ontology, taking the items in the domains of preference and probability to be different sorts of things, they differ in their views of the sorts of probabilities which it is appropriate to introduce, and they differ in how precisely they axiomatize the theory. But such differences still allow them to give a common endorsement to the sorts of principles presented. The presentation of those principles is sufficient for our purposes in this paper, but some may find it useful to see how the concepts involved in the theory can be given operational sense. Probably the best way to do this is to look at the approach suggested by Frank Ramsey which is described in the appendix.

3 THE EXPLICATION THESIS

The explication thesis requires two points to be established: first, that folk psychology involves a certain incontestable core of theory; second, that decision theory explicates that core. In practice the first stage in defending the thesis comes to a defense of the assumption of intentional agency, and the second to an argument for identifying subjective probabilities and utilities respectively with the desires and beliefs postulated under that assumption.

The assumption of intentional agency involves three components.

1 Every action issues from the agent's beliefs and desires.
2 Those beliefs and desires constitute a reason for the agent as to why the action should have been performed; they mean that he desired an action of a certain sort and that he believed that he would bring one about by doing what he did.
3 The beliefs and desires cause the action to occur in virtue of rationalizing it in this way, and not by a deviant route: not, for example, because their presence produces a temporary failure – say embarrassment – which has the fortuitous result of engendering the appropriate response.[3]

I shall not argue here either that the intentional assumption is implicit in folk psychology or that it is sound. Both points are generally, if not universally, granted among contemporary philosophers and I am happy to go along.[4]

The second stage in defending the explication thesis requires an argument that decision theory explicates the assumption of intentional agency. The argument might go like this. If an agent has the subjective probabilities and utilities postulated, then provided that their contents are suitable, those states serve, like the beliefs and desires assigned under the assumption of intentional agency, to give the agent reasons for choosing as he does; they do so, at least, provided that they are taken as more than fictions.[5] The most economical way of viewing such an agent will then be to identify the posits respectively of the theory and the assumption – to equate beliefs with subjective probabilities, and desires with subjective utilities. And that view amounts to seeing decision theory as explicating the assumption of intentional agency.

It may be thought to be an objection to the equation of the two sorts of states that only subjective probabilities and utilities come equipped with numbers. But the objection is not compelling, for the number can be seen as a way of coding the degree of strength of the corresponding belief or desire. I think that there are no persuasive objections of this kind to the equation and so I am prepared to go along with the explication thesis. Doing so without the ceremony of full-scale argument may be excusable, given that my ultimate purpose in the paper is to show that the thesis is subject to an important and little noticed limitation.

It is important to realize that the decision theory which explicates beliefs and desires involves a great amount of idealization. What the explication thesis says is that the subjective probabilities and utilities which an agent would have under the idealized circumstances described in the relevance conditions are his beliefs and desires. It does not say that, for any agent who has beliefs and desires, those states constitute subjective probabilities and utilities, or at least the full range of subjective probabilities and utilities ascribed in decision theory. Rather, what holds is the reverse, namely that if an agent has subjective probabilities and utilities, then they are his beliefs and desires by other names.

Finally, a caution. As I have stated it, the assumption of intentional agency is silent on how an agent's beliefs and desires should change in the light of certain changes of belief – changes reporting new evidence and the like. Equally, as I have stated it, decision theory is silent on how the agent's subjective probabilities and utilities should shift in response to certain changes in probabilities: this is the topic of probability kinematics. Thus the explication thesis has quite restricted scope. I have nothing against the enriched version, however, under which the thesis is that decision theory as enriched by a suitable probability kinematics explicates the assumption of intentional agency as enriched with a suitable assumption of attitudinal rationality. Indeed, henceforth I shall write as if the explication thesis takes this richer form.

4 THE ABSTRACTION THESIS

The best way into the abstraction thesis that I wish to defend is probably to identify the folk pyschological platitude which I claim that decision theory ignores. I call the platitude the assumption of *desiderative structure*. What it says is that there are two quite different sorts of object which desires may have – prospects and properties – and that the desires that we form for different prospects are determined by the properties that we think they have. Any prospects that we desire, any prospects that we prefer to the relevant alternatives, we desire for the properties they display or promise to display.

A *prospect*, in my usage, is what would more commonly be described as a state of affairs: something like the state of affairs involved in my

going to London this afternoon, in Western banks' extending the
repayment period on Third World loans, or in the greenhouse effect's
proving not to be a reality. It is any way that the world may be. At the
limit it is any token way that the world may be, that is, any particular
possible world; more usually, it is any type of way the world may be, that
is, any set of possible worlds. The prospect that p is just the set of possible
worlds at which it is the case that p, and so on.[6] I shall use a description
to pick out any prospect; usually I will present it via a sentence – say
"p" – expressing the state of affairs in question. But I can think of it as
a state of affairs satisfying other descriptions as well as the description
used to pick it out. The prospect is coarsely individuated so that it is an
a posteriori matter whether certain prospect-identifying descriptions pick
out the same prospect or not.

Every prospect involves the realization of a certain *property* or
properties, whether in a given individual or individuals, in a given
domain, or after a given pattern. The property involved may be of a
variety of forms; thus it may be relational or nonrelational, as in the
difference between the property of equality and the property of mass, it
may involve a particular, as in the property of speaking French, or it may
be universal, like the property of being intelligent, and so on. A property
can be seen as a distinct sort of entity which belongs to any prospect that
involves it, though there is a qualification to be made in a moment about
this claim; the property of traveling will belong to the prospect of my
going to London this afternoon, and so on. Like a prospect, a property
in this sense is a coarsely individuated entity – something such that for
at least some expressions in a language it is an *a posteriori* matter whether
they pick out the same property or not. I may discover that what I prize
as the elegance of certain paintings is just the classical quality for which
you admire them or that what I took to be the cruelty of certain actions
is what you described as their brutality. There are not as many properties
as property-expressions: properties are independent entities to which the
expressions help us refer.

But though properties can be seen in this way as distinct sorts of entities
which belong to the prospects that involve them, there is a qualification
to be made about that representation. This is that, for all we need to say,
a property can equally be represented as itself a type of prospect. Ignoring
some complications, we can represent the property of being an F as
equivalent in all significant respects, for example, to the prospect that
there is something which is F: that is, equivalent to the set of possible
worlds at which there are Fs. If this representation is preferred, then it
will affect the formulation of the assumption of desiderative structure,
but it will not alter the substance. The assumption will not be that we

desire properties as well as prospects and desire prospects for the properties that we think they have. Rather, it will be that among the set of prospects there is a special class – those corresponding, for appropriate properties, to sentences such as "there is something which is F" – and that, for any prospect we desire, we desire it because we see it as involving the realization of one such privileged sort of prospect. This principle will apply to prospects within the special class as well as to prospects outside it. It is important to recognize this possibility, for fear of misunderstanding, but in what follows I shall set it aside. I shall assume that properties are distinct sorts of entities from prospects and that they belong to the prospects that involve them.

The assumption of desiderative structure is that, not only do we desire prospects, we also desire properties, and that we always desire prospects for the properties we think they have. Take the notion of prospect-preference as given – the notion of ranking prospects in a preference-ordering.[7] This enables us to identify what it is to desire a prospect and what it is to desire a property. To desire a prospect is to prefer it to the prospects that you think of as the alternatives. To desire a property is to be disposed to prefer a prospect that has it, assuming that there is only one, among a set of prospects that otherwise leave you indifferent. More intuitively, to desire a prospect is to opt for it, or to form the intention of opting for it, among the set of available alternatives; to desire a property is to value it, being disposed, if other things are equal, to desire any prospect that displays the property. Notice that under these definitions we can think of desire as being involved in the same sense in each case. If there are two sorts of desire, that is not because there are two senses of the term; it is only because there are two sorts of objects for desire in the one and only sense of "desire" available. But enough of abstract definition. It is time to introduce our distinction with examples.

Consider the self-ascription of desire involved in my saying that I desire that p: for example, that I desire to have a teaching job, or to live in a warmer climate, or to be moral.[8] One context in which I may make such an ascription is where the proposition "p" picks out a particular prospect or state of affairs from among a set of fixed alternatives. I have a choice between staying in research and going to a teaching job, between living in Canberra and moving to Queensland, between doing something of questionable ethics and being more punctiliously moral. In such a context I shall indicate a desire for a particular prospect by reporting that I desire to teach or move nearer the tropics or be moral.

But now imagine that the context of ascription is different and that it is not assumed that "p" picks out one among a fixed set of alternatives. Suppose for example that I have been asked about the things that I would like in life and that I say that I have a desire to have a teaching job, to live in a warmer climate, and to be moral. Here these ascriptions clearly do not pick out desires for particular states of affairs or prospects. So what are the objects I claim to desire? The ready answer is that I desire the properties in question in the ascriptions. The presence of one of those properties will make any prospect the more attractive to me; at the limit its presence in one of a number of alternatives between which I am otherwise indifferent will lead me to prefer that alternative. Among a set of career prospects I will tend to prefer a teaching job, at least if other things are equal; among a set of residential alternatives, one near the tropics; among a set of behavioural options, one that is morally permissible. And so on. I may prefer a nonteaching job if presented with a certain set of alternatives, for it may be that the job scores very well in respect of other attractive properties. But that the job is not in teaching will still count against it; compared with the abstractly possible job which is identical except in this respect – a job not in fact available as an alternative – it will look inferior (see Jackson, 1985a).

The assumption of desiderative structure marks this sort of distinction between desires for prospects and properties. But it also goes further. It says that whenever an agent desires a prospect, he does so because of the properties it displays: he desires it for the desired properties that it promises to realize. In scholastic terms, the prospect is the material object of his desire, the properties the formal object. The observation is common to the Aristotelian way of thinking about these matters.[9] *Quidquid appetitur sub specie boni appetitur*: whatever is desired is desired for being good. This extra element in the assumption of desiderative structure ought not to be surprising. If there are independent desires for properties as well as prospects, and if they are not idle wheels in our psychology, the only obvious role that they can play is in the determination of prospect-desires.

There are three points that I maintain about the assumption of desiderative structure: first, that decision theory neglects it; second, that it is recognized in our folk psychology; third, that it is a reasonable assumption to make.

It ought to be clear, I think, that decision theory neglects the assumption.[10] In Bayesian theory we assume a domain of items – in effect, different states of affairs or prospects – over which the agent has preferences. We suppose that every option that the agent faces – the prospect of doing A, doing B, or whatever – appears among those items or can be equated with a suitable disjunction of items: the disjunct items will be subprospects of the prospect constituted by the disjunction. Then we postulate that if a rational agent ranks certain outcomes in a particular way in his preference ordering then he will rank disjunctions of those outcomes in a corresponding manner, and that as he ranks items or disjunctions of items which correspond to options so will he choose among them: he will choose so as to maximize expected utility. The outcomes and options invoked here are all particular states of affairs or prospects. What the theory does then is formulate a constraint of consistency which the rational agent will satisfy in the preferences and choices that he forms over such prospects.

The assumption of desiderative structure postulates a different constraint of consistency on the rational agent. It is not a constraint of consistency between a prospect-desire and the agent's preference-ranking over its subprospects and the subprospects of its alternatives. Rather, it is a constraint of consistency between a prospect-desire and the agent's property-desires, in particular, his desires for the properties exhibited by the prospect and its alternatives. In concentrating on the first constraint of consistency, decision theory neglects the second. It asks after what an agent's preferences over relevant outcomes rationally require of him in his decision between certain options. It ignores the other question, of what an agent's values – the properties he cherishes – require of him in the decision.

But while decision theory neglects the assumption of desiderative structure, and the constraint of rationality that it involves, nothing in the theory is strictly inconsistent with the assumption. The theory tells us what prospect an agent ought to desire, given his preferences over the relevant subprospects. Perhaps the assumption only tells us how he ought to form preferences over those subprospects, given his desires for the different properties they display. Perhaps it only bears on the original prospect-desire indirectly, so that there is no potential conflict between decision theory and the assumption. These matters will come up again in the next section, particularly in the discussion of the nonautonomy claim.

We have seen that decision theory neglects desiderative structure, though it does not rule it out. What then of folk psychology? Is it clear that in our everyday habits of thinking about desire we distinguish between property-desires and prospect-desires, and see the former as serving to determine the latter? I believe that this is clear and that little more needs to be said in defense of the claim than is already implicit in the remarks about the examples used in introducing the distinction. After all, those remarks appeal to what we all find familiar, and that they introduce the assumption of desiderative structure shows that this is part of our common lore.

But in case you are not persuaded, here is a thought which may convince you that we folk psychologists, even those of us schooled in decision theory, postulate property-desires at the source of desires for prospects.[11] There is a family of paradoxes acknowledged by decision-theorists which ought not to be paradoxes in the absence of desiderative structure; that we find them paradoxical therefore shows that we endorse that assumption. For example, consider someone who prefers to go to the other side of town to buy a bicycle for $50 less than he can buy it on this side – for $150 rather than $200 – but who does not prefer to go to the same trouble in order to save $50 on the price of a car – to buy it for $15,000 rather than $15,050. Thinking strictly in terms of prospect-desires, there is nothing even slightly irrational, and nothing therefore paradoxical, about such a pair of preferences. Yet most of us do feel some tension. Obviously the explanation is that most of us assume that property-desires drive prospect-desires and are therefore ill at ease with the notion that the property-desire that is apparently relevant in the first case – the desire to save $50 – is irrelevant in the second. If we regain our ease, it will probably be through coming to assume that the relevant property in the first case is not that feature but one which is absent in the second: say, if this makes economic sense, the feature of buying the commodity at 25 percent less.

Let us agree that as decision theory neglects desiderative structure, folk psychology recognizes it. The final question is whether it is in fact reasonable to postulate such a structure in our desires. I believe that it is, on the grounds that the structure offers the best explanation of a variety of phenomena. Consider first the ambiguity, noted above, in ascriptions of desire. In ascribing to myself or to any other agent the desire that p, I may be attributing a property-desire or a prospect-desire. That ambiguity may be capable of being otherwise explained, but the most natural explanation is the account in terms of desiderative structure which is assumed in my very characterization of it. This phenomenon of ambiguity is not the only one that can be nicely explained by positing desiderative structure. I shall offer four other examples here.

The first is the phenomenon of internal conflict in desires; in a recent paper Frank Jackson (1985b) has argued that this is best explained by a distinction like ours. Consider the conflict that I feel when confronted with a choice between, say, attending an important departmental meeting and seeing my son perform in the school play. Consider, more particularly, the conflict that I may continue to feel even after deciding for the meeting; that is, even after forming a preference or desire for that prospect rather than the other. How do we explain the continuing conflict, given that the first prospect has triumphed – given, in other words, that there is only one prospect-desire present, the desire for that prospect? An attractive explanation is offered by the assumption of desiderative structure, for it enables us to say that after coming to desire the meeting rather than the play I can continue to feel the pull of the property which put the play in the running, even if it was not enough to earn it victory – the property of enabling me to see my son on stage.

A second phenomenon which desiderative structure enables us to explain is the distinction, common in many quarters, between desire *simpliciter* for a state of affairs and *prima facie* desire. That distinction is often taken as a primitive, but the assumption of desiderative structure lets us see how it can be derived from more basic considerations. Under that assumption I come to form a desire for a prospect only so far as I identify it as the bearer of certain properties which I already desire. I come to desire that p, period, only so far as I desire that p, *qua* F. But then it is natural to say that the prospect-desire is the desire *simpliciter* that p, and the other state – the desire that p, *qua* F – the *prima facie* desire. Furthermore this goes with the fact that *prima facie* desire is sometimes also cast as desire *pro tanto* or desire *secundum quid* – desire in so far as something is true, desire in a certain respect.[12]

A third phenomenon explained by the assumption of desiderative structure is closely related to the last. It is the apparent fact that linguistic desire-contexts are not extensional: that even if A desires that p, and p if and only if q – so that the p-object of desire just is the q-object – still we cannot say that A desires that q without being misleading. John desires to go to the movies, and will disappoint his mother tonight if and only if he goes – so that going to the movies just is disappointing his mother – but he may not desire to disappoint his mother, or so we regularly say. The assumption of desiderative structure suggests a straightforward explanation of this phenomenon. When we use a sentence "p" to ascribe a prospect-desire, we naturally pick a sentence that serves to indicate the relevant property-desire also – a sentence involving predicates that alert us to the property in question. John desires to go to the movies and desires that prospect for the property of its involving him in going to the movies, or for a closely related property. Thus if we replace "p" in the original desire-ascription with a sentence that picks out the same prospect but under a different property, we run the risk of misleading our audience about the property desired. John desires the prospect which involves disappointing his mother but he does not desire it for the property of disappointing his mother; he may not even have realized that it would disappoint her. Hence it is misleading to say without qualification that John desires to disappoint his mother. The failure of extensionality is unsurprising.

The fourth phenomenon which desiderative structure lets us explain is the practice among human agents of seeking and giving certain sorts of reasons for choice. Consistently with the decision-theoretic picture, the picture involving prospect-desires only, an agent will have only one sort of reason to offer in explanation or justification of what he does: the fact, however elliptically expressed, that the option chosen best served his desires for prospects in general, according to his beliefs. But this sort of consideration will not do to answer challenges such as these. "How could you want anything so cruel?" "How could you desire such a comparatively unfair oucome?" "How could you ignore the self-destructive aspects of your decision?" To respond to these questions with a suitable reason, the agent will have to point to properties of the option, or of its potential outcomes, which made it attractive to him – ideally, to properties such that his interrogator can understand how someone might be moved as he was by desires for their instantiation. The availability of such answers, however, is explicable only under the assumption of desiderative structure.

Finally, an objection. The decision-theoretic picture, it may be said, can make room for the way in which properties are invoked in explanation of these four phenomena; there is no need to posit property-desires as independent of prospect-desires. The idea will be that although the only desires I have are desires for prospects, still I may often identify properties that are common as a matter of fact among the prospects I desire. Identifying such properties in an option forgone, I may experience conflict; identifying them in any option at all I may represent myself as having a *prima facie* desire for that option; identifying them in an ascription of desire, I may see the ascription as nonextensional; identifying them in an option chosen, I may succeed in making sense of the choice for another.

The objection comes of confusion. If I am oriented only to prospects, if properties are not objects of desire independently, then the trick suggested works in none of these cases. Consider the property of the option forgone in the earlier example: the property of enabling me to see my son on stage. If prospects are all that concern me then, even if this is generally a property found only in prospects desired, its presence in the option forgone will not explain any lingering desire. Why should it cause desire to linger given in this case that if the property had been realized then the undesired prospect would have eventuated in place of the one desired?

The point to which we are directed shows also why the trick will fail in the other cases. Identifying in an option before me a property present in prospects frequently desired in the past will not furnish me with a *prima facie* desire; at best it will provide a *prima facie* reason for predicting that

I will come to desire that option. Identifying a reference to a commonly featured property in an ascription of desire will not explain why we cannot substitute reference to another property of the prospect desired, at least if the other property is equally recognized as a property of the prospect; nothing distinctive will be signaled by reference to that property, if prospects are the only things we desire. Identifying in an option chosen a property present in prospects often desired by others will not justify the choice to them; at most it will show them that in one respect, as no doubt in countless others of equal irrelevance, the choice is like choices they make. I conclude that if phenomena like those cited are to be explained, then we need a robust distinction between prospect-desires and property-desires, a distinction such as the assumption of desiderative structure posits.

5 THE SIGNIFICANCE OF THE ABSTRACTION THESIS

The explication thesis has it that decision theory explicates, in David Lewis's words, certain well-chosen platitudes about belief, desire, preference, and choice. What we have seen is something not inconsistent with this, that equally decision theory ignores certain other platitudes about such intentional states and acts. That this is so may not be found particularly interesting, however, unless it has some lesson for the significance of decision theory. In this final section I shall try to show that our abstraction thesis does have such a lesson. I shall argue that the thesis implies that decision theory is first incomplete, second nonautonomous, and third nonpractical. The incompleteness claim bears on decision theory as a descriptive device; the nonpracticality claim bears on its status as a normative instrument. The nonautonomy claim is relevant to decision theory in both its roles.

5.1 Decision theory is incomplete

The incompleteness claim follows fairly directly from the considerations mentioned in discussion of desiderative structure. But it is probably worth spelling out in a little detail. The claim is that decision theory is an incomplete account of the matters relevant to decision-making. In decision-making the agent's preference-ordering over a certain set of prospects gets to be determined, whether consciously or unconsciously, deliberatively or mechanically. Decision theory charts some of the elements that play a role in such preference formation but if the incompleteness claim is correct then it systematically misses others.

Decision theory does not allege its own completeness. But it is natural, if only because of the name given to the theory, to think of it as a complete account of preference formation.[13] Decision theory is generally committed to the following principle of the co-determination of prospect-preferences and that principle is easily rendered as a principle of completeness.

> For every prospect, the place of that prospect in a rational agent's preference-ordering is determined – given his probability function – simultaneously with the places occupied by its subprospects; the place of each subprospect is co-determined in the same way with the places occupied by each of its subprospects; and so on down to the ultimate atomic subprospects, if there are any.[14]

If "p" expresses a possible state of affairs or prospect, and if there are two different ways in which it may be realized relative to another proposition "q" – the two ways will be expressed respectively by "p-and-q" and "p-and-not-q" – then they are subprospects of the original prospect. Any prospect can be partitioned into a variety of sets of subprospects, but most theorists suppose that there is a single set of maximally determinate subprospects on the basis of which all others are constructed. These are the different ways that things might be at the finest level of discrimination at which the agent works; they are, from his point of view, the different possible worlds.

The principle of the co-determination of preferences easily goes over into the principle of completeness. Two attractive assumptions are sufficient to generate the shift: first, that there are indeed ultimate atomic subprospects; second, that the rational agent's preferences for non-ultimate prospects are determined by his preferences for subprospects, so that his preferences for the ultimate subprospects come out then as basic. The completeness principle holds that the rational agent assigns a place in his preference-ordering to every possible world and that the place of every other prospect – in effect, every set of possible worlds – is determined by those rankings combined with the agent's probability function. The place of "p" may be fixed by the places of "p-and-q" and "p-and-not-q" or by the places of "p-and-r" and "p-and-not-r," and the places of each of those may be fixed in turn by further subprospects, but, however it goes, the place of everything will be fixed eventually by the agent's preferences over the ultimate subprospects he distinguishes, his subjectively different possible worlds.

The picture projected by the completeness principle, the picture usually associated with decision theory, is distinctively instrumentalist. The different possible worlds represent different possible outcomes or ends of action. The different desires which the rational agent has *vis-à-vis* those ends are given and beyond debate. The only job in rational decision-making then is for the agent to form his preferences over the relevant options on the basis of how, given his probability function, they promise to do by his desires for those ends.

The abstraction thesis defended in the last section gives the lie to the completeness principle and to this instrumentalist picture which it projects. It means that the picture is inadequate in at least two respects. First of all, an agent need not have determinate preferences over all the relevant subprospects before he can rationally form a preference over certain prospects. Second, even if he does have such preferences, even indeed if he has determinate preferences over the ultimate possible worlds involved, those preferences cannot be seen as basic, as the unmoved movers of the system.

This second point follows from the claim that in forming preferences over prospects, even prospects as specific as possible worlds, we are moved by our preferences over the properties which we see those prospects as displaying. That claim, in effect the assumption of desiderative structure, means that the rational agent's ultimate points of reference, his ultimate motivational bearings, must be given by abstract properties rather than by concrete outcomes. In more everyday language they must be given by the agent's values rather than by his ends. Certainly he may take his guidance in decision-making from the ends to which different choices are likely to lead, but how desirable he finds those ends will depend on his values.

The first point mentioned is that not only are values more basic than ends in rational decision-making, they may serve to determine a decision without the agent's preference-ordering over relevant ends becoming determinate. Consider a situation where an agent has to form a preference between two options, A and B, where the different outcomes that are relevant to him – they may or may not be as specific as possible worlds – are A_1 and A_2, B_1 and B_2. Suppose now that both A_1 and A_2 are certain to realize a certain property which is of supreme importance to the agent – in this circumstance, it is an overriding value – while at least one of the B options is certain to fail in this regard. In such a situation the rational agent will form a preference for A over B and may do so without having a determinate preference-ordering between A_1 and A_2 or between them and the B outcome, if there is one, which promises to realize the value in question. The decision may be rationally determined by values in a way that abstracts from concrete ends.

We have been documenting the incompleteness of decision theory, in particular the incompleteness which follows from the abstraction thesis of the last section. The incompleteness, in a slogan, is that decision theory looks only at ends, oblivious of the fact that values are more basic than ends and may even determine rational choice in abstraction from ends. But this incompleteness charge will not pass unchallenged. There is at least one line of objection that I can envisage.

According to a familiar style of behaviorism, preferring one state of affairs or prospect to another is simply being reliably disposed to choose it rather than the other, if you are given the choice; being indifferent between the two will then be failing to meet this condition in both directions. This approach means that you may prefer one prospect to another, or be indifferent between them, even if you have never considered them before. More generally, it means that preference and indifference between prospects are almost always given: they come on the cheap. The approach suggests two things: first that far from values being more basic than ends, an agent will have preferences over ends which outrun the control of values; second, that far from values determining choice in abstraction from ends, an agent will always have determinate preferences over the ends that are relevant to any choice.

But the assumption of desiderative structure dictates a clear response to this objection. If the rational agent forms preferences between prospects in the light of his preferences over the properties of those prospects, then preference comes to something significantly more than the disposition simply to choose. It may be that each of us has defined dispositions of this kind across the range of all prospects that we can distinguish – all our possible worlds – but the idea is that such dispositions should not be dignified with the title of "preferences." For a disposition to choose to count as a preference, it must be a disposition to choose with reason – a disposition to choose on the basis of the properties displayed by the alternatives.

This line of response is not unreasonable. The behaviorist explication must equate preference with the disposition, already determined by how the agent is constituted, to select one of the relevant alternatives as soon as they are presented. It is that explication which suggests that I may already have a preference between two prospects, even though I have never considered their properties, never weighed up the values that they realize. But the equation of preferences with such brute dispositions is bound to seem inappropriate under the assumption of desiderative structure. And rightly so. After all, even if a person is disposed to choose one unconsidered prospect rather than another, he will equally be disposed, if possible, to consider the properties of the two before making his choice. It is not unreasonable for someone who believes in desiderative structure to refuse to equate preference with the brute disposition, claiming that preference proper appears only after the consideration of properties or values.[15]

5.2 Decision theory is nonautonomous[16]

The second interesting result which follows from the abstraction thesis of section 4 is that decision theory is not as autonomous in relation to folk psychology as might otherwise be thought. The decision-theorist who wishes to apply his theory to determine what an agent will do, or ought rationally to do, must rely on folk psychological insight in identifying the required prediction or prescription. The best way to introduce this result will be by means of some examples.

Consider first an agent who is to be offered each of the following choices, perhaps on different days.[17]

1 Here is a (large) apple and an orange. Take your pick; I will have the other.
2 Here is an orange and a (small) apple. Take your pick; I will have the other.
3 Here is large apple and a small apple. Take your pick; I will have the other.

Imagine now that the agent has chosen the large apple over the orange and the orange over the small apple. If he is rational, what should we expect him to do in 3? By consistency or transitivity we ought, it seems, to expect him to take the large apple. But of course we know that being a well-bred young man he will not. So what do we say?

The obvious thing to say is that taking a large apple when the alternative left for another person is an orange is quite a different thing from taking a large apple when the alternative left is a small apple. Thus the three choices are not an instance of the intransitive sequence: A rather than B; B rather than C; C rather than A. The sequence, properly represented, is A^1 rather than B; B rather than C; C rather than A^2. A^1 is taking a large apple and leaving an orange for the other person; A^2 is taking a large apple and leaving a small apple for the other person.

Consider next an example which challenges, not transitivity of preference, but something called Independence or, in one version, the Surething Principle. The Independence assumption is implicit in the principle of rational preference mentioned in section 1. It says that if you prefer an option involving a certain probability of A to an option involving the same probability of B, where otherwise they are the same, then for any two options differing in such a way only, you ought to prefer the one involving A – this, no matter what the probability shared by A and B, and no matter what the alternative to A and B in each case. Thus you ought to prefer 3 to 4, if you prefer 1 to 2.

1   10 percent chance of A, 90 percent chance of C.
2   10 percent chance of B, 90 percent chance of C.
3   50 percent chance of A, 50 percent chance of D.
4   50 percent chance of B, 50 percent chance of D.

This principle is basic to traditional decision theory, since what it amounts to is the claim that an agent's preferences over the outcomes involved ought to impact on his choices homogeneously, without any difference being made by those differences in probabilities and alternatives that cancel out between options.

But this principle is subject to the same sorts of apparent counter-examples as transitivity. The most famous is the Allais Paradox but the one I prefer is this (derived from Diamond, 1967). I have to decide whether I am to give a candy to little Mary or little John, both of whom have equal claims. I prefer tossing a coin and giving the prize to Mary if the coin comes up heads and to John if it comes up tails, than giving it to John in either case. That is to say, I prefer 1 to 2.

1   Heads Mary wins; tails John wins.
2   Heads John wins; tails John wins.

But if my choice goes this way, then by Independence I ought to prefer 3 to 4.

3   Heads Mary wins; tails Mary wins.
4   Heads John wins; tails Mary wins.

But of course, being concerned with fairness, I shall prefer 4 to 3, not 3 to 4. So what are we to say?

Again, the obvious thing to say is that as the options differ in the case that challenged transitivity, so the outcomes differ here. The outcome under which Mary wins is different depending on whether or not the alternative possible outcome is that John wins. In the one case it is a fairly generated outcome; in the other it is not. Thus the example is not an instance of the scheme to which the Independence principle applies.

I hope that the two examples considered are sufficient to make clear that, if decision theory is to be applied to predictive or normative purpose, then it must be able to borrow from somewhere a principle for determining of two apparently equivalent options or outcomes, whether or not they really are relevantly similar. Of course decision theory might go to the extreme of saying that no two options or outcomes X and Y are ever suitably equivalent if they occur in the context of different alternatives. But that would be to make the theory useless in practice, since nothing would then follow from one choice as to what a rational agent would pick in a second.[18]

Clearly what is needed is a principle of equivalence for options and outcomes which is moderate in its effects; that is, which makes sufficient distinctions to handle the sort of counterexamples mentioned without making so many distinctions that no choice bears on any other.[19] What type of principle would do the trick? John Broome points us in the right direction, I believe, with this principle for individuating possibilities (for example, options or outcomes): "worlds should be classified as different possibilities if and only if they differ in a way that can justify a preference" (Broome, 1990a, p. 11). Taking the large apple is a different option when the alternative is an orange from what it is when the alternative is a small apple, because it differs in a way that can justify apparently intransitive preferences. For similar reasons, Mary's winning is a different outcome when the alternative is John's winning from what it is when the alternative also gives victory to Mary.

If we take up Broome's suggestion here, and it has overwhelming attractions to my mind, then we must agree that it is a sufficient condition for one option's being non-equivalent to another option, one outcome to another outcome, that they differ in regard to properties that are desired or undesired by the agent. This proposition will enable us to say, at least in principle, when contexts (of alternatives) affect what would otherwise count as a single option or outcome X in such a way that equivalence fails across those contexts: in one context we have X^1, say, and in another X^2. It enables us to tell whether the relational property of having such and such alternatives – and, in the outcome case, at such and such probabilities – is sufficient to affect the identity of the option or outcome. The property will suffice to make a difference just in case it is or it involves a property desired or undesired by the agent. The relational property of leaving a small apple rather than an orange means that taking the large apple is impolite and since politeness is likely to be a property that matters to the agent, it makes a difference to the identity of the option. The relational property of there having been an equal chance of John's winning means that Mary's victory is fair and since fairness is likely to count with any agent, it makes a difference to the identity of the outcome.

The upshot is that while decision theory abstracts from the assumption of desiderative structure in regimenting folk psychology, the application of the theory requires us to practice folk psychology in a way that relies on that very assumption. Does our reliance on the assumption jeopardize the status of decision theory, making it radically indeterminate in many cases whether an agent is faced with one or two options, one or two outcomes? I do not think so, since a property only has to matter in some measure, however miniscule, to make a difference. While there is probably great variety in how agents weight different properties, there seems to be less variation in which sorts of property they desire. In any case, what I wish to stress here is that, however this affects its status, decision theory does have to rely on the practice of a part of folk psychology from which it abstracts. Decision theory is a nonautonomous discipline.[20]

5.3 Decision theory is nonpractical

This is enough on the incompleteness and nonautonomy of decision theory. I turn now to the final proposition that I derive from the abstraction thesis: the claim that decision theory is nonpractical. Decision theory claims to identify the pattern of choice which a rational agent will make: it spells out an ideal of rational choice. But there are two ways in which such an ideal may relate to practice:[21] first as a *calculus* or procedure for getting the practice right; second as a *canon* or test for determining of any practice whether it is right.[22] An ideal may be a calculus for successful practice without being a canon, as when it offers a generally reliable way of achieving a certain desired standard, where the achievement of that standard is the canon of success. And an ideal may be a canon of successful practice without being a practical calculus for achieving success. When a stockmarket adviser tells you to buy low and sell high, you are certainly offered a relevant canon of success, but equally certainly you are not offered an effective recipe or calculus.

Whether decision theory is practical or not depends on whether it offers just a canon of rational choice – I assume that it offers that – or something that serves also as a calculus. When we are told that the rational agent maximizes expected utility, are we told how we manage, or perhaps should manage, to be rational, namely by attending to the task of maximizing expected utility? Or are we just told that, however the rational agent does it, what makes him distinctively rational is the fact that he maximizes expected utility? Imagine that we are informed that what makes for excellence in long-distance running is the efficient use of oxygen, where there is nothing we can do to affect this feature in ourselves. The issue is whether decision theory gives us the same sort of nonpractical information: a fine analysis perhaps, but useless advice.

The habit in business schools and the like may be to treat decision theory as a calculus, but it is not an uncommon view among philosophers that at most the theory serves as a canon of rationality. One ground on which that view has been defended is that human agents do not have the sort of access to their own utilities and probabilities that would be required for using decision theory as a calculus (see Harman, 1986, ch. 9). I believe that the abstraction thesis defended in this paper provides another reason for holding by this view, casting decision theory as a nonpractical normative device. I argue that the assumption of desiderative structure means that were an agent to try to use decision theory as a calculus, then he would be departing in a fundamental way from ordinary procedure; he would be changing the basis of his decision-making. I take it that this will be seen as a consideration against such a calculative employment of the theory, since no one admits the sort of transformative effect I allege.

If someone uses decision theory as a calculus, then he forms his preference over options on the basis of considerations such as "My subjective probability for 'p' is 3/4" and "My subjective utility for 'q' is 7." This means, given the explication thesis which equates such probabilities and utilities with beliefs and desires, that he forms his preference on the basis of self-ascriptions of beliefs and desires. The considerations deployed can equally well be cast as follows: "I believe to degree 3/4 that p" and "I desire that q with an intensity of degree 7." Why can they not be cast in a less subject-centered way as "It is 3/4 probable that p" and "It is desirable to degree 7 that q"? Because under the explication thesis subjective probability measures degree of belief, subjective utility degree of desire. The numbers given register the strength with which states like the belief that p and the desire that q are held, not aspects of the content of other states – states like the belief that it is probable that p or desirable that q.[23]

If the agent who uses decision theory as a calculus forms preferences over options on the basis of self-ascriptions of belief and desire, then this means that the property in virtue of which he comes to prefer one option to another ultimately refers back to his own desire-satisfaction. He prefers the option for the property of promising the most satisfaction of his preferences over relevant prospects. Suppose that I use decision theory as a calculus to decide between A and B, where the relevant possible outcomes are A_1 and A_2, B_1 and B_2. The lesson is that I will then come to prefer one or the other option for its property of answering in the most satisfactory way to my preferences over A_1, A_2, B_1, and B_2.

These considerations counsel against the calculative use of decision theory, for when in ordinary practice an agent comes to prefer one option to alternatives, he often prefers it for a property other than that of answering in a certain way to his prospect-desires; say, for the property of being an obligation of etiquette, being amusing, or being in the public interest. The agent's actual practice of decision-making is radically different from what it would be if he were to use decision theory as a calculus. Were he to apply decision theory in this way, then he would submit himself to the control of different property-desires from those which normally operate. He would be concerned in every decision with realizing the property of best satisfying his prospect-preferences, rather than with realizing independent properties like those of being mannerly, having fun, or advancing the common good.

But it may seem that I am overlooking an obvious objection. Suppose that I have a certain preference-ordering over the prospects A_1, A_2, B_1, and B_2, an ordering driven by my preferences over properties of those prospects: say, F_1, F_2, G_1, and G_2 respectively. If I make my decision between A and B in the ordinary way I will make it in the light of how the options do by F_1–G_2 properties; if I make it by using decision theory as a calculus, I shall make it in the light of how they answer to my A_1–B_2 preferences. But since the F_1–G_2 properties determine my A_1–B_2 preferences, this means that either way I shall make the same choice. And does that not entail that there is no significant difference between the two practices?

No, it does not. When I make a decision, forming a preference over certain options, desiderative structure means that two things become fixed: first the material object of my desire and second its formal object. Even if the two practices in our example generate a desire or preference for the same material object, the same option, the desire has a different formal object in each case; it brings a different value into play. In the one case the option is preferred for answering in a certain way to the agent's prospect-preferences over A_1, A_2, B_1, and B_2. In the other it is preferred for answering in a certain way to the properties F_1, F_2, G_1, and G_2.

The variation in formal object makes for a difference in the scope across times and modalities of the preference formed.[24] If I prefer an option for property K, then I prefer it here and now for any time or situation at which it retains that property; if I prefer it for property L, then I prefer it here and now for the different range of times and situations at which it retains that other property. If I prefer the option in our example for answering to my preferences over A_1–B_2, then assuming that I am concerned with my preferences at the time of action rather than now at the time of decision, I prefer it now only for times and situations at which I retain those preferences. If I prefer the option for how it answers to the F_1–G_2 properties, I prefer it now for times and situations where it continues to answer in that way. The scope is different in each case and that means that there is a sense of preference-satisfaction such that the preferences will have different satisfaction conditions. It will be possible to satisfy in that sense the preference with the one sort of formal object without satisfying the preference with the other.

Suppose, however, that in making my decision with regard to how the option answers to my preferences over A_1–B_2, I have my current actual prospect-preferences in view. Does that not mean, since these are driven by properties F_1–G_2 that the option-preference formed will have the same scope across times and modalities, regardless of difference in formal object? Yes, but there remains a difference in its scope across persons; I assume that the preference extends to different persons, given that it is driven by properties which abstract from the identity of the agent. If we ask in the two cases what course is preferred for the arbitrary agent facing exactly the same decision, then we are given different answers. In the one case the preference is that any agent with such and such prospect-preferences over A_1, A_2, B_1, and B_2 should choose the favored option. In the other case the preference is that any agent facing options that answer in the required way to properties F_1, F_2, G_1, and G_2 should do so. The difference in scope can scarcely be described as making for a difference in the satisfaction conditions of the preferences, since the notion of satisfaction suggests that one and the same agent is involved. What it makes for, more colloquially, is a difference in the universalization conditions of the two preferences (see Pettit 1987b, 1988a).

We have seen that the shift to using decision theory as a calculus, even if it has no effect on choice of option, will affect the values that drive an agent's decisions, the properties for which he prefers certain options over others. We have also seen that this change of value focus will mean a change in the satisfaction conditions, or at least the universalization conditions, of the agent's option-preferences. All of this said, however, an advocate of using decision theory as a calculus may still protest that it is unclear why we should worry about such a shift of value focus. The final question before us then is whether such a change is likely to make any practical difference to an agent.

The question, more generally, is whether it will make any practical difference for an agent to switch from one value set to another, if the sets yield the same output, supporting the same decisions. The answer is that the switch will make a difference if the value sets differ, as they are likely to do, on the input rather than on the output side: if they differ in the sorts of considerations that tend to support or subvert them. The answer in the general case dictates a negative response to the specific issue about using decision theory as a calculus, for the values that go with such an employment of the theory have a different profile on the input side from the values that more ordinarily move us.

One input to which it is generally appropriate to submit a set of values is the universalizability test. The challenge raised by this test is whether the agent can happily endorse, not just the decision dictated in his own case by the values he adopts, but also the decision dictated by those values for any other agent, including any agent whose action would affect him negatively. I submit that the values endorsed under a calculative use of decision theory are vulnerable to this test in a way in which the values endorsed in ordinary modes of decision-making are not.

Suppose that you are in the position of Socrates and that you are about to drink the hemlock, much to the distress of your friends, when you are challenged to put the values motivating that decision to the universalizability test. Imagine that you reached your decision out of concern that the option taken should be the honorable choice. In that case the universalizability test will hardly have any effect. You may acknowledge that you would probably feel differently about the option chosen were you in the position of your friends, but that need not cause you to weaken in your resolve; you will probably reckon that you would feel differently only because of being emotionally blinded, as they are surely blinded, to the importance of being honorable.

Imagine now that you reached your decision, using decision theory as a calculus, on the ground that the option taken promised the greatest satisfaction of your prospect-desires. It promised that satisfaction, of course, because it seemed to be the honorable choice, but the important thing in your calculations was not the source of the promised satisfaction, only the satisfaction itself. Consider then how this value orientation will fare under the universalizability test. Acknowledging that you would feel differently about the option chosen if you were in the position of any of your friends, acknowledging in other words that in their position you would not see the option as promising the greatest satisfaction of your prospect-desires, will you be as unshaken as before in your resolve to take the hemlock? Arguably not. You could think before that the feelings that you would have in the position of your friends should be discounted, being the product of blind emotion. Now you cannot take this view and you have to face the question: "Why should the satisfaction of the prospect-desires I have in the role of agent matter so much more than the satisfaction of the prospect-desires I would have in the position of my friends?"[25]

This line of thought shows that the values adopted in the switch to using decision theory as a calculus are more vulnerable to at least one sort of challenge than the values invoked in more regular decision-making. Even if the switch does not immediately mean that different options will be chosen, then, it is likely to be of practical significance. It is likely over the longer haul to generate a shift in the choices that the agent will make. In jargon that will ring a chord in decision-theorists, the switch may not directly alter the utilities that an agent attaches to various prospects but it will probably alter them indirectly, for it subjects the agent to a different utility kinematics.

We must conclude then that not only is decision theory an incomplete account of decision-making and a nonautonomous theory, it is also an impractical instrument for making decisions. This does not mean, of course, that decision theory has no value. On the contrary, it has the great merit of clearly explicating certain important features of our folk psychology. The lesson is only that the value of decision theory has to be carefully judged. While it explicates one part of folk psychology, it abstracts from another, and the abstraction places limitations on its utility as a descriptive and normative device.

APPENDIX

In "Truth and probability" Frank Ramsey begins with the assumption that, given his preferences, we can identify for each person an ethically neutral proposition with a probability of a half; a plausible example might be the proposition that a coin which is tossed in the air will come up heads.[26] Let this proposition be represented by "h." The proposition will be ethically neutral for the agent if and only if he is indifferent between two situations that differ only in whether it is true or false. It will have a probability of 1/2 for the agent if, for two possibilities A and B which leave the realization of "h" open and which are such that he prefers A to B, he is indifferent between the following gambles: A if h, B if not, and B if h, A if not. For short, he is indifferent between (AhB) and (BhA).

With this assumption in place, Ramsey suggests that we can operationalize a decision-theoretic view of the agent in roughly the following steps.

1 Among suitable items, find those items most preferred and least preferred by the agent, say A and Z, and assign these to the endpoints of an arbitrary scale, say between 0 and 1.

2 By a version of the Bayesian theory – the principle of rational preference – the gamble (AhZ) ought to appear at the midpoint of the scale, with a preference ranking or utility of 1/2. Find an item M such that the agent is indifferent between the gamble (AhZ) and M and assign this to the midpoint. (Alternatively, though this breaks with Ramsey, call the gamble "M.")

3 By the theory, the gambles (AhM) and (MhZ) ought to appear respectively on the quarter points of the scale, with utilities of 3/4 and 1/4. Find items F and R such that the agent is indifferent between (AhM) and F, (MhZ) and R, and assign these to the quarter points. (Alternatively, call these gambles "F" and "R" respectively.)

4 Continue filling in the scale by successive applications of this procedure.

5 If an item AA appears which the agent prefers to A, then find an item C on the scale such that he is indifferent betwen the gamble (AAhC) and A and assign a utility figure to AA on the basis of the theory. Use a similiar procedure to determine the utility of any item that appears to which Z is preferred.

6 Having established the utilities of relevant items, determine the probabilities of propositions other than h by the following procedure. For any proposition p, find items B, K, and V such that the agent prefers B to K to V but is indifferent between K and (BpV). Given the utilities for B, K, and V, the theory dictates the appropriate probability for p.

7 In order to establish the subjective expected utility of any option, find a gamble with which it can be equated and determine the expected utility that belongs to it.

The Ramsey procedure just described is useful, not just in showing how Bayesian decision theory might be made operational, but also in revealing that under this version of that theory an agent's subjective probabilities and utilities are all fixed by a relatively austere base – an appropriate preference ordering over appropriate items. That preference ordering enables us to identity an ethically neutral event with a probability of 1/2 and, as the seven steps show, it serves in principle to determine all the agent's subjective utilities and probabilities. Instead of our three relevance principles we might have postulated just that the agent has such an ordering. Equip an agent with that ordering and you will have done all that is required to equip him with a full set of subjective probabilities and utilities. Indeed, more than that, you will also have done all that is required to equip him with rational preferences.

But though this base is relatively austere, there is one way in which it is not so austere as it may seem. It assumes that there is no problem in determining the content of an agent's preference – in determining for example that in choosing this object over that he is expressing a preference for "a chair given he has a table" over "a table given he has a table" rather than for "a chair over a table," "something to sit on over something to write on," "something made of plastic over something made of wood," and so on. This feature of the procedure is worth noting, since it explains why decision theory does not get into trouble with the problem of determining the contents of subjective probabilities and utilities.[27] Decision theory assumes that that problem is solved. The point connects with the discussion of nonautonomy in section 4.

NOTES

I was helped by comments received when versions of this paper were read at seminars in the Australian National University and Oxford University. I was particularly helped by conversations with and comments from Paul Anand, Michael Bacharach, John Broome, Peter Gärdenfors, Susan Hurley, Frank

Jackson, David Lewis, Peter Menzies, Huw Price, and Michael Smith. I am also grateful for useful comments received from Edward Craig, Lloyd Humberstone, and Fred Schick.

1 The continuity assumption requires, roughly, that if P is preferred to Q, and there is a continuum of increasingly less preferred points as we move from P to Q, then for any S such that the agent prefers P to S and S to Q, there must be some point on the P–Q continuum such that he is indifferent between S and that point; there must not be a discontinuous leap from points preferred to S to points to which S is preferred. Continuity is broken by someone with strictly lexical preferences over the components of the packages on the P–Q continuum, someone for example who prefers any increase in X – any increase in the amount or chance of X – to any increase in Y, if each package has X and Y as components. If a person takes rights seriously then he may seem to have lexical preferences, for he will not sacrifice any increase, for example, in his own innocence or cleanness of hands (X), for an increase in certain other goods (Y) (see Pettit, 1987a, pp. 8–14). But rights may not introduce the offending sort of discontinuity, for even the most rights-respecting of people are willing to run a certain risk of imposing the ills against which rights are a protection for the attainment of goods that rights trump. I risk the taking of innocent life by driving to work and I do so, presumably, only for the convenience thereby attained.

2 For reviews, the first informal and the second technical, see Eells (1982, ch. 3) and Fishburn (1981, pp. 139–99).

3 This assumption is well characterized by Davidson (1980).

4 For a defence see Jackson and Pettit (forthcoming).

5 Notice, however, that to take them as more than fictions, in particular to identify utilities with desires – where desires are taken as more than fictions – need not be to equate utility with something felt, like pleasure. Desire satisfaction need not be something felt.

6 I ignore the complications required in virtue of the considerations raised in Lewis (1983a), Essay 10.

7 There is some further discussion of how to understand prospect-preference in section 4.

8 On this ambiguity see Jackson (1985b).

9 See the relevant essays in Raz (1978) and see Milligan (1980, ch. 3). The Gorman–Lancaster translation of commodities into characteristics offers a parallel in economics. See Sen (1982a, p. 30). The development of multi-attribute utility theory stems also from a recognition of the role of property-desires. See Keeney and Raiffa (1976) and Farquhar (1980, pp. 381–94).

10 Regular decision theory. I except the multi-attribute utility theory mentioned in note 9.

11 I owe the point to Frank Jackson. It is supported by the examples considered in the next section in the discussion of the nonautonomy claim.

12 For related points see Jackson (1985a). On desire *pro tanto*, and a difference between it and another sense of desire *prima facie*, see Hurley (1985–6). See

also her recent book (Hurley, 1989), which appeared after this paper was in near final draft.

13 Notice though that many decision theorists explicitly deny completeness (see, for example, Tversky, 1975, pp. 163–73). Notice too that multi-attribute utility theory, which was mentioned in note 9, stems from a recognition of the incompleteness of regular decision theory.

14 Some axiomizations of decision theory, most notably the Jeffrey–Bolker axiomatization, involve atomless algebras (see Jeffrey, 1983). While the principle of the co-determination of preferences is supported by decision theory generally, it should be noticed that it need not be fatal for decision theory if the rational agent's preference-ordering does not extend to all prospects (see Broome, 1990b).

15 Should he be reluctant not just to equate prospect-preference with brute disposition but also property-preference? Perhaps, for it is not clear that property-preference has to be brute in the same sense. After all, only some properties are taken by most of us to be desirable or undesirable and, aspiring as we do to attain agreement about which are which, most of us seem to think that if we only understand what is involved we shall agree about whether a given property makes for good or ill; of course, this is compatible with our weighting the properties in different ways.

16 I have been aided greatly in developing my thoughts here by conversations with Peter Gärdenfors and by reading Broome (1990a, b) and Hurley (1989).

17 The example is not mine but I do not know its provenance.

18 See Broome (1990a, b, ch. 4). For a different approach to the problem raised see Schick (1987).

19 Alternatively, as Broome notes, we might individuate options and outcomes to the finest level possible and then look for a principle to tell us which differences ought not rationally to matter.

20 A similar result follows on a different treatment of the counterexamples. We might say that the lesson of the Diamond example is that when inter-outcome properties, such as that related to fairness, serve to undermine Independence, then we reach a limit beyond which decision theory does not apply. But if we say this, then decision theory is nonautonomous in the sense of applying with in a boundary which it iself does not have the resources to discern.

21 This parallels a more familiar distinction in ethics (see Pettit and Brennan, 1986; Pettit, 1988b).

22 Of course there is a further looser sense in which an ideal like that offered by decision theory may relate to practice: by stimulating agents to be more systematic and rigorous in their thinking. I do not doubt but that decision theory often usefully plays this role.

23 Of course, this line is consistent with the claim that ordinary ascriptions of probability express degrees of belief, and that ordinary ascriptions of desirability degrees of desire.

24 Here I am indebted to collaborative work with Michael Smith; see Pettit and Smith (forthcoming).
   See Pettit (1987b, 1988a).

25 The general lesson in the offing is that universalizing decisions based on reasons of desire-satisfaction tends to generate utilitarianism (see Pettit, 1987b).

26 Reprinted in Ramsey (1978).

27 On that problem see, for example, Dretske (1986).

5

Decentralization, Duplicity, and Minimal Equity

John E. Roemer

1 INTRODUCTION

Imagine a social planner who has an endowment of n goods represented by a vector $\omega \in R^n$ to distribute to a population of agents whose utility functions for the goods he does not know. The planner's aim is to maximize some social welfare function W whose arguments are the utilities of the agents in the population. If he were to know that the ith agent has utility function u^i, he would find that allocation of goods $(x^1, \ldots, x^m)$, where $\Sigma x^i = \omega$, which maximizes $W[u^1(x^1), \ldots, u^m(x^m)]$. Not knowing the utility functions of the agents, what can he do? Suppose that the planner's goal is common knowledge; everyone knows that he seeks to maximize the social welfare function W. If he were to ask the agents to report their utility functions, or preferences, to him, it would in general be in the interest of an agent to misrepresent his preferences in order to appear, to the planner, to be the type of agent who should receive a large allocation of the goods. Can the planner design a system of reporting that, after all is said and done, will result in the allocation of goods that he would have assigned, had he in fact known the true preferences of the agents?

There are myriad applications to this problem of decentralization of resource allocation in the presence of asymmetric information. Consider a socialist planner, for instance, who has a stock of iron ore to distribute to a number of public enterprises for manufacture into steel. The enterprises have different production functions that are unknown to the planner. He seeks to find that distribution of the iron ore that will maximize total steel produced. He will, eventually, assign an amount of iron ore and an output quota to each enterprise manager. Each enterprise manager wants to fulfill his production quota with ease; it is in his interest to make the planner believe that his enterprise's production function is less good than it actually is. Can the planner design a method of reporting production functions, and consequent assignment of input–output quotas to the enterprises, that will result in the maximum possible output of steel, or something fairly close to it?

The second example illustrates a reason that the problem of decentralization of resource allocation in the presence of asymmetric information is interesting to someone, like myself, who believes that the future of socialism depends upon the substantial decentralization of economic activity in socialist economies. The failure of the model of central allocation in the twentieth-centry socialist experience, thus far, might be diagnosed as being due to its unsuccessful confrontation with the principal–agent problem,[1] in at least three forms: the planners are not perfect agents of the people, enterprise managers are not perfect agents of the planners, and the workers are not perfect agents of enterprise managers. One of the central claims of neoclassical economics is that a regime of private property and competitive markets is capable of overcoming a substantial fraction of the problems due to asymmetric information; unfortunately, there is associated with such a system a distribution of income and welfare that socialists often can not countenance. It is therefore of interest to know the extent to which a desirable distribution of income and welfare can be achieved in an economy whose transactions are characterized by asymmetric information, using institutions of decentralization other than the unfettered capitalist market.

During the past 15 years, economic theory has made substantial progress in understanding the extent to which problems like the ones posed above can be solved. An implementation theory has been constructed, which studies how a planner can implement a social welfare function, or, more generally, a social choice correspondence, when he does not know the preferences of (or technologies available to) the agents. The basic idea is that the planner designs a game that he requires the agents to play. It is assumed that the agents reach an equilibrium of this game. The planner announces a rule to the agents that assigns to each equilibrium of the game some allocation of the resources that he wishes to distribute. The game is cleverly designed so that, even though the planner does not know the preferences of the agents who are playing the game, the equilibria of the game induce, through the allocation rule, precisely the allocation of resources that the planner would have chosen, were he to have known the preferences of the agents in the beginning. Describing this procedure as a 'decentralized' one may puzzle the noneconomist, who is used to thinking of decentralization of resource allocation as synonymous with the use of markets. The procedure is so called because, once the planner announces publicly the rule by which the allocation is arrived at as a function of reports received, he has no further role in affecting resource allocation, which depends, from that point on, only upon the strategic decisions of the agents in the game that they play with each other.

In the next section of the paper, I shall provide an illustration of this procedure. However, there are a number of (what I consider to be) fatal weaknesses with implementation theory as a method of decentralizing transactions in actual societies. I shall summarize these after having presented the example in the next section. In the third section, I shall propose another approach to the implementation problem, based on some recent work, which, I shall argue, constitutes a more realistic approach to the problem.

Thus far, I have only motivated one word of the paper's title. The role of duplicity and equity will be clear later on: most briefly, minimal equity requires that the planner not penalize agents who report their true preferences to him,[2] and duplicity enters because it may be in the best interest of an agent to misrepresent his preferences when he reports to the planner. The political problem that is discussed in this paper is that, in a sense to made precise, it is impossible for the planner to expect honesty of the population, respect minimal equity, and maximize social welfare all at once. In general, one of these desiderata must be sacrificed.

2 NASH IMPLEMENTATION

We return to the original example of a planner who wishes to distribute a social endowment of, let us say, two goods to two agents whose preferences he does not know. The planner wishes to maximize social welfare, some function W of the utilities that the agents will have upon consuming the goods. In implementation theory he designs a game, which the agents must play, and an allocation rule, which associates with each equilibrium of the game an allocation. He hopes to construct the game and the allocation rule so that the allocation assigned to the game's equilibrium is precisely the allocation that he would have chosen had he known the preferences of the agents and computed the social welfare maximum directly. If, for a given aggregate endowment $\omega \in R^2$ and social welfare function W, a planner can construct a game G and an allocation rule φ which induce the welfare-maximizing allocation as described, we say that the pair (G, φ) is a *mechanism* that *implements W*.

Implementation theory can be divided into several chapters, depending upon the kind of game that the planner constructs and the equilibrium concept that is used. In dominant implementation, or implementation in dominant strategies, the planner constructs a game in normal form and requires an equilibrium in dominant strategies. It is almost never possible to implement a social welfare function *W* in dominant strategies, because there are so few games, so to speak, with dominant strategy equilibria. A special case of dominant implementation is Clarke–Groves implementation. If preferences are quite special (quasi-linear), then many social welfare functions can be "almost" implemented using the techniques of Clarke and Groves. I shall not describe these implementation theories here.

In the theory of Nash implementation, due to Eric Maskin, the planner constructs a game in normal form, and uses the Nash equilibrium concept.[3] In the following illustration of Nash implementation it is assumed that the two players are known by the planner to have "type A" preferences or "type B" preferences. In the Edgeworth box of figure 5.1, the indifference curves of the two agents, called Tom and Harry, are illustrated for all possible allocations of the two goods between them. (The length of the box is the aggregate endowment of the first good, and the height is the aggregate endowment of the second good.) The point T is the origin for reading Tom's indifference curves, and the point H is the origin for Harry's indifference curves. Suppose that it is known by the planner that either Tom and Harry both have type A preferences or they both have type B preferences. If it is the case that the preferences are both of type A, then the planner's social welfare function instructs him to implement the allocation labeled 'a', and if Tom and Harry have

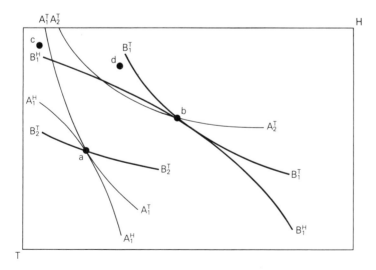

Figure 5.1

type B preferences he wishes to implement allocation b. Tom and Harry's type A indifference curves, labeled "A_1^T" and "A_1^H," through allocation a are drawn, and Tom's type A indifference curve A_2^T through b is drawn. Likewise, Tom and Harry's type B indifference curves B_1^T and B_1^H through b are drawn, and one of Tom's type B indifference curves B_2^T through a is drawn. We assume that both Tom and Harry know their own and each other's type.

Suppose, naively, that the planner simply asked Tom and Harry to report whether they had type A or type B preferences. Whether they each have type A or type B preferences, Tom will always say that they have B preferences, since he is better off at b than at a regardless, and Harry will always say that they have A preferences, since he is better off at a than at b in both cases. Thus the planner will learn nothing. He cannot deduce the true preferences from the reports, since he will receive the same reports in both cases AA and BB. He cannot, therefore, implement the desired allocation in this naive way.

The planner can implement his social welfare function, however, using the normal-form game with the matrix displayed in figure 5.2, which is to be read as follows. He specifies the allocations c and d in the Edgeworth box, as indicated, and constructs an allocation rule as indicated by the matrix. If Harry and Tom each report that the preference profile is AA, the planner distributes the goods according to allocation a. If Harry reports BB and Tom AA, then allocation d is implemented, and so on.

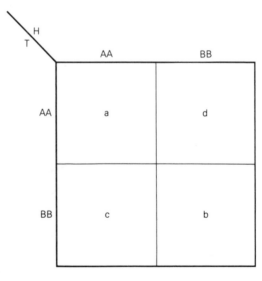

Figure 5.2

Let us suppose that the true preferences are in fact AA. I will show that it is a Nash equilibrium for both agents to report the truth, and that truthful reporting is the only Nash equilibrium. If Harry reports AA, would Tom deviate from the truth and report BB? No, because if he did then c would be implemented, which lies below Tom's A-type indifference curve through a. If Tom reports the truth, would Harry deviate and report BB? No, because d is worse than a for type-A Harry. This shows that truthful reporting is a Nash equilibrium. Is it the only one? The arguments just given also show that (AA, BB) and (BB, AA) are not Nash equilibria.[4] Is (BB, BB) a Nash equilibrium? Under this strategy pair, they receive b. If Tom deviates to AA, then d is implemented, which he prefers to b, and so it is not. Thus the unique Nash equilibrium of the game of figure 5.2, in the case when the true preferences are AA, is a. A similar argument shows that the unique Nash equilibrium of the game when the true preferences are BB is b. Thus the game in figure 5.2 implements the planner's social welfare function in Nash equilibrium: he can be assured that, whatever the true preferences, the game he has constructed will induce the players to report their true preferences in equilibrium, and that the desired allocation will be implemented.[5]

What Maskin did was to characterize precisely the class of social welfare functions (or social choice correspondences) that can be implemented in Nash equilibrium; that is, the set of W for which there exists a mechanism (G, φ) implementing W. (His characterization is considerably more general than the illustration indicates.) I shall argue, however, that, despite the beauty of Maskin's theory, it suffers from a number of practical defects – ones, that is, that would make it politically unfeasible in actual democratic societies.

First, in Maskin's theory, each agent must report to the planner the preferences of all the agents, not just his own.[6] This is not evident from my example: there, it suffices for each agent to report his own preferences because the planner knows *a priori* a good deal about the profile of preferences in the population (that is, that it is either AA or BB). The necessity to report a profile of preferences for the population is a practical defect because in real decentralization problems agents do not usually know the preferences of other agents and, even if they did, it is often not politically feasible to require some agents to report upon the traits of others. Welfare agencies do not collect information on the family status of their clients from the clients' neighbors.[7] There are some important exceptions: employers are asked to report the income of their employees to the Internal Revenue Service.

Second, it is often politically inappropriate to design a mechanism in which one agent is punished as a consequence of another's behavior.

Consider the illustrative game, in the case when the true preferences are AA. If both report truthfully, then a is implemented but if Tom lies, the allocation c is implemented which punishes Harry (as well as Tom).

Third, and this point is not well illustrated by the example, Nash implementation is fragile in this sense: an (irrational) deviation from optimal behavior by a very small number of players (even one) typically effects a large change in the assigned allocation. In particular, a small number of irrational agents can effect a large decrease in social welfare. This is an extreme practical defect in these mechanisms, since it cannot be expected that all agents will be rational. It certainly would be good policy for the planner to announce to each agent: "The mechanism has been constructed so that, if every agent but you announces the true profile of preferences, it is in your best interest to do likewise." However, it is still unlikely that such counsel will be followed by everyone.

Finally, and this is a more qualitative point, it is probably clear from the example that the games required to implement particular social welfare functions are complex; agents must be quite, and perhaps unrealistically, well educated to "play" them. One can say that the reasoning required of an agent in a mechanism to implement a particular social welfare function is considerably more complicated than is necessary to fill out an income tax schedule.

3 IMPLEMENTATION WITH INSPECTION

A central reason for the complex games needed to implement allocations in Nash equilibrium is that it is assumed, in the theory, that the planner knows very little about the actual profile of preferences in the population. In the illustration of the previous section, the planner does not know if he faces an AA population or a BB population. But in real-world situations, it is often the case that information about the relevant traits of the population is available to the planner; he has access to, for instance, survey information on a sample of the population.[8] Thus, while he may not know what the preferences or relevant trait of a particular agent are, he knows the statistical distribution of preferences in the population. Second, allocating agencies almost always have the ability to inspect the agents after they have made their reports, at a cost, at which time they can ascertain the relevant traits of the agent, but this capacity is not exploited in implementation theory. I shall describe how a planner, who knows the distribution of the relevant preferences or traits among the population, can implement a social welfare function, making use of the ability that he has to inspect the agents to verify their reports.

To return to the prototype example, we have a planner with an aggregate endowment of goods ω to distribute among a population with unknown preferences: now, however, he knows the statistical distribution of preferences in the population, but lacks information on the preferences of any individual. The planner will announce a policy, and require that each agent report his preferences. The policy consists of three parts: it will specify the *allocation* that an agent will receive as a function of the trait (preferences) he reports he has, the *probability* that he will be inspected as a function of the report he makes, and the *penalty allocation* he will receive should he be inspected and be discovered to have lied about his trait.[9] Suppose that the planner knows that there are r types in the population, where "type" means a specific set of preferences. The planner knows the types from survey data; label them 1 through r. A policy τ consists of a vector $t = (t_1, \ldots, t_r)$, a vector $q = (q_1, \ldots, q_r)$, and a vector $t^P = (t_1^P, \ldots, t_r^P)$, where t_i is the allocation of goods to an agent who reports that he is type i, q_i is the probability that such an agent will be inspected, and t_i^P is the penalty allocation that an agent who is discovered to have lied after inspection, and actually is of type i, receives. Thus, in an n-good allocation problem, t_i and t_i^P are vectors in R^n and q_i is a number between 0 and 1.

The planner's problem is to choose that policy $\tau = (t, q; t^P)$ that will maximize social welfare, subject to the constraint that the agents behave in a self-interested manner; that is, that facing a given policy each agent will make the report that maximizes his expected utility. For example, suppose that the von Neumann–Morgenstern utility function of a type i agent is u_i. Facing a policy τ, an agent of type i will calculate, for each $j \neq i$:

$$(1 - q_j)u_i(t_j) + q_j u_i(t_i^P) = u_{ij}(\tau) \qquad (5.1)$$

$u_{ij}(\tau)$ is the expected payoff to an agent of type i who reports that he is type j facing policy τ. He then compares the maximum expected payoff he can receive by dissembling with $u_i(t_i)$, which is his payoff if he reports truthfully facing τ. He reports to the planner that type that maximizes his expected payoff.

Let the expected payoff (in utility) to a player of type i facing a policy τ be $\varphi_i(\tau)$, calculated as just described:

$$\varphi_i(\tau) = \max\left[\max_j u_{ij}(t), u_i(t_i)\right]$$

The planner's problem is to calculate that policy τ from among all feasible policies that maximizes expected social welfare, which is $W[\varphi_1(\tau), \ldots,$

$\varphi_r(\tau)$]. It is the properties of this method for implementing social welfare functions that I wish to discuss. Formally, the implementation procedure is a Stackelberg game with the planner as leader.

3.1 The redistribution of income

Before proceeding, it will be useful to illustrate the method of implementation with inspection with some examples. Suppose there is a population with income levels $a_1, \ldots, a_r$. It is known that an agent of income a_i has a von Neumann–Morgenstern utility function u_i over money lotteries. The planner wishes to redistribute income in order to maximize a social welfare function W defined on the utilities that agents in the population receive. A *type* thus consists of a pair (a_i, u_i). The planner knows the distribution: there are N^i agents of type i in the population. The planner announces a policy $\tau = (t, q, t^P)$, where t_i is the transfer payment that an agent receives who reports that he is type i before inspection, q_i is the probability that such an agent will be inspected, and t_i^P is the transfer that an agent will receive if, upon inspection, he is discovered to have lied and is actually a type i. Negative transfers are taxes, and some agents will be taxed. Suppose that it costs the planner w_0 to carry out an inspection, and that inspection costs must come from the total taxes collected. Facing a proposed policy τ, the planner can compute the type that each (rational) agent will report – the expected-utility-maximizing type. He therefore knows which types will lie and which will report truthfully facing τ. Knowing the distribution of traits in the population, he can calculate his expected tax collection, transfers, and costs of inspections from the parameters of the policy. A policy is feasible in expectation if the sum of taxes collected minus transfers paid minus costs of inspection is nonnegative. For each feasible policy, he can calculate the expected utility $\varphi_i(\tau)$ of each type and associated expected social welfare $W[\varphi_1(\tau), \ldots, \varphi_r(\tau)]$. The planner's optimization problem is to choose that feasible policy which maximizes expected social welfare.

As described thus far, there is a simple thing for the planner to do which would in principle produce social welfare almost as high as could be achieved if he were actually to know the type of each agent, and were able to assign taxes and transfers to agents straightaway. Call the allocation that the planner would make, if he were to know the type of every agent, the first-best allocation. If the following procedure were to be acceptable, there would be almost no social cost due to the asymmetric information in the problem. The planner would simply announce small positive probabilities of inspection, but penalties so high that no agent would be willing to take the risk of lying. All agents would report truthfully (because of the expected disutility from lying); the planner would be committed to carrying out a small number of inspections, which costs something; except for these costs, he can assign the first-best allocation. Therefore, with arbitrarily severe penalties available, the planner could achieve social welfare arbitrarily close to the first-best allocation by making the inspection probabilities arbitrarily close to zero.

This procedure is unrealistic, however; it violates our requirement that the implementation mechanism be politically acceptable even when a small number of agents respond irrationally. Thus, in democratic societies at least, planners cannot announce the kind of severe penalties that would be required to induce all agents to tell the truth as just described.[10] Consequently, we shall further constrain the planner in the rest of the discussion. It will be assumed that he does not have the power to set penalties; they are provided to him by a legislature, which presumably sets them at a moderate level. The planner's only two policy instruments are now t and q. An alternative assumption is that the planner can choose the penalty allocations, but from a specified bounded set.

We can express this discussion formally as follows. First, we characterize the first-best allocation. There are N^i agents of type i and there are r types. We shall write the social welfare function of the planner as $W(\bar{u}_1, . . ., \bar{u}_r; N^1, . . ., N^r)$, where $\bar{u}_i$ is the utility enjoyed by an agent of type i. If the planner were to know the income–utility function pair of each agent, he would choose a transfer policy $t = (t_1, . . ., t_r)$ to

$$\max_t W[u_1(a_1 + t_1), . . ., u_r(a_r + t_r); N^1, . . ., N^r]$$

subject to (5.2)

$$\sum N^i t_i = 0 \qquad a_i + t_i \geq 0$$

The constraints in program (5.2) state that total transfers balance and no agent is reduced to an income less than zero. The solution to (5.2) is the *first-best policy*.

Now suppose that the planner knows only the distribution of income and preferences. He is given penalty transfers $t^P = (t_1^P, . . ., t_r^P)$ by the legislature. His problem is to choose a policy $\tau = (t, q; t^P)$ to

$$\max_{t,q} W[\varphi_1(\tau), . . ., \varphi_r(\tau); N^1, . . ., N^r]$$

subject to (5.3)

$$T(\tau) \leq 0 \qquad a_i + t_i \geq 0 \qquad t_i \geq t_i^P$$

where $T(\tau)$ is shorthand for the transfers paid plus inspection costs minus taxes collected when each agent responds optimally to the policy τ and the planner is committed to carrying out the inspections as stipulated by q. (The last constraint in (5.3) asserts that transfers assigned to an honest agent must be at least as great as what he would receive should he be penalized for dissembling.) To spell out the calculation of $T(\tau)$, let $N_{ji}(\tau)$ be the number of agents of type j who announce their type as i, facing a given policy τ, and let $N_i(\tau)$ be the total number of agents who announce that they are of type i facing τ. Then

$$T(t, q, t^P) = \sum_i \left\{ \sum_{j \neq i} [(1 - q_i)N_{ji}t_i + q_iN_{ji}t_j^P] + N_{ii}t_i + q_iw_0N_i \right\} \quad (5.4)$$

The relevant point is that the planner can calculate $T(\tau)$ for any policy, as he knows the traits (a_i, u_i) and their distribution $(N^1, \ldots, N^r)$. Thus, he can solve program (5.3) for the optimal policy. It is generally the case, of course, that the social welfare achieved in the solution of (5.3) is less than the social welfare achieved in the first-best solution of (5.2). We call the solution to (5.3) the second-best implementation of the problem, given the penalty allocations t^P. The difference between the values of the programs in (5.2) and (5.3) is the social cost of asymmetric information.

Before discussing some of the issues that arise with the method of implementation with inspection, I shall present three more examples of the allocation problems that can be implemented by using the procedure.

3.2 A production economy

There is an economy with two goods: the labor that the members of its population possess, and an output that can be produced from labor. People have utility functions over labor expended (or leisure consumed) and the output good. An agent's type is specified by his preferences and his endowment of labor (which can be taken to be a measure of his skill). There are r types; the utility function and labor endowment of type i are u_i and a_i respectively. There are N^i agents of type i. There is a production function $f(x) = y$ that converts labor x into output y. The planner knows the distribution of types and the production function.

The planner wishes to allocate labor and output among the population in order to maximize some social welfare function $W(\bar{u}_1, \ldots, \bar{u}_r; N^1, \ldots, N^r)$, where $\bar{u}_i$ is the expected utility that an agent of type i receives as a function of his expected labor-output allocation. Let the allocation of labor input required of an agent and output assigned to an agent of type i be (x_i, y_i). Suppose that the penalty allocations are given;

for type i it is (x_i^P, y_i^P). (If an agent of type i lies to the planner about his type and is discovered, he must contribute x_i^P labor and receive y_i^P output.) The planner's problem is to choose a policy $\tau = (x_1, y_1)$, $(x_2, y_2), \ldots, (x_r, y_r), q_1, \ldots, q_r]$, given the penalty allocations (x^P, y^P), to maximize expected social welfare, subject to the conditions that the total labor that the planner expects to collect from agents will suffice to produce the total output that he expects to distribute with the technology f, and subject to the requirement that

$$u(a_i - x_i, y_i) \geq u_i(a_i - x_i^P, y_i^P) \qquad \text{for all } i$$

which means that the penalty allocation for each type is no better for him than the allocation he receives for telling the truth.

This example is more complicated than the income distribution problem because there are two goods to allocate, an input and an output. More generally, implementation with inspection can be used, in principle, to allocate inputs and outputs in a many-good production economy.

3.3 The distribution of food stamps

A planner is endowed with a value C of food stamps, which he must distribute to a population as a function of some traits (income, number of children) that its members possess. The vector of traits of the ith type of agent is a_i, and there are N^i agents of type i. If an agent of type i receives x_i in food stamps, his utility is represented by a concave von Neumann–Morgenstern utility function $u(x_i, a_i)$. The planner wishes to maximize a social welfare function $W(\bar{u}_1, \ldots, \bar{u}_r; N^1, \ldots, N^r)$. He knows the distribution of the types in the population, but the traits of any particular agent are that agent's private information. Agents can be inspected, after their announcements, at a cost of w_0. If an agent of type i lies, he receives a penalty allocation of x_i^P in food stamps. The planner seeks that policy (x, q) that maximizes expected social welfare, subject to the constraint that the value of food stamps he expects to distribute when agents respond rationally to his policy announcement is less than or equal to C.

3.4 Distribution of an input to firms with unknown technologies

A planner has a stock $\bar{x}$ of an input (iron ore) to be used to produce an output y (steel). There is a population of enterprises that produce steel; an enterprise of type i has a production function

$$y = f(x, a_i)$$

where a_i is some vector of parameters. There are N^i firms of type i, and the planner knows the function f and the distribution of the a_i. He wishes to announce a policy $\tau = (x, y, q)$, where $x = (x_1, \ldots, x_r)$, $y = (y_1, \ldots, y_r)$, $q = (q_1, \ldots, q_r)$, and x_i is the amount of iron ore assigned to enterprises of type i, y_i is the amount of steel output assigned as a quota to that type, and q_i is the probability of inspecting an enterprise that announces that its type is a_i, which will maximize total steel output. Consider the penalty allocation (x^P, y^P) as given: if an enterprise of type i is discovered dissembling, it must produce y_i^P of steel from input x_i^P of iron ore.

The individual firm manager wants to maximize the output gap defined as $f(x_i, a_i) - y_i$, that is, the slack in his enterprise's plan. The utility function of the manager is $u(x_i, y_i, a_i) = v^i[f(x_i, a_i) - y_i]$, which is a von Neumann–Morgenstern utility of the output gap. In trying to maximize total output, the planner has some constraint set of workable plans, defined with respect to utilities it must allow the managers. The feasible set is defined by

$$W[u(x_1, y_1, a_1), \ldots, u(x_r, y_r, a_r); N^1, \ldots, N^r] \geq \overline{W}$$

where W is an increasing function of the utilities of the firm managers. We assume that f is concave in x and that the v^i are concave von Neumann–Morgenstern utility functions.

As in section 3.2, this example involves a two-dimensional allocation vector, of iron ore and steel.

4 THE POLITICAL TRADEOFFS

Consider the second-best solution to an implementation problem with inspection – the solution τ^* that maximizes expected social welfare under the inspection procedure. When facing the policy τ^*, is it necessarily the case that agents will report their traits truthfully to the planner? In the illustration I gave in section 2 of implementation in Nash equilibrium, this was the case. That is, does the planner's welfare-maximizing policy induce rational agents to be honest when reporting to the planner? The answer is, in general, no.[11]

This is, I think, unfortunate, because it is politically schizophrenic for a government to ask agents to report their traits and yet to depend upon some agents lying for the implementation of the optimal policy. The dissemblers are punished if caught, but the achievement of maximal expected social welfare depends upon them dissembling, and indeed depends upon many of the dissemblers escaping unpunished (for an agent is inspected only with some probability less than 1). To elaborate, the planner depends upon rational duplicity of agents in this sense: the policy he arrives at is optimal under the assumption that each agent chooses his announcement, when facing the policy, in order to maximize his expected utility, a choice which in general involves lying. If agents who optimally should lie do not, the social welfare associated with the policy will in general be lower than if they had responded optimally (and lied). It is, of course, critical to recall that duplicity as such does not count against social welfare as measured by W, although the point of this paragraph is that it is not right for a government to depend on it.

That the optimal policy may induce rational duplicity on the agents' part is a somewhat surprising result for those who have studied games with incomplete information, and requires some comment. In the theory of mechanism design, it is usually the case that a revelation principle can be proved, which states that the rational response of agents to the welfare-maximizing policy proposed by the principal is to report their traits truthfully.[12] It turns out that the reason why the revelation principle fails to hold in the model of implementation with inspections is due to our equity requirement: the requirement that an agent who announces his type as i, is inspected, and has told the truth, must not receive lower utility than an agent who announces his type as i and is not inspected. Suppose that we widen the class of feasible policies that the planner can assign to allow him to penalize truthful agents of type i who are inspected. The planner will now be able to achieve higher expected social welfare, in general, than in the second-best solution, as he is optimizing over a larger class of policies, and it can be proved that, in this case, the optimal policy will induce truthful reporting by all agents. But the tradeoff seems unacceptable, for to guarantee honesty from the agents, the planner must in general penalize some agents who tell the truth and are inspected.

If the government wants to respect the minimal equity requirement and to construct policies to which the rational response from agents is to report honestly, it must be content with what I will call third-best implementations of the welfare-maximizing problem. It can respect minimal equity and achieve honesty by restricting its set of feasible policies to a smaller set than the ones described in the four examples – to the set of feasible policies that will induce truth-telling from the agents. Formally, this is assured by appending to the constraints in the programs inequalities that guarantee truthful reporting. For instance, in (5.3), we would include additional inequalities of the form

$$u_i(a_i + t_i) \geq (1 - q_j)u_i(a_i + t_j) + q_j u_i(a_i + t_i^P)$$
$$\text{for all } i \text{ and } j \neq i \tag{5.5}$$

as constraints upon the choice of the policy τ. The right-hand side of inequality (5.5) is the expected utility that a type i agent receives from reporting that he is type j for some $j \neq i$, facing the policy $(t, q; t^P)$, and the left-hand side is the utility type i receives from reporting honestly. If constraints (5.5) are added to the planner's optimization problem, he is restricting his choice of policy to ones which make honesty the best response of the rational agent.

Because, in general, the third-best solution to the planner's problem achieves a lower social welfare than the second-best solution, social welfare must be sacrificed if the government insists upon this minimal equity requirement and rules out rational duplicity.

I have written the qualifier "in general" in describing the tradeoff between welfare and the two social norms because there is a class of problems in which the second-best solution does induce honest reporting by agents. Facing a policy τ, define $m(i, \tau)$, or $m(i)$ for short, to be the type that an agent of type i rationally announces to the planner. Our theorem (Ortuño-Ortin and Roemer, 1988) states that, if in the optimal policy $\tau^* = (t, q, t^P)$ the vector $t_{m(i)}$ dominates, componentwise, the vector t_i^P for all i, that is,

$$t_{m(i)} \geq t_i^P \qquad \text{for all } i \qquad (5.6)$$

then every agent will report truthfully to the planner. (That is, we shall have $m(i) = i$ for all i.)

Now there is a class of problems for which (5.6) automatically holds, and that is when there is only one commodity being distributed. Thus in the redistribution-of-income problem in section 3.1 and the food stamp problem in section 3.3, the second-best solution entails no rational duplicity. In the examples in sections 3.2 and 3.4, however, two goods are being allocated – in the first case, labor input and some output, and in the second case the input of iron ore and output of steel – and there is in general no guarantee that (5.6) will hold at the optimal policy. Nevertheless, the inequalities (5.6) are useful to the planner or the legislature, for if he (or it) is at liberty to choose the penalty allocations so that they are "small" in every component, then inequalities (5.6) are likely to hold at the optimal policy.

What if the planner cannot choose t^P so that (5.6) holds? Should he accept the possibility that he may put rational members of the population in a situation where they should lie to him, should he drop the equity requirement, or should he restrict himself to the third-best solution? I suppose that the answer depends on the numbers. If the welfare sacrifice involved in moving to the third-best solution is small, then it is probably worthwhile to do so. In any case, I do not think that it is a reasonable option to drop the equity requirement.

Finally, I remark that the four defects of implementation in Nash equilibrium outlined at the end of section 2 are rectified with the method of implementation with inspection. Each agent need only know his own trait, and need report only his trait to the planner. The mechanism is robust, in the sense that deviation by a small number of agents from their rational response to a policy will alter only trivially the allocation assigned to rational agents. (This may happen because a policy may not be quite feasible in the aggregate owing to the failure of some agents to optimize.) And if truth-telling turns out to be the optimal policy for agents, the planner can honestly announce that the agents need not carry out a complicated computation, since their best response is just to report their true trait to him.

On the other hand, if inspections are relatively costly, then the second-best implementation may not be terribly satisfactory in terms of social welfare. There is no general answer to the question of how many inspections the planner should carry out, except the trivial one: the optimal number, given the parameters of the problem. The more costly the inspections, the lower will be second-best social welfare.

5 CONCLUSION

The main points are these. Economists tend to be pessimistic about the possibilities of decentralizing resource allocation in a planned economy because the planner lacks knowledge of the traits of the agents involved. Their skepticism is reinforced by the theory of implementation of choice correspondence via game forms, which, on the whole, provides a negative answer to the question of whether a given social welfare function can be implemented by a suitably simple decentralized procedure. But the accepted theory of implementation begins with the extreme premise that the planner knows almost nothing about the traits of the population that are of concern to him, and in actual societies planners have access to survey data on the population's traits. We modeled this observation by assuming that the planner knows the frequency distribution of traits, although the trait of any specific individual is the agent's private information. When the planner has available an inspection procedure, then it is possible to implement, to an approximation, any social welfare function.

There are, however, some political tradeoffs involved in implementation with inspection. I proposed that a minimal equity condition and truthful reporting are political desiderata; the unfortunate conclusion is that insisting upon the first in general requires either dropping the second or not achieving the second-best level of social welfare.

More generally, the lesson is that decentralization of resource allocation using institutions other than markets involves its own political costs. (I have not discussed the political costs involved in using markets, which are a more common theme in the literature.) It should be pointed out that the problems in implementation with inspection that I have focused upon may be only of second order, while the first-order problems may be with the assumption that the planner has access to information on the frequency distribution of traits and that a workable inspection procedure exists. I have very little feel for the reasonableness of these assumptions.

It must be pointed out that the role of the kind of inspection procedure discussed here in (even) a socialist economy is necessarily limited. It is probable that for the allocation of thousands of commodities, markets, regulated in some fashion, must be used for decentralization, a topic that this paper does not study. I do not wish to leave readers with the false impression that I believe the institution of implementation with inspection to be the key to the decentralization of economic activity in a socialist economy. It may, however, be a partial answer.

NOTES

I am grateful to Ignacio Ortuño-Ortin for permission to report our joint work in this form. This work was supported by a research grant from the National Science Foundation. I thank the editors of this volume for helpful suggestions.
1 In a principal–agent problem, a principal wishes to achieve some goal, but must delegate tasks necessary for its achievement to agents whom he can only imperfectly observe or control. His problem is to design a system of incentives that induces the agents to act in a way that achieves the best possible result for him, given his inability to monitor them perfectly.
2 I call this minimal equity because the planner must not treat differently, in terms of resource allocation, agents who announce that they are a certain type and are not inspected, and those who announce that they are of that type, are inspected, and have told the truth.
3 Maskin's original paper (Maskin, 1977) is still unpublished; the material is available in a more recent paper (Maskin, 1985). Another early important contribution to implementation theory is that of Dasgupta et al. (1979).
4 By (AA, BB) I mean the strategy pair AA for Tom, BB for Harry.
5 In the Nash equilibrium of this game, each player reports the true profile. This is actually not necessary for implementation. It is only necessary that, whatever the agents report, they are assigned allocation a if their true preferences are AA and allocation b if their true preferences are BB.

6 In a recent paper, Saijo (1988) has shown that, in fact, this statement can be weakened. It suffices that each agent know and report the preferences of one other agent beside his own.

7 I am told that the Thatcher government in the United Kingdom violated this democratic norm.

8 One might question the accuracy of survey data; perhaps respondents will lie to the planner. This possibility is discounted here.

9 It is assumed that inspections always uncover the truth about an agent's type.

10 One reason, though certainly not the only one, for limitations on the size of penalties is that in reality inspection procedures are not perfect as is assumed here.

11 The social welfare functions in this paper do not include the welfare that a society might be said to derive when its population responds honestly to the planner. Nevertheless, I count such honesty as a desideratum.

12 For a discussion of the revelation principle, see Laffont (1988, ch. 5).

6

Deciding How to Decide: Is There a Regress Problem?

Holly Smith

Rational deliberation is itself an activity like any other, and the extent to which one should engage in it is subject to rational decision.

John Rawls, *A Theory of Justice*

A decision guide is a principle – such as "Maximize expected utility" – that evaluates actions and can be used by agents in selecting which action to perform. Most decision guides are designed to be usable in choosing actions even though the agent has incomplete knowledge about her options. Even so, an agent often wants or needs to acquire fuller information before making her choice. Thus choices are often preceded by activities in which the agent seeks, processes, and assesses relevant information. These activities, too, may be subject to choice. In deciding whether to invest her money in stocks or a money market account, should an agent consult government economic forecasters or the newsletter of her brokerage firm? It may be that the very same principle that guides an agent's choice of her target action can also be used to guide her choice of the kind of information-gathering that she should employ beforehand: consulting forecasts or newsletters, like investing in stocks or money markets, can be evaluated in terms of expected utilities.

Information-gathering includes a wide variety of processes, which I shall divide into two rough categories, *deliberation* and *research*. By "deliberation" I shall mean all those processes aimed at revealing to the agent, for purposes of making a decision, information that she already implicitly possesses. Deliberation includes recalling facts stored in memory, deducing implications of one's beliefs, working out one's subjective probability assignments, assigning values to the outcomes of one's choices, intellectually structuring the decision problem in order to apply one's decision-guiding principle to it, and so forth. Although much deliberation involves purely psychological operations, it need not: one often utilizes paper and pencil, or a hand calculator, to elicit the information desired. Research, on the other hand, involves acquiring information not already implicitly contained in the agent's "mental store." Straightforward examples of research include consulting authorities, conducting experiments, retrieving data from newspaper files, and similar activities.

Since deliberation and research are activities which one can choose, the selection of information-gathering activities may be guided by practical decision guides. Agents often have limited information, not only about their prospective acts, but also about their potential information-gathering activities. Hence they frequently have the need to gather information about information-gathering itself. In deciding whether consulting the government forecast or the brokerage newsletter has greater expected utility, the agent might ask advice from her economist friend. But she has other options as well: perhaps she can consult forecast track records in the financial journals. Which of these information-gathering activities should she employ? These options, too, may be evaluated, and a decision guide may be used in doing so.

It begins to appear that the use of decision guides in decision-making is threatened with some form of infinite regress. To decide how to act, we must first decide how to decide how to act. But to decide this, we must first decide how to decide how to decide how to act. But to decide this, we must first decide . . . *ad infinitum.* A variety of theorists have commented on this problem. A characteristic statement of it is given by Raiffa:

People often ask: "How do you know whether or not it is worth the effort to make a formal analysis of a decision problem? Is this a decision problem itself? Can you do a decision analysis of whether it is worth doing a decision analysis?" I don't know anyone who can give definitive answers to these questions, and I suspect one runs into a messy and explosive infinite regression if he tries to incorporate considerations of these questions into the formal structure of a decision-theoretic model. (Raiffa, 1968, p. 266)

Another statement is found in Elster, quoting Sidney Winter:

collecting information involves costs for the firm and therefore should be undertaken only to the extent that it is (expected to be) profitable. To acquire no information about the environment is irrational; to go on collecting information for a very long time equally so; and hence there must be some optimal amount of information that the firm should acquire. But once again this begs the question, since the "choice of a profit maximizing information structure itself requires information, and it is not apparent how the aspiring profit maximizer acquires this information or what guarantees that he does not pay an excessive price for it" [Winter, 1964–5, p. 262]. The demand for an optimal amount of evidence immediately leads to an infinite regress. (Elster, 1983, pp. 17–18)

Another expression of it can be found in Michael Resnik's recent introduction to decision theory:

The difficulty here can be put succinctly by observing that *whenever we apply decision theory we must make some choices*: At the least, we must pick the acts, states, and outcomes to be used in our problem specification. But if we use decision theory to make those choices, we must make yet another set of choices. This does not show that it is impossible to apply decision theory. But it does show that to avoid an infinite regress of decision analyses any application of the theory must be based ultimately on choices that are made without its benefit. Let us call such decisions *immediate decisions*. Now someone might object that insofar as decision theory defines rational decision making, only those decisions made with its benefit should count as rational. Thus immediate decisions are not rational, and because all decisions depend ultimately on these, no decisions are rational. (Resnik, 1987, p. 11)[1]

The problem has long been thought by a variety of moral philosophers to undermine utilitarianism as an ethical theory.[2] Russell Hardin, however, dismisses the problem. "It should embarrass philosophers that they have even taken this objection seriously," he states, and advises them to follow James March and Herbert Simon in escaping the quandary by noting that often we *satisfice*, we do not maximize: we stop calculating and considering when we find a merely adequate choice or action (Hardin, 1988, p. 4).

In this paper I shall investigate issues raised by the fact that decision guides can be used to guide choices over information-gathering activities as well as choices over the target acts themselves. Since most theorists have focused on the problem as it concerns deliberation rather than research, I shall confine my attention to the former. In a useful shorthand I shall call our topic the "regress problem." As we have seen, however, one of the issues is whether or not a regress need arise at all. I shall argue that it need not.

1 ALLEGED DIFFICULTIES RAISED BY THE REGRESS PROBLEM

It is commonly feared that the regress problem threatens the possibility of rational decision-making. But what exactly is the nature of the threat?

Many commentators fear that the regress problem will lead to "an infinite regress." This suggests that what is feared is an infinite regress of deliberations, each one a deliberation regarding the rationality of the subsequent deliberation. But very little reflection is required to see that no threat of this simple sort looms.

One possible way that the threat might arise is through the agent's being required to keep deferring – infinitely many times – the target acts while she deliberates further. (By "target acts" or "terminal acts" I shall mean those nondeliberative acts, the necessity for choosing among which originally creates the opportunity to deliberate.) But of course no such infinite postponement can take place. Even if the target acts can be deferred, there is only a finite length of time available for postponement. After some finite length of time, the agent (if human) will die, and by that point she has either performed a target act or failed to do so. She cannot deliberate indefinitely. Nor can she deliberate indefinitely in cases where the target acts cannot be deferred, but must be performed at some fixed time, say, t_n. Suppose that it is now any time t_1 in the agent's lifetime prior to t_n. The agent cannot move farther back in time in order to secure more time for deliberation about what to do at t_n. Hence there is no possibility of the agent's somehow being required to deliberate for an infinite amount of time before she performs some target act. If there is a genuine threat from the regress problem, it must arise in a more subtle fashion.

I suggest that the threat should be described as follows.

Universal Irrationality: the regress problem entails that there is no action which it is rational to perform.

Two arguments can be given in support of this threat. First, it can be argued that no act is rational, since there is always some superior act that it would have been more rational to perform, namely acquiring information about the act in question. But this is equally so when the act in question is an act of acquiring information. Thus *no* act is rational. Second, it can be argued (following Resnik) that to avoid an infinite regress, agents must make some initial decision without reference to relevant decision-guiding principles. Since such an unguided decision is irrational, so are all the subsequent decisions and actions that flow from it.

In what follows I shall investigate the extent to which Universal Irrationality represents a genuine threat to rational decision-making. In examining this threat, I shall ask whether solving the problem requires us to utilize satisficing rules, which would otherwise constitute less attractive decision guides.

It is helpful to distinguish (as I just did in rough form) between two different types of cases in which the regress problem may arise. In *nondeferral* cases, the agent possesses a set of alternative target actions performable only at a given time. The agent does not have the option of deferring any of these actions to any subsequent time. Any one of them must be performed at the given time; since the set of alternative acts is exhaustive, he must perform at least one of them at that time. In *deferral* cases at least some of the agent's set of alternatives can be deferred for future performance. In this paper I shall consider nondeferral cases only.

2 THE THREAT TO RATIONAL DECISION-MAKING WITH SIMPLE DECISION GUIDES

Agents' beliefs and information about their prospective actions vary enormously. Hence no single decision-guiding principle is adequate to the task of guiding every agent in every decision.[3] Some agents have fairly full and complex beliefs at the time of decision about their prospective actions. Such an agent could make a decision by utilizing, for example, the principle of maximizing expected utility (MEU). But some agents' beliefs are insufficient for them to derive any prescription from this principle. For example, an agent may lack beliefs about the probabilities of his actions' consequences.[4] Such an agent must employ a decision guide that requires a less comprehensive set of beliefs. He might do best to employ a satisficing rule or a maximining rule. The cognitive situation of every agent will be covered only if there is a hierarchy of decision guides, the joint range of which is sufficient to accommodate all the possible cognitive situations in which agents find themselves. If an agent's beliefs enable him to use either a higher or a lower decision guide in this hierarchy, then he ought to employ the higher one. For example, he ought to maximize expected utility rather than maximin. We can summarize this by saying that it is rational to choose an action if and only if it is prescribed by the highest decision guide that one is capable of using to make one's decision.[5]

Since to use a decision guide is to derive a prescription directly from it and one's beliefs, whether or not an agent can use a given decison guide depends on her actual beliefs at the time of decision. In determining what decision guide an agent can use, one must be strict about what beliefs an agent is counted as possessing. Suppose that proposition P = "Act A has an expected utility of 10 while its sole alternative, act B, has an expected utility of 8" and proposition Q = "Act A would maximize expected utility," and MEU states that an action is choiceworthy if and only if it would maximize expected utility. Further suppose that, at t_i, an agent believes P but not Q. (Perhaps she has not yet seen that P entails Q.) Because this agent would not derive a prescription from MEU in a one-step inferential process, she is not able at t_i to use MEU in deciding between A and B. Before she can use MEU, she must derive Q from P. This is a (very short) process of deliberation. She must perform it before she can use MEU.

Since an agent's beliefs can change over time, the highest usable decision guide available to her may change as well. In such a case the action that it would be rational for her to choose may also change. Suppose that an agent must choose between doing A or doing B on Wednesday. On Monday she calculates (correctly) that A would maximize her minimum gain. The maximin rule (MM) is the highest one she can employ: hence she would be rational on Monday to choose A for Wednesday. Suppose that she comes to believe on Tuesday that B would maximize expected utility. This belief renders the superior rule of maximizing expected utility usable by her as a decision guide. Assume that this rule prescribes B. Then on Tuesday, by contrast with Monday, she would be rational to choose B for Wednesday. Normally in this sort of case the agent's information improves. Of course it can also degenerate, for example if she forgets previously held beliefs. Either form of belief change shows that our previous meta-principle should incorporate temporal indexing in the following manner.

> M. It is rational to choose an action at t_i for performance at t_n if and only if that action is prescribed by the highest decision guide that the agent is capable of using at t_i to make her decision.

Note that this meta-principle is Janus-faced: it implicitly provides two evaluations. On the one hand it evaluates a choice at t_i as the one it would be rational to make, while on the other hand it evaluates an act at t_n as the one it would be rational to choose.

It is often thought that what it is rational to choose depends, not on the action's satisfying the relevant decision guide, but rather on the agent's justifiably believing that it does. This view is best interpreted as a view about the appropriate content of decision guides. On such a view, for example, the correct statement of MEU says that an action is choice-worthy if the agent is justified in believing it to maximize expected utility. I shall call such decision guides "justified-belief decision guides." The impact of the regress problem on decision-making utilizing justified-belief guides will be considered in section 3. For the remainder of this section and the next, I shall confine the discussion to what I call "simple" decision guides, ones that merely, for example, prescribe an act as choice-worthy if it maximizes expected utility.[6]

An agent who is attempting to decide which action to choose may have excellent reasons for engaging in deliberation. This form of information-gathering activity may be valuable in a variety of different ways. First, it may supply the agent with more accurate beliefs by which to judge, relative to a given decision guide (such as MEU), which options it prescribes as choiceworthy. Second, it may supply the agent with beliefs that will render a superior decision guide usable in his decision (for example, it may enable him to switch from using MM to using MEU). Third, it may improve the agent's assessment of which decision guide is superior. For example, deliberation may lead him to believe that maximining is superior to maximaxing. In all these ways it may enhance his chances of performing a superior act. Deliberation may also be valuable in ways not directly connected with the acquisition of information relevant to the problem at hand; for example, in using one's computer to generate spreadsheet information for a business decision, one may also discover that one's software should be replaced by a more powerful program.

Counterbalancing these possible gains are significant possible losses. First, some forms of deliberation possess intrinsic disvalue (for example, arithmetical calculation may be inherently unpleasant for the agent). Second, deliberation may involve opportunity costs (for example, tying up the computer in a prolonged statistical analysis prevents it from being put to other uses). Third, deliberation may have disadvantageous side-effects (for example, prolonged sessions in front of a video display terminal may cause the subsequent development of cataracts). Finally, deliberation may actually lead one to perform a less desirable act than one would have performed if one had thought less (for example, careful thought about the long-run consequences of a certain chess move blinds one to the immediate trap that it opens up).

Let us spell this out in terms of a concrete example in order to see how a regress problem might arise. Suppose that a physician must, at t_n^*, order one of two different types of chemotherapy (A or B) for a cancer patient. The physician believes that the outcome of this choice will be determined by the physiological origin of the cancer. He ascribes a probability of 0.6 to the cancer's having originated in the lungs (state S_1), and a probability of 0.4 to the cancer's having originated outside the lungs (state S_2). He believes that, if S_1 obtains, therapy A would produce 800 utiles, while therapy B would produce 600 utiles, and further that if S_2 obtains, therapy A would produce 700 utiles while therapy B would produce 1,200 utiles. He has not yet compared these figures to arrive at a belief as to which therapy would minimize the worst possible outcome, or which has the highest expected utility. It is now t_1, and the physician is choosing which therapy to prescribe. Part of his representation of the choice may be depicted as follows:

	$S_1(0.6)$	$S_2(0.4)$
A	800	700
B	600	1,200

Let us confine our attention to two possible decision guides, MEU and MM. I shall assume that MEU is superior to MM and ought to be used by any agent capable of using either. In this example I assume for simplicity that MM and MEU each select a unique act, but of course this is not generally the case.

At t_1 itself neither of these two decision guides can be used by the physician. However, if he engaged in suitable brief mental deliberation D_1 starting at t_1 he would shortly acquire beliefs sufficient for utilizing MM; if he engaged in slightly longer deliberation D_2 starting at t_1 he would acquire beliefs sufficient for utilizing MEU. Use of either decision guide would lead to his performance of the act actually prescribed by it. His options for t_1, and the acts that would follow them, can be represented as in figure 6.1. In this figure "D_1" represents the deliberative process that would enable the physician to apply MM to his options at t_n, and "D_2" represents the deliberative process that would enable him to apply MEU to the same options. "$(MM-t_n)$" and "$(MEU-t_n)$" represent the agent's deriving prescriptions for t_n from MM and MEU respectively. The dotted lines represent the duration of deliberation, while the broken lines represent the agent's "activities" following his derivation of a prescription. To simplify discussion of this case I shall assume that these activities (which of course may not involve overt actions at all) have zero utility. Thus in option 2 the physician calculates (D_2) the expected utilities of A and B, derives a prescription (MEU-t_n) for B as having the highest expected utility at t_n, and finally does B. Note that this figure represents the physician's possible choices as a very well-informed observer might understand it, not necessarily as the physician does. The physician, for example, does not realize at t_1 that his calculating which act would maximize expected utility would lead to his performing B at t_n. *His* mental representation of his choice

Figure 6.1

problem might refer to the act at t_n as "whatever terminal act is prescribed by MM."[7]

Because deliberation and immediate choice have their costs and benefits, which can be measured in utilities, we can ask which alternative at t_1 it is rational (according to meta-principle M) for the physician to adopt.[8] For example, suppose that MEU is the highest decision guide that the physician is capable of using with respect to his options at t_1. Does MEU recommend that the physician deliberate in order to apply MM (as in option 1), or does it recommend that he deliberate at greater length in order to apply MEU (as in option 2)? The physician himself may ask this question as he seeks guidance in choosing which form of deliberation to utilize. But this choice, too, may be assisted by deliberation at a higher level. For example, if he does not already know the expected consequences of deliberating in order to apply MEU, he may need to calculate these in order to apply MEU to *this* choice. But this calculation also has its costs and benefits according to various decision guides, and so a choice must be made as to whether or not to carry it out. And the agent may need to deliberate before making this choice. Any of these forms of deliberation could be carried out at t_1 as alternatives to D_1 and D_2.

Taking this into account, we can more fully represent the physician's set of options as in figure 6.2. This diagram can be read on the model of figure 6.1. For example, in option 3, the physician begins by deliberating about deliberation at a lower level. He calculates (D_1^*) the worst possible outcomes of (a) D_1, that is, calculating the security levels of A and B and then applying MM to his choice of A versus B, and (b) D_2, that is, calculating the expected utilities of A and B and then applying MEU to his choice of A versus B. On this basis he derives a prescription (MM-t_2) from MM to perform D_1. He then derives a prescription (MM-t_n) to perform act A at t_n and finally performs act A itself. (Note that I am here assuming that MM, when applied to the physician's choice

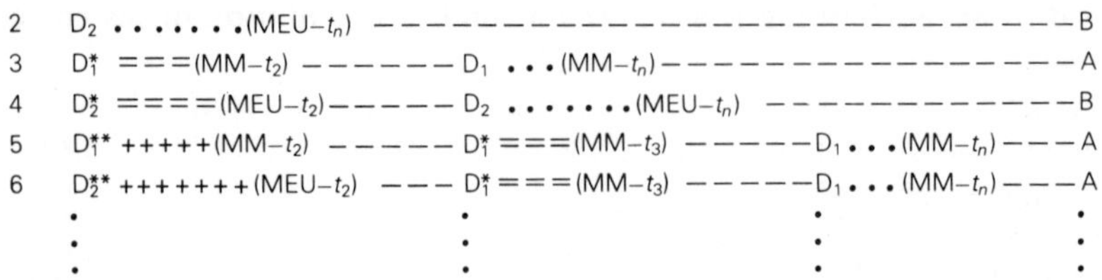

	t_1	t_2	t_3	t_n
1	D_1 ...(MM-t_n) —			A
2	D_2 ....(MEU-t_n) —			B
3	D_1^* ===(MM-t_2) — — — — — — D_1 ...(MM-t_n) — — — — — — — — — — — — —			A
4	D_2^* ====(MEU-t_2)— — — — — D_2 ....(MEU-t_n) — — — — — — — — — — —			B
5	D_1^{**} +++++(MM-t_2) — — — — — D_1^* ===(MM-t_3) — — — — —D_1 ...(MM-t_n) — — —A			
6	D_2^{**} +++++++(MEU-t_2) — — — D_1^* ===(MM-t_3) — — — — —D_1 ...(MM-t_n) — — —A			
	·	·	·	·
	·	·	·	·
	·	·	·	·

Figure 6.2

of what type of deliberation to engage in, prescribes deliberation relevant to the future application of MM itself. However, there is no reason to suppose that a decision guide will always prescribe deliberation leading to its subsequent own use. Option 6 reflects this fact. Note also that in order to carry out, say, D_1^*, the physician need not actually carry out the deliberations about which he deliberates.) In option 5, the physician calculates (D_1^{**}) the worst possible outcomes of performing D_1^* or D_2^* at t_2. On this basis he derives a prescription ($MM-t_2$) from MM to perform D_1^* at t_2. He then performs D_1^* as just described.

2.1 Universal irrationality: the first argument

We construed the threat posed by the regress problem as a threat of Universal Irrationality, according to which every action is irrational to perform. Two arguments were given for this threat. First, it was argued that no act is rational, since there is always some superior act that it would have been more rational to perform instead, namely acquiring information about the act in question. Second, it was argued that, to avoid an infinite regress, agents must make some initial decision without reference to relevant decision-guiding principles. Since such an unguided decision is irrational, so are all the subsequent decisions and actions that flow from it.

Let us examine the first of these arguments. In terms of figure 6.2 we can see that the argument assumes that (for example) it would not be rational for the physician to perform D_1 at t_1, because it would be more rational for him instead to deliberate about performing D_1. That is, it would be more rational for him to perform, say, D_1^* at t_1, deliberating about whether to perform D_1 at t_2. But by parallel reasoning it would not be rational for him to perform D_1^* at t_1 either, because it would be more rational instead to deliberate about performing D_1^* – for instance, to perform D_1^{**} at t_1, deliberating about whether to perform D_1^* at t_2. And similar reasons would be introduced for rejecting any deliberation at t_1 in favor of deliberating at t_1 about performing that deliberation later.

In order to conclude that no act at t_1 is rational, the argument requires that each agent possess an infinite number of alternatives for any given time, each alternative incorporating a higher level of deliberation about lower-level deliberations. (Otherwise the alternative incorporating the highest level of deliberation would emerge as the rational act, since no superior deliberation concerning it would be available to the agent.)

The descending dots in figure 6.2 suggest that the physician does indeed possess an infinite number of appropriate alternatives at t_1. But is this really the case? It is sometimes argued on metaphysical grounds that every agent, on every occasion, possesses an infinite number of alternatives. Even if true, however, this would not give rise to the problem of Universal Irrationality. This problem is only raised if the agent has a nonterminating ascending series of alternatives in each of which the agent deliberates about deliberating at the next lowest level. If the physician's alternatives, depicted in figure 6.2, ascend infinitely in the same pattern, this fact would provide a necessary condition for success of the first argument for Universal Irrationality of actions (necessary, but not sufficient, since the first argument for Universal Irrationality assumes *both* that there is an infinitely ascending set of deliberation alternatives *and* that each alternative involving a higher level of deliberation is superior to the alternatives involving any lower level of deliberation).

However, there is good reason to think that the alternatives available to the physician (or any other agent) cannot ascend infinitely in the same pattern. Any act must take some finite amount of time.[9] Hence an agent cannot, within a finite amount of time such as t_1 through t_n, perform a sequence of acts having infinitely many members. But this is what the existence of an infinite ascending series of deliberation alternatives on the model of figure 6.2. would require. For any option N, however densely packed with deliberations about deliberations, there would have to exist a higher-level option including an additional deliberation about those deliberations. At some point this would no longer be possible, since there are only so many acts of deliberation that an agent can squeeze into a finite span of time. When this point is reached, the terminal option has been reached in the agent's series of alternatives of the figure 6.2 type.

Unfortunately, even if the number of deliberations that can be packed into a finite time span is finite, we cannot infer from this that there is an upper limit on the *level* of deliberation that an agent may perform, for an agent might possess alternatives which involve "gappy" sequences of deliberation. In these options an episode of deliberation at one level is not followed by deliberation at the appropriate next-lowest level. Thus in our current example the physician might have the following gappy option:

$$D_1^{**} + + + + + (MM-t_n) - - - - - - - - - - - - - - - - - A$$

Here, although D_1^{**} consists of calculating the security levels of performing D_1^{*} and D_2^{*}, the physician does not appropriately proceed to either D_1^{*} or D_2^{*}, but rather leaps directly to applying MM to the choice of A versus B. Since it seems possible to perform such a sequence, the previous argument establishes no upper limit on the level of deliberation that an alternative might involve. For example, suppose that the agent can only

t_1	t_2	t_3	t_n
1	D_1 ...(MM–t_n) — A		
2	D_2 ....(MEU–t_n) — B		
3	D_1^* ===(MM–t_2) — — — — — — D_1 ...(MM–t_n) — — — — — — — — — — — — — A		
4	D_2^* =====(MEU–t_2) — — — D_2 ....(MEU–t_n) — — — — — — — — — — — B		
5	D_1^{**} +++++(MM–t_2) — — — — — D_1^* ===(MM–t_3) — — — — — D_1 ...(MM–t_n) — — A		
6	D_2^{**} +++++++(MEU–t_2) — — — D_1^* ===(MM–t_3) — — — — — D_1 ..(MM–t_n) — — — A		
7	D_1^{**} ....(MM–t_2) — — — — D_2^{**} +++++++(MEU–t_3) — — D_1^* ===(MM–t_n) — — B		
8	D_2^{**} ....(MEU–t_2) — — — D_2^{**} +++++++(MEU–t_3) — — D_1^* ===(MM–t_n) — — A		
9	D_1^{***} =======(MM–t_2) — — D_1^{**} ....(MM–t_3) — — — D_2^{**} +++++++++++A		
10	D_2^{***} ========(MEU–t_2) — D_2^{**} ....(MEU–t_3) — — D_1^{**} +++++++++ B		
11	D_1^{****} +++++++(MM–t_2) — — D_1^{***} =======(MM–t_3) — D_1^{**} .... A		

Figure 6.3

perform three deliberations between t_1 and t_n, as shown in figure 6.3.[10] Even so, if he performs gappy sequences, he would have the depicted ascending series of options available. Notice that (after option 6) as the level of the initial deliberation performed at t_1 goes up, lower-level deliberations drop out of the sequence in order to make room for the initial deliberation.

With the availability of gappy options of this sort it will be true that, for any given level of deliberation, the agent might perform a gappy option incorporating that level of deliberation as the initial act. Hence, for any given level of deliberation, the agent will have a (gappy) alternative initiated by a higher-level deliberation about that deliberation. Thus the threat of Universal Irrationality reasserts itself.

We should not forget, however, that human beings have severe constraints on their cognitive processing abilities. These constraints undoubtedly rule out any possibility of an agent's genuinely possessing the option of deliberating at a very high level, despite the possibility of performing gappy sequences. It already strains our capacities to grasp the physician's options as I have shown them in figures 6.2 and 6.3; any option much more complicated than D_1^{**} probably exceeds what any normal agent could actually perform.

But suppose that we waive this point. Let us grant, *arguendo*, that agents possess infinitely ascending series of (gappy) deliberation alternatives. Does this drive us to the conclusion that no act is ever rational to choose, because for any given act, some alternative act involving a higher level of deliberation would have been superior? The answer is no.

I shall argue for this answer in detail, but it is worth noting the intuitive plausibility of this answer. Deliberation, as we have seen, may have beneficial effects. But it may also have significant costs, and there is no reason to suppose in advance – as the first argument for Universal Irrationality supposes – that the benefits always outweigh the costs.

According to meta-principle M, two conditions must be met in order for an act to be rational for the agent to choose and perform. First, there must be at least one legitimate decision guide that the agent is capable of using to make his decision. Second, some act must be prescribed by the agent's highest usable decision guide. (This act is rational for him to choose and perform. Notice, as was pointed out in note 5, that the relevance of a decision guide in determining which act is rational for an agent is partly a function of the decision guide's usability for the agent. Its usability depends on the agent's stock of beliefs. But the rationality of the act is determined by its being prescribed by the decision guide, not by the agent's believing that it is prescribed by the decision guide. He may not believe this.) Are these conditions satisfied in the physician's case – is there an alternative at t_1 that the physician would be rational to choose immediately prior to t_1, say at t_0? I shall argue that there is such an alternative; it provides a counter example to Universal Irrationality. Indeed, I shall argue even more strongly that there is a significant class of such counterexamples. Let us suppose that the physician believes at t_0 that the maximin action for t_1 is D_1. This belief renders MM usable by the physician at t_0 with respect to his alternatives for t_1. Hence the first condition is met. Let us further assume that MM is the physician's highest usable decision guide. The only remaining question is whether MM prescribes any action for t_1. Given that the physician has – and, let us stipulate, believes that he has – an infinite number of alternatives for t_1, can MM prescribe any action for t_1?

Under certain plausible assumptions, MM does prescribe an alternative for t_1; in particular, it prescribes D_1. Moreover, these assumptions are ones that may frequently hold in cases having the same structure as the physician's present case. Any cases having this structure, and for which these assumptions hold, will be ones in which MM prescribes the analog to D_1. That is, it prescribes calculating what terminal action MM requires, and then performing that action. In these cases, contrary to the first argument for Universal Irrationality, meta-principle M does not imply that, for any alternative, it would always be better for the agent to deliberate about that alternative.

What are these assumptions? Examining the physician's case we can see that the security level (utility of the worst possible outcome) of any act at t_1 is determined by two variables: (a) the intrinsic security level of the physician's deliberative process between t_1 and t_n (for example, the process $D_1^* = = = (MM-t_2)D_1 \ldots (MM-t_n)$ in option 3), and (b) the intrinsic security level of the terminal act (for example, terminal act B in option 2) that he would perform at t_n. By "intrinsic security level of his deliberative process" I mean the security level it possesses *apart from* the possible terminal acts to which it may lead; by "intrinsic security level of the terminal act" I mean the security level it possesses apart from the processes leading up to it. Of course, in a realistic case a deliberative process may have side-effects that influence the act's security level. However, since the presence of such effects is immaterial to our concern, I shall assume that the only possible effects are those inherent in deliberation itself.

If a given alternative at t_1 involves (a) a deliberative process having an intrinsic security level at least as high as that of any alternative, and (b) a terminal action having an intrinsic security level at least as high as that of any alternative, then that alternative is prescribed by MM. There are plausible assumptions under which D_1 meets both these conditions. (Of course, D_1 might be prescribed by MM even if it met only one of these conditions. But I shall argue that it meets both. This fact makes it unnecessary to quantify and compare the values of the security levels in question.)

Let us first consider the intrinsic security level of the deliberative process involved in D_1. Suppose that deliberation in itself always has disutility for the agent, that longer deliberation has greater disutility than briefer deliberation, that higher-level deliberation has greater disutility than lower-level deliberation of the same duration, and that all alternatives to D_1 involve either longer or higher-level deliberation than D_1 itself. It follows that D_1's deliberative process has a higher intrinsic security level than the deliberative process involved in any of its alternatives, since D_1 (being the shortest and lowest-level deliberation) involves, for certain, less intrinsic disutility for the agent.

Let us next look at the intrinsic security level of the terminal action that the physician would perform if he performed D_1. Suppose that if the physician performs D_1 he will then perform, at t_n, the action that maximizes the minimum possible gain. The terminal action that follows any alternative to D_1 cannot have a higher intrinsic security level than this.[11]

Since the intrinsic security level of D_1's deliberative process surpasses those of its alternatives, and the intrinsic security level of its terminal act at least equals those of its alternatives, D_1's overall security level exceeds theirs. It is prescribed by MM as the maximin act.

The assumptions that led to this conclusion may hold in a number of cases. Moreover, the physician himself may have noted their truth in previous cases, and concluded that in all cases of this sort the maximin act involves calculating the security levels of the terminal acts. This conclusion may be what leads him to believe, as we assumed, that D_1 would maximize the minimum possible gain. (Recall that his having this belief makes MM usable by him for deciding what to do at t_1.) In describing the case I simply assumed that he had this belief. We can now see that the belief need not be unreasoned or arbitrary.

I have described assumptions under which MM prescribes an act for the physician, and under which the physician would be rational to choose and perform that act. These assumptions are not bizarre or outlandish. On the contrary, they are likely to hold in many cases having the structure of the physician's case. Hence we have undermined the threat of Universal Irrationality. There are at least some cases, and possibly a great many, in which some particular act would be rational for the agent to perform. It is notable that this act does not involve deliberation at a very high level. The quest for rationality need not drive agents to higher and higher realms of deliberation about deliberation. We may also note that this demonstration does not depend on idiosyncratic features of MM as a decision guide. Similar conclusions can be reached about MEU, an exercise that I shall leave to the reader.[12]

Of course there are other kinds of cases in which the agent cannot derive any prescription from MM. Suppose, contrary to our previous assumptions, that the physician derives substantial positive utility from deliberation, and greater utility from higher levels of deliberation. Then MM rates any act involving more and higher deliberation as superior to any act involving less and lower deliberation. If the physician genuinely possessed an infinitely ascending set of deliberation alternatives, then MM could not select any alternative at t_1 as the most rational.

But this kind of case does not pose a problem for the rationality of decision-making that needs to be taken seriously in the context of this discussion. First, such conditions are highly unlikely – much less likely than those previously laid out. Normal cases will resemble our previous case more than this one. Second, the underlying phenomenon that produces the untoward result in the revised case has nothing to do with the hierarchical structure of deliberation. The result only arises because of the bizarre character of the agent's preferences. Similar problems can arise in any case involving an infinitely large set of (nondeliberation) alternatives for which the agent has ever-increasing utility values. For example, if an agent derives higher utility the faster she drives her car, and for each speed at which she can drive her car there is another faster speed at which she could drive it instead, then (assuming all other possible outcomes remain stable across her alternatives) MM can select no action as the most rational one for her. The problem we see here has nothing to do with the hierarchical structure of deliberation. Moreover, the fact that in the unusual conditions just described MM prescribes no act for the physician only shows that he is unable to apply MM as a decision guide. There may be other decision guides that he can apply, and the highest of these will dictate what it is rational for him to do. A satisficing decision guide is one example of the kind of principle that can cope with this sort of situation. But the bottom line is this: we have found a general class of cases in which an action can be identified as rational, and so we can reject the claim that the regress problem shows that *no* action can ever be rational.

In general, there is no reason to think that an agent's highest applicable decision guide will require very high levels of deliberation. In normal cases (ones where the agent does not derive positive utility from the process of deliberation itself), the primary reason to deliberate is to enable oneself to make a better choice about the terminal acts (acts A and B in the physician's case). As we have seen, the only way in which an agent can engage in options involving very high levels of deliberation is for him to perform "gappy" sequences. We saw, however, that the proper sequence of deliberations in such options is broken, so that "pre-gap" deliberations do not exercise proper normative control over "post-gap" deliberations and acts. It is unlikely that the agent gains anything by pursuing such gappy options, since they are unlikely to enable him to make a better choice about his terminal acts. If any act of his is rational, it would normally involve a sufficiently low level of deliberation to avoid gappy sequences.

2.2 Universal irrationality: the second argument

Two arguments for Universal Irrationality were described. We have now examined the first of these and found it wanting. The second argument states that, to avoid an infinite regress, an agent must make some initial decision without reference to relevant decision-guiding principles. Since, according to the argument, such an unguided decision is irrational, so are all the subsequent deliberations and acts flowing from it. (Since, in conjunction with meta-principle M, we have already implicitly introduced the term "irrational" to express another concept, let us label unguided decisions "arbitrary" rather than "irrational.") This argument is mistaken. Consider again the case of the physician as described in connection with figure 6.2. In assessing the second argument we must consider two distinct scenarios. In the first the physician has never made a decision prior to his decision at t_0 with respect to his options at t_1; this decision is an "initial decision" in the fullest sense. In this scenario, any decision he makes at t_0 cannot be tainted by previous defective decisions. (Of course it is implausible that an adult agent should never have made a decision, but ignore this.) Despite his lack of decision-making experience, at t_0 the physician correctly believes that MM is his highest usable decision guide. Moreover he possesses enough beliefs at t_0 to enable him to derive a prescription from MM to perfrom D_1. Thus MM is usable by him. In deriving this prescription and choosing to perform D_1, he performs an "initial decision." But, *contra* the above argument, this decision is guided by a relevant decision-guiding principle, namely MM. The mere fact that the decision is the first decision that the agent has ever made in no way shows that it cannot be guided by a correct decision guide. Without making any prior decisions, the agent may nonetheless have acquired (say, through early education and through a combination of perception and natural induction) the beliefs about decision guides and about his circumstances necessary for making a guided decision. So his decision is not arbitrary, and it does not taint any of the acts or deliberations flowing from it. It need not be the case, then, that an infinite regress can only be avoided by engaging in arbitrarily unguided initial decisions.

Now let us consider the second scenario. In this scenario the physician does make an arbitrary decision, one unguided by any decision guide. Need this arbitrary decision taint the subsequent decisions and acts that issue from it? Suppose that the physician reads an article about decision theory at $t-1$. Reading this article influences his beliefs about his choice problem for t_0, but the act of reading the article itself is performed completely spontaneously, without reference to any decision-guiding principle. The decision to read the article is arbitrary. The decision to read the article results in the physician's deciding at t_0 to comply with MM by performing D_1 at t_1. Does this mean that the decision to perform D_1 is in some way defective? As far as I can see, the answer is no. Although the decision to read the article is arbitrary, and this decision leads to the decision to perform D_1, the decision to perform D_1 is nevertheless nonarbitrary – it is guided by a relevant decision guide. Moreover, if the highest decision guide usable by the agent at t_0 dictates his choosing D_1 at t_1, then that choice is rational (as is the performance of D_1 itself). In this circumstance both the decision to perform D_1 and the performance of D_1 itself are dictated by the Janus-faced meta-principle M. The fact that an arbitrary choice prior to a given decision provided information that influenced that decision has no tendency to show that the decision itself is arbitrary or irrational. Nor does there seem to be any other substantive sense in which this decision is irrational. We can conclude that the second argument for Universal Irrationality has even less foundation than the first.[13]

2.3 The role of satisficing principles

Let us note an important implication of our discussion. Many theorists such as Elster and Hardin appear to believe that the solution to the regress problem requires agents to utilize satisficing principles to guide their decisions (Elster, 1983, p. 18; Hardin, 1988, p. 4). Since such rules appear on other grounds to be inferior to traditional maximizing decision guides, the necessity of invoking this solution may show that the regress problem demonstrates an important deficiency in the rationality of decision-making.

But we must be careful before drawing this conclusion. On the one hand, we should remember our previous admission that, quite apart from the regress problem, agents need a large range of decision principles to guide their decision-making. Agents often lack sufficient beliefs about their terminal actions to use such decision guides as MEU or even MM, and so must turn to lower-ranking decision guides. Indeed, to assist all agents making all decisions, however cognitively impoverished those agents may be, a very large number of decision guides may be required. Some of these principles will undoubtedly be satisficing principles. Hence, even if there were no regress problem, satisficing principles would still be an important weapon in our arsenal of decision guides. Principles such as MEU cannot do the work alone. If the regress problem forces decision-makers to turn to satisficing principles, its doing so hardly introduces a new element into the practice of making decisions.

Second, we have seen that satisficing principles are *not* required to solve the regress problem. We have described a case in which the decision-maker's use of MM avoids any problem arising from potential regression in deliberation. In such cases the agent need not, and should not, follow a satisficing principle when a superior decision guide will serve.[14] Of course satisficing principles often enable agents to derive prescriptions for action quickly and on the basis of sparse information. Hence the rational agent will often deliberate in order to apply a satisficing principle rather than some other. Satisficing principles have their place in the hierarchy of decision guides. But the regress problem often can, and should, be defused without invoking them.

3 JUSTIFIED-BELIEF DECISION GUIDES

In section 2 we considered whether the regress problem threatens the rationality of decision-making with "simple" decision guides such as "An act is choiceworthy if and only if it would maximize expected utility." We noted that many theorists hold that the rationality of choosing an action depends, not on the action's satisfying the relevant decision guide, but rather on the agent's justifiably believing that it does. This view was interpreted as a view about the content of proper decision guides. On such a view, the above version of MEU should be rejected in favour of something like "An act is choiceworthy if and only if the agent *is justified* in believing that it would maximize expected utility." In this section we consider whether such "justified-belief" decision-guides are more vulnerable to difficulties raised by the regress problem than are simple decision guides.

We should note that not every decision-guide can be a justified-belief rule. For a justified-belief guide to be usable by an agent, the agent must believe that her beliefs about the features of her prospective acts are justified. (According to such rules, an act counts as choiceworthy if the agent has certain justified beliefs regarding it. Hence for her to be able to *use* the rule, she must believe that she has these justified beliefs.) However, an agent may have plenty of justified beliefs about the features of her prospective acts but be uncertain whether *any* of these beliefs is justified. (Perhaps she does not recall the source of her beliefs, or perhaps a philosophical skepticism has rendered her uncertain whether any beliefs are justified.) In such a case she could not apply any justified-belief rule to her decision. Yet she still needs to make a decision, and could do so by invoking a pertinent simple decision guide. Since this seems a rational strategy, it appears that the set of appropriate decision guides must include simple as well as justified-belief guides.

But, for the sake of argument, let us explore the view that *all* decision guides must be justified-belief rules. We may stipulate that no choice is rational for an agent who cannot apply any actual-justification rule. Does the regress problem raise difficulties for decision-making with justified-belief rules that do not arise when all decision guides are simple? I shall argue that it does not.

If justified-belief rules raise any difficulty, it would be a version of the problem of Universal Irrationality. One could argue as follows for the existence of such a difficulty. To avoid an infinite regress, agents must make an initial decision to perform some act without any prior deliberation about that decision. Suppose that this initial decision is the decision at t_1 to deliberate at t_2 about an act to be performed at t_3. Since, by hypothesis, the decision at t_1 is made without prior deliberation, then the beliefs in virtue of which the agent makes his decision at t_1 are unjustified. But if they are unjustified, then the decision is irrational, since it is not prescribed by any justified-belief decision guide. If it is irrational to decide at t_1 to deliberate at t_2, then (by Janus-faced meta-principle M) deliberating at t_2 is also irrational. If deliberating at t_2 is irrational, then it cannot provide justified beliefs for the decision to perform any act at t_3. Hence the choice to perform an act at t_3, and the chosen act itself, are similarly irrational. This argument can be generalized to show that every decision-making process is similarly flawed, and hence that every action is irrational.

Let us call this argument the "zipping-forward" argument. The argument has a persuasive appearance, but it is incorrect. The first flaw to notice is that it would not be accepted by anyone who accepts a current time-slice theory of epistemic justification – for example, foundationalism or coherentism.[15] According to such theories, a current belief is justified just in case it stands in the correct relationship to other current beliefs or quasi-doxastic states of the agent. Hence the agent's justification in believing something does not depend in any way on what kind of deliberation preceded or generated that belief. For example, coherentism holds that, if the agent makes a decision at t_1, and the decision rests on beliefs that are justified by their relation to other contemporaneous beliefs, then lack of prior deliberation in no way shows that the decision is irrational. For the coherentist, or other current time-slice epistemologist, the zipping-forward argument cannot get off the ground, and the rationality of decision-making is not impaired.

The argument looks more persuasive, however, for theorists who accept a *historical* account of justification. According to such accounts, the justificatory status of a current belief depends entirely on what prior processes generated it. For example, a simple "reliabilist" theory might state that a belief is justified just in case it is produced by a reliable belief-forming process such as deduction from true premises. Beliefs formed by unreliable processes (such as wishful thinking) are unjustified.[16] In the context of reliabilist accounts of justification, it appears as though the necessity for an agent to make some initial decision without prior deliberation validates the zipping-forward argument.

However, this appearance is an illusion. Although reliabilism stipulates that a belief must be generated by a reliable process, this process need not be a form of *deliberation*. Nor need it be any other process which the agent *chooses* to perform. To take a dramatic example, consider an agent who is kidnapped by terrorists and strapped to a chair. While strapped in, he is unavoidably exposed to certain sounds. These sounds initiate a perceptual process resulting in the agent's forming various beliefs ("Now my captors are leaving the building"). These processes may be reliable, and so the beliefs will be justified, even though they did not result from deliberation or from any other process that the agent chose to initiate or could have avoided. Hence, contrary to the assumption of the previous paragraph, an agent's beliefs can be justified even though they do not result from any previously chosen deliberational process. And if those beliefs form the basis for a decision (say, the decision to try to escape while one's captors are absent), then the decision can be rational, because it can be in accord with a suitable justified-belief decision guide. Of course, few of us fall into the hands of terrorists, but for most of us the processes that produce our beliefs as infants and young children are ones we do not choose and about which we do not deliberate. This fact does not prevent our beliefs or subsequent decisions from being rational. Even for historical accounts of justification, the zipping-forward argument is incorrect.

It is important to see that the zipping-forward argument goes wrong in an additional way. The argument begins by assuming that the beliefs in virtue of which the agent decides at t_1 to deliberate are unjustified because they do not result from any process of deliberation. We have just seen that this is a mistake; justified beliefs may arise from involuntary nondeliberational processes. But let us consider a case in which the beliefs on the basis of which the agent decides at t_1 to deliberate at t_2 are *not* justified. Since the decision is not prescribed by an appropriate justified-belief decision guide, it is irrational, and the agent's deliberating at t_2 is likewise irrational. The zipping-forward argument assumes that an irrational deliberation at t_2 cannot provide justified beliefs for the decision to perform any act at t_3. Hence any decision with regard to t_3, and any act at t_3, are themselves irrational. But this assumption is a mistake, arising from an illegitimate confusion of the evaluations of epistemology with those of practical decision-making. The deliberation at t_2 may have been irrationally chosen and performed. But as an epistemic process it may be perfectly reliable, and confer justification on any beliefs arising out of it.

To see this, consider an agent whose inordinate love of arithmetical calculation leads her to decide at t_1 to deliberate at t_2 about the expected utilities of her prospective acts at t_n. She is not justified in believing at t_1 that this form of deliberation would be best, since this belief arises as a result of an unreliable process in which her love of calculation plays an inappropriate role. Her evidence indicates that she ought instead to calculate the security levels of her prospective acts. Hence her decision to calculate expected utilities is irrational, and deliberating itself is an irrational act. However, the process of deliberating – her calculating the expected utilities – may be perfectly reliable as a epistemological process, and it may deliver the justified belief at t_3 that act A would maximize expected utility. Suppose that the justified-belief version of MEU is the agent's highest usable decision guide at t_3. If act A satisfies this decision guide, a decision at t_3 to perform A is rational, and so is the act itself. The mere fact that the agent irrationally chose to perform this deliberation on the basis of unjustified beliefs does *not* taint all her subsequent decisions and acts with irrationality.

What this example shows is that it is important to separate epistemological assessments from those of practical rationality. A deliberational process that is irrational from the perspective of practical rationality may nonetheless be justification-conferring from the point of view of epistemology. For this reason a single irrational decision in a sequence of decisions need not infect all the subsequent decisions with irrationality. Thus even if we were to accept the view that all decision guides must be justified-belief rules, and even if we accepted a purely historical account of what makes beliefs justified, we need not worry that a version of Universal Irrationality undermines practical rationality. As we saw before, some justification-conferring processes are not themselves the subject of decisions, and even those that are, and that are chosen irrationally, do not necessarily taint the decisions and acts that follow them.

4. CONCLUSION

Because information-gathering processes, and in particular deliberation, are themselves activities that can be chosen and about which an agent can deliberate, it has often been feared that decision-makers may be vulnerable to some kind of vicious regress undermining the rationality of decision-making. This fear is best articulated as the concern, supported by two distinct arguments, that decision-making is subject to Universal Irrationality: all acts and decisions are irrational. I have argued that this fear is ill founded, whether decision-making is guided by simple decision rules or by justified-belief decision rules. I have not attempted to rule out the possibility that the regress problem renders some acts and decisions irrational. But I have argued that in a substantial range of normal cases this threat can be dismissed.

NOTES

I am grateful to Robert Cummins, Alvin I. Goldman, Keith Lehrer, John Pollock, and the editors of this volume for helpful comments on an earlier version of this paper.

1 Resnik himself rejects this objection, advocating the employment of "policies" instructing us when to deliberate and when not. He admits that the use of such

policies may itself require reassessment, and so raise the same problem all over again. More detailed examination of such policies and their re-examination is contained in Bratman (1987, Chs 5, 6).

2 See Bales (1971, pp. 257–65) for references to holders of this view.

3 See Smith (1988, pp. 89–108) for development and defense of this claim, and discussion of issues in this section.

4 In some accounts, to have a subjective probability assignment for a given proposition is to have a certain disposition to act on that proposition (for example, to bet on it). These accounts often assume that such dispositions are always in existence, so that (contrary to the text) the agent never lacks beliefs about the probabilities of his actions' consequences. This simplistic functional account of belief states seems to me inadequate. However, even if true, there is no guarantee on such an account that the agent has knowledge (or even beliefs) about his own relevant behavioral dispositions. Thus it may take him time and a variety of thought experiments – that is, deliberation – to determine what his subjective probability assignments are. (See Raiffa (1968, ch. 5) for a description of a method of eliciting subjective probability judgments.) In some accounts, an agent's choices always reflect his subjective probability and utility assignments, even though he himself may be unaware of the content of these assignments. These accounts appear to leave little room for agents to reflect on, or need guidance in, decision-making.

5 The criterion for rank-ordering decision guides will not be discussed in this paper; the reader is invited to provide his or her own criterion.

   Through out this paper I assume that the relevant notion of "capable of using" does not entail that the agent makes, or can make, the *correct* derivation of a prescription from the decision guide. All it requires is that she be able to derive *a* prescription. See Smith (1988) for further discussion. Thus the agent might believe that A would maximize expected utility, and so be able to use MEU. However, if MEU actually prescribes B, then it is rational for her to choose B, not A.

6 An alternative interpretation of this view is possible, according to which the content of the decision guides remains simple (in my sense), but what enables an agent to apply a guide is his justified beliefs, rather than his actual beliefs. I shall not discuss this alternative interpretation here, but the conclusions reached in section 3 would remain roughly the same.

7 In this case I am assuming, for brevity of presentation, that the agent has only two alternatives available at t_n. In most cases of course the number of alternatives would be greater. Maximizing decision guides (such as MEU and MM) are often criticized on grounds that there are infinitely many alternatives for a given time. (This presents a *theoretical* difficulty only if, for any alternative act, there is another alternative that has a higher security level or expected utility. It presents a *pragmatic* difficulty for the usability of such decision guides if the agent does not have time or resources to discover, among the infinite set of alternatives, the one (if there is one) having the maximum security level or expected utility.) I shall set this alleged difficulty aside, since

it is distinct from the difficulties raised by the opportunity to deliberate. In any event, most agents do not consider themselves as having an infinite number of alternatives about which they *should* deliberate; their attention is restricted to a few salient alternatives.

8 I shall assume for the purposes of this paper that the rationality of a given option at t_1 is determined, in part, by the actions that would actually follow it. Thus the rationality of the physician's performing D_1 at t_1 is partly a function of the value or disvalue of his then performing A. This assumption is necessitated by the fact that agents' subsequent acts are often not the ones it would be rational for them to perform. Because of this assumption, I do not use the traditional decision tree to represent the agent's choice at t_1 in figure 6.2. For discussion and defense of this view, see Smith (1976, pp. 449–87).

9 If time can be divided into infinitely small intervals, then any bodily movement consists of nested shorter and shorter parts (for example, moving your hand for 1 second, moving your hand for 0.1 second, moving your hand for 0.01 second, . . .). In this way movements can be defined for any interval of time, however small. However, these arbitrarily small movements do not count as acts. In waving your hand for a minute, you also wave your hand for 0.00000001 second. But since you cannot effectively choose to wave your hand (as an independent motion) for 0.00000001 second, doing so does not count as an action, anymore than falling off a collapsing building counts as an action, even though it is a motion of your body.

10 I am assuming in this example that deliberations at the second level or above take no more time than those at the first level. If deliberations become longer as their level increases (a highly plausible thesis), there will be a highest-level deliberation (the highest-level deliberation just short enough to fit between t_1 and t_n) that could be performed by the agent between t_1 and t_n.

11 Alternatively, it may be uncertain whether the physician's performing D_1 would lead to his performing the maximin act at t_n – perhaps there is a possibility that he would miscalculate the security levels, or perhaps there is a possibility that he would fail to carry through by doing at t_n what he identifies at t_2 as correct. In this case, we must ascribe equal security levels to the terminal acts following each of the physician's alternatives at t_1 – since any of those alternatives may fail to lead to the maximin act at t_n. D1 would still be prescribed as choiceworthy by MM, since the security level of its terminal act is no less than the security level of the terminal act following any alternative.

12 It is easiest to demonstrate this result for MEU by concentrating on the kind of case in which deliberation provides the agent with better information for applying the same decision guide, e.g. MEU. For a helpful discussion of the rationality of obtaining information by research (as opposed to deliberation), see Raiffa (1968, chs 3 and 7).

13 At this point a pressing question might be raised, and has been raised by the editors of this volume. Suppose that an agent has to perform either action

X or action Y at time t_n. She has beliefs that would enable her at t_1 to apply either MM or MEU to the choice between X or Y. MM prescribes X, while MEU prescribes Y. The agent is familiar with both MM and MEU. We have assumed that MEU is a higher decision guide than MM. However, this agent falsely believes that MM is higher than MEU. According to meta-principle M, she would be rational at t_1 to choose Y, since Y is prescribed by the highest decision guide (namely MEU) that she is capable of using at t_1 to make her decision. But can it really be true that she would be rational to do Y, since she believes MM to be the higher decision guide, and MM prescribes X rather than Y?

The answer has to be both yes and no. The choice to perform Y is the most rational choice for her in one clear sense – a sense somewhat analogous to the sense in which an act Z is the right act for an agent to perform because it is prescribed by the correct moral code. It is correct in this sense even though the agent believes some alternative code to be correct, and the alternative code prescribes act W instead of Z. We can contrast the correctness (in this sense) of performing Z with the correctness, in a different sense, of performing the act W prescribed by the moral code that the agent believes to be correct. We might call this second sense the "putative" sense of correctness. Similarly we can contrast the rationality of choosing act Y in our original case with the rationality of choosing X, the act prescribed by the decision guide that the agent believes to be correct. In a different, equally clear, sense, it would be rational for the agent to choose X. We might call this the "putative" sense of rationality. There is, as far as I can see, no way to avoid the divergence between the first and the putative senses of rationality (and correctness in the case of codes). In this paper I have restricted myself to the first sense, rather than the putative sense, but it is clear that the latter has an important role to play. Part of what is interesting about the divergence between these senses of rationality/correctness is that the bifurcation cannot be avoided (as some theorists might hope) by shifting from "objective" norms, such as moral codes, to decision guides.

Note that in the putative sense of rationality/correctness there may be *no* act which it is rational to choose or correct to perform. If the agent does not believe of any moral code that it is correct, then there is no act which it would be correct (in the putative sense) for her to perform. Similarly, if the agent does not believe of any decision guide that it is the highest usable one for her, then there is no choice which it would be rational (in the putative sense) for her to perform. I have explored this problem, from a somewhat different point of view, in Smith (1988) where I argue that its existence places a limit on how widely usable we can expect moral codes to be, even when they are augmented with auxiliary decision guides of the sort represented by MM and MEU.

Does the possibility that an agent may be uncertain which decision guide is highest raise an infinite regress problem that has not been addressed by the arguments in this paper so far? I would argue that it does not. Suppose that our agent is at t_0, and suppose that she does not yet have the beliefs necessary to apply either MM or MEU, although she can obtain them by engaging in deliberation D_1 or D_2 respectively. Assume that she also has the option at t_0 of deliberating whether MM or MEU is the highest decision guide. Then her situation at t_0 might be represented as follows:

	t_0	t_1	t_2	t_3	t_n
1	D_1 .... (MM–t_n) --X
2	D_2 .... (MEU–t_n)----------------------------Y
3	D_3 .... (D_2–t_2) ---- D_2 .... (MEU–t_n) --------Y

If she engages in D_3, she comes to believe that MEU is the highest decision guide and so ought to be applied via D_2; she then engages in D_2, calculates whether X or Y has the greatest expected utility, and eventually does Y. Merely adding this option does not commit her to any infinite regress. If we ask "Which option at t_0 is rational for her to choose at t_{-1}, just before t_0?", the answer is given by meta-principle M, for our guiding sense of "rationality." What it is rational for her to choose at t_{-1} depends on which option is prescribed by the highest decision guide usable by her at t_{-1} for her options at t_0.

I have not tried in this note to spell out the conditions of rational choice for putative rationality. However, there is no apparent threat of infinite regress there either. What it is putatively rational for her to choose at t_{-1} depends on what she believes at t_{-1} to be her highest usable decision guide. If she had no belief about what her highest usable decision guide is, then there is nothing at t_{-1} that it is putatively rational for her to choose at t_0. She has a problem, but it is not an infinite regress problem.

14 In the case described in the text, a satisficing rule was not considered as one of the physician's possible decision guides. However, even if such a rule had been included, we cannot conclude that using it, or deliberating further in order to use it, would have been the rational choice for the agent. Employing a satisficing rule typically takes less deliberation than employing a decision guide such as MM, but its potential benefits may not be nearly so advantageous. Theorists often assume that a decision-maker maximizes overall expected utility by utilizing a satisficing rule in deciding how much information to obtain, but this need not be so. For recent expressions of this assumption, see Nozick (1981, p. 300) and Hollis (1987, ch. 8). Robert C. Richardson argues against this mistake in his unpublished manuscript, "Satisficing and optimizing."

15 Detailed versions of coherentism are provided by Lehrer (1974) and Bonjour (1985). Foundationalism is advocated by Chisholm (1977), and is discussed by Pollock (1986, ch. 2). The terms "current time-slice" and "historical theories of justification" were introduced by Goldman (1979).

16 A detailed reliabilist theory is developed by Goldman (1986).

7

Inductive Deliberation, Admissible Acts, and Perfect Equilibrium

Brian Skyrms

1 NAIVE BAYESIANS MEET THE THEORY OF GAMES

Bayesians take the principle of rational choice to be maximization of expected utility. Naive Bayesians[1] apply this principle in a naive manner. Consider what happens when two naive Bayesians, Row and Column, play a game. Independently, each chooses one of two possible acts, which jointly determine the following payoffs (example 1):

	C_1	C_2
R_1	(2, 1)	(0, 0)
R_2	(0, 0)	(1, 4)

Here Row's payoffs are listed first: so if, for example, Row chooses R_1 and Column chooses C_1, then Row gets a payoff of 2 and Column gets a payoff of 1. Let us suppose that our players each initially have equal subjective probabilities for the other player's two possible acts. Each calculates expected utility and opts for that act which maximizes her expected utility. Row calculates R_1 as having expected utility 1 (the average of 2 and 0) and R_2 as having an expected utility of 0.5 (the average of 0 and 1), and thus opts for R_1. Column calculates C_1 as having an expected utility of 0.5 and C_2 as having an expected utility of 2, and thus opts for C_2. Thus Row and Column end up at (R_1, C_2) with each getting a payoff of 0. They could not have done worse. And if each knew that the other was a Bayesian, could they not have foreseen this calamity and done something to avert it?

2 BANG-BANG BAYESIANS WITH INFORMATIONAL FEEDBACK

Row and Column, having played the last game and gotten 0, have decided that it is a good thing to think about the other player's reasoning, and feed the information thus gotten back into their strategic reasoning. Feeding in new information before deciding – if the cost of so doing is negligible – is, after all, quite consistent with Bayesian methodology. (We assume that it is common knowledge that both are expected utility maximizers, and that each starts with equiprobability for the other's acts.) Row reasons that Column has calculated expected utilities and will opt for C_2, in which case it is better for Row to opt for R_2. Column reasons that Row has calculated expected utilities and will opt for R_1, in which case it is better for her to opt for C_1. It looks as if our deliberators will arrive at (R_2, C_1), for a payoff no better than that achieved by naive Bayesians.

But our players know not only that the other players are expected utility maximizers but also that the other players know that they are. So each has enough knowledge to see that the other player can carry out the reasoning of the preceding paragraph. Reasoning in this manner, Row predicts that Column will choose C_1 and thus that it is best for her to choose R_1; likewise Column predicts that Row will choose R_2 and thus that it is best for him to choose C_2. This is where our players came in.

But they do not leave. For they have enough knowledge to carry out the reasoning of the last paragraph as well. Thus our deliberators climb the ladder of common knowledge, oscillating between (R_1, C_2) and (C_1, R_2). The oscillation is uncontrolled because at each stage our bang-bang deliberators believe with probability one that the other player will maximize expected utility as calculated in the previous stage and leap to the strategy which maximizes expected utility relative to that belief. Perhaps our deliberators should approach informational feedback with more caution and a certain amount of healthy skepticism.

3 DELIBERATIONAL DYNAMICS

If deliberators generate and feed back information during deliberation, then deliberation should be studied as a dynamic process. In cases of strategic interaction such as those studied by the theory of games, the deliberation of all the players forms a complex dynamical system. The study of the dynamics of such systems is of fundamental importance for the theory of strategic rationality. In certain models, dynamical properties of the system of deliberators will correspond to game-theoretic concepts. At the most fundamental level, one can identify conditions under which a joint deliberational equilibrium of the players corresponds to a Nash equilibrium of the game. It is also of interest to investigate strengthenings of the Nash equilibrium concept that have a natural motivation in the dynamics. In this way one can have a unified theory of rational action which includes classical game theory as a special case. The assumptions required to get classical game theory out of deliberational dynamics turn out to be very strong, and so a theory of rationality based on dynamic deliberation must also be interested in phenomena not covered by that theory.

This is a large and rich territory, where a great variety of models are of interest. I have considered a number of different models of dynamic deliberation in other publications (Skyrms, 1986, 1988, 1990, forthcoming). In this paper I would like to introduce some models of dynamic deliberation· driven by inductive rules and explore the connections between them and the game-theoretic concepts of admissibility and perfection. Models of deliberation driven by inductive rules are conceptually rather different from models that I have considered elsewhere that are driven by adaptive rules.

4 CAUTIOUS DELIBERATORS WITH ADAPTIVE RULES

Cautious deliberators take the moral of section 2 to be that one should not immediately leap to the option having currently the highest expected utility, but rather should incline in its direction. After all, things may change. This sort of decision-maker calculates expected utilities, modifies her probabilities of her available acts according to an adaptive rule which gives higher probabilities to currently more attractive acts, discovers other players' calculations and modifications of their probabilities by emulating their reasoning, and uses this information to recalculate expected utilities.

One example of an adaptive rule is the Nash dynamics. A player calculates the expected utility of the status quo as the average of the probabilities of her pure acts, weighted by the probabilities that she will do them:

$$\text{Row's utility of the status quo} = \sum_i \text{pr}(R_i) U(R_i)$$

Take as the *covetability* of a pure act the difference in expected utility between it and the status quo if it looks better than the status quo and zero otherwise:

$$\text{covet}(R_i) = \max \left[0, \; U(R_i) - U(\text{status quo})\right]$$

Then the *Nash map* with caution parameter k takes old probabilities pr to new ones pr′ such that

$$\text{pr}'(R_i) = \frac{k\text{pr}(R_i) + \text{covet}(R_i)}{k + \sum_i \text{covet}(R_i)}$$

When a player modifies her probabilities according to the Nash map or a similar adaptive rule, her probabilities for the currently attractive acts are raised, but she does not leap to a decision and give probability one to the act with currently maximal expected utility. The Nash dynamics *seeks the good*: that is, it raises the total of the probabilities of all acts with expected utility greater than the status quo and raises the probability of an act only if it has expected utility greater than that of the status quo. If dynamic deliberators start out with a common prior probability and an adaptive rule which seeks the good, and update by emulation, and all this is common knowledge, then they are at a joint deliberational equilibrium if and only if they are at a Nash equilibrium of the game.

As another somewhat different example of an adaptive rule, consider the *Darwin map*:

$$\text{pr}'(A) = \text{pr}(A)\frac{U(A)}{U(\text{status quo})}$$

where utility is measured on some standard nonnegative scale. Darwin seeks the good on the interior of the space of indecision, that is, where no act has probability zero. However, if an act has probability zero or one, Darwin leaves its probability unchanged whether or not it is optimal. Darwin is the dynamics investigated in the evolutionary game theory of Maynard Smith (1982). We can move from these discrete maps to the associated continuous Nash and Darwin flows. I discuss both the Darwin and Nash dynamics in Skyrms (1990).

If we apply Nash or Darwin deliberation to example 1, we get a happier outcome than that achieved by naive or bang-bang Bayesians. Instead of wild oscillation or selection of a nonequilibrium point, the *trajectory* of deliberation starting with equiprobable beliefs converges to the Nash equilibrium at (R_2, C_2). This is shown in figure 7.1 for Nash dynamics with $k = 1$.

The interpretation of adaptive rules in the context of deliberational dynamics, however, raises certain delicate philosophical questions. The decision-maker must think about her own probabilities of action under the dual aspect of optimal control and rational prediction, and do so

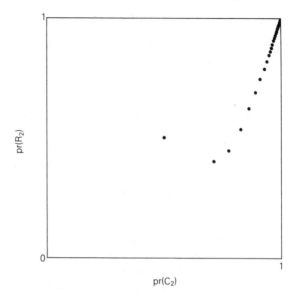

Figure 7.1   Nash dynamics on example 1.

consistently. Credence and degree of decidedness must coincide. Some authors, for example Spohn (1977), have argued vigorously that the decision-maker should never have to think about probabilities of her own acts at all. Even if this objection is put aside, the idea of the decision-maker altering her own probabilities by an act of will may seem strange and perhaps inconsistent with her probabilities being her actual degrees of belief about what – in the end – she will do. I believe that the apparent difficulties can be resolved and that adaptive deliberational dynamics does make sense, but not everyone will agree.

5 INDUCTIVE DYNAMIC DELIBERATION

Here I wish to introduce an alternative kind of deliberational dynamics which is driven by an *inductive* rule. Rather than thinking of a player as altering her own probabilities of her own acts by an act of will, we shall consider *other* players' probabilities for her acts. Given other players' probabilities (for acts of players other than themselves), a player can calculate their expected utilities for their options just as they do. On some form of the hypothesis that the players are optimizers, each player makes an inductive inference about the eventual play of other players, and updates her probabilities accordingly. Given sufficient common knowledge, these calculations can be emulated. Then each player again knows the probabilities that other players have (for acts of players other than themselves) and thus can calculate their expected utilities, starting the cycle anew. On the inductive dynamics, no player needs to have subjective probabilities for her own acts. She only needs to have probabilities for other players' acts, and to think about other players' probabilities for her acts.

An equilibrium in inductive dynamics is thus an equilibrium in degrees of belief. This is of special interest in connection with the theory of games because of a growing conviction among game theorists that the most viable interpretation of mixed equilibria is as equilibria in beliefs (see Harsanyi, 1973; Aumann, 1987; Binmore, 1988). In traditional expositions of game theory we are asked to think of a mixed strategy as a decision-maker turning her decision over to a random device. The problematic aspects of this interpretation of mixed equilibria are well known.

What would you think of a general or an executive who made his decisions by flipping coins? If you are really at a mixed equilibrium, expected utility considerations give you no reason to randomize. Each act which gets positive probability in your mixed strategy has expected utility equal to that of the mixed strategy. Why, then, not choose a pure act? The conventional answer is that mixing guarantees that the other players cannot "find out" what pure strategy you are going to play. But in normal – form games it is assumed that the players choose independently and simultaneously. Suppose that the unique mixed equilibrium requires that we each randomize between two possible plays with equal probability. We go into separate rooms to decide on our plays and phone them to the game master. You flip a coin like a good game theorist. It comes up heads. You phone the game master. I forgot my coin, so I just play heads. Am I any the worse off for not having randomized?

The essential aspect of the metaphor of my flipping a fair coin lies in your having equiprobable beliefs over my actions. Everything else is irrelevant. Mixed equilibrium should then be thought of as equilibrium in degrees of belief. This, of course, is compatible with the coin actually being flipped, but does not require it. Under suitably strong conditions of common knowledge, one can show that inductive deliberational equilibria coincide with Nash equilibria of the game, so interpreted.

Once one has a game played by inductive dynamic deliberators in which joint deliberational equilibria correspond to Nash equilibria, one also has natural refinements of the Nash equilibrium concept motivated by the dynamics of deliberation. In this paper I shall focus on one of these refinements, *accessibility*. A system of belief states for the players will be said to be accessible under deliberation if deliberation starting at some system of completely mixed belief states converges to it.

The characteristics of accessible points will depend to some extent on the inductive rule or rules involved. As illustrations, we look at dynamic deliberators who implement inductive rules due to Bayes, Laplace, and Carnap. It can be shown in each case that if a point is *accessible* under the dynamics then it is a Nash equilibrium which only gives positive probability to *admissible* acts. (An admissible act is one which is not weakly dominated by some alternative act.) It follows that in two-person games accessible equilibria are *perfect* in the sense of Selten (1975). Given sufficient initial common knowledge, this remains true for a class of subjective Bayesian models which generalize the Carnap dynamics.

6 FICTITIOUS PLAY BY LAPLACIAN DELIBERATORS IN 2-BY-2 TWO-PERSON NONCOOPERATIVE GAMES

Let us look at inductive deliberational dynamics first in the simplest context of 2-by-2 noncooperative games. Two players, Row and Column, must each pick between one of two possible actions. The results of their possible joint choices are specified in a payoff matrix; for example (example 2, with Row's payoff listed first),

$$
\begin{array}{ccc}
 & C_1 & C_2 \\
R_1 & (1, 1) & (-2, -2) \\
R_2 & (0, 0) & (0, 0)
\end{array}
$$

The players are to choose independently. One may think of them in separate rooms, simultaneously sending their choices to a referee, who then awards the prizes. Each player may then think of the other player's act as a state of the world that her acts cannot influence and that – together with her act – determines her payoff. From the point of view of expected utility maximization, each player faces two problems. The first is settling on initial probabilities of the other player's acts in order to calculate expected utility. The second – which is characteristic of games – is knowledge that the other player may be calculating expected utilities, and that the other player's changing perception of expected utilities is evidence that may be relevant to the first player's probability assignment over the other player's acts.

Let us suppose that our two players deal with these problems by a cookbook application of inductive logic; they rely on Laplace's rule of succession, treating each round of deliberation as a virtual trial.[2] Suppose too that it is common knowledge between them that they are such

Laplacian deliberators. Then each can emulate the other's calculations and discover the other's current expected utilities and utilities at each stage of deliberation.

Laplace's rule is that given n instantiations of a given act A_i in N trials, the probability of an instantiation on a new trial is

$$\mathrm{pr}(A_i) = \frac{n + 1}{N + 2} \tag{L}$$

So initially our players each assign the other probability $\frac{1}{2}$ for each act. Each player then calculates the other player's expected utilities, identifies the act with highest expected utility and counts that act as exemplified on the first trial to get an updated probability over the other player's acts.[3] Each player can now emulate the other player's calculation in this process to find the other player's updated probability. This process is then repeated, generating a *trajectory* in the *joint belief space* of the players.

This space can be represented as the unit square with the y axis measuring Column's degree of belief that Row will play R_2 and the x axis representing Row's degree of belief that Column will play C_2. This two-dimensional space suffices to represent the players' relevant beliefs since each is assumed to know the other's belief state at each stage of the deliberational process. (If we allowed each to have mistaken beliefs about the other's degree of belief, Row would have a belief-space on the unit square, with x representing Row's degree of belief that Column will play C_2 and y representing the degree of belief that Row believes Column to have that Row will play R_2. If each player were allowed to have degrees of belief about the other player's degrees of belief, then each player's belief state would be represented by an infinite hierarchy of degrees of belief. By virtue of the common knowledge that the players are Laplacian deliberators, these hierarchies collapse.)

The trajectory of belief for example 2 under the Laplacian belief dynamics is shown in figure 7.2. The trajectory starts at $(\frac{1}{2}, \frac{1}{2})$ and converges to $(0, 0)$, which is a Nash equilibrium. Starting with each act having probability $\frac{1}{2}$, we can calculate the expected utilities of R_1, R_2, C_1, and C_2 as $-\frac{1}{2}$, 0, $\frac{1}{2}$, and -1 respectively. R_2 and C_1 have the highest expected utility, and so they are winners on this virtual trial. Applying the rule of succession, their probabilities now change to $\frac{1}{3}$, $\frac{2}{3}$, $\frac{2}{3}$, and $\frac{1}{3}$ respectively. These are used to calculate new expected utilities, and so on. Belief starts at a state where no player has a clue as to what the other player will do (that is, each possible act is judged equally likely) and converges to a state in which each player is certain what the other player will do. Furthermore, this is a state in which neither player has anything to gain by doing something different from what the other player thinks she

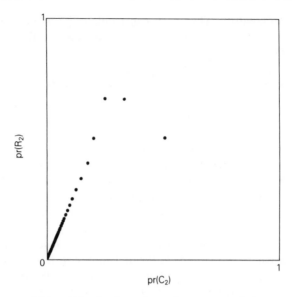

Figure 7.2   Laplace dynamics on example 2.

will do, provided that the other player does what she thinks he will do; it is a Nash equilibrium in belief states.

A different example shows that Laplacian deliberators need not converge to certainty. In the following game (example 3), at every state of certainty a player has an incentive to deviate from the act that the other is certain that she will do.

	C_1	C_2
R_1	$(1, 0)$	$(0, 1)$
R_2	$(0, 3)$	$(1, 0)$

In this game Laplacian deliberators converge to a mixed equilibrium in beliefs at $pr(R_2) = 0.25$, $pr(C_2) = 0.5$. The trajectory is shown in figure 7.3. The inductive interpretation of this equilibrium is that, with her beliefs about Column, Row finds her two options equally attractive and that, with his beliefs about Row, Column finds his two options equally attractive. Hence, by our rule for ties, each option is counted as having a "fractional success," the fractions being proportional to the other player's current probabilities for the tied options. Then the inductive rules do not move the probabilities.

This equilibrium in beliefs does not necessarily mean that the players do not know what they themselves are going to do at the end of deliberation – that they are committed to turning their choice over to a randomiz-

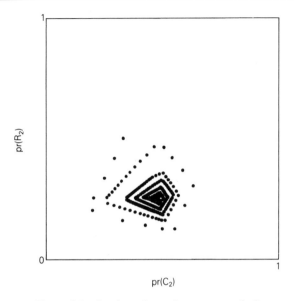

Figure 7.3   Laplace dynamics on example 3.

ing fiducial agent or some such thing. Each may know perfectly well how he or she will break a tie in expected utility. The essential point is that the other player does not know it and relies rather on his or her inductive rule.

7 CARNAPIAN DELIBERATORS IN FINITE NONCOOPERATIVE GAMES

The spirit of the foregoing scheme extends smoothly to finite two-person games. Here we assume that our players have studied some of Carnap's inductive logic. Suppose that Column has m possible acts, $A_1, \ldots, A_m$. After N trials in which act A_i has been chosen n times,

$$\text{pr}(A_i) = \frac{n + 1}{N + m} \qquad \text{(C)}$$

This natural generalization of Laplace's rule sets the acts as equiprobable on no evidence and updates using a simple frequency count.[4]

When we move to games with more than two players, it is not as clear what the natural extension of these techniques would be. One simple approach would be to assume that each player updates her beliefs regarding each of the other individual players according to rule (C) and to assume that each player takes the other $n - 1$ players' actions to be

probabilistically independent. We shall call this the mechanical independence approach to n-person games. For the time being we shall assume
this approach. Some alternatives will be discussed later.

8 BAYESIAN GENERALIZATIONS OF CARNAPIAN DELIBERATION

Laplace's rule of succession and rule (C) postulate initial beliefs for the
decision-makers based on symmetry and indifference. But perhaps we
would like to consider decision-makers who do not begin deliberation
with these symmetry-based beliefs but rather have other initial degrees of
belief based on whatever life experience they may bring to this game.

Laplace's rule of succession can be gotten by assuming a Bernoulli process with unknown parameter (for example, flipping a coin with unknown
bias), assuming a uniform prior probability on the parameter and
updating by applying Bayes's theorem. In the coin flipping example, the
parameter can be taken as the chance of heads. As Bayes himself showed,
the uniform prior leads to initial equiprobability of heads and tails and
to updating after N tosses of the coin by the rule of succession. Bayes
justified the uniform prior on the basis of ignorance, by an application
of the "principle of insufficient reason." He took the fact that this quan-
tification of ignorance leads to inductive inference via the rule of succession as an answer to the inductive skepticism of David Hume. Inductive
rule (C) is the natural generalization to the multinomial case. The process
is modeled as rolling a die with unknown bias, or sampling with replacement from an urn of unknown composition. Taking the prior as uniform
yields rule (C), as was shown by Lidstone (1920) and Johnson (1924).[5]

Carnap's continuum of inductive methods[6] adds another parameter k,
which determines how quickly the empirical frequency overwhelms the
prior probability:[7]

$$\mathrm{pr}(A_i) = \frac{n + k}{N + km} \qquad \text{(CC)}$$

The end-user of Carnap's continuum is supposed to decide the value of
k. But if we allow this choice of parameters in the inductive method, why
not allow a little more? From a parametric Bayesian point of view, the
natural way to handle flipping a coin with unknown bias is to pick a prior
over the bias parameter in the natural conjugate prior[8] family of beta
distributions. The beta distribution has two parameters α and β, both
positive, and $\alpha < \beta$. This leads to a general rule of succession for coin
flipping:

$$\text{pr(A)} = \frac{n + \alpha}{N + \beta} \tag{β}$$

Laplace's rule is just the special case in which $\alpha = 1$ and $\beta = 2$, which gives the uniform beta.

Similarly, in the case of the die or sampling from an urn with replacement, the natural conjugate prior is the Dirichlet distribution. If there are m possible outcomes then the Dirichlet distribution is characterized by positive parameters $\alpha_1, \ldots, \alpha_m$. Take $\beta = \alpha_1 + \ldots + \alpha_m$. Then if n is the number of occurrences of A_i in N trials we get the general rule

$$\text{pr}(A_i) = \frac{n + \alpha_i}{N + \beta} \tag{D}$$

If the α_i are all unity we get (C); if they are all equal we get Carnap's continuum (CC). In his posthumously published basic system (Carnap, 1980) Carnap, in fact, moved to the parametric Bayesian rule, rule (D).[9]

In analyzing games played by deliberators using rule (D), we are faced with a question which did not arise for rule (C): are the parameters $\alpha_1, \ldots, \alpha_m$ of the deliberators' Dirichlet priors common knowledge at the onset of deliberation? If so, then updating by emulation makes sense and common knowledge of belief states is preserved by the process of deliberation. If not, then a whole range of different kinds of failure is possible. The players might believe that they have such common knowledge but be mistaken, or they might have some prior over the parameters of other players' Dirichlets, with attendant complications of the deliberational process. We shall need to make assumptions of common knowledge to recover the Nash equilibrium concept of classical game theory. These are in general less plausible for personalist deliberators than for consumers of inductive logic who swallow the implicit flat prior as part of inductive methodology. This is because inductive *logic* – at least as Carnap originally conceptualized it – is supposed to be an essential feature of rationality, whereas for a subjective Bayesian any coherent prior belief state is considered rational.

9 NASH EQUILIBRIUM, ADMISSIBLE ACTS AND PERFECT EQUILIBRIUM

We shall consider only finite noncooperative normal-form games. Each player has a finite number of pure acts. Each has at any time a belief state which specifies a probability on the product-space of the act-spaces of all the other players. This is a space whose points consist of combinations of acts of all the other players. These points are the relevant states of the world for the player in question. In the case of independence in beliefs, this measure is a product measure. That is, the player gets a probability for a combination of actions of all the others just by multiplying the probabilities of the individual constituent acts.

The players will be said to be at a *Nash equilibrium in beliefs* if the following hold.

1 Each player's beliefs treat the other players' acts as probabilistically independent.

2 All players' beliefs are consistent with each other: if player i and player j have beliefs over player k's act-space then these beliefs agree.

3 If an act of player i does not maximize player i's expected utility according to player i's beliefs, then the other players give it probability zero.

This definition is mathematically equivalent to the usual definition of a Nash equilibrium in mixed strategies, but the reinterpretation of the mixing probabilities radically alters our perspective.

Some Nash equilibria appear to be highly suspect. Consider example 2. There is a Nash equilibrium in beliefs with Row believing with probability one that Column will do C_2 and Column believing with probability one that Row will do R_2. Doing R_2 maximizes expected utility for Row and doing either act has maximal expected utility for Column. Thus condition (3) is fulfilled. (Conditions 1 and 2 are fulfilled vacuously because there are only two players.) Should the players have such beliefs?

Column's act C_2 is *weakly dominated* by C_1. That is, for some state of the world (i.e. R_1) C_1 gives Column greater payoff than C_2, and for all states of the world C_1 gives Column at least as great a payoff as C_2. Acts which are not weakly dominated are called *admissible*. Since C_2 is inadmissible, if Column is not absolutely certain about row choosing R_2 – if Column assigns each of Row's choices positive probability – then C_2 would no longer maximize expected utility for Column.

It is often assumed that a rational player will never choose an inadmissible act (see Luce and Raiffa, 1957, p. 287; Kohlberg and Mertens, 1986, pp. 1013ff.). However, this conclusion is not a consequence of the postulate that players maximize expected utility. If Column's probability of R_2 is one, then his choice of the inadmissible act C_2 *does* maximize expected utility. If, however, players are never certain of anything – if their belief states are *completely mixed* giving some nonzero probability to every state of the world – then an inadmissible act will never maximize expected utility.

Perhaps rational agents – at least in decision problems with a finite number of states of nature – should always be in a completely mixed belief state regarding the states of nature. This point of view is given some support by the argument of Shimony (1955) that *strict* coherence requires a completely mixed belief state.

However, an attempt to found game theory on common knowledge of Bayesian rationality with strict coherence runs into logical difficulties. Consider example 2 again. Column has only one admissible act, C_1. Row must have probability one that Column will do the admissible act, because she knows that Column is strictly coherent. That is, she knows that Column will maximize expected utility because Column is coherent, and that Column will assign some positive probability to each of Row's acts because Column is *strictly* coherent, from which it follows that Column will do C_1. Row must *not* have probability one that Column will do the admissible act because Row is strictly coherent. Thus the assumption that both the game and the strict coherence of the players is common knowledge for the players is inconsistent.

Selten (1975) introduced the concept of a *perfect* equilibrium in a section entitled "A Model of Slight Mistakes." Selten was motivated by problems with extensive-form games, but here we restrict ourselves to games in normal form. His leading idea is that for a given game G we consider perturbed games G' in which the players do not completely control their choices. There is some small probability ϵ that rational choice will break down and some unspecified psychological mechanism will take over and determine the act. Thus in the perturbed game the players do not choose between "Do A_1," "Do A_2," and "Do a randomized act $(0.4A_1, 0.6A_2)$," but rather between "Try to do A_1," "Try to do A_2" and "Try to do the $(0.4A_1, 0.6A_2)$ mixture." If the player selects the latter, for example, there is $1 - \epsilon$ probability that trying succeeds and ϵ probability that "the hand trembles" and the unspecified mechanism makes the choice. Then the probability of A_1 that arises from trying to do the $(0.4A_1, 0.6A_2)$ mixed act is really $0.4(1 - \epsilon) + \text{Trembleprob }(A_1)(\epsilon)$. Trembles of different players away from the Nash equilibrium are assumed to be uncorrelated. A perfect equilibrium is defined as the limit of a sequence of Nash equilibria in *at least one* such sequence of perturbed games as the magnitude of ϵ shrinks to zero. Thus this concept of perfection embodies "a point of view which looks at complete rationality as a limiting case of incomplete rationality" (Selten, 1975, p. 35).

Myerson (1978) gave a mathematically equivalent reformulation of the concept of perfection. In Myerson's definition, we need not consider perturbed games. Rather, we define an ϵ-perfect equilibrium as a combination of completely mixed acts such that any pure strategies which do not maximize expected utility get probability less than ϵ. Myerson showed that an equilibrium is perfect if it is the limit of some sequence of ϵ-perfect equilibria.

Selten (1975) gave a third equivalent characterization of perfection: A mixed strategy combination s is perfect if and only if s is a limit point of some sequence $\{s(\epsilon)\}$ as ϵ goes to 0 of completely mixed strategy combinations, with the property that s is a best reply against every element $s(\epsilon)$ in this sequence. (s is a best reply to $s(\epsilon)$ if and only if each player's constituent of s maximizes her expected utility at $s(\epsilon)$.)

Every perfect equilibrium is a Nash equilibrium but not conversely. In example 1, (R_2, C_2) is Nash but not perfect. Every completely mixed Nash equilibrium, however, is perfect. This is evident from Myerson's definition and from Selten's alternative characterization of perfection, since an infinite sequence $\{s(\epsilon)\}$ all of whose members $s(\epsilon)$ are just the equilibrium itself satisfies this characterization. The equilibrium is completely mixed by hypothesis, and – since it is an equilibrium – it is a best reply to itself.

Van Damme (1983) shows that in two-person games the perfect equilibria coincide with the Nash equilibria which give positive probability only to admissible acts. This result fails for three-person games, as van Damme shows with the following (example 4):

	M_1		M_2	
	C_1	C_2	C_1	C_2
R_1	$(1, 1, 1)$	$(1, 0, 1)$	$(1, 1, 0)$	$(0, 0, 0)$
R_2	$(1, 1, 1)$	$(0, 0, 1)$	$(0, 1, 0)$	$(1, 0, 0)$

Player 1 chooses the row, player 2 the column, and player 3 the matrix. There is an equilibrium at (R_2, C_1, M_1). Each of these acts is undominated (R_2 because of the possibility of (C_2, M_2)). But the equilibrium is imperfect. If $pr(M_1)$ is close to one in a completely mixed point, then at that point R_1 has higher expected utility than R_2.

10 EQUILIBRIUM AND INDUCTIVE DELIBERATION

In this section we shall assume that in the case of games for $n > 2$ persons, each player treats the plays of the others as probabilistically independent. The consequences of departing from this assumption will be discussed briefly in a subsequent section. We shall also assume, as before, that the players are parametric inductive deliberators, using rule (D) with some choice of parameters $\alpha_1, \ldots, \alpha_n$. Players may or may not have the same initial values of the parameters. The payoff matrix for the game, that the players are inductive deliberators using rule (D), and the values of each player's initial parameters are all assumed to be common knowledge at the onset of deliberation. This model subsumes the use of inductive rules (C) and (L) as special cases where, in effect, certain initial values of the parameters are implicit in the inductive rule. Under these assumptions connections emerge between the game-theoretic equilibrium concepts and dynamical equilibria of the system of deliberators.

PROPOSITION 7.1:   A completely mixed point is a Nash equilibrium if and only if it is a joint deliberational equilibrium.

Proof: A completely mixed point is a Nash equilibrium if and only if at it all pure strategies maximize expected utility for all players. Suppose this is so. Then the tie breaking rule awards fractional successes in a way that changes no probabilities. This, by definition, is a deliberational equilibrium. Conversely, if the point is not a Nash equilibrium, some pure strategy of some player does not maximize expected utility, and inspection of the inductive rules shows that its probability is decreased.

All the rules that we have discussed yield a completely mixed point at the onset of deliberation. And, for each of them, no matter how long deliberation proceeds the belief states of all deliberators remain completely mixed. However, deliberation can approach asymptotically points which are not completely mixed. This raises the question of the game-theoretic character of such *accessible* points.

PROPOSITION 7.2:   Accessible points are Nash equilibria.

Proof: Suppose not. Then at the point p some pure act, A, which does not maximize expected utility gets positive probability. By continuity of expected utility of the acts as a function of the probabilities, there is some neighborhood of p throughout which A does not maximize expected utility. Inspection of the inductive rules shows that, if deliberation converges to p, then the probability of A must – contrary to hypothesis – converge to zero.

PROPOSITION 7.3:   Accessible points give positive probability only to admissible acts.

Proof: Suppose not. Then there is a weakly dominated act A which has positive probability at the accessible point p. Since A is weakly dominated it does not maximize expected utility at any completely mixed point. Inspection of the rules shows that, if deliberation converges to p, then the probability of A must converge to zero.[10]

COROLLARY: In two-person games, accessible equilibria are perfect.

We do not have the corollary for n-person games because there, as we have seen, Nash equilibria in admissible acts can be imperfect. However, we have the following proposition for n-person games.

PROPOSITION 7.4:   In finite n-person games, accessible equilibria in pure strategies are perfect.

Proof: Let s be an accessible pure equilibrium. At s each player i plays a pure strategy s_i. Note that from the form of rule (D) deliberators starting at a completely mixed state can only converge to s if the trajectory of deliberation contains an infinite number of points in every neighborhood of s. Now let $_0p_1$, $_0p_2$,. . ., be a trajectory of deliberators starting at a completely mixed state and converging to s. Select out a subsequence, $_1p_1$, $_1p_2$,. . ., by deleting each point in the original sequence (if any) to which s_1 is not a best reply. The subsequence must still have an infinite number of points in every neighborhood of s. Otherwise rule (D) would have driven the probability of s to 0 rather than to 1. Continue from subsequence n to subsequence $n + 1$ in like manner, deleting the points to which s_{n+1} is not a best reply. Since there are only a finite number of players, this process terminates, leaving the sequence $s(\epsilon)$ which converges to s and is such that s is a best reply to every member of it. Thus by Selten's second characterization of perfection, s is perfect.

The connection with admissibility need not hold for all models of dynamic deliberation. For instance, Darwin deliberation can converge to an imperfect equilibrium which uses inadmissible strategies in the 2-by-2 game of example 2. This is shown in figure 7.4, with the Darwin map

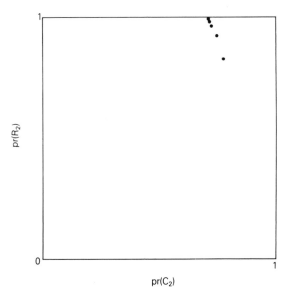

Figure 7.4   Darwin dynamics on example 2.

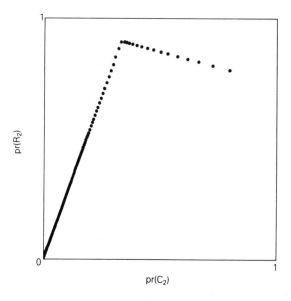

Figure 7.5   Beta dynamics on example 2.

starting at the initial point $(0.8, 0.8)$.[11] For comparison figure 7.5 shows beta deliberators starting from the same point (with $\alpha = 8$ and $\beta = 10$ for each deliberator) converging to the perfect equilibrium of example 2.

11 ANALOGY AND CORRELATION

So far we have used the assumption of mechanical independence for $n > 2$ person games, but if the interpretation of the mixing probabilities is in terms of *beliefs* we must ask why a player's beliefs about other players' actions should necessarily satisfy independence. Why should not one player notice that two other players' payoffs are symmetric, know that they use the same inductive rule (or have the same parameters for rule (D)), and incorporate this analogy in her inductive reasoning? How might this be done?

In the inductive logic literature we find some useful discussions but hardly any canonical treatment of the problem of analogy. One of the most suggestive discussions appears already in de Finetti (1938). He considers the case of two odd-shaped coins of unknown bias. A range of judgments of similarity are possible. At one extreme, the coins may be judged to be so dissimilar that a flip of one gives no information about the flip of the other. At the other extreme, the coins may be judged to be exact replicas so that a toss of coin B gives as much information about coin C as a toss of coin C itself does. In between lie cases of partial analogy.

The prior here can be thought of as a measure on the unit square, with the y axis representing the bias of coin B and the x axis representing the bias of coin C. A flat prior gives no analogy, while a prior concentrated on the diagonal gives perfect analogy. Either way, if there really is independence then in the limit the outcomes of tosses of each coin approach independence in belief. As one becomes more certain of the bias of a given coin, another toss of it is judged to give one less information about it. Likewise, in the limit, outcomes of tosses of coin B and coin C give no information about each other's bias. If we were to choose this as the model of correlation of beliefs in deliberation, then we could have trajectories of belief in which initial high correlation washes out as players converge to a deliberational equilibrium. Nevertheless, such a modification would have a profound effect on the dynamics, which remains to be fully assessed.

On the other hand, one might want to allow for the possibility that there is a correlation and that players learn it during deliberation, and converge to a deliberational equilibrium which incorporates correlated beliefs. This could be done in various ways. A simple one would be to treat a player in an n-person game as sampling $(n - 1)$-tuples of acts of the other players. Carnap seems to have considered the possibility of using a weighted average of this sort of model and the mechanical independence model in inductive logic.[12] If this sort of model were used deliberators might converge to correlated equilibria which are not Nash equilibria.

12 OTHER CRITICAL INDUCTIVE ASSUMPTIONS

Bracketing the assumption of independence, there are a number of additional assumptions implicit in the use of inductive logic with which this paper began. These assumptions become explicit in the parametric Bayesian models to which they were generalized.

One is the assumption of a flat prior on grounds of symmetry or ignorance, which turned out not to be essential to the connection with admissibility. A wide range of Dirichlet priors will do just as well. This point could be pressed further – if one wished to take the trouble – by using mixtures of Dirichlet priors to approximate arbitrary subjective priors (see Diaconis and Ylvisaker, 1984).

That would be to strain at a gnat. The camel is the imputed statistical model – that the process of deliberation is to be thought of like sampling optimal plays from an infinite urn. In the first place, each round of computation generates a lot of information for a deliberator. I see no good reason to assume that the current optimal play is a sufficient statistic (that it captures all the information relevant to predicting the act ultimately chosen). In the second place, as the deliberational process has been modeled, the "samples" are patently *not* independent. Where one has been in preceding iterations of the deliberative process is relevant to where one may be on the next round, both for the mundane reason that after a while the probabilities do not move very quickly and for the more interesting reason that there may be patterns (for example, limit cycles)[13] in deliberation. In subjectivistic terms, the trials are not exchangeable – order makes a difference.

A more adequate treatment of inductive deliberational dynamics will have to deal with these concerns, as well as with the question of correlation raised in the last section. At this point the conceit that the players are following an inductive logic cookbook will have to be dropped. The cookbook for this dish does not yet exist.

NOTES

Research on which this paper is based was partially supported by the National Science Foundation.

1 Here I am echoing the criticism of naive Bayesians made by Harsanyi and Selten (1988). For a more sympathetic view of naive Bayesians see Kadane and Larkey (1982). Harsanyi and Selten propose a solution procedure for non-cooperative games called the Tracing Procedure. The Tracing Procedure can be regarded as a kind of dynamic deliberation for strategically naive but computationally sophisticated deliberators. It is not clear, however, how to interpret the Tracing Procedure as involving Bayesian updating. I discuss the relation of the Tracing Procedure to Nash, Darwin, and other models of dynamic deliberation in Skyrms (1990, ch. 7).

2 The method of fictitious play was introduced by Brown (1951) as a way of finding solutions to finite two-person zero-sum games. This method resembles the methods to be examined here except that Brown uses the empirical average over past virtual plays as the probability for the next virtual play, rather than using one of the rules of succession. Robinson (1951) showed that Brown fictitious play always converges to a Nash equilibrium in finite two-person zero-sum games. Miyasawa (1961) showed that it converges for two-person nonzero-sum games where each person has a choice of two actions. It is evident that these results carry over to Bayes–Laplace–Carnap–Dirichlet deliberation which must converge where Brown fictitious play does. Convergence is not guaranteed, however, in larger games. See Diaconis and Ylvisaker (1984).

3 In the case of a tie we shall award "fractional successes" with the fractions proportional to the tied strategies' current relative probabilities and summing to one.

4 Ties for maximum expected utility are handled in the way specified in note 3.

5 Lidstone (1920) gives a parametric Bayesian derivation by taking the uniform prior on multimonials and integrating. Johnson (1924) gives a subjective Bayesian derivation from two postulates on subjective probability: (a) permutation and (b) combination. Permutation is the property made famous by de Finetti as *exchangeability*, that is, invariance of the probability under finite permutations of trials. The combination postulate says that in a fixed number of trials any proportion among types is as probable as any other, *a priori*. For example, in the case of coin flipping it says that in two tosses the prior probabilities are equal for two heads, two tails, one head, and one tail. See Good (1965) and Zabell (1982).

6 Johnson (1932) already has this continuum. Furthermore, he deduced it from the assumption that the posterior probability of a type on the evidence of a sequence of trials only depends on how many times the instances of that type occurred. (The theorem only goes through if the number of types is at least three.) See Zabell (1982).

7 In Carnap's notation, $k = \lambda/m$.

8 See De Groot (1970), Raiffa and Schlaifer (1961), and Diaconis and Ylvisaker (1979) on natural conjugate priors.

9 α is the product of Carnap's λ and γ. β is Carnap's γ. Carnap's interpretation of these parameters, however, has a nonpersonalist flavor.

10 This is due to the ordinal nature of the inductive dynamics. The dynamics only depends on which acts have maximal expected utility, not on the degree to which this expected utility exceeds that of alternatives. Compare the closely related discussion in Samuelson (1988). For an example of a kind of dynamic deliberation for which this proposition is not true see the discussion of the Darwin dynamics in Skyrms (1990).

11 This is also true of the Darwin flow.

12 See Pietarinen (1972, pp. 63ff.) for a discussion.

13 As in the game in Shapley (1964):

$$
\begin{array}{cccc}
 & C_1 & C_2 & C_3 \\
R_1 & (1, 0) & (0, 0) & (0, 1) \\
R_2 & (0, 1) & (1, 0) & (0, 0) \\
R_3 & (0, 0) & (0, 1) & (1, 0)
\end{array}
$$

Shapley used this example to show that Brown fictitious play need not converge for 3-by-3 two-person games. There is a unique mixed equilibrium at $[(\frac{1}{3}, \frac{1}{3}, \frac{1}{3}), (\frac{1}{3}, \frac{1}{3}, \frac{1}{3})]$. However, almost every starting point leads to a stable limit cycle. Dirichlet deliberators find themselves similarly embarrassed. The moral is that they should reconsider their statistical model and use a more sophisticated form of inductive reasoning.

8

Two Notions of Ratifiability and Equilibrium in Games

Hyun Song Shin

1 INTRODUCTION

Consider the following situation. A pollster faces the problem of predicting the outcome of a forthcoming election. There are two candidates: the Republican and the Democrat. The pollster gets a payoff of 1 if he chooses the same candidate as the electorate and zero otherwise. The payoffs are given in figure 8.1(a).

However, let us suppose that the pollster is an incorrigible pessimist and that his subjective probability distribution over the actions is given by figure 8.1(b). The probability of the Republican being elected is exactly $\frac{1}{2}$, as is the probability of the Democrat being elected. However, whenever the pollster predicts one candidate, the electorate invariably chooses the other.

Given the situation as it is, the pollster resigns himself to getting zero always. However, suppose we embellish story as follows. The night before polling day, the pollster submits his prediction of the winning candidate to a morning newspaper where his prediction will appear in print. The newspaper typesetter is usually very reliable, but there is a small probability that he makes a mistake and reverses the pollster's prediction. In this new scenario, we must distinguish between the pollster's *prediction* of the winner, and the actual *report* of his prediction in the newspaper. Crucially, suppose that the probability distribution above now pertains to the pollster's predictions, while his payoff matrix pertains to the actual report of this prediction in print. (He is only concerned with his reputation as a pundit.)

On the eve of polling day, the pollster appeals to his decision rule, which indicates that he pick a particular candidate – the Republican, say. He then has the following beliefs.

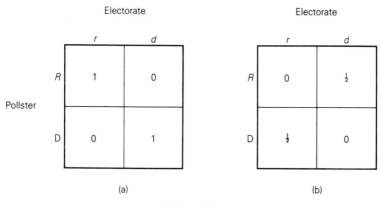

Figure 8.1

1 My decision procedure has produced an answer, namely, that I should pick the Republican.
2 However, given (1), I believe that the Democrat will win with probability 1.

The pollster is struggling with an internal conflict. He believes that, taking everything into account, his decision procedure dictates that he predict a certain candidate to win. But given his decision, he is better off if the typesetter makes a mistake and reverses his prediction. We could describe this situation as one in which the decision-maker suffers from *dissonance*. An agent's belief that a certain decision is best "all things considered" conflicts with a concurrent belief that, nevertheless, this "best" decision is actually worse than the implementation of some other decision.

Jeffrey's (1983) notion of *ratifiability* is a criterion of rational choice which makes essential use of this distinction between decisions and performances. In his own words,

The notion of ratifiability is applicable only where, during deliberation, the agent finds it conceivable that he will not manage to perform the act he finally decides to perform, but will find himself performing one of the other available acts instead. (Jeffrey, 1983, p. 18)

Having thus driven a wedge between decisions and performances, the criterion of ratifiability picks out as rational those actions which do not give rise to dissonance.

The option in question is ratifiable or not depending on whether or not the expected desirability of actually carrying it out (having chosen it) is at least as great as the expected desirability of actually carrying out each of the alternatives (in spite of having chosen to carry out a different option, as hypothesized). (Jeffrey, 1983, p. 20)

To understand the motivation behind the notion of ratifiability, we need to consider the underpinnings of Jeffrey's framework for decisions. In abolishing Savage's (1954) distinction between "acts," "states of the world," and "consequences," Jeffrey (1965) was able to construct a unified framework for decisions in which the consequences of an individual's action and the action itself is as much a part of the description of the world as any other feature of the world. To choose an act in Jeffrey's framework is to make a certain proposition true. Thus, when Ω is the state space consisting of all states of the world ω, an act can be seen as a subset of Ω. To choose an act a_k is to ensure that the true state of the world is an element of a_k.

However, there are two problems in developing this idea. Let $\{a_1, a_2, \ldots a_m\}$ be the set of acts for the decision-maker. This set partitions Ω, reflecting the condition that one, and only one, act is chosen. It is assumed that the decision-maker has a probability distribution p over Ω. The desirability $u(\omega)$ of the state ω is thus the value of a random variable u at ω. Denote by $E(u|a_k)$ the conditional expectation of u on a_k. Then, it might seem that the following is a natural criterion of rationality.

a_k is rational whenever $E(u|a_k) \geqslant E(u|a_l)$ for all actions a_l for which the payoff $E(u|a_l)$ is defined   (8.1)

Of the two problems mentioned above, one has been discussed at length; namely, when p is not independent, (8.1) may advocate the choice of a strictly dominated act. We shall not dwell on this issue here but merely refer the reader to the huge literature on Newcomb's Problem (see, for example, the survey by Eells (1982)).

There is a second, more basic, problem. We have supposed that the decision-maker has a probability distribution p over Ω. An act is a subset of Ω, and so the decision-maker attaches a probability to each of his own acts. Moreover, let us suppose that the decision-maker is aware that he holds the beliefs implied by p. In particular, suppose p is the probability distribution obtained after full deliberation by the decision-maker about his choice problem. In this case, the probability attached to an act is the probability attached by the decision-maker to his choosing that act. Among other things, this would mean that when the decision-maker decides against an act he attaches probability zero to his choosing this act. That is,

$$\text{If } a_k \text{ is not chosen then } p(a_k) = 0 \qquad (8.2)$$

This would seem to be uncontroversial in the extreme. It nevertheless generates a problem for our initial definition of rationality. When a_k is chosen, $p(a_l) = 0$ for all $l \neq k$, and so $E(u|a_l)$ is undefined for all $l \neq k$. Since $E(u|a_k)$ is equal to itself, (8.1) is satisfied trivially, and any act that is chosen is rational. At the root of this difficulty is the fact that, when we abolish Savage's distinction between states of the world and consequences, the distribution p over Ω cannot be specified independently of the act chosen.

Let us draw this point out more fully. There is something of a dilemma. On the one hand, in order to compare the desirability of various actions, the decision-maker needs a set of beliefs about the world. That is, p must be specified before the individual can assess the desirability of an action. However, as soon as the decision-maker forms a probability distribution p, this implies a choice by the decision-maker among the available acts, and thus prejudges the comparison of desirability among acts. In short, p is needed *before* deliberation takes place, but p implies the *conclusion* of such a deliberation.

Ratifiability is a device which is designed to overcome this problem. By introducing the distinction between decisions and performances, it is possible to ensure that all acts have positive probability. However, by attributing these probabilities to "mistakes" rather than to informed choice, the individual is not prejudging the desirability of actions.

The notion of ratifiability is a comparative newcomer in decision theory, but the basic theme of introducing perturbations has a longer history in the physical sciences. The pioneering work of Selten (1975) has popularized the device of introducing perturbations in the analysis of games. His notion of "trembling hands" has exercised a profound influence on the subsequent development of game theory. Admittedly, the game-theorist's motive in introducing perturbations is somewhat different from the motivation underlying ratifiability. Game-theorists are often interested in the "robustness" of equilibria, and perturbations are introduced to test for such robustness. Nevertheless, the vocabulary of game theory can help us in analysing ratifiability. Indeed, the central theme of this paper is that ratifiability can be given a precise formal representation in terms of game-theoretic concepts.

In our formal characterization of ratifiability I draw on two solution concepts in game theory. The first is Aumann's (1974, 1987) notion of correlated equilibrium and the second is Selten's (1975) notion of perfect equilibrium. I present two alternative formalizations. The first coincides with the notion of correlated equilibrium, while the second yields a refinement of correlated equilibrium akin to Selten's perfect equilibrium.

Inevitably, much of our discussion is concerned with formal structures, and some readers may find this unpalatable. However, it is hoped that the formalism is seen not to be gratuitous. There are important insights to be gained from the formalism. In particular, we can isolate two distinct notions of ratifiability depending on how we choose to model the notion of "trembles." Moreover, by showing that ratifiability can be understood in terms of game theory, we can tap the accumulated body of knowledge provided by game theory in understanding ratifiability.

2 FIRST NOTION OF RATIFIABILITY

I shall conduct the discussion in terms of a two-player normal-form game. This allows us to formalize the notion of ratifiability in a perspicuous way and focus attention on substantive issues of interpretation. A one-person decision problem is construed as a game between the decision-maker and Nature.

2.1 The game G

Let G: $= (S^1, S^2, h^1, h^2)$ be a two-player normal-form game, where S^i is player i's strategy set and h^i is player i's payoff function which associates a number (i's payoff) with each pair of strategies, one from each of S^1 and S^2. We assume that both S^1 and S^2 are finite, with K^1 and K^2 elements respectively. We denote by s^i_j the jth strategy of player i. For the rest of this paper, we shall follow the notational convention of denoting individuals by superscripts and strategies by subscripts. The superscript $-i$ refers to player i's opponent.

2.2 The state space Ω

We define a set of *propositions* Ψ consisting of the following propositions.

$$D^i_k: = \text{"player } t \text{ decides to play } s^i_k\text{"}$$

$$P^i_k: = \text{"player } t \text{ performs } s^i_k\text{"}$$

where k ranges over $\{1, \ldots K^i\}$. Ψ has $2(K^1 + K^2)$ elements.

Consider any function ω defined on the elements of Ψ which takes the value 0 and 1. I shall say that ω is a *state* if, for all i, k and $l \neq k$,

$$\omega(D_k^i) = 1 \Leftrightarrow \omega(D_l^i) = 0 \text{ and } \omega(P_k^i) = 1 \Leftrightarrow \omega(P_l^i) = 0 \qquad (8.3)$$

The interpretation is that a proposition q is true at ω if $\omega(q) = 1$ and q is false at ω if $\omega(q) = 0$. Let Ω denote, as before, the set of all states. Ω has $(K^1 K^2)^2$ elements. Define the following subsets of Ω.

$$\delta_k^i := \{\omega \,|\, \omega(D_k^i) = 1\} \qquad (8.4)$$

$$\pi_k^i := \{\omega \,|\, \omega(P_k^i) = 1\}$$

δ_k^i is the event that i decides to play s_k^i, and π_k^i is the event that i performs s_k^i. These events do not coincide by construction, and we leave open as a logical possibility the divergence between decisions and performances. The mnemonics of δ for "decision" and π for "performance" should help the reader keep track of the notation.

Write Δ^i for $\{\delta_k^i\}$ and Π^i for $\{\pi_k^i\}$, where $k \in \{1, \ldots, K^i\}$. By (8.3) both Δ^i and Π^i partition Ω. Denote by Δ the meet of the partitions Δ^1 and Δ^2 and by Π the meet of the partitions Π^1 and Π^2. That is,

$$\Delta := \{\delta^1 \cap \delta^2 \,|\, \delta^1 \in \Delta^1 \text{ and } \delta^2 \in \Delta^2\}$$
$$\Pi := \{\pi^1 \cap \pi^2 \,|\, \pi^1 \in \Pi^1 \text{ and } \pi^2 \in \Pi^2\} \qquad (8.5)$$

Thus, Δ is a partition of Ω whose generic element is the event that 1 decides on one of his acts and 2 decides on one of hers.

2.3 ϵ-Ratifiability

Suppose player i has a probability distribution p over Ω. We define the function H^i as follows.

$$H^i(k|j) := \sum_{l=1}^{K^{-i}} p(\pi_l^{-i} \,|\, \delta_j^i \cap \pi_k^i) h^i(s_k^i, s_l^{-i}) \qquad (8.6)$$

$H^i(k|j)$ is the payoff expected by player i when he decides on s_j^i but performs s_k^i. $H^i(k|j)$ is defined whenever p assigns nonzero probability to $\delta_j^i \cap \pi_k^i$.

Let some $\epsilon > 0$ be given. We take ϵ to be small. In particular,

$$\epsilon < \min_i \left\{ \frac{1}{K^i} \right\}.$$

Consider the following conditions on p.

$$p(\pi_j^i \,|\, \delta_k^i) = \epsilon \qquad \forall j \neq k, \text{ whenever defined} \qquad (A1)$$

$$p(\pi^i|\delta^i \cap \delta^{-i}) = p(\pi^i|\delta^i) \qquad \forall \pi^i,\, \delta^i,\, \delta^{-i},\ \text{whenever defined} \quad (A2)$$

$$H^i(j\,|j) \geqslant H^i(k\,|j) \qquad \forall j,\, k,\ \text{whenever defined} \qquad (A3)$$

(A1) formalizes the existence of trembles of size ϵ so that, given a decision to play a certain strategy, each of the other strategies may be performed with probability ϵ. (A2) states that such trembles are independent of the opponent's decisions. (A3) formalizes the absence of dissonance. It states that, whenever an individual decides on an action, he cannot do better than to perform that action.

DEFINITION 8.1. p is ϵ-ratifiable for i if p satisfies (A1), (A2), and (A3).

Note that we have applied the term "ratifiable" to the probability distribution p itself rather than to particular actions. The rationale for this is that p specifies, among other things, the decisions of the individual.

The notion of ϵ-ratifiability is very close in spirit to Jeffrey's own informal discussion of ratifiability. However, the prescriptions delivered by the notion of ϵ-ratifiability will depend on the particular ϵ chosen. For any particular decision problem, the notion of ϵ-ratifiability will specify a whole family of prescriptions, depending on what value of ϵ is chosen. Arguably, this is a shortcoming. The motive for introducing trembles at all was merely to avoid attaching probability zero to any act. The precise magnitude of such trembles should play no part in the analysis. Rather, what matters is that such trembles exist, and that they be "small."

An elegant way of overcoming this sort of problem is a method used by Selten (1975) in which we work with those tremble-free distributions (that is, those distributions with $\epsilon = 0$) which can be obtained as the limit of a sequence of distributions with trembles.

As one might expect, there is more than one way of implementing such a project, and we shall present just two. In the first, a player believes that whereas he himself is susceptible to trembles his opponent is free from such a handicap. In the second, we try to incorporate the common recognition on the part of the players of their common fallibility. The former leads to correlated equilibrium, while the latter leads to a robust refinement of correlated equilibrium, closely related to Selten's perfect equilibrium. We shall discuss the significance of these results as they appear.

2.4 First notion of ratifiability

Consider the following condition on p.

$$p(\pi_k^{-i}) = p(\delta_k^{-i}) \qquad \forall k \qquad (A4)$$

We say that p is *modest* for i if it satisfies (A4). When i has a modest distribution, he believes that his opponent is not susceptible to trembles. We define our first notion of ratifiability as follows.

DEFINITION 8.2. p is *modestly ratifiable* for i if there are sequences $\langle p_t \rangle$ and $\langle \epsilon_t \rangle$ such that, for all t, p_t is modest for i and ϵ_t-ratifiable for i, and $p_t \to p$ as $\epsilon_t \to 0$.

At this point, I shall introduce the idea that the two players' probability distributions may be identical. That is, they hold the same beliefs about the world. Note that this idea is not as innocuous as it may seem, since the "world" specifies the actions of both players.

In essence, the idea of a shared belief over actions is part of the assumption that the players' actions are in equilibrium. It is as if both players are correctly predicting each other's actions and answering with their best replies. By allowing shared beliefs, it is possible to compare the results of this paper directly with those of game theory. On the other hand, if we choose to steer clear of the idea of shared beliefs, we can still develop the ideas which follow, but at a cost. All our results would have to be prefixed with the phrase "player i believes that . . .," or words to that effect.

We shall take the first course and allow for the possibility of a shared probability distribution. Without wishing to downgrade the problems associated with this move, we can say that our "sin" is no graver than that of game theory itself.

Thus, I shall say that a shared probability distribution p is modestly ratifiable if p is modestly ratifiable for both players.

2.5 Correlated equilibrium

Our first result is that the class of modestly ratifiable distributions coincides with the class of correlated equilibrium distributions. We begin by reviewing the notion of correlated equilibrium. Let p be a tremble-free distribution on Ω, that is, one for which $p(\delta_k^i) = p(\pi_k^i)$ for all i and k. In such a case, p defines an unambiguous probability to each strategy pair. Define

$$\phi^i(l|j) := p(\delta_l^{-i}|\delta_j^i) \qquad (8.7)$$

The distribution p is said to be a *correlated equilibrium distribution* if, for all i, j, and k, whenever $\phi^i(l|j)$ is defined

$$\sum_{l=1}^{K^{-i}} \phi^i(l|j)[h^i(s_j^i, s_l^{-i}) - h^i(s_k^i, s_l^{-i})] \geq 0 \qquad (8.8)$$

The notion of correlated equilibrium is due to Aumann (1974, 1987), and has the following interpretation. Suppose there is an impartial arbitrator who administers an experiment in which a random outcome is observed. The space of outcomes is the strategy set $S^1 \times S^2$, and both players know the distribution of probabilities over this set. However, only the arbitrator can observe the actual outcome of the experiment. When the arbitrator observes the outcome $s = (s^1, s^2)$, he recommends to player 1 that s^1 should be played, and recommends to player 2 that s^2 should be played. Crucially, one player does not know the recommendation made to his opponent. A probability distribution over $S^1 \times S^2$ is a correlated equilibrium distribution if no player can achieve a higher expected payoff by departing from the arbitrator's recommendations, given that his opponent heeds the recommendations.

We illustrate this concept with an example. Consider the game in figure 8.2 – the familiar game of Chicken. There are three Nash equilibria in this game: (T, R), (B, L), and a mixed strategy equilibrium in which each player receives $4\frac{2}{3}$. However, both players can receive an expected payoff of 5 if they agree to the following coordination scheme. Before the game is played, they appoint an impartial arbitrator who will administer an experiment in which a fair die is cast. The arbitrator then issues suggestions to each player on which action should be performed. A player only hears his own message and can only make probability judgments about the likely messages received by his opponent. The rule followed by the arbitrator is as follows.

Outcome	Suggestion to 1	Suggestion to 2
1 or 2	Play T	Play L
3 or 4	Play T	Play R
5 or 6	Play B	Play L

It can readily be verified that neither player obtains a higher payoff by departing from the suggestions (given that his opponent follows the

	L	R
T	(6, 6)	(2, 7)
B	(7, 2)	(0, 0)

Figure 8.2

suggestions). For example, if player 1 is recommended to play T, he infers from the rule that the outcome of the die is in {1, 2, 3, 4}. Conditional on this information, he infers that player 2 has been suggested L and R with equal probability. Thus, on the assumption that 2 follows the arbitrator's suggestions, if 1 plays T his expected payoff is $\frac{1}{2}(6) + \frac{1}{2}(2)$ = 4, whereas if he departs from the suggestion and plays B his payoff is $\frac{1}{2}(7) + \frac{1}{2}(0) = 3\frac{1}{2}$. By agreeing to follow the mechanism above, both players can expect a payoff of $\frac{1}{3}(7) + \frac{1}{3}(2) + \frac{1}{3}(6) = 5$, which exceeds the maximum symmetric payoff obtainable as a Nash equilibrium.

On a point of terminology, when p is a correlated equilibrium distribution, we shall simply refer to p as a correlated equilibrium.

THEOREM 8.1. p is modestly ratifiable if and only if p is a correlated equilibrium.

The proofs of this and all other theorems appear in the appendix. For now, we remark on the interpretation of modest ratifiability supplied by the notion of correlated equilibrium. The distinction between decisions and performances is exactly analogous to the distinction between the recommendations issued by the arbitrator and the actions taken by the players. Notice the crucial role played by the assumption that p is shared by both players. Without it, we could not obtain an equilibrium.

In addition to the interpretation supplied by the notion of correlated equilibrium, we can draw on the discussions of the properties of correlated equilibrium (as in Aumann, 1974), and translate them directly into the idiom of ratifiability. Thus, when p is modestly ratifiable we have the following corollaries.

1 No player will place positive probability on a strictly dominated strategy (so that, in Newcomb's problem, both boxes are taken, and in the Prisoners' Dilemma, the players confess).

2 In a two-person zero-sum game, the payoffs achievable by modest ratifiability cannot exceed the "value" of the game.

3 However, in nonzero-sum games, the payoffs achieveable by modest ratifiability can exceed the payoffs achievable as a Nash equilibrium (as in our example above).

3 SECOND NOTION OF RATIFIABILITY

3.1 Motivation

We motivate our second formalization of ratifiability with the example shown in figure 8.3. Consider the game on the left and the distribution

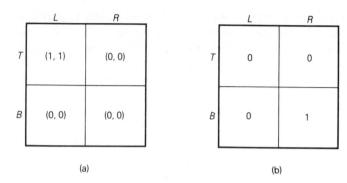

Figure 8.3

over the strategy combinations on the right. This distribution is over the *decisions* of the players. The distribution on the right represents the situation in which the player choosing rows chooses B and the player choosing columns chooses R. It is a correlated equilibrium of the game on the left, and by theorem 8.1 is modestly ratifiable. Also, as long as players are modest, the existence of small trembles will not alter their assessments of their prospects. Each expects a payoff of zero whether he believes he trembles or not. Consider now a situation in which not only are both players susceptible to trembles but both players recognize each other's fallibility. Then player 1 believes that player 2 trembles and performs L with a small probability. But then, player 1's payoff when he trembles will be higher than that when he does not. The reasoning is symmetric for player 2, and the distribution above is no longer ratifiable.

This example is an illustration of the fragility of modest ratifiability. In a situation such as the one above, as soon as a player recognizes that his opponent is fallible in the same way as he is, he recognizes that trembles on his part would promote his own interest. It could be argued that, if we are to take the notion of trembles seriously, we must allow for the common recognition of this fallibility.

3.2 Second notion of ratifiability

Our second formalization of ratifiability incorporates the common recognition of trembles. As with modest ratifiability, we examine those tremble-free distributions which can be obtained as the limit of ϵ-ratifiable distributions, but we dispense with the condition of modesty. As soon as a player recognizes that both players tremble, his distribution p over Ω determines the degree of correlation between his own trembles and those of his opponent. We shall consider the simplest case, namely, that in which the trembles across players are independent. Denote by δ a typical element of Δ. This condition can be stated as follows.

$$p(\pi^i | \delta) = p(\pi^i | \delta \cap \pi^{-i}) \qquad \forall \pi^i, \delta, \pi^{-i}, \qquad \text{(A5)}$$

It is important to understand the precise sense in which trembles are independent across players. (A5) states that whether one player trembles or not is probabilistically independent of whether his opponent trembles or not. It does *not* imply that the decisions of the players are themselves independent.

As an intermediate step in our formalization, we characterize ϵ-ratifiability under (A5). For a given $\epsilon > 0$ and a distribution p over Ω, define the following quantity, which will be given an interpretation shortly:

$$\theta^i(l|j) := \left[1 - (K^{-i} - 1)\epsilon\right]\rho(\delta_l^{-i}|\delta_j^i) + \left[\sum_{m \neq l} p(\delta_m^{-i}|\delta_j^i)\right]\epsilon \qquad \text{(8.9)}$$

THEOREM 8.2. Under (A5), if p is ϵ-ratifiable for both players, then for all i, j, and k, whenever $\theta^i(l|j)$ is defined

$$\sum_{l=1}^{K^{-i}} \theta^i(l|j)\left[h^i(s_j^i, s_l^{-i}) - h^i(s_k^i, s_l^{-i})\right] \geq 0 \qquad \text{(8.10)}$$

Comparing (8.10) with the definition of correlated equilibrium given in (8.8) we see that $\phi^i(l|j)$ has been replaced by $\theta^i(l|j)$. $\theta^i(l|j)$ is the probability that i's opponent performs s_l^i given that i has decided to play s_j^i . It is the sum of two expressions – the probability of i's opponent's performing s_l^{-i} intentionally, and the probability of his performing s_l^{-i} by mistake.

Note one important corallary of theorem 8.2. As $\epsilon \to 0$, $\theta^i(l|j) \to \phi^i(l|j)$. Thus, under (A5), the limit of a sequence of ϵ-ratifiable distributions as ϵ tends to zero is modestly ratifiable. However, as our example at the beginning of this section shows, there are modestly ratifiable distributions which cannot be obtained as the limit of such a sequence. It will be useful to have a term for the smaller class of distributions, the limits of ϵ-ratifiable distributions satisfying (A5).

DEFINITION 8.3. p is *ratifiable* if there are sequences $\langle p_t \rangle$ and $\langle \epsilon_t \rangle$ such that, for all t, p_t is ϵ_t-ratifiable for both players, satisfies (A5) for both players, and $p_t \to p$ as $\epsilon_t \to 0$.

Since $\theta^i(l|j) \to \phi^i(l|j)$ as ϵ tends to zero, the set of ratifiable distributions is a subset of the set of modestly ratifiable distributions, and so by theorem 8.1 is a subset of correlated equilibria. Moreover, since we have seen a counterexample to the converse inclusion, the inclusion is strict. We thus arrive at a refinement of correlated equilibrium. Indeed, if we modify definition 8.3 to incorporate independence of the decisions of the players, any ratifiable distribution defines a perfect equilibrium in the sense of Selten (1975). Our third theorem makes this claim precise. To state it, we begin by reviewing the notion of perfect equilibrium.

3.3 Perfect equilibrium and ratifiability

A pair of strategies which are best replies to each other is called a Nash equilibrium. A perfect equilibrium is a Nash equilibrium which also has the property that, even if the players were susceptible to small trembles, the strategies remain best replies to each other.

The formal definition of perfect equilibrium rests on the notion of mixed strategies in which each pure strategy has a "minimum" prescribed weight in the following sense. For pure strategy s_j^i of player i, associate a strictly positive number η_j^i. The n-tuple of these numbers, one for each pure strategy of i, is denoted by η^i. These numbers sum to less than 1. Let $M^i(\eta^i)$ denote the set of all mixed strategies for i in which he plays his jth pure strategy with probability at least η_j^i.

For a pair (η^1, η^2), a *perturbed game* associated with a game G is a game in which player i is constrained to play mixed strategies in $M^i(\eta^i)$. That is, each player is constrained to play s_j^i with probability at least η_j^i.

It is easy to see that a pair of strategies (m^1, m^2) $(m^1 \in M^1(\eta^1)$, $m^2 \in M^2(\eta^2))$ is a Nash equilibrium of this perturbed game if and only if any pure strategy $s_j^i \in S^i$ which is not a best reply to m^{-i} is chosen with the minimum prescribed probability in m^i. More precisely, $m = (m^1, m^2)$ is a Nash equilibrium of the perturbed game $[G, \eta]$ if and only if, for any i, j, k,

$$\sum_{l=1}^{K^{-1}} m_l^{-i} [h^i(s_j^i, s_l^{-i}) - h^i(s_k^i, s_l^{-i})] < 0 \Rightarrow m_j^i = \eta_j^i \qquad (8.11)$$

A perfect equilibrium of the game G is defined to be the limit of a sequence of Nash equilibria of perturbed games $[G, \eta_t]$ as $\eta_t \to 0$. More precisely, m is a *perfect equilibrium* of G if there are sequences $\langle m_t \rangle$ and $\langle \eta_t \rangle$ such that, for all t, m_t is a Nash equilibrium of $[G, \eta_t]$ and $m_t \to m$ as $\eta_t \to 0$.

We show that, if we impose the condition that p is independent to our notion of ratifiability (so that, among other things, the decisions of the players are independent), we obtain a perfect equilibrium. Consider the following strengthening of definition 8.3.

DEFINITION 8.4. p is *independently ratifiable* if there are sequences $\langle p_t \rangle$ and $\langle \epsilon_t \rangle$ such that, for all t, p_t is independent, p_t is ϵ_t-ratifiable for both players, and $p_t \rightarrow p$ as $\epsilon_t \rightarrow 0$.

Notice that we can dispense with condition (A5) since it is automatically satisfied by independence. Notice also that this definition is strictly stronger than definition 8.3, since it ensures the independence of *decisions* as well as the independence of *trembles*. Denote by $\lambda^i(p)$ the K^i-tuple of numbers representing the distribution over performances given by p, and let $\lambda(p) := [\lambda^1(p), \lambda^2(p)]$.

THEOREM 8.3. If p is independently ratifiable, then $\lambda(p)$ is a perfect equilibrium.

The converse need not hold. Ratifiability characterizes robustness to a particular type of perturbation, namely, perturbations which are uniform in the sense of (A1). Perfectness, however, is defined with reference to any arbitrary perturbation. Thus, an equilibrium may be perfect without being robust to perturbations satisfying our assumptions.

Since our second notion of ratifiability is a special case of the first, the interpretation provided by the notion of correlated equilibrium is still applicable. However, we now have an additional twist to the scenario involving the impartial arbitrator. When an individual receives a recommendation to choose an action, the individual takes into account the possibility that his opponent will make errors in implementing the recommendations of the arbitrator. This has the effect that the rules governing the recommendations of this sort must be robust to small perturbations. That is, following them must be optimal for a player who regards it as possible that others will err in playing their respective parts. Those actions which satisfy our first notion of ratifiability but fail our second are actions which are fragile to such perturbations. To put it crudely, such an action ceases to be optimal when even a tiny amount of sand is thrown into the system.

In many ways, our second notion of ratifiability is a natural extension of the first. If trembles are to be given a role in the analysis of decisions at all, there is a case for allowing the individuals to be aware of them.

Even a partially rational person who realizes that he sometimes makes mistakes must realize that others do too. Robustness follows from this recognition and expected utility maximization.

4 BEYOND RATIFIABILITY

The purpose of this paper has been to make precise the consequences of drawing the distinction between decisions and performances and to see what restrictions are implied by ratifiability. This, of course, leaves open the much more fundamental issue of whether such an approach to decision theory is the best.

The objection is clear enough – that, although we are working with tremble-free distributions, as long as we make reference to trembles of any form in the definition of ratifiability we cannot remain untinged of associations therewith. This is a criticism which must be taken seriously, and it is sufficiently forceful to persuade us to search for alternative formulations of rational choice which go beyond ratifiability. We conclude this paper with a few remarks on one possible approach.

As was mentioned in section 1, the device of trembles is brought in, not because of the intrinsic interest of players "trembling," but because we want to compare the desirability of each available act. Since an act which is not chosen is assigned a probability of zero, the desirability of any act which is not chosen can only be assessed in a counterfactual sense. The device of trembles makes this counterfactual evaluation possible. The sentence

"I have decided to play x, but if I were to tremble and perform
y instead, the consequence would be z."   (8.12)

could be regarded as a surrogate for the more direct statement

I play x, but if I were to play y, the consequence would be z."
                                                            (8.13)

In other words, ratifiability can be regarded as a device for formalizing counterfactual beliefs about those acts which are given zero probability in equilibrium. The postulates (A1)–(A5) are instrumental in providing a particular theory of counterfactuals within which to evaluate these statements.

This suggests an alternative to ratifiability which evaluates these counterfactuals directly. By tackling counterfactuals head on, we could bypass the philosophically dubious enterprise of defining rationality in terms of concepts such as trembles. Rather than packing away all the assumptions into the postulates (A1)–(A5), we could try to lay bare the workings of the relevant counterfactuals.

This theme is taken up in another paper (Shin, 1989). By specifying a theory of counterfactuals in the spirit of Stalnaker and Lewis, we arrive at formal structures which deliver the same answers as ratifiability but without the baggage. For instance, correlated equilibrium is obtained by imposing a natural metric on the space of possible worlds. Robust refinements are also obtained with little extra cost.

One implication of this is rather interesting. Reading some of the papers in the literature, one might be forgiven for thinking that Bayesian decision theory and causal decision theory are poles apart, and implacably opposed to each other. The results we have alluded to suggest otherwise. Given the appropriate formalization, they deliver identical recommendations.

APPENDIX: PROOFS OF THEOREMS

Proof of Theorem 8.1

We begin with some preliminary remarks. Let some $\epsilon > 0$ be given. Since Π^i partitions Ω,

$$p\left(\pi_k^i \mid \delta_j^i\right) = 1 - \sum_{m \neq k} p\left(\pi_m^i \mid \delta_j^i\right)$$

Thus, when p satisfies (A1) for player i,

$$p\left(\pi_k^i \mid \delta_j^i\right) = \begin{cases} \epsilon & \text{if } j \neq k \\ 1 - (K^i - 1)\epsilon & \text{if } j = k \end{cases} \qquad (8.\text{A1})$$

Then, since $p(\delta_j^i \cap \pi_k^i) = p(\pi_k^i \mid \delta_j^i)\,p(\delta_j^i)$, we have

$$p(\delta_j^i \cap \pi_k^i) = 0 \Leftrightarrow p(\delta_j^i) = 0 \qquad (8.\text{A2})$$

Suppose p satisfies (A1) and (A2) for i and is modest for i. Then, consider the probability $p(\pi_l^{-i} \mid \delta_j^i \cap \pi_k^i)$ when $p(\delta_j^i) > 0$. We have two cases.

Case (i) $p(\delta_j^i \cap \delta_l^{-i}) > 0$

$$p\left(\pi_l^{-i} \mid \delta_j^i \cap \pi_k^i\right) = \frac{p\left(\pi_l^{-i} \cap \delta_j^i \cap \pi_k^i\right)}{p\left(\delta_j^i \cap \pi_k^i\right)}$$

$$= \frac{p\left(\delta_l^{-i} \cap \delta_j^i \cap \pi_k^i\right)}{p\left(\delta_j^i \cap \pi_k^i\right)} \quad \text{by modesty}$$

$$= \frac{p\left(\pi_k^i \mid \delta_l^{-i} \cap \delta_j^i\right) p\left(\delta_l^{-i} \cap \delta_j^i\right)}{p\left(\pi_k^i \mid \delta_j^i\right) p\left(\delta_j^i\right)}$$

$$= \frac{p\left(\delta_l^{-i} \cap \delta_j^i\right)}{p\left(\delta_j^i\right)} \text{ by (A2)}$$

Case (ii) $p\left(\delta_j^i \cap \delta_l^{-i}\right) = 0$

$$p\left(\pi_l^{-i} \mid \delta_j^i \cap \pi_k^i\right) = \frac{p\left(\pi_l^{-i} \cap \delta_j^i \cap \pi_k^i\right)}{p\left(\delta_j^i \cap \pi_k^i\right)}$$

$$= \frac{p\left(\delta_l^{-i} \cap \delta_j^i \cap \pi_k^i\right)}{p\left(\delta_j^i \cap \pi_k^i\right)} \text{ by modesty}$$

$$= 0$$

$$= \frac{p\left(\delta_l^{-i} \cap \delta_j^i\right)}{p\left(\delta_j^i\right)}$$

In other words, when p satisfies (A1), (A2), and modesty for i, whenever $p(\delta_j^i) > 0$,

$$p\left(\pi_l^{-i} \mid \delta_j^i \cap \pi_k^i\right) = p\left(\delta_l^{-i} \mid \delta_j^i\right) \qquad \forall l, j, k \qquad \text{(8.A3)}$$

We can then prove theorem 8.1. First, we show that when p is modestly ratifiable p is a correlated equilibrium. We fix a player i and let $\langle p_t \rangle$ and $\langle \epsilon_t \rangle$ be sequences such that p_t is ϵ_t-ratifiable for i for all t, p_t is modest for i for all t, and $p_t \to p$ as $\epsilon_t \to 0$. Then, by (A3) and (8.A2), whenever $p_t(\delta_j^i) > 0$,

$$\sum_l p_t\left(\pi_l^{-i} \mid \delta_j^i \cap \pi_j^i\right) h^i\left(s_j^i, s_l^{-i}\right) \geqslant \sum_l p_t\left(\pi_l^{-i} \mid \delta_j^i \cap \pi_k^i\right) h^i\left(s_k^i, s_l^{-i}\right) \qquad \forall j, k \qquad \text{(8.A4)}$$

where l ranges over $\{1, \ldots, K^{-i}\}$. Denote the left-hand side of (8.A4) by L_t and the right-hand side by R_t. Then

$$\lim_{t \to \infty} L_t = \sum_{l=1}^{K^{-i}} \lim_{t \to \infty} p_t\left(\pi_l^{-i} \mid \delta_j^i \cap \pi_j^i\right) h^i\left(s_j^i, s_l^{-i}\right)$$

$$= \sum_{l=1}^{K^{-i}} \lim_{t \to \infty} p_t\left(\delta_l^{-i} \mid \delta_j^i\right) h^i\left(s_j^i, s_l^{-i}\right) \qquad \text{by (8.A3)}$$

$$= \sum_{l=1}^{K^{-i}} p\left(\delta_l^{-i} \mid \delta_j^i\right) h^i\left(s_j^i, s_l^{-i}\right) \qquad \text{since } p_t \to p$$

Similarly,

$$\lim_{t \to \infty} R_t = \sum_{l=1}^{K^{-i}} p_t\left(\delta_l^{-i} \mid \delta_j^i\right) h^i\left(s_k^i, s_l^{-i}\right)$$

Since $L_t \geqslant R_t$ for all t, $\lim_{t \to \infty} L_t \geqslant \lim_{t \to \infty} R_t$. This argument can be repeated for both players. Thus, whenever δ_j^i is non-null,

$$\sum_{l=1}^{K^{-i}} \phi^i(l|j)\left[h^i(s_j^i, s_l^{-i}) - h^i(s_k^i, s_l^{-i})\right] \geq 0 \qquad \forall i, j, k \qquad (8.\text{A}5)$$

which is the condition for p to be a correlated equilibrium.

We now prove the converse, namely, that when (8.A5) holds for non-null δ_j^i, p is modestly ratifiable. Consider some player i. Let $\langle \epsilon_t \rangle$ be some sequence which converges to zero. We construct a sequence $\langle p_t \rangle$ as follows.

1 $p_t(\delta) = p(\delta)$, $\forall \delta$, t.
2 p_t is modest for i, $\forall t$.
3 p_t satisfies (A1) and (A2) for i, where $\epsilon = \epsilon_t$, $\forall t$.

Then $p_t \to p$ as $\epsilon_t \to 0$. Moreover, p_t is modest for i, for all t. Thus, to prove that p is modestly ratifiable for i, it remains to check that p_t is ϵ_t-ratifiable for i, for all t. Of the three conditions for ϵ_t-ratifiability, (A1) and (A2) hold by construction. To see that (A3) holds as well, note that from 1 and (8.A5), whenever δ_j^i is non-null,

$$\sum_{l=1}^{K^{-i}} p_t(\delta_l^{-i}|\delta_j^i)\left[h^i(s_j^i, s_l^{-i}) - h^i(s_k^i, s_l^{-i})\right] \geq 0 \qquad \forall j, k, t \qquad (8.\text{A}6)$$

Then, from (8.A3) and (8.A2),

$$\sum_l p_t(\pi_l^{-i}|\delta_j^i \cap \pi_j^i)\, h^i(s_j^i, s_l^{-i}) \geq \sum_l p_t(\pi_l^{-i}|\delta_j^i \cap \pi_k^i)\, h^i(s_k^i, s_l^{-i}) \qquad \forall j, k, t \qquad (8.\text{A}7)$$

whenever such expressions are defined. This is condition (A3). Thus p is modestly ratifiable for i. We can construct such a sequence for both players, so that p is modestly ratifiable for both players. This proves our theorem.

Proof of Theorem 8.2

Let some $\epsilon > 0$ be given and suppose p satisfies (A1) and (A2) for both players. Consider $p(\pi^{-i} \cap \delta^{-i} \cap \delta^i)$. When $\delta^{-i} \cap \delta^i$ is non-null,

$$p(\pi^i \cap \delta^i \cap \delta^{-i}) = p(\pi^{-i}|\delta^i \cap \delta^{-i})\, p(\delta^i \cap \delta^{-i})$$

$$= p(\pi^{-i}|\delta^{-i})\, p(\delta^i \cap \delta^{-i}) \qquad \text{by (A2)}$$

$$> 0 \qquad \text{by (8.A1)}$$

Thus, when p also satisfies (A5) for both players and $p(\delta^i \cap \delta^{-i}) > 0$,

$$p(\pi^i \cap \pi^{-i} \cap \delta^i \cap \delta^{-i}) = p(\pi^i|\pi^{-i} \cap \delta^i \cap \delta^{-i})\, p(\pi^{-i}|\delta^i \cap \delta^{-i})\, p(\delta^i \cap \delta^{-i})$$

$$= p(\pi^i|\delta^i \cap \delta^{-i})\, p(\pi^{-i}|\delta^i \cap \delta^{-i})\, p(\delta^i \cap \delta^{-i}) \quad \text{by (A5)}$$

$$= p(\pi^i|\delta^{-i})\, p(\pi^{-i}|\delta^{-i})\, p(\delta^i \cap \delta^{-i}) \quad \text{by (A2)} \qquad (8.\text{A}8)$$

Define the function α^i such that, for any $j, k \in \{1, \ldots, K^i\}$,

$$\alpha^i(j, k) = \begin{cases} \epsilon & \text{if } j \neq k \\ 1 - (K^i - 1)\epsilon & \text{if } j = k \end{cases} \tag{8.A9}$$

Thus, from (8.A1) we can express (8.A8) more succinctly by saying that, whenever $p(\delta_j^i \cap \delta_m^{-i}) > 0$, $p(\pi_k^i \cap \pi_l^{-i} \cap \delta_j^i \cap \delta_m^{-i}) = \alpha^i(j, k)\alpha^{-i}(l, m)p(\delta_j^i \cap \delta_m^{-i})$. But this also holds when $p(\delta_j^i \cap \delta_m^{-i}) = 0$. In short, when p satisfies (A1), (A2), and (A5) for both players,

$$p(\pi_k^i \cap \pi_l^{-i} \cap \delta_j^i \cap \delta_m^{-i}) = \alpha^i(j, k)\alpha^{-i}(l, m)p(\delta_j^i \cap \delta_m^{-i}) \qquad \forall i, j, k, l, m \tag{8.A10}$$

Suppose $p(\delta_j^i) > 0$ and consider $p(\pi_l^{-i}|\delta_j^i \cap \pi_k^i)$.

$$
\begin{aligned}
p(\pi_l^{-i}|\delta_j^i \cap \pi_k^i) &= \frac{p(\pi_l^{-i} \cap \delta_j^i \cap \pi_k^i)}{p(\delta_j^i \cap \pi_k^i)} \\
&= \frac{\Sigma_m p(\delta_m^{-i} \cap \pi_l^{-i} \cap \delta_j^i \cap \pi_k^i)}{p(\pi_k^i|\delta_j^i)p(\delta_j^i)} \\
&= \frac{\Sigma_m \alpha^i(j, k)\alpha^{-i}(l, m)p(\delta_j^i \cap \delta_m^{-i})}{\alpha^i(j, k)p(\delta_j^i)} \qquad \text{by (8.A10) and (8.A1)} \\
&= \sum_{m=1}^{K^{-i}} \alpha^{-i}(l, m)p(\delta_m^{-i}|\delta_j^i) \\
&= [1 - (K^{-i} - 1)\epsilon]p(\delta_l^{-i}|\delta_j^i) + \left[\sum_{m \neq l} p(\delta_m^{-i}|\delta_j^i)\right]\epsilon \\
&= \theta^i(l|j)
\end{aligned}
$$

That is, when p satisfies (A1), (A2), and (A5) for all i and $p(\delta_j^i) > 0$,

$$p(\pi_l^{-i}|\delta_j^i \cap \pi_k^i) = \theta^i(l|j) \qquad \forall i, j, k, l \tag{8.A11}$$

Theorem 8.2 now follows immediately. Together with (A3), (8.A11) implies that, whenever $p(\delta_j^i) > 0$,

$$\sum_{l=1}^{K^{-i}} \theta^i(l|j)[h^i(s_j^i, s_l^{-i}) - h^i(s_k^i, s_l^{-i})] \geq 0 \qquad \forall i, j, k \tag{8.A12}$$

which proves theorem 8.2.

Proof of Theorem 8.3

Let some $\epsilon > 0$ be given, and suppose p satisfies (A1) and (A3) for both players. Consider the probability $p(\pi_l^{-i}|\delta_j^i \cap \pi_k^i)$. When p is independent and $\delta_j^i \cap \pi_k^i$ is non-null,

$$p(\pi_l^{-i}|\delta_j^i \cap \pi_k^i) = p(\pi_l^{-i}) \tag{8.A13}$$

By (8.A2), $\delta_j^i \cap \pi_k^i$ is non-null if and only if δ_j^i is non-null. Thus, under independence, (A3) can be stated as the conditional: for all j and k, when δ_j^i is non-null,

$$\sum_{l=1}^{K^{-i}} p\left(\pi_l^{-i}\right)\left[h^i\left(s_j^i, s_l^{-i}\right) - h^i\left(s_k^i, s_l^{-i}\right)\right] \geqslant 0 \qquad (8.\text{A}14)$$

Equivalently, for all j and k, if

$$\sum_{l=1}^{K^{-i}} p\left(\pi_l^{-i}\right)\left[h^i\left(s_j^i, s_l^{-i}\right) - h^i\left(s_k^i, s_l^{-i}\right)\right] < 0 \qquad (8.\text{A}15)$$

then $p(\delta_j^i) = 0$. But when $p(\delta_j^i) = 0$,

$$p\left(\pi_j^i\right) = \sum_{s=1}^{K^i} p\left(\pi_j^i \cap \delta_s^i\right)$$

$$= \sum_{s=1}^{K^i} p\left(\pi_j^i \mid \delta_s^i\right) p\left(\delta_s^i\right)$$

$$= \left[\sum_{s \neq j} p\left(\delta_s^i\right)\right] \epsilon + \left[1 - (K^i - 1)\epsilon\right] p\left(\delta_j^i\right) \qquad \text{by (8.A1)}$$

$$= \left[\sum_{s \neq j} p\left(\delta_s^i\right)\right] \epsilon$$

Thus, when p is independent and satisfies (A3) for both players, we have the following condition. For all j and k,

$$\sum_{l=1}^{K^{-i}} p\left(\pi_l^{-i}\right)\left[h^i\left(s_j^i, s_l^{-i}\right) - h^i\left(s_k^i, s_l^{-i}\right)\right] < 0 \Rightarrow p\left(\pi_j^i\right) = \left[\sum_{s \neq j} p\left(\delta_s^i\right)\right] \epsilon \qquad (8.\text{A}16)$$

Define the K^i-vector η^i as

$$\eta_j^i = \left[\sum_{s \neq j} p\left(\delta_s^i\right)\right]_\epsilon \qquad (8.\text{A}16)$$

and let η be the $[K^1 + K^2]$-vector (η^1, η^2). Then (8.A16) is the condition for the vector of performances $\lambda(p)$ to be a Nash equilibrium of the perturbed game $\langle G, \eta \rangle$. It states that, if s_j^i is not a best reply to $-i$'s mixed strategy $\lambda^{-i}(p)$, then s_j^i is performed with minimum probability η_j^i.

Theorem 8.3 follows from this. When p is independently ratifiable, there is a sequence $\langle p_t \rangle$ of independent distributions and a sequence $\langle \epsilon_t \rangle$ converging to zero such that each p_t is ϵ_t-ratifiable for all i. By the argument above, each p_t is a distribution associated with a Nash equilibrium of a perturbed game defined by ϵ_t. More precisely, for all t, $\lambda(p_t)$ is a Nash equilibrium of the perturbed game

$\langle G, \eta_t \rangle$, with η_t defined as in (8.A16). Moreover, as $\epsilon_t \to 0$, $\eta_t \to 0$ and $\lambda(p_t) \to \lambda(p)$. Thus, there are sequences $\langle \eta_t \rangle$ and $\langle \lambda(p_t) \rangle$ such that $\lambda(p_t)$ is a Nash equilibrium of the perturbed game $\langle G, \eta_t \rangle$, and $\lambda(p_t) \to \lambda(p)$ as $\eta_t \to 0$. Thus, $\lambda(p)$ is a perfect equilibrium.

NOTE

I thank Michael Bacharach and James Mirrlees for discussions while preparing this paper, and to Christopher Harris for suggesting the example of the Pollster's Dilemma. I am particularly indebted to Susan Hurley for drawing my attention to lapses in the exposition of earlier drafts.

9

Ratifiability and Refinements (in Two-person Noncooperative Games)

William Harper

1 INTRODUCTION AND BACKGROUND

Consider the following game. You get to write down one of three options T, M or B (or some probability mixture of them, for example (0.5T, 0.1M, 0.4B)). A referee picks up your card and goes to the other player. That player gets to write down one of three options a, b, or c (or a probability mixture of them). The second player does not get to see your card and neither of you gets to communicate with the other. The referee reads the cards and then assigns the payoffs according to the following matrix (mixed choice payoffs are determined by first performing a chance experiment according to the specified probabilities):

	a	b	c
T	(300, 200)	(200, 200)	(0, 0)
M	(100, 100)	(0, 0)	(0, 100)
B	(0, 100)	(200, 0)	(100, 0)

The payoffs are in dollars. Assume that each of you has utilities that are linear with these dollar amounts. You are row chooser. Your payoffs are on the left. This game is noncooperative because you and the other player do not have any opportunity to make binding agreements as would be the case in a bargaining game. I shall use it to introduce some background for an exposition of some of the recent work on refining the concept of a solution for noncooperative games and an exposition of my proposal to use some recent ideas from individual decision theory to contribute to this refinement program.

The matrix is a normal-form representation of your game. A *normal-*

form representation of a game is an assignment of utilities representing each player's preferences for the outcomes corresponding to each combination of pure strategies. A *pure strategy* for a player is a complete plan for how that player would choose at each choice the game might offer. In this game each player gets to choose only once so that their pure strategies are just their basic options in that choice – T, M, and B for player 1, and a, b, and c for player 2. A *mixed strategy* is a probability mixture of pure strategies. In this game players get to play mixed strategies by writing down probability mixtures of their basic acts. A *utility* for a player is an assignment of numbers to outcomes representing that player's relative preference differences between pairs of those outcomes.[1] One of the idealizations of game theory is that all that matters to strategic reasoning about any player's preferences over outcomes are the ratios of these preference differences. This makes any scale transformation (multiplying the utility assigned to each outcome by the same positive number) or any change of zero point (adding the same positive or negative number to the utility assigned to each outcome) for either one player or both players irrelevant to the analysis of the game. The assumption that each player has utilities that are linear with the dollar amounts of the payoffs allows the dollar amounts to function as utilities representing the relevant ratios of preference differences of these players.

Another representation of this game is shown in figure 9.1. In this representation player 1's utilities are shown on top. Another change is that the utilities are scaled differently. In this case the units are 100 times larger.

This tree is an *extensive-form* representation of the game. It represents

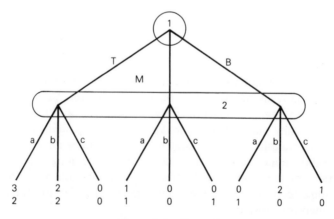

Figure 9.1   Game 0.

explicitly some relevant causal structure in the story. In the story you get to move first. In the tree your (player 1's) choice is the initial node. Player 2's choice is represented by three nodes with a line drawn round them. This is player 2's information set. It represents that player 2 must choose without getting to observe or otherwise be empirically informed what your choice was. This tree represents explicitly that neither of you can causally influence the other by the way you make your own choice. That your choice comes earlier in the tree represents that it cannot be influenced by player 2's. That player 2's information set does not distinguish among any of your options represents that you cannot influence player 2's choice by informing him of yours.

Assume that as you consider your choice in this game the game structure (as given in the extensive-form tree) and each of your utilities (that is, preferences over the outcomes up to ratios of differences) are common knowledge, as is the assumption that each of you is rational. In classical game theory the players' beliefs about what each other's choices will be are not assumed to be common knowledge at the outset. Rather, the players are expected to use strategic reasoning about the situation to form their beliefs about each other's choices as well as to figure out what their own choices should be. You are now ready to reason your way through the strategic circumstances to figure out what to expect the other to do and what to do yourself.

According to John Nash (1950, p. 290) your game is solvable if the set of all its equilibrium pairs of strategies is interchangeable. A pair of strategies is an *equilibrium* if each is a best reply to the other. A set of pairs of strategies is *interchangeable* if each pairing of a strategy for player 1 from any pair in it with a strategy for player 2 from any other pair in it is itself an equilibrium pair. The game you are facing does have a Nash solution. It is the set of all pairs consisting of the pure strategy T for player 1 and any mixture $(y\text{a}, (1 - y)\text{b})$ for player 2. Any such pair

$$(\text{T}, (y\text{a}, (1 - y)b))$$

is an equilibrium, and all the equilibrium pairs belong to this interchangeable set. According to traditional game theory the important thing about such a solution is that if it became common knowledge that each of you was committed to doing your part to reach it, then neither of you should expect to gain by defecting to a nonsolution strategy.

Von Neumann and Morgenstern (1944, pp. 147–8) offered an argument (the Indirect Argument) designed to defend the requirement that solutions be equilibria. If you assume that the game has a solution that rational players will figure out and commit themselves to, then you should assume that if you play your part in it the other player will be able to figure out what your part is and will choose a best reply to whatever strategy you choose. Notice that this best-reply assumption does not depend upon the solution being a single equilibrium pair. What is required is that there be an interchangeable set which it becomes common knowledge both players will do their part to realize.

I shall be exploring a proposal to use two ideas from individual decision theory to explicate an application of the Indirect Argument as the first stage of what Binmore (1987-8) would call an "eductive" procedure whereby rational agents in the position you are in as you begin to analyze the game can discover the solution. The explication of the Indirect Argument is as a *reductio* test of the assumption that a given strategy would satisfy your part of a solution. The first stage in the procedure is to throw out candidate strategies that fail the test in an attempt to eliminate all but the strategies in an interchangeable set.

One of the ideas from individual decision theory is to use probabilities of subjunctive conditionals as the probabilities for evaluating expected utility (see Gibbard and Harper, 1978). This is one of several equivalent formulations of what has come to be called *causal decision theory* (see Lewis (1981) and Skyrms (1982) for other formulations). On this formulation the expected utility of M is

$$U(\text{M}) = P(\text{M} \,\square\!\!\rightarrow a)(1) + P(\text{M} \,\square\!\!\rightarrow b)(0) + P(\text{M} \,\square\!\!\rightarrow c)(0)$$

Read the subjunctive conditional

$$\text{M} \,\square\!\!\rightarrow a$$

as

"If I were to play M then a would be played"

Causal decision theory was motivated by examples (for instance Newcomb's Problem) where subjective conditional probabilities do not adequately represent relevant beliefs of agents about what they can and cannot causally influence by their choices. We shall see that probability assignments to such subjunctive conditionals by rational players are adequately sensitive to their knowledge of relevant causal dependencies and independencies represented in extensive-form game trees. Using such probabilities will be a convenient way to generate expectations appropriate to the eductive reasoning that our players are engaged in as they attempt to find a solution to their game.

The second idea from individual decision theory is that a rational decision is *ratifiable*. A choice is unratifiable if and only if the assumption that you are going to commit yourself to it leads you to conclude that you would be better off doing something else instead.[2] When more than one of your alternatives is ratifiable the natural recommendation is to choose from among these ratifiable options by maximizing expected utility (Harper, 1986b, 1988, 1989).

Evaluating the ratifiability of an act requires evaluating alternatives conditional on the assumption that you are going to do the given act. Causal decision theory allows such evaluations to be explicitly formulated. For example,

$$U_B(M) = P(M \,\square\!\!\rightarrow a \,|\, B)(1) + P(M \,\square\!\!\rightarrow b \,|\, B)(0) + P(M \,\square\!\!\rightarrow c \,|\, B)(0)$$

is the evaluation on the assumption that you are going to do B of what you would expect if you were to do M instead. We can now formulate the ratifiability requirement for any act A:

$$U_A(A) \geqslant U_A(A') \text{ for all alternatives } A' \text{ to } A$$

Now we are ready to illustrate how these ideas operate in our explication of an application of the Indirect Argument to rule out B as a candidate for realizing your part in a solution.

You are assuming that there is a solution which both of you will end up finding. Now assume B realizes your part in it. On this assumption the other player will optimize relative to your part and thus will make a best reply to B. This is represented by using a best-reply prior, that is, by assigning

$$P(y \,|\, B) = 0$$

unless y (a mixed or pure strategy) is a best reply to B. You assign $P(a \,|\, B) = 1$ since a is the unique best reply to B. In evaluating the conditional probabilities of the subjunctive conditional we use the general facts that

(SA) $$P(A \,\square\!\!\rightarrow y \,|\, A) = P(y \,|\, A)$$

and that

(CI) $P(A' \,\square\!\!\rightarrow y \,|\, A) = P(y \,|\, A)$ if y is causally independent of the choice between A and A'

These constraints ensure that

$$U_B(B) = 0 < U_B(M) = 1$$

which shows that B is not ratifiable by *any P* which is a best-reply prior. This rules B out as a candidate for your part of the solution to the game.

This is a game in which the Indirect Argument succeeds in cutting down the candidate strategies to those in an interchangeable set. The best-reply ratifiable strategies are exactly the equilibrium strategies T for player 1 and all mixtures (ya, $(1 - y)$b) for player 2 that form the set of interchangeable pairs that is the Nash solution. I have argued (Harper, 1989) that such a successful application of the Indirect Argument vindicates the presumption that the game has a solution which rational players can be expected to do their parts to realize.

So far I have been working out the procedure for two-person games. I shall continue to postpone application to n-person games until the application to two-person games is more fully worked out. Among the general results for two-person games are (Harper, 1988)

(T1) Only equilibrium strategies are best-reply ratifiable
(T2) All equilibrium strategies are best-reply ratifiable if all choices in the game are causally independent

Most games (even most two-person games) have multiple noninterchangeable equilibria. Such games have no Nash solutions. In some of these games causal dependencies represented in the extensive-form tree can be exploited to show that the best-reply ratifiability test can successfully cut the candidates down to an interchangeable set (Harper, 1988, pp. 39–43). The ratifiability idea also suggests some natural extensions of the procedure that can be applied when the best-reply ratifiable strategies do not form an interchangeable set (Harper, 1988, pp. 38–9). This suggests that our eductive procedure can be developed into an interesting refinement of the Nash solution concept.

2 CLASSICAL REFINEMENTS

2.1 Sequential reasoning

Noncredible threats   In 1965 Reinhard Selten pointed out that in some extensive-form games certain Nash equilibria were obviously not sensible because they depended upon noncredible threat strategies. The idea that one could find principled ways of ruling out equilibria which are not sensible offered the exciting prospect of extending the class of games for which solutions exist.

Puccini's opera *Gianni Schicchi* provides a vivid example of the sort of noncredible threat Selten discussed.[3] For our purposes the relevant part of the story can be rendered as follows. A very wealthy man has just died. His relatives discover the death and that the man has willed his fortune to the monks instead of to them. They call in a fixer: Gianni Schicchi. Schicchi suggests that they let him impersonate the wealthy man and make out a new will. Here is Schicchi disguised as the rich man beginning to make out the new will in the presence of the relatives and the appropriate officials, but instead of naming the relatives he names himself (Gianni Schicchi) as beneficiary of the fortune. A salient background assumption is that the state in which all this happens has a very strict penalty for anyone found guilty of colluding to interfere with a will. The penalty is loss of one's right hand and banishment.

We can represent the game-theoretic reasoning in the story by the following extensive-form game. Player 1 in figure 9.2 represents Gianni Schicchi. His pure options are either C (to cooperate with the relatives) or D (to deceive them by naming himself as beneficiary). He gets to move first. Player 2 represents the relatives. Their pure options are either a (to accuse Schicchi) or b (to back down). Player 1's utility is the top number and player 2's utility is the bottom number. I also use upper case letters for player 1's *strategies* and lower case letters for player 2's. Each information set is labeled by the number of the player to which it belongs. The information set I of player 2 represents that the relatives know that Schicchi has already chosen D if and when they get to make their own choice.

There are two pure strategy equilibria (D, b) and (C, a). Any pair (C, (ya, $(1 - y)$b)) where the mixed strategy for player 2 assigns $y \geq \frac{1}{3}$ is also a Nash equilibrium of this game. The problem with any of the equilibria involving C is that neither player 2's threat strategy a nor player 1's cooperative strategy C is credible. By choosing D rather than C, Schicchi can put the relatives into the information set I. At this information set they know that the choice is between losing the fortune (to Schicchi) or losing the fortune (to the monks) together with losing their right hands and banishment. This is a choice in which backing down is the only sensible option. Schicchi's cooperation is also not credible. The relatives know that he knows they would back down if he were to choose D instead

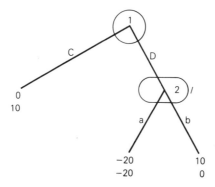

Figure 9.2 Game 1.

of C and therefore that he can get the fortune for himself by choosing D instead of C.

Our best-reply ratifiability test throws out strategy C in this game. The key here is that the relatives' choice is *causally dependent* on Schicchi's. In the tree this is shown by the fact that the D branch leads to their information set *I* while the C branch does not. This represents that Schicchi can put them into that information set by choosing D rather than C. We have a general principle relating such causal dependencies with conditional probability assignments to subjunctive conditionals.

(CD) $P(A' \mathbin{\Box\!\!\rightarrow} b | A) = P(b | \text{player is at } I)$ for any strategy b of player *i*, if choosing A' rather than A would put player *i* into information set *I*.

When Schicchi evaluates the conditional probability on C of the subjunctive conditional

"They would carry out a if I were to do D instead of C"

he assigns

$$P(D \mathbin{\Box\!\!\rightarrow} a | C) = P(a | \text{they are at } I)$$

since he would put them in *I* by choosing D instead of C. Schicchi knows that b is the only rational choice for the relatives at this information set so he assigns

$$P(a | \text{they are at } I) = 0$$

He reasons that even if the relatives had attempted to commit themselves to the threat strategy a they would not be able rationally to stick to the choice corresponding to that strategy if he were to put them in the information set by doing D rather than C. Even if Schicchi assigns $P(a | c) = 1$ as he applies the best-reply ratifiability test to C he will assign $P(D \mathbin{\Box\!\!\rightarrow} a | C) = 0$. Therefore

$$\begin{aligned} U_C(D) &= P(D \mathbin{\Box\!\!\rightarrow} a | C)(-20) + P(D \mathbin{\Box\!\!\rightarrow} b | C)\,(10) \\ &= 0(-20) + 1(10) \\ &= 10 > U_C(C) = 0 \end{aligned}$$

and so strategy C fails the test.

Strategy D is the only best-reply ratifiable strategy for Schicchi. All of the relatives' equilibrium strategies are best-reply ratifiable, since Schicchi's choices are causally independent of theirs. The first stage of our eductive procedure fixed Schicchi's choice, but leaves the relatives with the problem of choosing from among their equilibrium strategies. The basic decision-theoretic recommendation is to choose from among your ratifiable options one which maximizes expected utility. This suggests a second stage for our eductive procedure. Choose from among your best-reply ratifiable strategies one which optimizes expected utility given appropriate unconditional probabilities over the other player's best-reply ratifiable strategies. In this game the expectations generated in the first stage settle the second stage as well. The relatives expect that Schicchi will play his only best-reply ratifiable strategy D; therefore, they will choose b, which is their only optimal choice given that expectation. Our eductive procedure yields the equilibrium (D, b) as the unique solution to this game.

Subgame perfection   Our explication of the Indirect Argument can exploit causal dependencies in the extensive form of the game to generate a refinement of the Nash equilibrium solution concept by ruling out equilibria that include unratifiable strategies. A number of interesting refinement concepts that appeal to extensive-form structure have been proposed. Selten's (1965) original proposal was what he later (1975) came to call a *subgame-perfect equilibrium*. A subgame-perfect equilibrium is one which remains an equilibrium as the strategies are restricted to *subgames*. In the Gianni Schicchi game, player 2's choice node initiates the subgame shown in figure 9.3. Clearly any strategy assigning positive probability to a is not an equilibrium strategy in this subgame. So, the subgame-perfect refinement agrees with our proposal in generating the unique equilibrium (D, b) as the solution of this game.

Consider the variation on our game shown in figure 9.4. Here we add a strategy for player 1. Player 2's information set does not distinguish between the node where player 1 plays the new strategy E and the node where player 1 plays D, but it does exclude the C branch. This represents that the empirical information available to player 2 when they get to choose specifies that C did not get played, but does not specify which of E or D got played.

The equilibrium (C, a) is subgame-perfect in this game because there

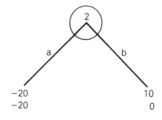

Figure 9.3   Subgame 1.1.

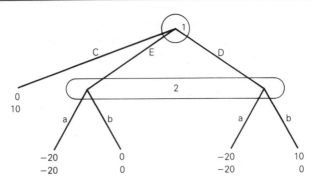

Figure 9.4   Game 2.

is no subgame, but it is no better in this game than in the original one because strategy a is strictly dominated by b in player 2's information set.

Our explication of the Indirect Argument also gets the right answer here. Strategy C still fails the test:

$$P(D \mathbin{\square\!\!\rightarrow} a \,|\, C) = 0$$

Strategy b is the only optimal choice for player 2 at the information set into which player 1 can put them by choosing D rather than C. So, once again,

$$U_C(C) = 0 < U_C(D) = 10$$

No best-reply prior that respects the causal structure shown by the extensive form of this game can ratify C.

Sequential equilibrium   When we look at game 2 from the point of view of players who are committed to the equilibrium (C, a) we see that player 2 does not expect to reach the information set *I*. Kreps and Wilson (1982) introduced *sequential equilibrium* as a refinement concept which would be sensitive to probability assignments at information sets off the equilibrium path even when the information set does not initiate a subgame.

An assessment specifies a profile π of strategies (one for each player) and also a profile μ of beliefs. At each information set μ and π together fix a probability over outcomes. This probability is to be the one assigned at that information set by its player on the assumption that the strategies specified in π are being played. An assessment is *completely mixed* if the strategy profile π assigns strictly positive probability to all pure strategies. An equilibrium is *sequential* if it can be specified as a limit of some sequence of completely mixed assessments such that

(SC1) the probability assigned at each information set must agree with what would result from the player's updating belief by sequentially conditionalizing on information sets reached on the way to the given information set;

(SC2) each strategy in the equilibrium must be such that the choice it specifies at any information set must maximize the agent's expected utility with respect to the limiting conditional probability assigned to that information set.

The requirement that assessments in the series be completely mixed ensures that limiting conditional probabilities are defined even for information sets off the equilibrium path. Condition SC1 is designed to ensure that the conditional probability on any information set reflect what the agent would have learned empirically by playing through the tree to reach it. Condition SC2 ensures that this sequential information would have rationalized the choice made at that information set.

The defective equilibrium (C, a) in game 2 fails to be sequential because no assessment could make strategy a maximize expected utility at player 2's information set. This is obvious because b strictly dominates a. Kreps and Wilson's sequential equilibrium refinement agrees with our proposal in generating the unique equilibrium (D, b) as the solution to game 2.

2.2 Sure-thing reasoning

Gianni Schicchi with causal independence   Consider the following alternative version of Gianni Schicchi. The relatives get to move first. Their strategy a is to instruct a confederate ahead of time to be committed to blow the whistle on all the principles if Schicchi chooses D. By choosing this strategy they can put a doomsday arrangement in place to carry out the threat automatically if Schicchi chooses to deceive them. Their strategy b would be to refrain from putting the doomsday arrangement into place. Schicchi is not informed which act they have chosen before he makes his own choice. This is illustrated by the two nodes in the information set at which Schicchi must make his choice (figure 9.5). In this alternative game the relatives are represented by player 1 and Schicchi by player 2. As usual player 1's utilities are on top.

In this game the equilibrium (C, a) is sequential, even though it fails to be sequential in the original Gianni Schicchi game. Consider an assessment assigning completely mixed strategies $((1 - \epsilon)a, \epsilon b)$ and $((1 - \epsilon)C, \epsilon D)$. The limit as $\epsilon \to 0$ of a sequence of such assessments will yield the equilibrium pair (C, a). Neither player gets to update by conditionalization so the first condition applies trivially. The second con-

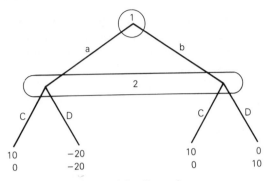

Figure 9.5   Game 3.

dition is met because C and a each maximize expected utility with respect to the belief probabilities reached at the limit, which assign $P_1(C) = 1$ as the relatives' belief about Schicchi at their information set and $P_2(a) = 1$ as Schicchi's belief about the relatives at his information set.

Game 3 has the same normal form as the original Gianni Schicchi game.[4] Representing Schicchi as row chooser we have

$$
\begin{array}{ccc}
 & \text{a} & \text{b} \\
\text{C} & (0, 10) & (0, 10) \\
\text{D} & (-20, -20) & (10, 0)
\end{array}
$$

Schicchi's utilities are on the left. So, this game has the same set of Nash equilibria as the original Gianni Schicchi game – the two pure strategy pairs (D, b) and (C, a) as well as all pairs (C,(ya,(1 − y)b)) where the mixed strategy assigns $y \geqslant \frac{1}{3}$ as the probability of a. All these equilibria are sequential. The sequential equilibrium refinement does not yield a solution to this game. These equilibria do not satisfy the basic inter-changeability condition that a player's strategy in one of them would be a best reply to the other player's strategy in any one of the others.

In developing the sequential equilibrium concept Kreps and Wilson focused on the demands generated by respecting the empirical informa-tion that would have been afforded to an agent had that agent or the other traversed an off-equilibrium path. They left out desirable features that had been incorporated into some earlier refinement concepts in order to isolate and develop their basic sequential requirement. In game 3 neither player can get any empirical information about the choices of the other as they traverse the tree, and so neither can use their choices to give the other player any empirical information about themselves. It should be no surprise, therefore, that a game such as this affords no purchase for the sequential equilibrium constraint to act as a refinement.

Our initial best-reply ratifiability test does as badly in this game as the sequential equilibrium concept. The game structure ensures that causal independence holds. Therefore, T2 applies to make every equilibrium strategy pass the test. To illustrate, let us look at how strategies C and a pass the test. Begin with C. Here you are as Schicchi making the hypothetical assumption that C is your part of a solution. You assume the relatives have made some best reply, but this assumption does not fix your conditional belief. Any of their strategies is a best reply to C. Among these are ones which assign a probability of $\frac{1}{3}$ or more to a. Strategy C is best-reply ratifiable as long as *some* best-reply prior will ratify it, and any such that $P_1(a|C) \geqslant \frac{1}{3}$ will do it. As an example take $P_1(a|C) = 1$.

$$U_C(D) = P_1(D \;\square\!\!\rightarrow a|C)(-20) + P_1(D \;\square\!\!\rightarrow b|C)(10)$$

Here we have *causal independence*, and so

$$P_1(D \;\square\!\!\rightarrow a|C) = P_1(a|C) = 1$$

Thus on this best-reply prior

$$U_C(D) = -20$$

Clearly, under causal independence these priors will not lead you to judge that you would have been better off choosing D instead.

Now let us look at strategy a. The unique best reply to a is C, and so we only have to consider assigning $P_2(C|a) = 1$. We have

$$U_a(a) = P_2(a \;\square\!\!\rightarrow C|a)(10) + P_2(a \;\square\!\!\rightarrow D|a)(-20)$$

while

$$U_a(b) = P_2(b \;\square\!\!\rightarrow C|a)(10) + P_2(b \;\square\!\!\rightarrow D|a)(0)$$

Causal independence makes the probabilities agree, so that

$$U_a(a) = P(C|a)(10) + P(D|a)(-20)$$

and

$$U_a(b) = P(C|a)(10) + P(D|a)(0)$$

but the best-reply prior assigns zero as $P_2(D|a)$, so that $U_a(a) = U_a(b)$ even though b weakly dominates a.

Trembling-hand perfection In 1975 Selten introduced ("trembling-hand") perfection. The idea is that a good equilibrium should not be destroyed by allowing a little probability for mistakes. Here is a formulation of the normal-form version of Selten's requirement. An ϵ-*perfect equilibrium* is a vector of completely mixed strategies such that each assigns probability less than ϵ to any pure strategy which fails to maximize expected utility given the mixed strategies assigned to the other players. A *perfect equilibrium* is the limit as $\epsilon \rightarrow 0$ of some sequence of ϵ-perfect equilibria.[5]

This refinement generates a solution to game 3. The equilibrium (C, a) and all the equilibria (C, $(y$a, $(1 - y)$b$)$) fail to be perfect. This is because a cannot maximize expected utility relative to any completely mixed strategy $(x$C, $(1 - x)$D$)$. Any strategy of player 1 (the relatives) in any ϵ-perfect equilibrium must therefore assign less than ϵ as the probability of a, so that b is the only strategy for player 1 that can be reached as $\epsilon \rightarrow 0$. The only equilibrium that meets this condition is (D, b). This same reasoning provides an alternative argument for the (D, b) solution in the original Gianni Schicchi game.

Weakly dominated strategies are widely regarded as problematic. Kohlberg and Mertens (1986, p. 1020) are among those who classify weakly dominated strategies as inadmissible along with the obviously inadmissible strongly dominated strategies. They take *admissibility* (the exclusion of weakly dominated strategies) to be a condition on any adequate solution concept. The salient advantage of Selten's trembling-hand refinement is that it only allows equilibria with admissible strategies. Indeed, van Damme (1983, p. 53) has shown that in two-person normal-form games the perfect equilibria are exactly those which have no inadmissible strategies.

We could tinker with the best-reply ratifiability test to get rid of strategies like a, but we have no need to. The role of ratifiability in individual decision-making offers a natural framework within which to apply additional reasoning if the initial test of best-reply ratifiability fails to yield a solution. As we have seen, determining which acts are ratifiable is only the first step in solving a decision problem. If there are several alternative ratifiable options the agent is to choose from among them by maximizing unconditional expected utility.

Put yourself in the position of the relatives in game 3. Your ratifiable options are b and all strategies $y = (y$a, $(1 - y)$b$)$ where $y \geqslant 1/3$. These a options include, of course, your pure strategy a. Any of your a options is *weakly dominated* by b. You are indifferent between the outcome of the a act and the outcome of b if Schicchi chooses C, but you strictly prefer the outcome of b to the outcome of the a act if he chooses D. This suggests a sure-thing argument of the sort Savage (1954, pp. 21–6) made into one of his fundamental rationality principles. Your preferences between any a option and b ought to be guided by your preferences conditional on D, since these acts agree in outcome if not-D (i.e. C) is the case. Therefore, if you prefer b to the a option given D you should unconditionally prefer b to it as well.

Causal independence and sure-thing reasoning This sort of sure-thing reasoning can be fallacious if causal independence fails, as the following variation on the original Gianni Schicchi game should make clear. In this version (figure 9.6) the relatives not only get to move first, they also get to have their move observed by Schicchi before he makes his choice. Once again, the relatives are player 1 and their utilities are on top. Suppose you are faced with their choice. In this version of the story you can make your threat credible because if you choose a Schicchi will know that the dooms-day arrangement is already in place when he faces his own choice.

Here is the incorrect application of the Sure-thing Principle to your choice between a and b.

a and b agree in outcome if not-D. Therefore your preference between a and b ought to agree with your conditional preference given D.

It is incorrect because D is not causally independent of your choice between a and b. If you choose a, then Schicchi will choose C (not-D) because he will know that you have chosen a and he strictly prefers the (a, C) outcome to the (a, D) outcome. Causal decision theory is sensitive to this. We have

$$U(a) = P(a \mathbin{\square\!\!\rightarrow} C)(10) + P(a \mathbin{\square\!\!\rightarrow} D)(-20)$$

and

$$U(b) = P(b \mathbin{\square\!\!\rightarrow} C)(10) + P(b \mathbin{\square\!\!\rightarrow} D)(0)$$

so that the sure-thing argument is blocked when $P(a \mathbin{\square\!\!\rightarrow} C) \neq P(b \mathbin{\square\!\!\rightarrow} C)$, as in this game.

One advantage of causal decision theory is that it can sort between cor-rect and incorrect applications of sure-thing reasoning even if one uses

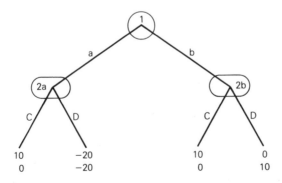

Figure 9.6 Game 4.

the states of the agent-normal form.[6] In the agent-normal form for game 4 Schicchi has two agents, one for each of his information sets, as shown in figure 9.6. The proposition that Schicchi chooses C has two states in it, one for the a agent and one for the b agent. The causal dependence is represented by the fact that one of these states is appropriate for evaluating $P(a \ \Box\!\!\rightarrow C)$ while the other is appropriate for evaluating $P(b \ \Box\!\!\rightarrow C)$.

Let us return to game 3, where Schicchi is not informed about your choice before he makes his. In this game Schicchi's information set does not distinguish between the node resulting from your choice a and the node resulting from your choice b. No choice you can make from among these options and their mixtures will generate any empirical information that Schicchi can use. Unlike in game 4, in game 3 you cannot influence him to choose C by yourself choosing a instead of b. This independence is nicely represented in the agent-normal form. The two choice nodes in Schicchi's information set belong to only one agent. Therefore, all the relevant conditionals for your choices among a, b and any mixtures $ya = (ya, (1 - y)b)$ will be evaluated on the states of this same agent. One state is the one that would make proposition C true while the other is the one that would make proposition D true. All the conditionals $a \ \Box\!\!\rightarrow C$, $b \ \Box\!\!\rightarrow C$ and $ya \ \Box\!\!\rightarrow C$ will be true just in case C is. Similarly, all the conditionals $a \ \Box\!\!\rightarrow D$, $b \ \Box\!\!\rightarrow D$ and $ya \ \Box\!\!\rightarrow D$ will be true just in case D is.

This supports the assignment of probabilities appropriate to causal independence. For any mixture ya (including the two pure acts b, where $y = 0$, and a, where $y = 1$) we have

$$P(ya \ \Box\!\!\rightarrow C) = P(C)$$

and

$$P(ya \ \Box\!\!\rightarrow D) = P(D)$$

Therefore, for any mixture we have

$$U(ya) = P(C)\,(10) + P(D)\,y\,(-20)$$

while

$$U(b) = P(C)\,(10) + P(D)\,(0)$$

So, the expected utility of any a option ($y > 0$) will be strictly less than that of b as long as $P(D) > 0$. Any nonzero probability for D will make b the unique act that maximizes your expected utility.

Selten's trembling-hand idea is designed to motivate probability assignments that will reject weakly dominated acts like your a acts, even if you are already sure that Schicchi has committed himself to C. According to Selten you should allow a small probability that Schicchi will end up doing D by mistake. If you are an agent who applies the eductive method advocated in this paper you will have just reasoned out that both of Schicchi's pure strategies have passed the best-reply ratifiable test. You do not need to appeal to the possibility of mistakes to motivate allowing some nonzero probability to D. The most precise expectation that your strategic reasoning has been able to deliver up to this stage of your analysis is that Schicchi will choose one or the other of his two pure strategies. In this context ordinary everyday prudence is quite enough to support allowing nonzero probability to D and so rejecting your a options.[7]

Savage's Sure-thing Principle can be applied to reinforce the argument for rejecting a. Schicchi's choices are causally independent of yours and acts a and b agree in C; therefore, according to the Sure-thing Principle, your unconditional preference between a and b should agree with your conditional preference between those given D. Therefore, if you strictly prefer b to a conditional on D you should unconditionally prefer b to a. Savage (1954, p. 24) defines a *null* proposition as one such that conditional on it you are indifferent between any two acts. When you strictly prefer b to a conditional on D you show that you do not treat D as null, but, according to Savage, this also shows that you do not treat it as having zero probability.[8]

Proper equilibrium Myerson (1978, p. 77) used the following normal-form game to motivate a stronger refinement than Selten's concept of trembling-hand perfect equilibrium.

	a	b	c
A	(1, 1)	(0, 0)	(−9, −9)
B	(0, 0)	(0, 0)	(−7, −7)
C	(−9, −9)	(−7, −7)	(−7, −7)

This game has three equilibria, (A, a), (B, b) and (C, c). The very bad (C, c) equilibrium is not perfect, but the (A, a) and (B, b) equilibria are both perfect even though only (A, a) seems sensible. To see that (B, b) is perfect consider the pair of completely mixed strategies (ϵA, $(1 - 2\epsilon)$B, ϵC) and (ϵa, $(1 - 2\epsilon)$b, ϵc). They are ϵ-perfect (for any ϵ) and (B, b) is their limit as $\epsilon \to 0$.

Myerson (1978) argues that it is not enough to allow some probability for mistakes. According to him these probabilities should be assigned so that a worse mistake occurs with a much lower probability than one which is not so bad. An ϵ-*proper equilibrium* is a pair (n-tuple) of completely mixed strategies such that if pure strategy a is better than pure strategy b (given the strategy(ies) assigned to the other player(s)) then the probability assigned to strategy b is at most ϵ times the probability assigned to a (pp. 77–8). A *proper equilibrium* is a limit as $\epsilon \rightarrow 0$ of a sequence of ϵ-proper equilibria (p. 78).[9] The only proper equilibrium for this game is the sensible pair (A, a). This pair is reached as $\epsilon \rightarrow 0$ for a sequence of ϵ-proper equilibria of the form $((1 - \epsilon - \epsilon^2)A, \epsilon B, \epsilon^2 C), ((1 - \epsilon - \epsilon^2)a, \epsilon b, \epsilon^2 c)$.

To see that (B, b) fails to be proper, put yourself in the place of agents who want to commit themselves to this equilibrium as the solution. Note that only mixtures such as $(\epsilon a, (1 - \epsilon - \epsilon^2)b, \epsilon^2 c)$ and $(\epsilon A, (1 - \epsilon - \epsilon^2)B, \epsilon^2 C)$, which make the worst mistakes c and C at most ϵ times as probable as what you regard as the not so bad mistakes a and A, are candidates for ϵ-proper equilibria that might reach (B, b) as $\epsilon \rightarrow 0$. But, as ϵ gets small, the best replies will become A and a rather than B and b. Therefore (B, b) cannot be reached as the limit as $\epsilon \rightarrow 0$ of any sequence of ϵ-proper equilibria.

Let us see what happens when we apply our eductive reasoning to Myerson's game. Suppose there is complete causal independence among all choices (as in game 0). Under this condition all the equilibrium strategies A, B, and C for row chooser and a, b, and c for column chooser pass the best-reply ratifiability test. Put yourself in row chooser's situation. Savage's Sure-thing Principle applies to rule out your worst strategy C (it agrees with B if c is played and does strictly worse if anything else is played). You can also expect that column chooser will similarly use sure-thing reasoning to reject their worst strategy c. These worst strategies are both weakly dominated and (at this stage of the analysis) are the only dominated strategies. After this first round of sure-thing reasoning only the strategies in the two perfect equilibria (A, a) and (B, b) will remain as candidates. Once these worst strategies have been eliminated the way is open to apply a second round of sure-thing reasoning.[10] Your strategy A agrees with B if b is played and beats it if a is played. So, at this second round, the B and b strategies are eliminated leaving only the strategies in the proper equilibrium (A, a).

Once again we see that the second stage of analysis in our eductive procedure is a natural arena for using sure-thing reasoning to motivate a refinement. On our analysis Myerson's "worse mistakes" turn out to be strategies which can be eliminated in earlier rounds of sure-thing reasoning. This may provide an alternative rationale for restricting solutions to strategies in proper equilibria for many other games as well.

3 FORWARD INDUCTION

A number of games having a quite similar structure have been used with variations to motivate new refinements and to make trouble for all the classic proposals. The game that Kreps and Wilson (1982, p. 878) label as "Fig. 9" is one of the early examples. Kohlberg and Mertens (1986) have generated some of the most important variations and have used them to explore interesting themes about game-theoretic reasoning. One of these themes is a kind of forward induction reasoning that seems to be at the heart of all these games. Our best-reply ratifiability test seems to generate a particularly strong form of this forward induction reasoning. It can be used to support Kohlberg and Mertens' recommendations against Harsanyi and Selten's commitment to a very strong version of backward induction.

3.1 Backward and forward induction

The Harsanyi and Selten subgame game   Figure 9.7 shows the game given in Harsanyi and Selten (1988, p. 351) as "Fig. 10.9". They argue for the equilibrium (AC, e) as follows:

In this game player 1's second information set [I_2] and the one information set [I_3] belonging to player 2 form a subgame Γ^*, whose solution is the equilibrium (C, e), which risk dominates the other pure strategy equilibrium (D, f). (There is

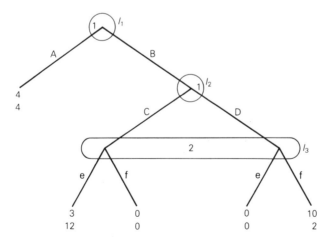

Figure 9.7   Game Γ.

no payoff dominance either way.)[11] If the players use the strategies (C, e) required by this solution they will obtain the payoff vector $u = (3, 12)$. [our notation]

When the subgame is solved first and the payoff vector is substituted for it we have the "truncation game" Γ^{**} shown in figure 9.8, in which A is the only optimal move for player 1.

Harsanyi and Selten (1988, pp. 351–2) note that if one looked only at the normal form of the main game it would be natural to argue for the equilibrium (BD, f) by noting that BC is dominated by AC and AD. They argue, however, that backward induction requires the strong subgame analysis that leads to (AC, e).

> Backward-induction rationality requires that the players should first decide how to act in subgame Γ^*. Once this has been decided, it will be obvious for player 1 whether or not to choose move A or move B before subgame Γ^* is reached. This means we cannot delete move C in subgame Γ^* because it is an undominated move within this subgame. The fact that in the entire game Γ, strategy BC is a dominated strategy is irrelevant because backward-induction rationality requires us to decompose the analysis of game Γ into two separate steps, the first involving analysis of subgame Γ^* and the second involving analysis of the truncation game Γ^{**}. Thus, if the internal mathematical structure of subgame Γ^* makes (C, e) the solution of Γ^*, we cannot refuse accepting (AC, e) as the solution of the entire game Γ, even though BC is a dominated strategy is the entire game Γ – as long as no similar dominance relations appear in subgame Γ^* and in truncation game Γ^{**} themselves. (p. 352; our notation)

They regard the strong subgame analysis in the extensive form as carrying more weight than the dominance argument generated in the normal form of the game.

They also discuss and dismiss an informal argument for (BD, f) that is suggested by Kohlberg and Mertens (1986, especially p. 1013). By giving up the sure payoff 4 obtainable by choosing A, player 1 can signal player

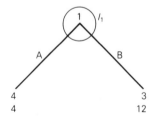

Figure 9.8

2 that she has played BD in order to obtain the higher payoff 10 associated with (BD, f). If player 2 believes that player 1 has played BD then player 2 must play f. According to Harsanyi and Selten (p. 353) we must carry out the subgame truncation analysis before we can decide whether or not player 1 can signal player 2 in the way Kohlberg and Mertens suggest.

Before deciding whether player 1 can effectively signal his strategic intentions, we must first decide what strategies are the rational strategies for the two players in subgame Γ*, and accordingly what strategy is the rational strategy for player 1 in the truncation game Γ**. Suppose we find as we did that in Γ* the only rational strategies are C and e and that because of this in Γ** the only rational strategy is A. Then we are no longer logically free to argue that if player 1 never-theless makes move B, this should be interpreted by player 2 as a *signal* of player 1's intention to make move D later on. Rather we must say that player 2 must interpret move B by player 1 as a *mistake* – such that rational players in player 1's position will make with a very small, yet positive, probability. . . .

Thus, even if at the first stage of the game player 1 made the "mistaken" move B, player 2 cannot rationally infer that at the second stage player 1 will again make the "mistaken" move D. Rather, 2 must expect 1 to make the "rational" move C with near-unity probability, and to make the mistaken move D only with a very small probability. By the same token, player 1 must expect player 2 to make the rational move e with near-unity probability and to make the mistaken move f only with very small probability. As a result of these expectations, even if player 1 makes the mistaken move B in the resulting subgame Γ*, both players will have a strong incentive to use strategies C and e as required by the solution of Γ*. (p. 353; our notation)

Harsanyi and Selten claim that consistency with the strong subgame trun-cation application of backward induction is a requirement of rational play. If player 2 accepts this assumption that any rational choice must agree with the version of backward induction that they recommend (and accepts that player 1 is rational), then Harsanyi and Selten are correct in claiming that player 2 will regard player 1's playing of B as a mistake rather than as a signal of player 1's intention to play BD.

The best-reply ratifiability analysis On the eductive procedure I am recommending the players assume (provisionally) that the game has a solution, but they are not already committed to any particular theory about what this solution is. They simply apply the Indirect Argument as a *reductio* test to rule out strategies as candidates for their part in any such solution. Let us see what happens when such players reason about this Harsanyi–Selten game.

Consider strategy BC. Player 1 is now hypothetically assuming that BC realizes her part in the solution to this game. She knows that e is player 2's unique best reply to BC. Therefore she assigns

$$U_{BC}(BC) = 3$$

Now she asks "What would happen if I were to play A instead of BC?" She can see that choice A will give her 4, whatever strategy player 2 may have chosen; therefore, she will expect 4 if she were to choose A even if BC is assumed to be her part of the unique rational solution. She assigns

$$U_{BC}(A) = 4 > U_{BC}(BC)$$

and so BC is not ratifiable by any best-reply prior. We think of the reasoning of the Indirect Argument as carried out before the agent actually commits herself to choosing a strategy. Choice A is an option that could be chosen instead of BC. When A beats BC, on the assumption that BC is player 1's part of the unique solution we have a *reductio* argument which rules out that assumption.

Any mixture $x = (x_1 A, x_2 BC, x_3 BD)$ such that x could reach player 2's information set I_3 (that is, such that $x_2 + x_3 > 0$) and such that $x_2 > 0$ will also fail to be best-reply ratifiable.[12] Strategy BD is best-reply ratifiable. Strategy f is player 2's best reply to BD, and so

$$U_{BD}(BD) = 10 \geqslant U_{BD}(x)$$

for any mixture x (including the pure strategies) available to player 1. Therefore, BD is the one and only best-reply ratifiable strategy of player 1 that can reach player 2's information set I_3.

Now we are ready to look at Harsanyi and Selten's recommended choice A. On the provisional assumption that A is her part in the unique solution player 1 asks what would happen if she were to play BD instead.

$$U_A(BD) = P(BD \;\square\!\!\rightarrow e\,|\,A)(0) + P(BD \;\square\!\!\rightarrow f\,|\,A)(10)$$

The game tree shows that there is causal dependence in that player 1 can put player 2 into the information set I_3 by choosing BD instead of A. So, in accordance with our causal dependence principle, we have

$$P_1(BD \;\square\!\!\rightarrow f\,|\,A) = P_1(f\,|\,\text{player 2 is at } I_3)$$

Player 1 must consider player 2's assessment at information set I_3.

Players applying the best-reply ratifiability test in this part of our eductive procedure will expect that a player at an information set will assume that the presumed solution reaches that information set unless that assumption is explicitly ruled out by showing that no best-reply ratifiable strategy can reach that information set. We have the following general principle constraining expectations at information sets in the best-reply ratifiability test.

(BRRI) A player at an information set assigns positive probability only to those strategies of the other player that can reach that information set and are also best-reply ratifiable, provided that any best-reply ratifiable strategy can reach that information set.

Our presumption that the game has a solution that rational players can be expected to do their parts to reach and the basic game-theoretic presumption that the rationality of the players, the structure of the game, and the preferences of the players are common knowledge are regarded as more fundamental than the hypothetical assumption that the choice being tested realizes the players' part of the presumed solution.

Player 1 knows that player 2 knows that the only best-reply ratifiable strategy of player 1 that can reach I_3 is BD, and so player 1 knows that player 2 will assign $P_2(BD | I_3) = 1$ as her assessment of the probability of BD conditional on her information set I_3. Player 1 also knows that player 2 will make a best reply to this assessment. Strategy f is player 2's unique best reply to BD; therefore,

$$P_1(f | \text{player 2 is at } I_3) = 1$$

Thus

$$U_A(BC) = 10 > U_A(A) = 4$$

This shows that strategy A fails the test of the Indirect Argument.

Strategy BD is the unique best-reply ratifiable strategy for player 1 in this game. Strategy f is player 2's unique best reply to BD, and strategy f itself is best-reply ratifiable. Our eductive procedure yields uniquely the solution (BD, f) rather than the putative solution (AC, e) recommended by Harsanyi and Selten.

Implications for forward versus backward induction Kohlberg and Mertens (1986, p. 1012) distinguish four backward induction properties. The very strong subgame truncation analysis proposed by Harsanyi and Selten satisfies all four properties.

(BI0) A solution of a one-player game should be consistent with payoff maximization
(BI1) A solution of a game induces a solution for any subgame
(BI2) Any solution of a subgame is part of a solution of the game
(BI3) Any solution of a game remains a solution when a subgame

is replaced by a terminal position at which the players receive their expected payoffs (according to this solution) in the subgame

If Harsanyi and Selten are correct in their risk dominance argument for (C, c) as the solution of the subgame on its own and we are correct in arguing that (BD, f) is the solution of the whole game, then both (BI2) and (BI3) fail.

Kohlberg and Mertens (1986) characterize their signaling argument as a *forward induction* argument.

Essentially what is involved here is an argument of "forward induction": a subgame should not be treated as a separate game, because it was preceded by a very specific form of preplay communication – the play leading up to the subgame. (p. 1013)

Our application of best-reply ratifiability is a kind of forward induction argument. It is the availability of A as an alternative against which BC must prevail when evaluated on its best-reply prior that throws this option out in the game as a whole. This alternative would not be available if we were looking at the subgame as a completely separate game. The context of the Indirect Argument supports this feature of our best-reply ratifiability explication of it. The whole argument is to be worked out before the players actually commit themselves to any of their choices. This is what makes it appropriate to consider A as an alternative against which the BC option must be evaluated, even if player 1 would not be able to recover her chance to do A once she had actually executed choice B.

3.2 Kreps and Wilson's Fig. 9 Game

Kreps and Wilson (1982, p. 876) point out that the Fig. 9 game (figure 9.9) has an infinite set of sequential equilibria. There are two kinds of sequential equilibria, the pair (L, l) and pairs (A, ((1 − y), yr)) where $y > 2/5$.[13] In this game the sequential equilibria do not constitute a solution. Neither do the perfect or the proper equilibria, since both pure strategy equilibria (A, r) as well as (L, r) are proper and therefore also perfect.[14]

Unlike the games we have been exploring so far there are no inadmissible (weakly or strongly dominated) acts at any information set. The straightforward version of the Kohlberg–Mertens signaling argument also does not apply, since both strategies L and R offer chances of payoffs that are better than the payoff guaranteed at A. Nevertheless, the version

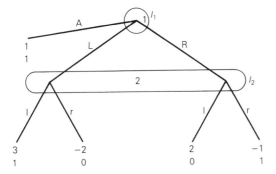

Figure 9.9   Kreps and Wilson's Fig. 9 game.

of forward induction reasoning generated by the best-reply ratifiability test does apply to generate (L, *l*) as the solution.

Consider R. Let player 1 assume hypothetically that R is her part of a solution. Player 2's unique best reply to R is r, and so for any best-reply prior P for player 1 we have

$$P(r|R) = 1$$
$$U_R(R) = P(l|R)(2) + P(r|R)(-1)$$
$$U_R(R) = -1$$

R is not BR-ratifiable because $U_R(A) = 1 > U_R(R) = -1$.

Consider any mixture $x = (xL, (1-x)R)$ such that $x < 1$. If $x > \frac{1}{2}$ then *l* is the unique best response so that $P(l|x) = 1$ and $U_x(x) < U_x(L)$. If $x < \frac{1}{2}$ then r is the unique best response, so that $P(r|x) = 1$ and $U_x(A) > U_x(x)$. Suppose that $x = \frac{1}{2}$. Then all strategies of player 2 are best replies, so that $P(l|x)$ can be any number in $(0, 1)$; however, if $P(l|x) > \frac{1}{2}$ then $U_x(L) > U_x(x)$; and if $P(l|x) < \frac{5}{8}$ then $U_x(A) > U_x(x)$. Thus no mixture $x = (xL, (1-x)R)$ such that $x < 1$ is best-reply ratifiable.

Now check L. $U_L(L) = 3$, as *l* is the unique best reply to L. Since 3 is the maximum payoff for player 1, we have $U_L(L) > U_L(x_1, x_2, x_3)$ for any strategy $(x_1 A, x_2 L, x_3 R)$. Thus L is ratifiable. We now have that L is the unique best-reply ratifiable strategy that can reach player 2's information set I_2.

Now let us consider A.

$$U_A(A) = 1$$
$$U_A(L) = P(L \:\square\!\!\rightarrow l|A)(3) + P(L \:\square\!\!\rightarrow r|A)(-2)$$

Once again, we have causal dependence. By choosing L rather than A player 1 can put player 2 into the information set I_2. So we have

$$P(\text{L} \;\square\!\!\rightarrow\; l\,|\,\text{A}) = P(l\,|\,I_2)$$

where $P(l\,|\,I_2)$ is the probability that player 1 attributes to player 2's playing l given that player 2 is in the information set I_2.

Now player 1 knows that player 2 knows that the only best-reply ratifiable strategy of player 1 that can reach I_2 is L. Therefore, player 1 can attribute to player 2 at I_2 an assessment P_2 such that $P_2(\text{L}) = 1$. Now player 1 can be confident that player 2 will optimize relative to her assessment. Therefore $P(l\,|\,I_2) = 1$ and $U_A(\text{L}) = 3 > U_A(\text{A}) = 1$, and so A is not ratifiable.

Thus L is the unique best-reply ratifiable option for player 1. Now when we look at it from player 2's point of view, l and r are both best-reply ratifiable, but l is the best-reply ratifiable strategy that is best with respect to player 2's assessment. So the only solution allowed by the Indirect Argument is the desirable equilibrium (L, l).

3.3 Kohlberg and Mertens' Fig. 6 game

Kohlberg and Mertens (1986, p. 1016) offer the game given in figure 9.10 to show that the elimination of inadmissible choices at every choice point is not sufficient to reject all equilibria which are not sensible. For our purposes the game is interesting because it shows that our procedure rejects the backward induction principle (BI1) as well as (BI2) and (BI3). Our solution concept does not require that the solution to the whole game also determines a solution to the off-equilibrium path zero-sum subgame.

It will turn out that, as in the simpler forward induction games, one and only one best reply strategy of player 1 can reach player 2's information set I_3. This is the choice M. At this information set player 2 can be sure that M will have been played and will therefore play r, which is the best reply to M. This makes T unratifiable and makes the ratifiable pair of acts (M, r) specify the solution outcome which is (3, 3). What we want to go into now is what the solution ought to specify at the unreached information sets I_4 and I_5 in the zero-sum subgame.

First let us go back to look at the unratifiability of act B. This is what ensures that the subgame will not be reached. You are player 1. Assume hypothetically that act B is your part of a solution. What you need to maintain this assumption as a possibility is a best reply to B for player 2 that gives you a payoff of at least 2. Anything less than 2 for you will make act T do better than B. If l is the best reply then the most you can expect from B will be 1. What is needed is a strategy pair in the zero-sum game that will assign at least 1 to player 2, so that some mixture assigning positive probability to r can be a best reply to B, and which assigns at

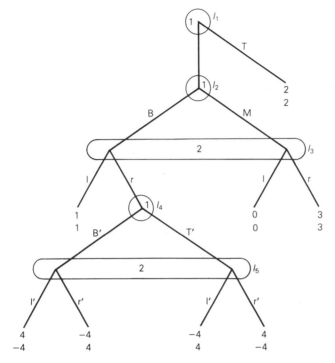

Figure 9.10   Kohlberg and Mertens' Fig. 6 game.

least 2 to player 1 to prevent act T from beating B. But there is no such pair in this zero-sum subgame.

Having settled on the (M, r) outcome (3, 3), we need only specify that the off-equilibrium acts will not entice either player away from the acts that give the solution. Thus, we allow the whole set of mixed strategies $(x\text{B}', (1 - x)\text{T}')$ where $\frac{1}{8} < x < \frac{7}{8}$ and $(y\text{l}', (1 - y)\text{r}')$ where $\frac{1}{8} < y < \frac{7}{8}$. This set of strategies: (M, x) such that $\frac{1}{8} < x < \frac{7}{8}$ for player 1 and (r, y) such that $\frac{1}{8} < y < \frac{7}{8}$ for player 2 does satisfy the interchangeability property demanded for a Nash solution. Therefore it counts as a successful application of the Indirect Argument to find a solution. Moreover, no more fine grained solution can be forthcoming from the Indirect Argument.

If this set-valued solution is correct then the subgame principle (BI1) is violated in that the solution to the whole game need not induce any solution at all in the subgame. I see nothing wrong with allowing this sort of violation of subgame principle (BI1). Such violations seem a natural implication of forward induction reasoning. They also seem to be invited

by the philosophy of the indirect argument approach, which offers no
reason to exclude any strategies which are included in the interchangeable
class generated by any proposed solution.

NOTES

This is a much revised version of a talk given at the International Conference on
Knowledge, Belief, and Strategic Interaction, Castiglioncello, Italy, June 1989.
A version was also presented at the University of California at Los Angeles in
December 1989. I have benefited from discussion at both talks. Phillip Reny and
Brian Skyrms were especially helpful, as were the comments by Susan Hurley and
the extensive comments and corrections suggested by Michael Bacharach.

  1 A utility assignment represents an agent's preferences over outcomes just in
    case the agent's preference ordering among gambles (objective probability
    mixtures) over those outcomes agrees with the ordering of the expected utilities
    $Eu(P_1O_1,\ldots, P_nO_n) = P_1(u(O_1)) + \ldots + P_n(u(O_n))$ of those gambles
    according to the specified probabilities and the assigned utilities. See Savage
    (1972), pp. 91–104 for useful historical and critical comments on utility.
  2 Richard Jeffrey (e.g. 1983, pp. 15–20) introduced the idea of ratifiability in
    an unsuccessful attempt to use it to make his "evidential" decision theory agree
    with the recommendations of causal decision theory in some of the examples
    that were used to motivate causal decision theory. The present formulation
    of ratifiability was introduced in Harper (1986a) and developed further in
    Harper (1986b).
  3 This game is also structurally isomorphic to a one-round version of the Chain
    Store game that Selten (1978) made so familiar to economists. The Puccini
    story, however, may provide a more vivid example of a noncredible threat.
  4 Here we have two games with the same normal form. The equilibrium (C, a)
    is sequential in one game but fails to be sequential in the other. Kreps and
    Wilson (1982, p. 886) use this sort of dependence of the sequential equilibrium
    concept on the extensive-form tree to argue that the normal form is inadequate
    to represent all the strategic considerations that should determine solutions
    to games. Since Kreps and Wilson's paper there has been widespread agree-
    ment that the normal form is inadequate and rapidly growing interest in refine-
    ment concepts that appeal to extensive-form structure. Kohlberg and Mertens
    (1986), however, have defended the claim that any two games which have the
    same normal form must have the same solution. They issued a challenge to
    opponents of the normal form to produce a pair of games with the same nor-
    mal form and two different solutions each of which is intuitively the correct
    solution for its game. Reverse Gianni Schicchi and Gianni Schicchi do not
    meet this challenge unless it can be made intuitively clear that some of the
    (C, a) equilibria are the unique rational solutions to the reverse game. This
    does not seem to be a likely prospect in classical game theory, though it might

perhaps be realized in one of the new approaches to game theory that specify initial beliefs as well as utilities in the formulation of a game.

5 A version of perfection that requires the strategies to specify choices that maximize expected utility at each choice node is appropriate for extensive-form games. Such a version can be generated by demanding that the version specified above be satisfied by the agent-normal form for the extensive-form game. The agent-normal form specifies separate agents at each of a player's information sets. These agents all assign the same utilities to outcomes as the player they belong to (see Kohlberg and Mertens, 1986, p. 1006; Selten, 1975). Van Damme (1983, p. 128) points out interesting games in which a perfect equilibrium of the normal form fails to satisfy the extensive-form concept. Van Damme (p. 127) also points out a degenerate game where a perfect equilibrium in the extensive form fails to be a perfect equilibrium in the normal form.

6 These agent-normal form states will not do for an application of Savage's theory to player 1's choices in game 4. Savage (1954) does not allow for causal relations between acts and states. Acts are represented as functions from states into consequences. His whole framework is designed for states on which the Sure-thing Principle is valid. If we can assume that Schicchi's choices among strategies (complete plans for how to choose at each choice node in the game) are causally independent of the relatives' choices, then we can represent appropriate Savage states by going to the usual *strategic normal form*.

	s_1	s_2	s_3	s_4
	C if a	D if a	C if a	D if a
	C if a	D if b	D if b	C if b
a	$(10, 0)$	$(-20, -20)$	$(10, 0)$	$(-20, -20)$
b	$(10, 0)$	$(0, 10)$	$(0, 10)$	$(10, 0)$

We have the relatives' utilities on the left. The Savage utility of player 1 for a is

$$U(a) = \sum_i P(s_i)u(a, s_i)$$

where the $u(a, s_i)$ are the left-hand numbers in the a row of the matrix. A glance at these numbers for rows a and b shows that the weak dominance of b over a has been broken up by the addition of state s_3 on which a does better than b. Thus, we have no violation of the Sure-thing Principle if a is chosen. There is, of course, a valid sure-thing argument for Schicchi to choose s_3. Savage's theory gets the right answer on these states.

7 Suppose we represent your uncertainty by a family of probability assignments to D – all those left open by your reasoning so far. We can generate a sure-thing argument for b appropriate to such an indeterminate representation of belief. The argument is that none of these assignments makes a do better than b, while some (indeed almost all) of them will make b strictly better than a.

8 Savage's restriction of null propositions to those such that conditional on them

you are indifferent between any acts also supports Selten's suggestion that you should always allow a little probability for mistakes. The test, in the present example, would be to see whether you are indifferent between a and b given that D was done by mistake. If not then, on Savage's account, you do not treat the proposition that such a mistake is made as *null*, that is, you do not really assign it probability zero.

If we allowed for non-Archimedian belief we could make room for a weaker notion of null proposition. This weaker notion would correspond to assigning a nonzero degree of belief that, nevertheless, would be smaller than any positive real number. On such a representation the sure-thing argument against a would apply, even if D were assigned only such an infinitesmal probability. Such representations have interesting connections with work on acceptance and Bayesian learning models which allow for revisions of corrigible evidence (see Harper, 1978). They have recently been independently developed and applied to generate refinements in game theory (Brandenburger and Dekel, 1986).

9 Proper equilibria have some desirable features. Every proper equilibrium is perfect. Every game has (at least) one proper equilibrium (Myerson, 1978, p. 79). Most interestingly, Kohlberg and Mertens (1986, p. 1009) showed that every proper equilibrium in a normal-form game corresponds to a sequential equilibrium in every extensive-form game with that same normal form. Van Damme (1983) strengthened this to show that the corresponding equilibrium is also perfect in the extensive-form game.

10 Iterative elimination of weakly dominated strategies can yield outcomes that depend on the order in which the strategies are eliminated. The following example illustrates the point (van Damme, 1983, section 1.5.5).

	a	b	c
A	$(1, 1)$	$(1, 0)$	$(0, 0)$
B	$(1, 1)$	$(0, 0)$	$(1, 0)$

If c is eliminated first for player 2 and player 1 applies sure-thing reasoning to the resulting matrix then the outcome will be (A, a). On the other hand, if b is eliminated first the outcome may be (B, a). Our procedure for applying sure-thing reasoning requires eliminating all dominated strategies at a single round. In this example this would lead to the strategies corresponding to the set of pairs (A, a) and (B, a).

This interchangeable set is the solution recommended by our eductive procedure. Our procedure begins by eliminating strategies which fail the best-reply ratifiability test and applies sure-thing reasoning as part of a second stage of analysis. In this game the best-reply admissible strategies are exactly those in this interchangeable set. In this game there is no need or opportunity for applications of sure-thing reasoning at a second stage of analysis. Kohlberg and Mertens (1986, p. 1015) also argue for such a set-valued solution for a similar game.

11 Equilibrium (A, a) *outcome (payoff) dominates* equilibrium (B, b) just in case both players strictly prefer the (A, a) outcome to the (B, b) outcome (see

Harsanyi and Selten, 1988, p. 81). Consider a 2-by-2 game with two strong equilibria (A, a) and (B, b). Let u_1 and u_2 be the payoffs to players 1 and 2 respectively in the outcome of equilibrium (A, a), and v_1 and v_2 be the payoffs to players 1 and 2 at the equilibrium (B, b). Equilibrium (A, a) *risk-dominates* (B, b) just in case $u_1 u_2 > v_1 v_2$. Consider the matrix representation of the subgame:

$$
\begin{array}{ccc}
 & e & f \\
C & (3, 12) & (0, 0) \\
D & (0, 0) & (10, 2)
\end{array}
$$

We have $u_1 = 3$ and $u_2 = 12$, while $v_1 = 10$ and $v_2 = 2$ so that

$$u_1 u_2 = 3 \times 12 = 36 > 20 = 10 \times 2 = v_1 v_2$$

Harsanyi and Selten (1988, pp. 82-8) argue that these products are inversely related to the comparative riskiness of the two equilibria. That (C, e) risk dominates (D, f) shows that it is the less risky of the two equilibria. I shall assume that Harsanyi and Selten have made a compelling case for their risk-dominance solution to independent games having the structure of this subgame.

12 On the assumption that x is the unique rational strategy for player 1, player 2 will know this and will assign $u = x_2 / (x_2 + x_3)$ as her assessment of the probability of BC conditional on player 2 reaching her information set I_3. If $u > 1/7$ then e is the unique best reply to x and $U_x(A) = 4 > U_x(x)$. If $u < 1/7$ then f is the unique best reply to x and $U_x(BD) > U_x(x)$ for $x_2 > 0$. If $u = 1/7$ then all mixtures of e and f are equally good against x; however, no best-reply prior P for player 1 will ratify x. If $P(e|x) < 10/13$ then $U_x(BD) > U_x(x)$.

13 Here is an assessment that supports (A, ($\frac{3}{5}$ l, $\frac{2}{5}$ r)). We have $(1 - 2\epsilon, \epsilon, \epsilon)$ for player 2 about player 1 and ($\frac{3}{5}$ l, $\frac{2}{5}$ r) for player 1 about player 2. The limit as $\epsilon \to 0$ of player 2's assessment is (1, 0, 0) or the assignment $P_2(A) = 1$. Each assessment in this sequence makes $P_2(L|I_2) = \frac{1}{2} = P_2(R|I_2)$, so that the limiting conditional probability on I_2 of this sequence makes 2's strategy ($\frac{3}{5}$ l, $\frac{2}{5}$ r) optimize expected utility at that information set. Player 1's strategy A is optimal against the assessment ($\frac{3}{5}$ l, $\frac{2}{5}$ r). Strategy A does as well as L and better than R against this assessment and so it does as well against it as any mixture.

14 The sequence as $\epsilon \to 0$ of completely mixed strategies $(1 - \epsilon - \epsilon^2, \epsilon^2, \epsilon)$ for player 1 and $(\epsilon, 1 - \epsilon)$ for player 2 shows (A, r) to be proper, while the sequence as $\epsilon \to 0$ of $(\epsilon_2, 1 - \epsilon - \epsilon^2, \epsilon)$ and $(1 - \epsilon, \epsilon)$ shows (L, l) to be proper.

10

Rational Bargaining

Robert Sugden

1 INTRODUCTION

Suppose two individuals are able to produce some benefit through cooperating with one another, but they have to agree on how to divide this benefit between them. If they fail to agree, neither will benefit at all. If they are rational, how should they act? This problem can stand as a model for many problems of bargaining: consider a buyer and a seller of a house or a second-hand car haggling over the price, or a worker with special skills negotiating a contract with an employer. In the literature of economics, two types of solution are commonly offered to this problem; both derive from the work of John Nash (1950, 1953).

One approach, the axiomatic approach, does not attempt to model the moves open to the players of bargaining games (how offers and counteroffers are made, who moves first, how delay in reaching agreement imposes costs on the players, and so on). The idea is to describe bargaining problems in as compact a way as possible, stripping out any inessential details that would be irrelevant to the deliberations of rational players, and then to formulate a set of axioms which refer to this stripped-down form of the game. Each axiom is claimed to represent a necessary property of any rational solution to a bargaining problem, irrespective of the details of the bargaining process. Finally, it is shown that these axioms identify a unique solution. Nash (1950) formulated a set of such axioms, which generate the Nash solution – a solution that has been widely used in the economics of bargaining.

In recent years, however, it has become fashionable to criticize the axiomatic approach. There is no good reason, it is said, to suppose that the outcome of rational bargaining will be independent of the structure of the bargaining game. We ought therefore to model the bargaining process explicitly, as a noncooperative game, and then to apply the standard equilibrium concepts of game theory. This approach is sometimes called the Nash program, in recognition of an early attempt by Nash (1953) to specify a noncooperative bargaining game whose unique equilibrium corresponded to the Nash solution.

One reason for taking this approach stems from the fact that real bargaining takes place over time and that delay in reaching agreement is usually costly for both parties. This suggests that the outcome of bargaining may depend on the relative costs of delay to the two players, since the player with the higher cost of delay seems to be in a weaker bargaining position than the other. If this is right, then we cannot determine the outcome of rational bargaining without specifying the process by which delay imposes costs. Ariel Rubinstein (1982) models such a process as part of a noncooperative game and shows that this game has a unique "trembling-hand" equilibrium. Many game theorists regard trembling-hand equilibrium as a necessary property of a rational solution for any noncooperative game. On this view, then, Rubinstein has identified a uniquely rational solution to a bargaining problem. In Rubinstein's solution, the player with the higher cost of delay settles on the less favorable terms: this corresponds to the intuition that this player is in the weaker position. If the cost of delay is the same for both players, Rubinstein's solution reduces to the Nash solution (Binmore et al., 1986).

The idea that bargaining problems have uniquely rational solutions is very attractive, particularly for economists who want to predict the outcomes of real bargaining, in labor markets for example. It is also attractive to contractarian philosophers like David Gauthier (1986) who want to show that rational individuals would agree to accept particular constraints on their actions – or, as Gauthier puts it, that morals can emerge by agreement, as the uniquely rational solution to a bargaining problem. But we must be careful not to be misled by wishful thinking: what matters is not whether we *want* bargaining problems to have uniquely rational solutions, but whether they really *do* have such solutions.

In this paper I shall try to show that neither Nash's axiomatic approach nor Rubinstein's development of the Nash program succeeds in showing that bargaining problems have uniquely rational solutions. Both approaches, I shall argue, *assume* the existence of unique solutions; at best, they can tell us what the unique solution must be, given the premise that such a solution exists. This argument, if correct, applies not only to bargaining problems but to any attempt to use Nash equilibrium or related concepts to "solve" one-off noncooperative games. From a theoretical point of view, bargaining games merely provide a concrete class of games with which to fix ideas.

The main conclusion of the paper is skeptical: we have no good reason to assume that bargaining games have uniquely rational solutions. Towards the end of the paper, however, I go beyond skepticism and offer some reasons for thinking that neither Nash's nor Rubinstein's solution can be uniquely rational. A rational player, I shall suggest, could hold beliefs that would lead him to choose strategies other than those of the Nash or Rubinstein solutions.

2 THE NASH SOLUTION

A two-person Nash bargaining game involves two players A (whom I shall make male) and B (whom I shall make female). There is a set P of possible agreements. Each agreement is represented by a *payoff vector* (u_A, u_B). This describes the *utility* that each player would get from the relevant outcome, utility being defined in accordance with the axioms of expected utility theory (von Neumann and Morgenstern, 1947). The set P is assumed to be convex. Given that utility is interpreted in terms of expected utility theory, this assumption says no more than that the players are free to design their own lotteries. Thus, for example, if X and Y are possible agreements, the players are free to agree to toss a coin to determine whether they will settle on X or Y. (P is also assumed to be closed and bounded, but these assumptions are of technical interest only.) One point in P is the *conflict point* $c = (c_A, c_B)$. This represents the utilities the players would get if they failed to agree. To put this another way, each player independently has the power to ensure that the outcome is c, while the two players jointly have the power to reach any point in P provided that they agree to do so. A Nash bargaining game is fully described by the pair (P, c).

A simple example may help here. Suppose A and B are told that they may have £10 provided that they can agree on how to divide the money between them; if they cannot agree, neither will get anything. Suppose also that A and B are risk neutral, so that for each of them utility is a linear function of wealth. Then, for each player, we can fix the utility scale by setting the utility of winning £10 at 10 and the utility of winning nothing at zero. Then P is the set of all payoff vectors such that $u_A \geqslant 0$, $u_B \geqslant 0$, and $u_A + u_B \leqslant 10$; c is the payoff vector $(0, 0)$.

Nash's (1950) theorem may be presented as follows. First, we must state a principle that defines the problem to be addressed:

Rational Determinacy: there exists a function s which assigns a unique payoff vector $s(P, c) = (s_A(P, c), s_B(P, c)) \in P$ to every game

(P, c). The payoff vector $s(P, c)$ is the *solution* of the game, as defined by the function s.

The idea here is that we are trying to discover what the outcome of a Nash bargaining game would be, given rational play. (What this means will be discussed in more detail shortly.) A function s is to be interpreted as a theory that, for every Nash game (P, c), determines a *unique* outcome as the one that would result from rational play. The Principle of Rational Determinacy states that such a theory exists. Given this principle, the problem is to narrow down the class of admissible functions. Nash's theorem can be presented in terms of four axioms,[1] each of which imposes some restriction on the function s.

1 Individual rationality. For any game (P, c): $s_A(P, c) \geqslant c_A$ and $s_B(P, c) \geqslant c_B$.

2 Linear invariance. Let (P, c) be any game and let u be any payoff vector in P. Now define a new game (P', c') and a corresponding payoff vector u' in P', by subjecting one of the players' utility functions to some positive linear transformation.[2] Then $u = s(P, c)$ implies $u' = s(P', c')$.

3 Symmetry. Let (P, c) be any game such that P is symmetrical around the line $u_A = u_B$ and such that c is a point on this line. Then $s_A(c, P) = s_B(c, P)$.

4 Independence of irrelevant alternatives. Let (P, c), (P', c) be any two games with a common conflict point, and such that $P' \subset P$. Then $s(P, c) \in P'$ implies $s(P', c) = s(P, c)$.

The theorem is that there is one and only one function s that satisfies axioms 1–4. For any game (P, c), this function identifies as the solution the payoff vector (u_A, u_B) in P that maximizes the value of $(u_A - c_A)(u_B - c_B)$ subject to the constraint that $u_A \geqslant c_A$ and $u_B \geqslant c_B$. This is the "Nash solution."

To examine the status of this result, we need to consider what is meant by "rational play." Nash himself says very little about this; he says only that

> In general terms, we idealize the bargaining problem by assuming that the two individuals are highly rational, that each can accurately compare his desires for various things, that they are equal in bargaining skill, and that each has full knowledge of the tastes and preferences of the other. (1950, p. 155)

However, my main concern is not with exegesis but with the way in which Nash's theorem has subsequently been used by economists and game theorists. I shall therefore interpret the theorem in the light of the conventions of modern game theory. Such an interpretation is, I think, reasonably faithful to Nash's intentions.

In game theory, it is conventional to describe games in terms of a few mathematical properties. Which properties are used differs between theories; in Nash's theory, a game is described by the pair (P, c). It is assumed that each player believes himself to be playing a game with these properties, and this is a matter of *common belief* (that is, each player believes that his opponent believes this, that his opponent believes that he believes it, and so on). Notice that this does not rule out the possibility that other features of the game, not included in the mathematical description, may also be known to the players. (For example, in a Nash bargaining game, the players may know that they are bargaining over the division of a certain sum of money, and thus know the money value of each outcome to each player *as well as* knowing its utility value.) As I understand it, the object of game theory is to derive conclusions that hold for all games that have a given mathematical description, whatever differences there may be between these games in other respects.

It is conventional to suppose that game-players are completely rational, and that this too is a matter of common belief. The concept of complete rationality has two components. First, each player maximizes his expected utility, given his beliefs (which may be expressed in terms of probabilities) about what his opponent will do. (I shall call this the *best-reply principle*.) Second, every true theorem about the game is known by each player. Because this is a matter of common belief, there is *transparency of reason*: if, given a particular set of data, player A is able to deduce that rationality requires him to hold a particular belief or to act in a particular way, and if B believes him to have these data and to be rational, then B must believe that A will hold that belief or act in that way. (This principle is formulated more precisely by Michael Bacharach (1987).)

Finally, it is conventional to treat a game as a one-off interaction (that is, the players have no previous experience of playing against one another and do not expect to play against one another again) and to suppose that this is a matter of common belief.

I shall use the term *rational play* for the behavior of players for whom all these conventional suppositions are true. The project of game theory is to determine the nature of rational play, so defined. In Nash's theory, the object is to determine the outcome of rational play (measured in terms of the player's utilities). Some theories are designed to determine the strategies that rational players would follow, or to determine the beliefs that rational players would hold about the strategy choices of their opponents. We may say that a game has a *uniquely rational solution* if, given an appropriate description of the game, there is a unique outcome (in the case of a theory like Nash's) or a unique combination of strategies or a unique set of beliefs that would necessarily result from rational play. Nash's theorem can be given a very natural interpretation if we interpret his concept of a "solution" as a uniquely rational solution.

On this interpretation, the Principle of Rational Determinacy asserts the existence of a theory that identifies a uniquely rational solution for every Nash bargaining game. For the purposes of this theory, a game is fully described by the pair (P, c); the theory is supposed to show that a particular payoff vector must be the outcome of rational play in any bargaining game which fits this description. That such a theory exists is not itself a theorem: it is an assumption. (In the original presentation of his theorem, Nash (1950) does not state the Principle of Rational Determinacy explicitly; the idea that any given game must have a unique solution seems to be treated as self-evident. In a later presentation, Nash (1953, p. 137) does state the principle as an axiom, but in support of it says only: "There is little need to comment on [it]; it is just a statement on the type of solution desired.") Taking this principle as given, the four axioms then represent properties that any such theory should possess.

The justification for axiom 1 is quite obvious. Suppose, contrary to axiom 1, that the uniquely rational solution is such that $s_A(P, c) < c_A$. Then rational play must lead to an outcome in which A is worse off than at the conflict point c. And A, being rational, must believe this to be the case. But the definition of "conflict point" entails that A has the power to ensure that c is the outcome of the game. Thus A's supposedly rational behavior cannot be consistent with the best-reply principle: the original supposition has generated a contradiction.

Axiom 2 is equally easy to justify. Recall that utility is to be interpreted in terms of expected utility theory. In this theory, the measurement of utility is unique only up to positive linear transformations. Thus the information content of utility vectors of the form (u_A, u_B) is unchanged if either person's utility is subjected to positive linear transformations: such transformations should not affect the nature of a solution that is uniquely rational.

Now consider Axiom 3. Suppose that some game (P, c) is symmetrical in the sense of this axiom. By the Principle of Rational Determinacy, there exists a theory which shows that any game which fits the description (P, c) has the same uniquely rational solution. Thus the theory must show each player how it is possible to deduce the nature of this outcome from the information contained in this description. But if this description is completely symmetrical as between the players, any deduction that A makes about how he should play the game must be exactly mirrored by a deduction that B can make about how she should play it. Thus the uniquely rational outcome must be symmetrical.

Axiom 4 is not quite so compelling as the others, but there is still a good argument in its favor. The effect of this axiom is to require that, if some payoff vector is the solution to a given game, it must be so in virtue of properties of *P in the locality of that solution*. I suspect that it is not possible to prove that if a solution is uniquely rational it *must* satisfy this axiom. However, it is a recurring feature of theories across the whole range of economics that optimal solutions and equilibria can be characterized in terms of local properties of functions. This is a consequence of the pervasive use of the mathematics of the calculus in economics, which in turn reflects the role of maximization in economic theory. Game theory is no exception: recall that rationality is interpreted in terms of the maximizing of expected utility. Thus if a theory of rational behavior implies that a particular outcome must occur, we might expect that this outcome would be describable in terms of the local properties of some function or functions. More particularly, if a theory of rational behavior implies that a particular outcome of a Nash game (P, c) must occur, and if the only information that the theory has used is contained in the description of P and c, then we might expect the outcome to be describable in terms of some local property of P. (Since c is a point, it has no local properties in the relevant sense.) Nash (1953, p. 138) puts this more intuitively: "It is as if a proposed deal is to compete with small modifications of itself and that utimately the negotiation will be understood to be restricted to a narrow range of alternative deals and to be unconcerned with more remote alternatives."

All this suggests the following interpretation of Nash's theorem. Suppose that the Principle of Rational Determinacy is correct, and that there exists a theory which identifies a uniquely rational solution for every Nash bargaining game. Then there must be some proof that shows that rational play does indeed lead to this outcome: this, presumably, is what the theory in question consists of. This proof will be accessible to the fully rational players of game theory, even if it is not yet accessible to us. Nash's theorem gives us strong (if not absolutely compelling) reasons for expecting that, *if such a proof is possible*, it will identify the Nash solution as the uniquely rational outcome.

But this does not imply that the Nash solution *is* uniquely rational. The problem is that we have no proof for the Principle of Rational Determinacy. In the absence of such a proof, we cannot be sure that Nash bargaining games have uniquely rational solutions: it may be that the rationality and common-belief assumptions of game theory are insufficient to determine how bargaining games will be played.

The difficulty here is an instance of a much more general problem in game theory. As Bacharach (1987) shows, game theory relies heavily on indirect arguments which assume the existence of solutions and then use this assumption to help establish what these solutions must be. (I shall discuss another example of this kind of reasoning in section 5.) Such indirect arguments assume that particular truths about rational choice are accessible to perfectly rational players – and thus, presumably, can be proved as theorems – even though we have as yet failed to discover them. We are entitled to be skeptical of claims about the existence of valid proofs which no one knows how to construct.

3 TREMBLING-HAND EQUILIBRIUM

As a first step towards understanding Rubinstein's very different analysis of bargaining, consider a simple bargaining game. A well-wisher has given a £5 note and a £10 note to A and B. This gift, however, is conditional on A and B's agreeing about which of them is to have which note. The procedure for bargaining is to be as follows. First A must decide whether he wishes to claim the £5 note or the £10 note. If he claims the £5 note, that is the end of the game: A gets £5 and B gets £10. If instead A claims the £10 note, B is told of this and then must decide which of the two notes she wishes to claim. If she claims the £5 note, the game ends in agreement: A gets £10 and B gets £5. If, however, B also claims the £10 note, neither player gets anything. No other communication between the players is permitted, and side-payments are forbidden.

This problem can be modeled as a noncooperative game. A has two strategies: "Claim £10" (T) and "Claim £5" (F). B also has two strategies: "If A claims £10, claim £10" (t) and "If A claims £10, claim £5" (f). If we assume A and B to be risk neutral and measure utility in money units, we can associate a payoff vector with each possible pair of strategies. The strategy pair (T, t) leads to the payoff vector (0, 0); (T, f) leads to (10, 5); and (F, t) and (F, f) both lead to (5, 10). The standard solution concept for noncooperative games is Nash equilibrium.[3] In a game for two players, a Nash equilibrium is a pair of strategies such that each player's strategy is a best reply to the other's. The usual interpretation of this concept is that each player believes that his opponent will play his equilibrium strategy; given this belief, each player is rational (in the sense of the best-reply principle) in playing his own equilibrium strategy.

My game has a Nash equilibrium in which A plays T and B plays f. Given that A claims £10, B's best strategy is clearly to claim £5; and given that B will claim £5, A's best strategy is to claim £10. But the game also has a second type of Nash equilibrium, in which A plays F (with certainty) and B plays t with a probability of 0.5 or more. If B is more likely to claim £10 than £5, A's best strategy is to claim £5. And given that A claims £5, the outcome for B is the same whatever strategy she plays (she wins £10); thus any probability mixture of f and t is *a* best reply for her.

Game theorists usually regard Nash equilibrium as a necessary property of a "reasonable" solution to a game. (I am being deliberately vague: I wish to postpone discussion of the rationale for Nash equilibrium.) However, Reinhard Selten (1965, 1975) has argued that not all Nash equilibria can be regarded as reasonable solutions, and his argument is now widely accepted among game theorists. The argument may be presented in terms of my bargaining game (which has the same formal structure as the One-round Chain Store game that Selten (1978) uses as an illustration). Is the second type of equilibrium reasonable? To keep things simple, consider the pure-strategy equilibrium in which A plays F and B plays t. A claims £5 because he believes that, were he to claim £10, B would claim £10 too. A's belief might be interpreted as a belief in some kind of implicit threat by B. But, Selten argues, such a threat is not credible. Were A to claim £10, B would be in the position of having to choose between carrying out the threat, in which case she would get nothing, and not carrying it out, in which case she would get £5. As a rational person, she must go for the £5. Being rational too, A must be able to foresee this; so he can safely ignore the threat. (The thought that it might be rational for B to carry out the threat in order to build up a reputation for future bargaining must be resisted: Selten is working in the classic tradition of game theory, in which games are one-off interactions.)

Selten (1975) formulates this idea of an unreasonable Nash equilibrium by way of the concept of a *trembling-hand equilibrium*. Games involving a sequence of moves can be represented as trees in which all the logically possible lines of play branch out successively. Consider the tree of a two-person game. The nodes of the tree are points at which one or other player has to make a choice between moves. Suppose that at each node there is some nonzero probability that the relevant player's rationality "breaks down," "some unspecified psychological mechanism" taking over (Selten, 1975, p. 35). Which move is then made is taken to be determined by a random process: it as though the player has to use his hands to put his rational decisions into operation and cannot be absolutely sure that his hands will not tremble.

Let us say that a *theory of trembles* specifies, for each node, the probability that such a breakdown of rationality will take place and the random process that will take over in that event. Selten imposes two restrictions on such theories. First, the probability of a breakdown of rationality at any node must be independent of the corresponding probability for any other node. Second, in the event of a breakdown of rationality at any node, every move that could possibly be made at that node must have a nonzero probability. This has the effect of ensuring that every point in the tree has a nonzero probability of being reached as a result of nonrational play.

Given any game, we may *perturb* it by adding a theory of trembles. Now suppose that the theory of trembles, like the other characteristics of the game, is a matter of common belief among the players (that is, each believes the theory to be true, each believes the other to believe this, and so on). Then we may identify Nash equilibria for the perturbed game. If we consider a sequence of such theories of trembles in which the probability of trembles tends to zero, we may construct a corresponding sequence of perturbed games and then find the limits to which the Nash equilibria of these games tend. Selten sees this as a way of preserving as much as possible of the classic game-theoretic assumption of fully rational players: we should, he says, regard complete rationality as a limiting case of incomplete rationality (1975, p. 35). A pair of strategies in the original unperturbed game is a trembling-hand equilibrium if it is the limiting case of a sequence of Nash equilibria in some such sequence of perturbations of the game.

This idea can be illustrated by my bargaining game. In any perturbation of this game, the probability that A will play T must be nonzero. (Even if A's rational decision was not to play T, he might still make this move as the result of a breakdown of rationality.) Given this, f is a strictly dominant strategy for B: whatever A's *rational choice* of strategy, f is B's unique best reply. Thus B's rationally playing t can be no part of a Nash equilibrium for any perturbed game. In contrast, (T, f) is a Nash equilibrium in every perturbation of the game, and so is the unique trembling-hand equilibrium.

4 RUBINSTEIN'S SOLUTION

The bargaining game analyzed by Rubinstein has a sequential structure rather like that of the game with the £5 and £10 notes. Two players A and B are faced with an infinitely divisible resource. This resource will be theirs if, but only if, they can agree on how to divide it between them. The bargaining process works as follows. In period 0 of the game, A makes a proposal about how to divide up the resource. This proposal is represented by the number a_0, where $0 \leqslant a_0 \leqslant 1$: this is the proportion of the resource that A is proposing to take for himself, leaving $1 - a_0$

for B. B then decides whether to accept or reject this proposal. If she accepts, the game ends, and the resource is divided in the proportions $a_0:(1 - a_0)$. If instead she rejects the proposal, there is a delay until period 1. Now it is B's turn to make a proposal a_1, which represents the proportion of the resource she is prepared to offer to A, keeping $1 - a_1$ for herself. If A accepts, the game ends, and the resource is divided in the proportions $a_1:(1 - a_1)$. If he rejects the proposal, there is a delay until period 2, when it is A's turn to make a proposal again. And so on indefinitely.

The inducement to reach agreement is that delay is costly. This is modeled by supposing A and B to have strictly positive rates of time discount, denoted by r_A and r_B (expressed in terms of a unit of time equal to the interval between proposals). Suppose that agreement is reached in period t, and that the agreement is that the resource should be divided in the proportions $a_t:(1 - a_t)$. Then (assuming utility to be a linear function of the quantity of the resource), the payoff vector may be written as $[a_t/(1 + r_A)^t, (1 - a_t)/(1 + r_B)^t]$.

Rubinstein shows, by means of an elegant proof, that his game has a unique trembling-hand equilibrium.[4] This solution has the property that agreement is reached in period 0: A makes a proposal a_0 and B immediately accepts. Other things being equal, this solution gives some advantage to A, as the player who makes the first proposal. This first-mover advantage vanishes if we take the limit as the interval of time between proposals tends to zero, holding constant the players' rates of time discount per unit of real time (hours or days). Mathematically, this is equivalent to holding r_B/r_A constant and taking the limit of Rubinstein's solution as r_A tends to zero. In this limit, we find that $a_0 = r_B/(r_A + r_B)$. Thus a_0 is greater than, equal to, or less than $\frac{1}{2}$ according to whether r_B is greater than, equal to, or less than r_A. In other words, if the players' discount rates differ, the player with the higher discount rate (the one for whom delay is relatively more costly) gets the smaller share.

Some insight into the logic of Rubinstein's proof can be gained by seeing how some Nash equilibria can be eliminated as "unreasonable." Consider any a^* where $0 < a^* < 1$. Consider the following pair of strategies. A's strategy is: "In periods 0, 2, 4,. . ., propose a^*; in periods 1, 3, 5,. . ., accept B's proposal if and only if it is no less than a^*." B's strategy is: "In periods 1, 3, 5,. . ., propose a^*; in periods 0, 2, 4,. . ., accept A's proposal if and only if it is no greater than a^*." It is easy to check that these strategies are best replies to one another and thus constitute a Nash equilibrium. In other words, any exact division of the resource between A and B (provided that each player's share is nonzero) is consistent with Nash equilibrium. Such a solution is supported by a set of implicit threats:

A will reject any proposal that offers him less than a^* and B will reject any proposal that offers her less than $1 - a^*$. But are these threats credible?

To examine this issue, consider any perturbation of the game. Then there must be some nonzero probability that in period 0 A will propose $a^* + \epsilon$ (where ϵ is some small positive number) as the result of a breakdown of rationality. If the strategies we are considering constitute a trembling-hand equilibrium, it must be a best reply for B to reject A's proposal and then, in period 1, to propose a^*. Since the probability that A will suffer from a breakdown of rationality in period 1 is vanishingly small (remember that the probability of breakdown at one node is independent of the probability at any other node), B can be virtually certain that A will accept this proposal. But then B's payoff will be $(1 - a^*)/(1 + r_B)$. Had she accepted A's original proposal, her payoff would have been $1 - a^* - \epsilon$. Thus, if ϵ is sufficiently small, B's best reply is *not* to reject A's original proposal: it is better to settle for $1 - a^* - \epsilon$ in period 0 than to wait until period 1 to get $1 - a^*$. And so the strategies we are considering cannot constitute a trembling-hand equilibrium. To put this another way: if we accept Selten's criterion for identifying non-credible threats, B's implicit threat to reject any proposal from A that offers her less than $1 - a^*$ is not credible.

5 THE RATIONALE FOR TREMBLING-HAND EQUILIBRIUM

If we accept that rational players must choose strategies that are in trembling-hand equilibrium with one another, Rubinstein has shown that his particular bargaining game has a uniquely rational solution. But must we accept this? Since trembling-hand equilibrium is a special case of Nash equilibrium, it is useful to begin by asking whether rational players must choose strategies that are in Nash equilibrium with one another.

One answer to this question is provided by von Neumann and Morgenstern. Justifying their concept of equilibrium for two-person zero-sum games, they argue as follows:

[In searching for a theory of rational play] it is perfectly legitimate for us to use the conventional tools of logics, and in particular that of the *indirect proof*. This consists in imagining that we have a satisfactory theory of a certain desired type, trying to picture the consequences of this imaginary intellectual situation, and then in drawing conclusions from this as to what the hypothetical theory must be like in detail. If this process is applied successfully, it may narrow down the possibilities for the hypothetical theory of the type in question to such an extent that only one possibility is left, – i.e. that the theory is determined, discovered by this device. . . .

Let us now imagine that there exists a complete theory of the zero-sum two-person game which tells a player what to do, and which is absolutely convincing. If the players knew such a theory then each player would have to assume that his strategy has been "found out" by his opponent. The opponent knows the theory, and he knows that a player would be unwise not to follow it. Thus the hypothesis of the existence of a satisfactory theory legitimizes our investigation of the situation when a player's strategy is "found out" by his opponent. (1947, pp. 147–8)

In other words, suppose that for a given game there exists a theory that prescribes a uniquely rational strategy for each player, and that this theory is accessible to rational players. Then if the players of a game are rational, and if their rationality is a matter of common belief, each player must follow his uniquely rational strategy while believing that his opponent will follow her uniquely rational strategy. But we also know that a rational player's strategy must be a best reply to the strategy he expects his opponent to follow. Therefore, uniquely rational strategies must be best replies to one another. Von Neumann and Morgenstern's solution concept for zero-sum games (the principle that each player chooses his maximin strategy) has this mutual-best-reply property; more generally, this property is the defining characteristic of Nash equilibrium. So this argument establishes that, if a game has a uniquely rational solution, that solution must be a Nash equilibrium.

Robert Aumann (1987) has recently re-stated this argument in slightly different terms.[5] For a game between two fully rational players A and B, Aumann interprets "A's strategy" as equivalent to "B's expectations about what A will choose." Thus a mixed strategy for A is interpreted in terms of B's uncertainty as to what A will choose, with probability being understood in the subjective Bayesian sense axiomatized by Leonard Savage (1954). Let B's expectations about A be described by the strategy x_A and let A's expectations about B be described by the strategy x_B. Now suppose that these expectations are matters of common belief between A and B. Thus A believes that B's expectations about him are x_A. If A believes B to be rational, he must expect B's choice to be optimal with respect to her expectations about him. This implies that x_B (A's expectations about B) must be a best reply to x_A (A's beliefs about B's expectations about him). Similarly, x_A must be a best reply to x_B. In other words, x_A and x_B must be in Nash equilibrium with one another. This amounts to the theorem that, if the players' beliefs about one another are matters of common belief, those beliefs must be in Nash equilibrium.

But does this imply that the beliefs of rational players must be in equilibrium? Aumann claims to prove this, but his proof turns out to depend on the common prior assumption (or "Harsanyi doctrine"): "that people with different information may legitimately entertain different probabilities, but there is no rational basis for people who have always been fed precisely the same information to do so" (1987, pp. 13–14). The idea behind this assumption seems to be that there is a uniquely rational way of deriving expectations from any given information. If this is so, and if the players of a game start with the same information about the nature of the game they are playing, then any expectations they form about one another must be matters of common belief. (This follows from the transparency of reason.)

But to suppose that there is a uniquely rational way of deriving beliefs from any given information is tantamount to supposing that all games have uniquely rational solutions. (Recall that, for Aumann, a solution *is* a set of beliefs.) Aumann offers no real reasons for accepting the common prior assumption. Indeed, he seems to have some doubts about its validity: his ultimate defence of the assumption is simply that it is what economists and game theorists usually assume (1987, pp. 12–15). Thus Aumann's line of argument proves no more than von Neumann and Morgenstern's: that *if* a game has a uniquely rational solution, that solution must be a Nash equilibrium.

My conclusion here is the same as Bacharach's (1987). Bacharach presents a formal logic for the analysis of games. Within this logic it is a theorem that only Nash equilibria can be solutions of games, essentially for the reasons given by von Neumann and Morgenstern. (A "solution," for Bacharach, corresponds with my concept of a uniquely rational solution.) But Bacharach, unlike Aumann, denies that this implies that rational players must choose Nash equilibrium strategies, even if a unique Nash equilibrium exists. There is no reason, he argues, to presume that because a game has a unique Nash equilibrium it must also have a solution.

Now consider how these arguments carry over from Nash equilibrium to trembling-hand equilibrium. Suppose that the players of a game are subject to lapses of rationality of the kind assumed by Selten. These lapses are explained by a theory of trembles, and the nature of this theory is a matter of common belief among the players. This "perturbed game" may equally well be thought of as a game for completely rational players, but in which there is an element of pure chance: a "lapse of rationality" may be thought of as a random event, part of the game but outside the control of the players (just as the deal of the cards is outside the control of the players of a game of bridge). Then the players may be assumed to act with full rationality in the light of their beliefs about the random process that controls trembles. Given this interpretation of trembles, we may make use of the theorem that uniquely rational solutions are Nash equilibria. If, from the information contained in the description of the game (which now includes the theory of trembles), it is possible to deduce a uniquely rational strategy for each player, these strategies must be in Nash equilibrium. So if we allow for the possibility of trembles, if we accept the restrictions that Selten imposes on the theory of trembles, and if we take the limiting case in which the probability of trembles tends to zero, we must conclude that any uniquely rational solution to a game must be a trembling-hand equilibrium.

In this sense, then, trembling-hand equilibrium is a natural development of, or refinement of, Nash equilibrium.[6] But like Nash equilibrium, its relevance for the choices of rational players is conditional on the presupposition that games have uniquely rational solutions. And so Rubinstein's analysis of bargaining turns out to have the same inconclusive character as Nash's axiomatic analysis: it can claim to do no more than to show us what the uniquely rational solution to a bargaining game would be, were such a solution to exist. But we still have no proof that a uniquely rational solution exists.

6 GOING BEYOND SKEPTICISM: NASH BARGAINING GAMES

So far, my argument has been negative and skeptical: I have argued only that there is no proof that rational play in a Nash bargaining game must lead to the Nash solution, or that rational play in Rubinstein's bargaining game must lead to Rubinstein's solution. I now wish to suggest that no such proof is possible, because outcomes other than those identified by Nash and Rubinstein can result from rational play. I say "suggest" rather than "prove" because this part of my argument is speculative in character. It depends on an interpretation of "rational" that derives from the literature of rationalizability.

This literature questions the idea that rational individuals must always play Nash equilibrium strategies or hold Nash equilibrium beliefs. Douglas Bernheim (1984) and David Pearce (1984) argue that, in general, we have no reason to expect that the expectations of players in one-off games will be matters of common belief. In their approach, a player's beliefs are *rationalizable* if they form an infinite chain of successively higher-order beliefs, and if every link in the chain is consistent with the rationality of the players being a matter of common belief. A strategy is rationalizable if it is optimal in relation to such beliefs. Rationalizable beliefs, then, are ones that could consistently he held by a rational player, even though these beliefs may not be capable of being derived by rational calculation. The idea is that beliefs may be underdetermined by such calculation, and that a rational player is someone who acts on rational calculation *whenever this is possible.*

For example, suppose that A is playing B at Scissors, Stone, Paper. A reasons as follows: "I shall play Scissors, because I expect B to play Paper. I expect her to play Paper because I believe that she expects me to play Stone. I believe that she expects this because I believe that she believes that I expect her to play Scissors. . . ." These are rationalizable beliefs, even though they cannot form part of a system of *common* beliefs. (A expects B to play Paper but he also believes that B believes that he expects her to play Scissors.) We should be entitled to conclude that such noncommon beliefs were irrational *if* we were entitled to assume that a uniquely rational set of beliefs existed. (If A must rationally expect B to play Paper then he must expect B, as a rational person who believes him to be rational, to believe that he holds this expectation.) But if we allow beliefs to be underdetermined by rational calculation, then it seems that rational players might hold noncommon beliefs. This implies that the beliefs of rational players need not always be in Nash equilibrium with one another.

A somewhat similar idea can be found in Robin Cubitt's (1989) axiomatic theory. Cubitt starts from the assumption that the strategies available to a player can be divided into those for which rational justifications exist and those for which such justifications do not exist. Which strategies fall into which class is a matter of common belief among the players. However, a player may have more than one rationally justifiable strategy, and there is no presumption that he must be indifferent between them. This framework thus allows for the possibility that a player's choice of strategy may be underdetermined by the assumption of rational play.

Consider the implications of this kind of approach for Nash bargaining games. Take, for example, the Nash bargaining game I described in section 2, in which A and B have to divide £10 between themselves, with each getting nothing if they fail to agree. Suppose the bargaining process is carried out according to the following simple rules. The players are not allowed to communicate with one another. Each player is called on to make a demand, which is a sum of money in the range from nothing to £10; neither player knows the other's demand before making his or her own. If the two demands are compatible – that is, if they sum to £10 or less – then each player gets what he has demanded. If the demands are not compatible, neither player gets anything. This constitutes a conceivable bargaining game, and one which captures at least some of the flavor of real bargaining. In the language of Thomas Schelling (1960, pp. 58–67), it is a game of tacit bargaining.

To find the Nash solution of this game, it is necessary to know the players' utility functions. If A and B happened to have identical utility functions, the game would be symmetrical in utility terms, and so the Nash solution would be symmetrical: this would imply a £5:£5 split. But suppose instead that one player is more risk averse than the other, so that the Nash solution is not symmetrical – say, that A (who is more risk averse) gets £4.62 and B gets £5.38. Does rationality therefore require A to demand £4.62? Would it, for example, be clearly irrational for A to demand £5?

It is easy to see that the strategy of demanding £5 is rationalizable for A. If A expects B to demand £5, demanding £5 is optimal for A. And if B expects A to demand £5, demanding £5 is optimal for B. Thus A may reason: "I shall demand £5 because I expect B to demand £5. I expect her to do this because I believe that she expects me to demand £5. I believe that she expects this because I believe that she believes that I expect her to demand £5. . . ." So A's demanding £5 can be supported by an infinite chain of successively higher-order beliefs. (In this case, there need be no noncommon beliefs, since B might reason in a symmetrical fashion and demand £5 too. This corresponds to the fact that it is a Nash equilibrium for each player to demand £5, even though this is not the Nash solution.)

It might be objected that these beliefs, even if held in common, are irrational: *on what grounds*, it might be asked, does A hold them? These beliefs do not seem to be derivable by deduction from the premises of rationality: although there is an infinite chain of beliefs in which each belief is justified in terms of a higher-order belief, we never reach a belief that can be justified in its own right. A's beliefs, then, seem to be internally consistent and yet rationally ungrounded. But must all the beliefs of a rational player be rationally grounded? If a set of rationally grounded beliefs – a set of beliefs that can be arrived at by rational analysis from premises that are available to the player – exists, then it would clearly be irrational for him not to hold them. But unless we have a proof that such a set of beliefs exists, we seem to have no grounds for claiming that ungrounded beliefs are necessarily irrational.

We may go further: A's expectation that B will demand £5 may not be completely ungrounded. Schelling (1960, pp. 53–67) argues that ordinary human beings are remarkably successful at coordinating their strategies in tacit bargaining games. He describes various games which he has tried out on a small and "unscientific" sample of people. One of these games was exactly like the game between A and B that I have just described, except that the players had to divide $100 between them; 36 out of 40 players made demands of exactly $50. In another game, two players A and B had each to name Heads or Tails. If both chose Heads, A would get $3 and B would get $2; if both chose Tails, B would get $3 and A would get $2; if they chose differently, neither would get anything. There were 22 A-players and 22 B-players in Schelling's sample; of these, 16 A-players and 15 B-players chose heads. In each case, it seems that many players were able to recognize a particular solution to their tacit bargaining problem as in some way "prominent" or "salient" – as sticking out from the others – and to see this as a reason for choosing the corresponding strategies. This approach has since been developed by Alvin Roth (1985b). Roth and his collaborators have carried out various experiments, the results of which support Schelling's hypothesis that bargaining behavior is influenced by considerations of prominence (e.g. Roth and Murnighan, 1982).

What kind of reasoning are players using when they choose strategies because they are prominent? There are really two questions here. First, we can ask how the two players in a game manage to identify the same solution as being prominent. Second, we can ask why, even granted that they have a common belief that a particular solution is prominent, they choose the strategies that bring that solution about.

As far as the first question is concerned, prominence often seems to depend on the existence of common beliefs, or common modes of thinking, that lie outside the scope of conventional game theory. For example, the prominence of an equal division of a sum of money may arise from ideas of fairness. The point is not that the players *want* the division to be fair: each might be concerned only to get as much as possible for himself or herself. It is not even necessary that they *believe* an equal distribution to be fair. It may be sufficient that they have a common experience of living in a society in which equal divisions are generally regarded as fair (and that their having such experience is a matter of common belief). Or it may be that the prominence of equality arises out of shared ideas of symmetry or balance. If the players have a common experience of a culture in which symmetry is seen as aesthetically pleasing, this may be sufficient to make an equal division prominent.

Conventional game theory treats beliefs such as these as irrelevant to the problem of defining the solutions of games. Nash's theory of bargaining belongs to this tradition. In Nash's axiomatic system, the solution of a bargaining game is required to depend only on the game's mathematical structure – that is, on the set of possible agreements and the conflict point, both of which are described purely in terms of utilities. (This is an implication of the Principle of Rational Determinacy. According to this principle, every game with the mathematical description (P, c) must have the same solution $s(P, c)$.) This amounts to saying that any information about a game that is not contained in the mathematical description (P, c) must be treated as irrelevant by rational players. But if the players are looking for prominence, some of this "irrelevant" information may in fact be very relevant. In the game of dividing £10, for example, the players need to know that a particular payoff vector corresponds to an equal division *of the money* if they are to recognize its prominence; this information is stripped away if the game is described only in terms of utilities.

But why would rational players be concerned with prominence? How can the prominence of a strategy be a reason for choosing it? Following Schelling, we can define a pair of strategies as constituting a *focal point* if (a) they are in Nash equilibrium with one another, (b) relative to other Nash equilibria for the relevant game, this equilibrium is prominent, and (c) the prominence of this equilibrium is a matter of common belief. It seems that in Schelling's games players are following a principle of the form, "If focal points exist, choose strategies that lead to focal points." I shall call this the Focal-point Principle. Clearly, each player is rational to act on this principle, provided that he believes that the other player will act on it too. (This follows from the stipulation that focal points must not only be prominent but must also be Nash equilibria.)

But what, it might be asked, is the ground for this belief? Such a belief cannot, I think, be deduced from premises of rationality of the kind that are used in game theory. (That it cannot be so deduced is argued convincingly by Margaret Gilbert (1989).) Ultimately, I suspect, we can say no more than that, in our society, it *is* a matter of common belief that people will tend to chose strategies that lead to focal points. There is no logical or rational necessity about this. But given the existence of this belief, it is rational for each individual to follow the Focal-point Principle.

Of course, it is possible to imagine a world in which it is a matter of common belief that people tend to follow the principle: "In bargaining games, choose strategies that lead to Nash solutions." Given such beliefs, it would be rational for each person to follow that principle. So the Nash solution may be said to have essentially the same theoretical status as a focal point. Or, as Schelling (1960, pp. 113–15) puts it, Nash's solution is just one of many possible focal points. That this solution is implied by an elegant system of axioms might be enough to make it focal in a community of mathematicians. But this is not to say that the mathematicians are more rational than the rest of us.

7 GOING BEYOND SCEPTICISM: RUBINSTEIN'S GAME

Now consider the implications of the rationalizability approach for Rubinstein's bargaining game. Suppose that A and B are playing a Rubinstein game in which they have to divide £10. Suppose also that their discount rates are such that, in the unique trembling-hand equilibrium, A opens the game by proposing that he takes £4.62, and B immediately accepts this proposal. Can we therefore conclude that it would be irrational for A to open the game by proposing a £5:£5 split?

In this case, we cannot defend A's rationality by claiming that an equal division of the £10 is a focal point. Recall that a focal point must be a Nash equilibrium. If it really is a matter of common belief that the players are liable to lapses of rationality, that these lapses occur with vanishingly small probability, and that they can be explained by a theory of trembles of the kind proposed by Selten, then A and B are playing a "perturbed" game in which the only Nash equilibrium is one in which A proposes a £4.62:£5.38 split. If we are to argue that it might nevertheless be rational for A to demand £5, we must argue that it might be rational for him to play something other than a Nash equilibrium strategy.

Suppose that A plays the strategy of proposing a £5:£5 split each time he is called on to make a proposal, accepting any proposal from B that gives him at least £5, and rejecting any less favorable proposal. Could this be rational? The force of Rubinstein's argument is that this could not be *uniquely* rational. Adapting the general argument presented in section 4, if this strategy were uniquely rational, B would expect A to play it. Even if A were to depart from this strategy in round 1, B would expect him to revert to it in subsequent rounds. (If rationality requires A to propose a £5:£5 split in round 1, then his failure to do so can be explained only as the result of a lapse into irrationality, and by assumption such lapses are uncorrelated.) Thus whatever A does in round 1, B must expect that if and when round 2 is played A will be prepared to settle for £5, but not to settle for less. So if A demands £5 + ϵ in round 1, and if ϵ is sufficiently small, it will be a best reply for B to concede in round 1. And this implies that it would be rational for A to demand £5 + ϵ rather than £5, contradicting the original supposition.

But to say that A's strategy is not uniquely rational is not to say that it is irrational. Perhaps this is one of several strategies, any one of which could rationally be played by A. Suppose, for example, that A believes that B has the initial expectation that A will play his Rubinstein strategy, and thus will be prepared to settle for £4.62. (Notice that this supposition implies that the Rubinstein strategy is *one of* the strategies that could rationally be played by A, since B must expect A to play rationally.) Given this belief, A might try to convince B that he is not in fact prepared to settle for less than a half share. He tries to do this by following the strategy I have described, repeatedly proposing a £5:£5 split and rejecting B's proposals as long as they offer him less than £5. By sticking to this plan he hopes to induce B to believe that he will continue to stick to it; if B does come to believe this, she will see that her best reply is to accept A's terms. If she comes to this belief sufficiently quickly, A will have done better than he would have done by settling immediately on the terms that B initially expected.

It seems, then, that A might believe that the strategy of demanding £5 would yield him a greater expected utility than would the Rubinstein strategy. Of course, he might equally well believe the contrary. (He might, for example, believe that if he were repeatedly to demand £5 B would recognize the pattern in his play but still try to hold out for a £4.62:£5.38 split, in the belief that she could induce A to back down.) Either belief, I think, could be consistent with the assumption that A and B are rational and that their rationality is a matter of common belief.

These considerations lead me to the following conjecture: there are beliefs that A could rationally hold, consistently with there being a common belief in the rationality of the two players, that would lead him to play something other than the Rubinstein strategy. I must concede that I have as yet no formal proof for this. (Such a proof would require a more careful specification of the concept of rationality that I am using.) What is clear, however, is that equilibrium reasoning of the kind that is conventionally used in game theory is not sufficient to establish that rational players *must* follow Rubinstein strategies.

8 CONCLUSION

If the argument of this paper is right, conventional game theory can tell us relatively little about the outcome of bargaining between rational individuals. Game theorists have tried to describe bargaining problems in an abstract mathematical form, discarding as irrelevant a great deal of the bargainers' knowledge about the social, cultural, and historical background to their actions. They have then tried to show, by pure deductive reasoning, that such problems have determinate solutions – solutions that fully rational individuals could not fail to find. This project, I have argued, has so far met with failure. I suspect that it cannot succeed.

NOTES

I wish to thank Michael Bacharach, Robin Cubitt, and Susan Hurley for their comments on earlier drafts of this paper.

1 Nash's presentation of the theorem uses an axiom requiring the solution to be Pareto efficient, in place of the more compelling axiom of individual rationality. On the equivalence of these two systems of axioms, see Roth (1977).

2 A function is subjected to a positive linear transformation by adding any constant to every value of the function and/or by multiplying every value of the function by any positive constant; thus if $g(x) = a + bf(x)$ and $b > 0$, g is a positive linear transformation of f.

3 It is perhaps unfortunate that so many different concepts in game theory have been named after Nash, but these terms have become established by long usage.

4 Rubinstein's proof is formulated in terms of the concept of "subgame perfection," a precursor of trembling-hand equilibrium (Selten, 1965). Selten (1975) has proved that every extensive game with perfect recall has at least one trembling-hand equilibrium, and that all trembling-hand equilibria are subgame-perfect. Thus a unique subgame-perfect equilibrium must be a unique trembling-hand equilibrium.

5 Aumann's argument is presented in terms of "correlated equilibrium" rather than Nash equilibrium. The mixed strategies of two players are *correlated* if they involve probabilities that are nonindependent. Aumann shows that, if correlated mixed strategies are possible, common beliefs must be in correlated equilibrium. The argument I have given is the analog of Aumann's for the case in which correlated mixed strategies are not possible. Throughout this paper I am assuming that such strategies are not possible.

6 We might wish to question the particular restrictions that Selten imposes on the theory of trembles, and in particular the restriction that trembles are uncorrelated. For a discussion of this issue, see Binmore (1987–8, part I). But the idea of postulating *some* theory of mistakes or trembles, and supposing this theory to be a matter of common belief among rational players, does seem to fit naturally with the interpretation of Nash equilibrium that I have been outlining.

Bibliography

Allais, Maurice (1953a) "Fondements d'une théorie positive des choix comportant un risque et critique des postulats et axiomes de l'école americaine," *Econométrie* (Colloques Internationaux du Centre National de la Recherche Scientifique, Paris) 40, 257–332.

Allais, Maurice (1953b) "Le comportement de l'homme rationnel devant le risque, critique des postulats et axiomes de l'école americaine,' *Econometrica* 21, 503–46 (summarized version of Allais (1953a)).

Allais, Maurice (1979a) "The foundations of a positive theory of choice involving risk and a criticism of the postulates and axioms of the American School,' in M. Allais and O. Hagen, *Expected Utility Hypotheses and the Allais Paradox*, Dordrecht: Reidel (English translation of Allais (1953a)).

Allais, Maurice (1979b) "The so-called Allais Paradox and rational decisions under uncertainty," in M. Allais and O. Hagen *Expected Utility Hypotheses and the Allais Paradox*, Dordrecht: Reidel.

Allais, Maurice and Hagen, Ole (eds) (1979) *Expected Utility Hypotheses and the Allais Paradox*, Dordrecht: Reidel.

Anand, Paul (1987) "Are the preference axioms really rational?," *Theory and Decision* 23, 189–214.

Aumann, Robert (1974) "Subjectivity and correlation in randomized strategies," *Journal of Mathematical Economics* 1, 67–96.

Aumann, Robert (1976) "Agreeing to disagree," *Annals of Statistics* 4, 1236–9.

Aumann, Robert (1987) "Correlated equilibrium as an expression of Bayesian rationality," *Econometrica* 55, 1–18.

Aumann, Robert and Maschler, Michael (1972) "Some thoughts on the minimax principle," *Management Science* 18, 54–63.

Axelrod, Robert (1984) *The Evolution of Cooperation*. New York: Basic Books.

Bacharach, Michael (1975) "Group decisions in the face of differences of opinion," *Management Science* 22, 182–91.

Bacharach, Michael (1976) *Economics and the Theory of Games*. London: Macmillan.

Bacharach, Michael (1987) "A theory of rational decision in games," *Erkenntnis* 27, 17–55.

Bales, R. Eugene (1971) "Act-utilitarianism: account of right-making characteristics or decision-making procedure?," *American Philosophical Quarterly* 8, 257–65.

Barcan Marcus, Ruth et al. (eds) (1986) *Logic, Methodology and Philosophy of Science*, vol. VII. New York: Elsevier, 351–65.

Battalio, Raymond C., Kagel, John H. and MacDonald, Don N. (1985) "Animal choices over uncertain outcomes: some initial experimental results," *American Economic Review* 75, 597–613.

Bayes, Thomas (1765) "An essay towards solving a problem in the doctrine of chances," *Philosophical Transactions of the Royal Society of London* 53, 370–418.

Bell, D.E. (1985) "Disappointment in decision making under uncertainty," *Operations Research* 33, 1–27.

Bell, D.E., Keeney, Ralph L. and Raiffa, Howard (eds) (1977) *Conflicting Objectives in Decisions*. New York: Wiley.

Bernardo, J.M. et al. (eds) (1984) *Bayesian Statistics*, vol. 2. Amsterdam: North-Holland.

Bernheim, B. Douglas (1984) "Rationalizable strategic behavior," *Econometrica* 52, 1007–28.

Bernoulli, Daniel (1954) "Exposition of a new theory on the measurement of risk," translated by Louise Sommer, *Econometrica* 22, 23–36.

Binmore, Kenneth (1987–8) "Modelling rational players," Parts I, II, *Economics and Philosophy* 3, 179–214; 4, 9–55.

Binmore, Kenneth (1988) "Game theory and the social contract: Mark II," manuscript, London School of Economics.

Binmore, Kenneth and Dasgupta, Partha (1988) "Nash bargaining theory: an introduction," in K. Binmore and P. Dasgupta (eds) *The Economics of Bargaining*. Oxford: Blackwell.

Binmore, Kenneth, Rubinstein, Ariel and Wolinsky, Asher (1986) "The Nash bargaining solution in economic modelling," *Rand Journal of Economics* 17, 176–88.

Bjerring, Andrew K. (1978) "The Tracing Procedure and a theory of rational interaction," in C.A. Hooker, J.J. Leach and E.F. McClennen (eds), *Foundations and Applications of Decision Theory*, Dordrecht: Reidel.

Bogdan, R. (ed.) (1986) *Belief.* Oxford: Oxford University Press.

Bonjour, Laurence (1985) *The Structure of Empirical Knowledge.* Cambridge, MA: Harvard University Press.

Borch, Karl and Mossin, J. (eds) (1968) *Risk and Uncertainty.* London: Macmillan.

Border, K. (1987) "Stochastic dominance and choice of lotteries," manuscript, Division of Humanities and Social Sciences, California Institute of Technology.

Brandenburger, Adam and Dekel, Eddie (1986) "On an axiomatic approach to refinements of Nash equilibrium," Economic Theory Discussion Paper, Cambridge University.

Brandenburger, Adam and Dekel, Eddie (1987) "Rationalizability and correlated equilibria," *Econometrica* 55, 1391–1402.

Bratman, Michael (1987) *Intentions, Plans, and Practical Reason.* Cambridge, MA: Harvard University Press.

Broome, John (1982) "Equity in risk bearing," *Operations Research* 30, 412–14.

Broome, John (1984) "Uncertainty and fairness," *Economic Journal* 94, 624–32.

Broome, John (1987) "Utilitarianism and expected utility," *Journal of Philosophy* 84, 405–22.

Broome, John (1991a) "Bernoulli, Harsanyi and the principle of temporal good," in Reinhardt Setten (ed.), *Essays in Honor of John Harsanyi*, Berlin: Springer.

Broome, John (1991b) "Rationality and the sure-thing principle," in G. Meeks, (ed.), *Thoughtful Economic Man*, Cambridge: Cambridge University Press.

Broome, John (1991c) *Weighing Goods.* Oxford: Blackwell.

Broome, John (1991d) "Utilitarian metaphysics?," in J. Elster and J. Roemer (eds), *Interpersonal Comparisons of Well-being*, Cambridge: Cambridge University Press.

Brown, G.W. (1951) "Iterative solutions of games by fictitious play," in T.C. Koopmans (ed.), *Activity Analysis of Production and Allocation*, Cowles Commission Monograph, New York: Wiley, 374–6.

Campbell, Richmond and Sowden, Lanning (eds) (1985) *Paradoxes of Rationality and Cooperation: Prisoner's Dilemma and Newcomb's Problem.* Vancouver: University of British Columbia Press.

Carnap, Rudolf (1950) *Logical Foundations of Probability.* Chicago, IL: University of Chicago Press.

Carnap, Rudolf (1952) *The Continuum of Inductive Methods* Chicago, IL: University of Chicago Press.

Carnap, Rudolf (1980) "A basic system of inductive logic, Part 2," in R.C. Jeffrey (ed.), *Studies in Inductive Logic and Probability*, vol. II,

Berkeley, CA: University of California Press.

Chew, S. (1983) "A generalization of the quasilinear mean with applications to the measurement of inequality and decision theory resolving the Allais Paradox," *Econometrica* 51, 1065–92.

Chew, S. and MacCrimmon, K. (1979) "Alpha–nu choice theory: a generalization of expected utility theory," manuscript, Faculty of Commerce and Business Administration, University of British Columbia.

Chew, S. and Waller, W. (1986) "Empirical tests of weighted utility theory," *Journal of Mathematical Psychology* 30, 55–72.

Chew, S., Karni, E. and Safra, Z. (1987) "Risk aversion in the theory of expected utility with rank dependent probabilities," *Journal of Economic Theory* 42, 370–81.

Chew, S., Epstein, L. and Segal, U. (1988) "Mixture symmetric utility theory," manuscript, Department of Economics, University of Toronto.

Chisholm, Roderick (1977) *Theory of Knowledge*, 2nd edn. Englewood Cliffs, NJ: Prentice-Hall.

Cochrane, James L. and Zeleny, M. (eds) (1973) *Multiple Criteria Decision Making*. Columbia, SC: South Carolina University Press.

Cohen, L. Jonathan (1981, 1983) "Can human irrationality be experimentally demonstrated?," with Open Peer Commentary, Continuing Commentary, Author's Response, and Continuing Commentary, *Behavioral and Brain Sciences* 4, 317–70; 6, 487–517.

Coleman, James (1979) "Rational actors in macrosociological analysis," in R. Harrison (ed.), *Rational Action*, Cambridge: Cambridge University Press.

Colman, Andrew (1982) *Game Theory and Experimental Games*. Oxford: Pergamon.

Cubitt, Robin (1989) "Refinements of Nash equilibrium: a critique," *Theory and Decision* 26, 107–31.

van Damme, Eric (1983) *Refinements of the Nash Equilibrium Concept*. Berlin: Springer.

Dasgupta, Partha, Hammond, Peter and Maskin, Eric (1979) "The implementation of social choice rules: some general results on incentive compatibility," *Review of Economic Studies* 46, 185–216.

Davidson, Donald (1980) *Essays on Actions and Events*. Oxford: Oxford University Press.

Davidson, Donald (1985) "A new basis for decision theory," *Theory and Decision* 18, 87–98.

Davidson, Donald and Suppes, Patrick (1956) "A finitistic axiomatization of subjective probability and utility," *Econometrica* 24, 264–75.

Davidson, Donald, McKinsey, J. and Suppes, Patrick (1955) "Outlines of a formal theory of value, I," *Philosophy of Science* 22, 140–60.

Davidson, Donald, Suppes, Patrick and Siegel, Sidney (1957) *Decision Making: An Experimental Approach* Stanford, CA: Stanford University Press.

De Finetti, Bruno (1937) "La prévision: ses lois logiques, ses sources subjectives," *Annales de l'Institut Henri Poincaré* 7, 1–68. English translation: "Foresight: its logical laws, its subjective sources," in H. Kyburg and H. Smokler (eds) (1980) *Studies in Subjective Probability*, 2nd edn, Huntington, NY: Robert E. Krieger.

De Finetti, Bruno (1938) "Sur la condition d'équivalence partielle," *Actualités Scientifique et Industrielles No. 793*. Paris: Hermann. Translated by Paul Benacerraf and Richard Jeffrey as "On the condition of partial exchangeability," in R. C. Jeffrey (ed.) (1980) *Studies in Inductive Logic and Probability*, vol. II, Berkeley, CA: University of California Press, 193–205.

De Groot, Morris H. (1970) *Optimal Statistical Decisions*. New York: McGraw-Hill.

Dekel, Eddie (1986) "An axiomatic characterization of preferences under uncertainty: weakening the Independence Axiom," *Journal of Economic Theory* 40, 304–18.

Dekel, Eddie (1989) "Asset demands without the Independence Axiom," *Econometrica* 57, 163–9.

Diaconis, P. and Ylvisaker, D. (1979) "Conjugate priors for exponential families," *Annals of Statistics* 7, 269–81.

Diaconis, P. and Ylvisaker, D. (1984) "Quantifying prior opinion," in J. M. Bernardo et al. (eds), *Bayesian Statistics*, vol. 2, Amsterdam: North-Holland.

Diamond, Peter (1967) "Cardinal welfare, individualistic ethics, and interpersonal comparison of utility: comment," *Journal of Political Economy* 75, 765–6.

Donaldson, J. and Selden, L. (1981) "Arrow–Debreu preferences and the reopening of contingent claims markets," *Economics Letters* 8, 209–16.

Dresher, M., Shapley, L. S. and Tucker, A. W. (eds) (1964) *Advances in Game Theory* Princeton, NJ: Princeton University Press.

Dretske, Fred (1986) "Misrepresentation," in R. Bogdan (ed.), *Belief*, Oxford: Oxford University Press.

Dreze, Jacques (1974) "Axiomatic theories of choice, cardinal utility and subjective probability," in J. Dreze (ed.), *Allocation Under Uncertainty: Equilibrium and Optimality*, London: Macmillan.

Edwards, Ward (1955) "The prediction of decisions among bets," *Journal of Experimental Psychology* 50, 201–14.

Edwards, Ward (1962) "Subjective probabilities inferred from decisions," *Psychological Review* 69, 109–35.

Eells, Ellery (1982) *Rational Decision and Causality*. Cambridge: Cambridge University Press.

Einhorn, Hillel and Hogarth, Robin (1981) "Behavioral decision theory: processes of judgment and choice," *Annual Review of Psychology* 32, 53–88.

Ellsberg, Daniel (1956) "Theory of the reluctant duellist," *American Economic Review* 46, 909–23.

Ellsberg, Daniel (1961) "Risk, ambiguity, and the Savage axioms," *Economic Journal* 64, 643–69; also in P. Gärdenfors and N.-E. Sahlin (eds) (1988) *Decision, Probability and Utility*, Cambridge: Cambridge University Press.

Elster, Jon (1979) *Ulysses and the Sirens*. Cambridge: Cambridge University Press.

Elster, Jon (1983) *Sour Grapes*. Cambridge: Cambridge University Press.

Elster, Jon and Roemer, John (eds) (1991) *Interpersonal Comparisons of Well-being*. Cambridge: Cambridge University Press.

Farquhar, P.H. (1980) "Advances in multi-attribute utility theory," *Theory and Decision* 12, 381–94.

Fine, A. and Lepin, J. (eds) (1989) *Philosophy of Science Association 1988*, vol. 2. East Lancing, MI: Philosophy of Science Association.

Fishburn, Peter (1970) *Utility for Decision Making*. New York: Wiley.

Fishburn, Peter (1981) "Subjective expected utility: a review of normative theories," *Theory and Decision* 13, 139–99.

Fishburn, Peter (1982a) *The Foundations of Expected Utility*. Dordrecht: Reidel.

Fishburn, Peter (1982b) "Nontransitive measurable utility," *Journal of Mathematical Psychology* 26, 31–67.

Fishburn, Peter (1983) "Transitive measurable utility," *Journal of Economic Theory* 31, 293–317.

Fishburn, Peter (1984a) "SSB utility theory: an economic perspective," *Mathematical Social Sciences* 8, 63–94.

Fishburn, Peter (1984b) "Equity axioms for public risk," *Operations Research* 32, 901–8.

Fishburn, Peter (1988) *Nonlinear Preference and Utility Theory*. Baltimore, MD: Johns Hopkins University Press.

Fisher, Franklin and Rothenberg, Jerome (1961) "How income ought to be distributed: paradox lost," *Journal of Political Economy* 69, 162–80.

Fisher, Franklin and Rothenberg, Jerome (1962) "How income ought to be distributed: paradox enow," *Journal of Political Economy* 70, 88–93.

Foot, Philippa (1985) "Utilitarianism and the virtues," *Mind* 94, 196–209; also in S. Scheffler (ed.) (1988) *Consequentialism and its Critics*, Oxford: Oxford University Press.

Gärdenfors, Peter and Sahlin, Nils-Eric (1982) "Unreliable probabilities, risk taking, and decision making," *Synthèse* 53, 361–86.

Gärdenfors, Peter and Sahlin, Nils-Eric (eds) (1988) *Decision, Probability and Utility*. Cambridge: Cambridge University Press.

Gauthier, David (1986) *Morals by Agreement*. Oxford: Oxford University Press.

Gibbard, Allan and Harper, William (1978) "Counterfactuals and two kinds of expected utility," in C. A. Hooker, J. J. Leach and E. F. McClennen (eds), *Foundations and Applications of Decision Theory*, Dordrecht: Reidel; also in P. Gärdenfors and N.-E. Sahlin (eds) (1988) *Decision, Probability and Utility*, Cambridge: Cambridge University Press; also in R. Campbell and L. Sowden (eds) (1985) *Paradoxes of Rationality and Cooperation: Prisoner's Dilemma and Newcomb's Problem*, Vancouver: University of British Columbia Press.

Gibson, Mary (ed.) (1985) *To Breathe Freely*. Totowa, NJ: Rowman & Allanheld.

Gilbert, Margaret (1989) "Rationality and salience," *Philosophical Studies* 57, 61–77.

Goldman, Alvin I. (1979) "What is justified belief?," in G. Pappas (ed.), *Justification and Knowledge*, Dordrecht: Reidel.

Goldman, Alvin I. (1986) *Epistemology and Cognition*. Cambridge, MA: Harvard University Press.

Good, I. J. (1965) *The Estimation of Probabilities: An Essay on Modern Bayesian Methods*. Cambridge, MA: MIT Press.

Good, I. J. (1983) *Good Thinking: The Foundations of Probability and Its Applications*. Minneapolis, MN: University of Minnesota Press.

Gorman, W. M. (1968) "The structure of utility functions," *Review of Economic Studies* 35, 367–90.

Green, J. (1987) " 'Making book against oneself': the Independence Axiom and nonlinear utility theory," *Quarterly Journal of Economics* 102, 785–96.

Green, J. and Jullien, B. (1988) "Ordinal independence in non-linear utility theory," *Journal of Risk and Uncertainty* 1, 355–87.

Grice, Paul (1957) "Meaning," *Philosophical Review* 66, 377–88.

Groves, Theodore (1973) "Incentives in teams," *Econometrica* 41, 617–31.

Hagen, Ole (1979) "Towards a positive theory of preferences under risk," in M. Allais and O. Hagen (eds), *Expected Utility Hypotheses and the Allais Paradox*, Dordrecht: Reidel.

Hammond, Peter (1976) "Changing tastes and coherent dynamic choice," *Review of Economic Studies* 43, 159–173.

Hammond, Peter (1977) "Dynamic restrictions on metastatic choice," *Economica* 44, 337–50.

Hammond, Peter (1983) *"Ex post* optimality as a dynamically consistent objective for collective choice under uncertainty," in P. Pattanaik and M. Salles (eds), *Social Choice and Welfare*, Amsterdam: North-Holland.

Hammond, Peter (1988a) "Consequentialism and the Independence Axiom," in B. Munier (ed.), *Risk, Decision and Rationality*, Dordrecht: Reidel.

Hammond, Peter (1988b) "Consequentialist foundations for expected utility," *Theory and Decision* 25, 25–78.

Hammond, Peter (1988c), "Orderly decision theory: a comment on Professor Seidenfeld," *Economics and Philosophy* 4, 292–7.

Hammond, Peter (1989) "Consistent plans, consequentialism, and expected utility," *Econometrica* 57, 1445–9.

Hampshire, Stuart (ed.) (1978) *Public and Private Morality.* Cambridge: Cambridge University Press.

Hardin, Russell (1988) *Morality within the Limits of Reason.* Chicago, IL: University of Chicago Press.

Harman, Gilbert (1986) *Change in View.* Cambridge, MA: MIT Press.

Harper, William (1978) "Bayesian learning models with revision of evidence," *Philosophia* 7, 357–67.

Harper, William (1986a) "Mixed strategies and ratifiability in causal decision theory," *Erkenntnis* 24, 25–36.

Harper, William (1986b) "Ratifiability and causal decision theory: comments on Eells and Seidenfeld," *Philosophy of Science Association 1984*, vol. 2. East Lancing, MI: Philosophy of Science Association.

Harper, William (1988) "Causal decision theory and game theory: a classic argument for equilibrium solutions, a defense of weak equilibria, and a new problem for the normal form representation," in W. Harper and B. Skyrms (eds), *Causation in Decision, Belief Change, and Statistics*, Dordrecht: Kluwer.

Harper, William (1989) "Decisions, games and equilibrium solutions," in A. Fine and J. Lepin (eds), *Philosophy of Science Association 1988*, vol. 2, East Lancing, MI: Philosophy of Science Association.

Harper, William and Skyrms, Brian (eds) (1988) *Causation in Decision, Belief Change, and Statistics.* Dordrecht: Kluwer.

Harrison, Ross (ed.) (1979) *Rational Action.* Cambridge: Cambridge University Press.

Harsanyi, John (1955) "Cardinal welfare, individualistic ethics, and interpersonal comparisons of utility," *Journal of Political Economy* 63, 309–21; also in J. Harsanyi (1976) *Essays on Ethics, Social Behavior, and Scientific Explanation*, Dordrecht: Reidel.

Harsanyi, John (1967–8) "Games with incompete information played by 'Bayesian' players," Parts I–III, *Management Science* 14, 159–82, 320–34, 486–502.

Harsanyi, John (1973) "Games with randomly disturbed payoffs: a new rationale for mixed strategy equilibrium points," *International Journal of Game Theory* 2, 1–23.

Harsanyi, John (1975) "Nonlinear social welfare functions: do welfare economists have a special exemption from Bayesian rationality?," *Theory and Decision* 6, 311–32.

Harsanyi, John (1976) *Essays on Ethics, Social Behavior, and Scientific Explanation*. Dordrecht: Reidel, 6–23.

Harsanyi, John (1978) "Bayesian decision theory and utilitarian ethics," *American Economic Review* 68, 223–8.

Harsanyi, John and Selten, Reinhard (1988) *A General Theory of Equilibrium Selection in Games*. Cambridge, MA: MIT Press.

Hart, Herbert and Hampshire, Stuart (1958) "Decision, intention and certainty," *Mind* 67, 1–12.

Hazen, G. (1987) "Does rolling back decision trees really require the Independence Axiom?," *Management Science* 33, 807–9.

Heller, Walter, Starr, Ross and Starrett, David (eds) (1986) *Social Choice and Public Decision Making: Essays in Honor of Kenneth J. Arrow*, vol. 1. Cambridge: Cambridge University Press.

Herstein, I. and Milnor, J. (1953) "An axiomatic approach to measurable utility," *Econometrica* 21, 291–7.

Hey, John (1984) "The economics of optimism and pessimism: a definition and some applications," *Kyklos* 37, 181–205.

Hilton, R. (1989) "Failure of Blackwell's theorem under Machina's generalization of expected-utility analysis without the Independence Axiom," *Journal of Economic Behavior and Organization*, forthcoming.

Hogarth, Robin and Reder, Melvin (eds) (1986) *Rational Choice: the Contrast Between Economics and Psychology*. Chicago, IL: University of Chicago Press.

Hollis, Martin (1987) *The Cunning of Reason*. Cambridge: Cambridge University Press.

Hooker, C. A., Leach, J. J. and McClennen, E. F. (eds) (1978) *Foundations and Applications of Decision Theory*. Dordrecht: Reidel.

Hurley, S. L. (1985–6) "Conflict, *akrasia* and cognitivism," *Proceedings of the Aristotelian Society* 86, 23–50.

Hurley, S. L. (1989) *Natural Reasons: Personality and Polity*. New York: Oxford University Press.

Hurwicz, Leonid (1973) "The design of mechanisms for resource allocation," *American Economic Review* 63, 1–30.

Hurwicz, L., Schmeider, E. and Sonnenschein, H. (eds) (1985) *Social Goals and Social Organization*. Cambridge: Cambridge University Press.

Hwang, Ching-Lai and Yoon, Kwangsun (1981) *Multiple Attribute Decision Making*. Berlin: Springer.

Jackson, Frank (1985a) "Davidson on moral conflict," in E. Le Pore and B. McLaughlin (eds), *Actions and Events*, Oxford: Blackwell.

Jackson, Frank (1985b) "Internal conflicts in desires and morals," *American Philosophical Quarterly* 22, 105–14.

Jackson, Frank (1986) "A probabilistic approach to moral responsibility," in R. Barcan Marcus et al. (eds), *Logic, Methodology and Philosophy of Science*, vol. VII, New York: Elsevier.

Jackson, Frank (forthcoming) "Decision theoretic consequentialism and the nearest and dearest objection," *Ethics*.

Jackson, Frank and Pettit, Philip (forthcoming) "In defence of folk psychology," *Philosophical Studies*.

Jeffrey, Richard C. (1965) *The Logic of Decision* New York: McGraw-Hill.

Jeffrey, Richard C. (1971) "On interpersonal utility theory," *Journal of Philosophy* 68, 647–56.

Jeffrey, Richard C. (1974) "Preference among preferences," *Journal of Philosophy* 71, 377–91.

Jeffrey, Richard C. (1977) "A note on the kinematics of preference," *Erkenntnis* 11, 135–41.

Jeffrey, Richard C. (ed.) (1980) *Studies in Inductive Logic and Probability*, vol. II. Berkeley, CA: University of California Press.

Jeffrey, Richard C. (1983) *The Logic of Decision*, 2nd ed. Chicago, IL: University of Chicago Press.

Johnson, W. E. (1924) *Logic, Part III: The Logical Foundations of Science*. Cambridge: Cambridge University Press.

Johnson, W. E. (1932) "Probability: the deductive and inductive problems," *Mind* 41, 409–23.

Johnsen, T. and Donaldson, J. (1985) "The structure of intertemporal preferences under uncertainty and time consistent plans," *Econometrica* 53, 1451–8.

Kadane, J. B. and Larkey, P. D. (1982) "Subjective probability and the theory of games," *Management Science* 28, 113–20.

Kagel, John H. (1987) "Economics according to the rats (and pigeons too): what have we learned and what can we hope to learn?," in A. E. Roth (ed.), *Laboratory Experimentation in Economics*, Cambridge: Cambridge University Press.

Kahneman, Daniel and Tversky, Amos (1979) "Prospect theory: an analysis of decision under risk," *Econometrica* 47, 263–91.

Kahneman, Daniel, Slovic, Paul and Tversky, Amos (eds) (1982) *Judgement under Uncertainty: Heuristics and Biases*. Cambridge: Cambridge University Press.

Kanbur, Ravi (1987) "The standard of living: uncertainty, inequality and opportunity," in A. Sen, *The Standard of Living*, Cambridge: Cambridge University Press.

Karmarkar, U. (1978) "Subjectively weighted utility: a descriptive extension of the expected utility model," *Organizational Behavior and Human Performance* 21, 61–72.

Karmarkar, U. (1979) "Subjectively weighted utility and the Allais Paradox," *Organizational Behavior and Human Performance* 24, 67–72.

Karni, E. (1987) "Generalized expected utility analysis with state-dependent preferences," *International Economic Review* 28, 229–40.

Karni, E. and Safra, Z. (1986) "Vickrey auctions in the theory of expected utility with rank-dependent probabilities," *Economics Letters* 20, 15–18.

Karni, E. and Safra, Z. (1988) "Behavioral consistency in sequential decisions," manuscript, Department of Political Economy, Johns Hopkins University.

Keasey, K. (1984) "Regret theory and information: a note," *Economic Journal 94, 645–8.*

Keeney, R. L. (1980) "Equity and public risk," *Operations Research* 28, 527–34.

Keeney, R. L. and Raiffa, Howard (1976) *Decisions with Multiple Objectives.* New York: Wiley.

Keeney, R. L. and Winkler, R. (1985) "Evaluating decision strategies for equity of public risks," *Operations Research* 33, 955–70.

Kohlberg, Elan and Mertens, Jean-Francois (1986) "On the strategic stability of equilibria," *Econometrica* 54, 1003–37.

Kreps, David (1988) *Notes on the Theory of Choice.* Boulder, CO: Westview Press.

Kreps, David and Porteus, E. (1979) "Temporal von Neumann-Morgenstern and induced preferences," *Journal of Economic Theory* 20, 81–109.

Kreps, David M. and Wilson, Robert (1982) "Sequential equilibria," *Econometrica* 50, 863–94.

Kyburg, H. and Smokler, H. (eds) (1980) *Studies in Subjective*

Probability, 2nd edn. Huntington, NY: Robert E. Krieger.

Laffont, Jean-Jacques (1988) *Fundamentals of Public Economics*. Cambridge, MA: MIT Press.

Laplace, P.S. (1774) "Mémoire sur la probabilité des causes par les évènements," *Memoires de l'Academie Royale des Sciences Presentés par Divers Savants* 6, 621–56.

Latsis, S.J. (ed.) (1976) *Method and Appraisal in Economics*. Cambridge: Cambridge University Press.

La Valle, I. and Wapman, K. (1986) "Rolling back decision trees requires the Independence Axiom!," *Management Science* 32, 382–5.

La Valle, I, and Fishburn, Peter (1987) "Equivalent decision trees and their associated strategy sets," *Theory and Decision* 23, 37–63.

Lehrer, Keith (1974) *Knowledge*. Oxford: Clarendon Press.

Le Pore, Ernest and Brian, McLaughlin, Brian (eds) (1985) *Actions and Events*. Oxford: Blackwell.

Levi, Isaac (1974) "On indeterminate probabilities," *Journal of Philosophy* 71, 391–418; also in P. Gärdenfors and N.-E. Sahlin (eds) (1988) *Decision, Probability and Utility*, Cambridge: Cambridge University Press.

Levi, Isaac (1977) "Subjunctives, dispositions and chances," *Synthèse* 34, 423–55; also in I. Levi (1984) *Decisions and Revisions*, Cambridge: Cambridge University Press.

Levi, Isaac (1979) "Serious possibility," in E. Saarinen (ed.) *Essays in Honour of Jaakko Hintikka*, Dordrecht: Reidel; also in I. Levi (1984) *Decisions and Revisions*, Cambridge: Cambridge University Press.

Levi, Issac (1980) *The Enterprise of Knowledge*. Cambridge, MA: MIT Press.

Levi, Isaac (1984) *Decisions and Revisions*. Cambridge: Cambridge University Press.

Levi, Isaac (1986a) *Hard Choices*. Cambridge: Cambridge University Press.

Levi, Isaac (1986b) "The paradoxes of Allais and Ellsberg," *Economics and Philosophy* 2, 23–54.

Levi, Isaac (1987) "The demons of decision," *The Monist* 70, 193–211.

Levi, Isaac (1988) "Iteration of conditionals and the Ramsey test," *Synthèse* 76, 49–81.

Lewis, D.K. (1969) *Convention: A Philosophical Study*. Cambridge, MA: Harvard University Press.

Lewis, David K. (1979) "Prisoner's Dilemma is a Newcomb Problem," *Philosophy and Public Affairs* 8, 235–40; also in D.K. Lewis (1986) *Philosophical Papers*, vol. 2, New York: Oxford University Press.

Lewis, David K. (1981) "Causal decision theory," *Australasian Journal of Philosophy* 59, 5–30; also in D.K. Lewis, (1986) *Philosophical Papers*, vol. 2, New York: Oxford University Press, 305–39.

Lewis, David K. (1983a) *Philosophical Papers*, vol. 1. New York: Oxford University Press.

Lewis, David K. (1983b) "Radical interpretation," in D.K. Lewis, *Philosophical Papers*, vol. 1, New York: Oxford University Press.

Lewis, David K. (1986) *Philosophical Papers*, vol. 2. New York: Oxford University Press.

Lidstone, G. J, (1920) "Note on the general case of the Bayes–Laplace formula for inductive or *a posteriori* probabilities," *Transactions of the Faculty of Actuaries* 8, 182–92.

Loomes, Graham and Sugden, Robert (1982) "Regret theory: an alternative theory of rational choice under uncertainty," *Economic Journal* 92, 805–24.

Loomes, Graham and Sugden, Robert (1984a) "The importance of what might have been," in O. Hagen and F. Wenstop (eds) *Progress in Utility and Risk Theory*, Dordrecht: Reidel.

Loomes, Graham and Sugden, Robert (1984b) "Regret theory and information: a reply," *Economic Journal* 94, 649–50.

Loomes, Graham and Sugden, Robert (1986) "Disappointment and dynamic consistency in choice under uncertainty," *Review of Economic Studies* 53, 271–82.

Luce, R. Duncan and Raiffa, Howard (1957) *Games and Decisions: Introduction and Critical Survey*. New York: Wiley.

MacCrimmon, K. (1968) "Descriptive and normative implications of the decision-theory postulates," in K. Borch and J. Mossin (eds), *Risk and Uncertainty*, London: Macmillan.

MacCrimmon, K. and Larsson, S. (1979) "Utility theory: axioms versus paradoxes," in M. Allais and O. Hagen (eds), *Expected Utility Hypotheses and the Allais Paradox*, Dordrecht: Reidel.

Machina, Mark J. (1981) " 'Rational' decision making versus 'rational' decision modelling? A review of Allais and Hagen (eds.), *Expected Utility Hypotheses and the Allais Paradox*," *Journal of Mathematical Psychology* 24, 163–75.

Machina, Mark J. (1982a) " 'Expected utility' analysis without the Independence Axiom," *Econometrica* 50, 277–323.

Machina, Mark J. (1982b) "A stronger characterization of declining risk aversion," *Econometrica* 50, 1069–79.

Machina, Mark J. (1983a) "Generalized expected utility analysis and the nature of observed violations of the Independence Axiom," in B. Stigum and F. Wenstop (eds), *Foundations of Utility and Risk Theory with Applications*, Dordrecht: Reidel.

Machina, Mark J. (1983b) "The economic theory of individual behavior toward risk: theory, evidence and new directions," Technical Report, Institute for Mathematical Studies in the Social Sciences, Stanford University.

Machina, Mark J. (1984) "Temporal risk and the nature of induced preferences," *Journal of Economic Theory* 33, 199–231.

Machina, Mark J. (1987) "Choice under uncertainty: problems solved and unsolved," *Journal of Economic Perspectives* 1, 121–54.

Markowitz, H. (1959) *Portfolio Selection: Efficient Diversification of Investments*. New Haven, CN: Yale University Press.

Marschak, Jacob (1950) "Rational behavior, uncertain prospects and expected utility," *Econometrica* 18, 111–41 ("Errata," *Econometrica* 18, 312).

Marschak, Thomas (1986) "Independence versus dominance in personal probability axioms," in W. Heller, R. Starr and D. Starrett (eds), *Social Choice and Public Decision Making: Essays in Honor of Kenneth J. Arrow*, vol. 1, Cambridge: Cambridge University Press.

Maskin, Eric (forthcoming) "Nash equilibrium and welfare optimality," *Mathematics of Operations Research*.

Maskin, Eric (1985) "The theory of implementation in Nash equilibrium: a survey," in L. Hurwicz, E. Schmeider and H. Sonnenschein (eds), *Social Goals and Social Organization*, Cambridge: Cambridge University Press.

May, Kenneth (1954) "Intransitivity, utility and the aggregation of preference patterns," *Econometrica* 22, 1–13.

Maynard Smith, John (1982) *Evolution and the Theory of Games*. Cambridge: Cambridge University Press.

McClennen, Edward F. (1988a) "Dynamic choice and rationality," in B. Munier (ed.), *Risk, Decision and Rationality*, Dordrecht: Reidel.

McClennen, Edward F. (1988b) "Ordering and independence: a comment on Professor Seidenfeld," *Economics and Philosophy* 4, 298–308.

McClennen, Edward F. (1989) *Rationality and Dynamic Choice: Foundational Explorations*. Cambridge: Cambridge University Press.

McGuire, C. B. and Radner, Roy (eds) (1972) *Decision and Organization*. Amsterdam: North-Holland.

Meeks, Gay (ed.) (1990) *Thoughtful Economic Man*. Cambridge: Cambridge University Press.

Milligan, David (1980) *Reasoning and the Explanation of Actions*. Brighton: Harvester Press.

Miyasawa, K. (1961) "On the convergence of a learning process in a 2 × 2 non-zero-sum two-person game," Research Memorandum 33, Princeton University.

Moore, G.E. (1966) *Ethics*, 2nd edn. Oxford: Oxford University Press.

Morrison, D. (1967) "On the consistency of preferences in Allais' Paradox," *Behavioral Science* 12, 373–83.

Morton, Adam (1987) "Hypercomparatives," manuscript, Department of Philosophy, University of Bristol.

Moskowitz, H. (1974) "Effects of problem representation and feedback on rational behavior in Allais and Morlat-type problems," *Decision Sciences* 5, 225–42.

Mossin, J. (1969) "A note on uncertainty and preferences in a temporal context," *American Economic Review* 59, 172–4.

Munier, B (ed.) (1988) *Risk, Decision and Rationality*. Dordrecht: Reidel.

Myerson, Roger (1978) "Refinements of the Nash equilibrium concept," *International Journal of Game Theory* 7, 73–80.

Nagel, Thomas (1970) *The Possibility of Altruism*. Oxford: Oxford University Press.

Nash, John F. (1950) "The bargaining problem." *Econometrica* 28, 155–62.

Nash, John F. (1951) "Non-cooperative games," *Annals of Mathematics* 54, 286–95.

Nash, John F. (1953) "Two-person cooperative games," *Econometrica* 21, 128–40.

von Neumann, John and Morgenstern, Oskar (1944) *Theory of Games and Economic Behavior*. Princeton, NJ: Princeton University Press.

Nozick, Robert (1969) "Newcomb's problem and two principles of choice," in N. Rescher (ed.), *Essays in Honour of Carl Hempel*, Dordrecht: Reidel; also in R. Campbell and L. Sowden (eds) (1985) *Paradoxes of Rationality and Cooperation: Prisoner's Dilemma and Newcomb's Problem*, Vancouver: University of British Columbia Press.

Nozick, Robert (1974) *Anarchy, State and Utopia*. New York: Basic Books.

Nozick, Robert (1981) *Philosophical Explanations*. Cambridge, MA: Harvard University Press.

Ordeshook, Peter C. (1986) *Game Theory and Political Theory*. Cambridge: Cambridge University Press.

Ortuño-Ortin, Ignacio and Roemer, John (1988) "Implementation with inspection," Working Paper 327, Department of Economics, University of California, Davis.

Pappas, (ed.) (1979) *Justification and Knowledge*. Dordrecht: Reidel.

Parfit, Derek (1984) *Reasons and Persons*. Oxford: Oxford University Press.

Pattanaik, P. and Salles, M. (eds) (1983) *Social Choice and Welfare*. Amsterdam: North-Holland.

Pearce, David G. (1984) "Rationalizable strategic behavior and the problem of perfection," *Econometrica* 52, 1029–50.

Pettit, Philip (1987a) "Rights, constraints and trumps," *Analysis* 47, 8–14.

Pettit, Philip (1987b) "Universalizability without utilitarianism," *Mind* 96, 74–82.

Pettit, Philip (1988a) "The paradox of loyalty," *American Philosophical Quarterly* 25, 163–71.

Pettit, Philip (1988b) "The consequentialist can recognise rights," *Philosophical Quarterly* 25, 537–51.

Pettit, Philip and Brennan, Geoffrey (1986) "Restrictive consequentialism," *Australasian Journal of Philosophy* 64, 438–55.

Pettit, Philip and Sugden, Robert (1989) "The backward induction paradox," *Journal of Philosophy* 86, 169–82.

Pettit, Philip and Smith, Michael (forthcoming) "Backgrounding desire," *Philosophical Review*.

Pietarinen, J. (1972) *Lawlikeness, Analogy and Inductive Logic*. Amsterdam: North-Holland.

Pollack, R.A. (1967–8) "Consistent planning," *Review of Economic Studies* 35, 201–8.

Pollock, John L. (1986) *Contemporary Theories of Knowledge*. Totowa, NJ: Rowman & Littlefield.

Quiggin, J. (1982) "A theory of anticipated utility," *Journal of Economic Behavior and Organization* 3, 323–43.

Raiffa, Howard (1968) *Decision Analysis: Introductory Lectures on Choices Under Uncertainty*. Reading, MA: Addison-Wesley.

Raiffa, Howard and Schlaifer, Robert (1961) *Applied Statistical Decision Theory*. Boston, MA: Harvard Graduate School of Business Administration.

Ramsey, Frank P. (1926) "Truth and probability," in *The Foundations of Mathematics*, ed. R.B. Braithwaite, London: Routledge & Kegan Paul, 1931; also in D.H. Mellor (ed.) (1978) *Foundations*, London: Routledge & Kegan Paul; also in H. Kyburg and H. Smokler (eds) (1980) *Studies in Subjective Probability*, 2nd edn, Huntington, NY: Robert E. Krieger; also in P. Gärdenfors and N.-E. Sahlin (eds) (1988), *Decision, Probability and Utility*, Cambridge: Cambridge University Press.

Rasmusen, Eric (1989) *Games and Information*. Oxford: Blackwell.

Rawls, John (1971) *A Theory of Justice*. Cambridge, MA: Harvard University Press.

Raz, Joseph (ed.) (1978) *Practical Reasoning*. Oxford: Oxford University Press.

Rescher, Nicholas (ed.) (1969) *Essays in Honour of Carl Hempel*. Dordrecht: Reidel.

Resnik, Michael (1987) *Choices: An Introduction to Decision Theory*. Minneapolis, MN: University of Minnesota Press.

Robinson, J. (1951) "An interactive method of solving a game," *Annals of Mathematics* 54, 296–301.

Roell, A. (1987) "Risk aversion in Quiggin and Yaari's rank-order model of choice under uncertainty," *Economic Journal* 97 (Supplement), 143–59.

Roth, Alvin E. (1977) "Individual rationality and Nash's solution to the bargaining problem," *Mathematics of Operations Research* 2, 64–6.

Roth, Alvin E. (1985) *Game-Theoretic Models of Bargaining*. Cambridge: Cambridge University Press.

Roth, Alvin E. (ed.) (1987) *Laboratory Experimentation in Economics*. Cambridge: Cambridge University Press.

Rubinstein, Ariel (1982) "Perfect equilibrium in a bargaining model," *Econometrica* 50, 97–109.

Rubinstein, Ariel (1988) "Similarity and decision making under risk (is there a utility theory resolution to the Allais Paradox?)," *Journal of Economic Theory* 46, 145–53.

Saarinen, E. (ed.) (1979) *Essays in Honour of Jaakko Hintikka*. Dordrecht: Reidel.

Sahlin, Nils-Eric (1981) "Preference among preferences as a method for obtaining a higher-ordered metric scale," *British Journal of Mathematical and Statistical Psychology* 34, 62–75.

Saijo, Tatsuyoshi (1988) "Strategy space reduction in Maskin's theorem: sufficient conditions for Nash implementation," *Econometrica* 56, 693–700.

Samuelson, L. (1988) "Evolutionary foundations for solution concepts for finite, two-player, normal-form games," in M. Vardi (ed.), *Proceedings of the Second Conference on Theoretical Aspects of Reasoning about Knowledge*, Los Altos, CA: Morgan Kaufmann, 211–26.

Samuelson, Paul A. (1952a) "Utility, preference, and probability" (abstract), in *Collected Scientific Papers of Paul A. Samuelson*, vol. 1, ed. J.E. Stiglitz, Cambridge, MA: MIT Press, 1966.

Samuelson, Paul A. (1952b) "Probability, utility, and the Independence Axiom," *Econometrica* 20, 670–8; also in *Collected Scientific Papers of Paul A. Samuelson*, vol. 1, ed. J.E. Stiglitz, Cambridge, MA: MIT Press, 1966.

Samuelson, Paul A. (1966) *Collected Scientific Papers of Paul A. Samuelson*, vol. 1, ed. J.E. Stiglitz Cambridge, MA: MIT Press.

Savage, Leonard J. (1954) *The Foundations of Statistics*. New York: Wiley.

Savage, Leonard J. (1972) *The Foundations of Statistics*, 2nd edn. New York: Dover.

Scanlon, T.M. (1978) "Rights, goals and fairness," in S. Hampshire (ed.), *Public and Private Morality*, Cambridge: Cambridge University Press, 93–111; also in S. Scheffler (ed.) (1988) *Consequentialism and its Critics*, Oxford: Oxford Unversity Press, 74–92.

Scheffler, Samuel (1982) *The Rejection of Consequentialism*. Oxford: Oxford University Press.

Scheffler, Samuel (ed.) (1988) *Consequentialism and its Critics*. Oxford: Oxford University Press.

Schelling, Thomas (1960) *The Strategy of Conflict*. Cambridge, MA: Harvard University Press.

Schick, Frederic (1979) "Self-knowledge, uncertainty and choice," *British Journal for the Philosophy of Science* 30, 235–52; also in P. Gärdenfors and N.-E. Sahlin (eds) (1988) *Decision, Probability and Utility*, Cambridge: Cambridge University Press.

Schick, Frederic (1986) "Dutch bookies and money pumps," *Journal of Philosophy* 83, 112–19.

Schick, Frederic (1987) "Rationality: a third dimension," *Economics and Philosophy* 3, 49–66.

Segal, U. (1984) "Nonlinear decision weights with the Independence Axiom," manuscript, Department of Economics, University of California, Los Angeles.

Segal, U. (1987) "The Ellsberg paradox and risk aversion: an anticipated utility approach," *International Economic Review* 28, 175–202.

Seidenfeld, Teddy (1988a) "Decision theory without 'Independence' or without 'Ordering': what is the difference?," *Economics and Philosophy* 4, 267–90.

Seidenfeld, Teddy (1988b) "Rejoinder," *Economics and Philosophy* 4, 309–15.

Selden, L. (1978) "A new representation of preferences over 'certain × uncertain' consumption pairs: the 'ordinal certainty equivalent' hypothesis," *Econometrica* 46, 1045–60.

Selten, Reinhard (1965) "Spieltheoretische Behandlung eines Oligopolmodells mit Naschfragetragheit," *Zeitschrift für die gesamkte Staatswissenschaft* 121, 301–24, 667–89.

Selten, Reinhard (1975) "Reexamination of the perfectness concept of equilibrium in extensive games," *International Journal of Game Theory* 4, 25–55.

Selten, Reinhard (1978) "The chain store paradox," *Theory and Decision* 9, 127–59.

Sen, Amartya (1970) *Collective Choice and Social Welfare.* San Francisco, CA: Holden-Day.

Sen, Amartya (1973) "Behaviour and the concept of preference," *Economica* 40, 241–59; also in A. Sen (1982) *Choice, Welfare and Measurement*, Oxford: Blackwell.

Sen, Amartya (1982a) *Choice, Welfare and Measurement.* Oxford: Blackwell.

Sen, Amartya (1982b) "Rights and agency," *Philosophy and Public Affairs* 11, 3–39; also in S. Scheffler (ed.) (1988) *Consequentialism and its Critics*, Oxford: Oxford University Press.

Sen, Amartya (1985) "Rationality and uncertainty," *Theory and Decision* 18, 109–27.

Sen, Amartya (1986) "Information and invariance in normative choice," in W. Heller, R. Starr and D. Starrett (eds), *Social Choice and Public Decision Making: Essays in Honor of Kenneth J. Arrow*, vol. 1, Cambridge: Cambridge University Press.

Sen, Amartya (1987) *The Standard of Living.* Cambridge: Cambridge University Press, 59–69.

Sen, Amartya and Williams, Bernard (eds) (1982) *Utilitarianism and Beyond.* Cambridge: Cambridge University Press.

Shackle, G. L. S. (1969) *Decision, Order and Time.* Cambridge: Cambridge University Press.

Shafer, G. (1986) "Savage revisited," *Statistical Science* 1, 463–501.

Shapley, Lloyd (1964) "Some topics in two person games," in M. Dresher, L. S. Shapley and A. W. Tucker (eds), *Advances in Game Theory*, Princeton, NJ: Princeton University Press, 1–28.

Shimony, A. (1955) "Coherence and the axioms of confirmation," *Journal of Symbolic Logic* 20, 1–28.

Shin, Hyun Song (1989) "Counterfactuals and a theory of equilibrium in games," mimeo, Magdalen College, Oxford.

Shubik, Martin (1982) *Game Theory in the Social Sciences: Concepts and Solutions.* Cambridge, MA: MIT Press.

Simon, Herbert (1955) "A behavioral model of rational choice," *Quarterly Journal of Economics* 69, 99–118.

Simon, Herbert (1976) "From substantive to procedural rationality," S. J. Latsis (ed.), *Method and Appraisal in Economics*, Cambridge: Cambridge University Press.

Simon, Herbert (1978) "Rationality as process and as product of thought," *American Economic Review* 68, 1–16.

Simon, Herbert (1986) "Rationality in psychology and economics," in R. Hogarth and M. Reder (eds), *Rational Choice: the Contrast Between Economics and Psychology*, Chicago, IL: University of Chicago Press.

Skyrms, Brian (1975) *Choice and Chance*, 2nd edn. Encino, CA: Dickenson.

Skyrms, Brian (1982) "Causal decision theory," *Journal of Philosophy* 79, 695–711.

Skyrms, Brian (1986) "Deliberational equilibria," *Topoi* 5, 59–67.

Skyrms, Brian (1988) "Deliberational dynamics and the foundations of Bayesian game theory," in J.E. Tomberlin (ed.) *Epistemology, Philosophical Perspectives*, vol. 2, Northridge: Ridgeview.

Skyrms, Brian (1990) *The Dynamics of Rational Deliberation*. Cambridge, MA: Harvard University Press.

Skyrms, Brian (forthcoming a), "Correlated equilibria and the dynamics of rational deliberation," *Erkenntnis*.

Skyrms, Brian (forthcoming b), "Ratifiability and the logic of decision," *Philosophy of the Human Sciences*, Midwest Studies in Philosophy, vol. 15. Minneapolis, MN: University of Minnesota Press.

Slote, Michael (1989) *Beyond Optimizing: A Study of Rational Choice*. Cambridge, MA: Harvard University Press.

Slovic, Paul and Tversky, Amos (1974) "Who accepts Savage's axiom?," *Behavioral Science* 19, 368–73.

Slovic, Paul, Fischoff, Baruch and Lichtenstein, Sarah (1977) "Behavioral decision theory," *Annual Review of Psychology* 28, 1–39.

Smart, J.J.C. and Williams, Bernard (1973) *Utilitarianism: For and Against*. Cambridge: Cambridge University Press.

Smith, Holly (1976) "Dated rightness and moral imperfection," *Philosophical Review* 85, 449–87.

Smith, Holly (1988) "Making moral decisions," *Nous* 22, 89–108.

Sosa, E. (ed.) (1975) *Causation and Conditionals*. Oxford: Oxford University Press.

Spence, M. and Zeckhauser, R. (1972) "The effect of the timing of consumption decisions and the resolution of lotteries on the choice of lotteries," *Econometrica* 40, 401–3.

Spohn, Wolfgang (1977) "Where Luce and Krantz do really generalize Savage's decision model," *Erkenntnis* 11, 113–34.

Spohn, Wolfgang (1978) *Grundlagen der Entscheidungstheorie*. Copenhagen: Scriptor.

Spohn, Wolfgang (1982) "How to make sense of game theory," in

W. Stegmuller et al. (eds), *Studies in Contemporary Economics,* vol. 2, *Philosophy of Economics,* Heidelberg and New York: Springer.

Stalnaker, Robert (1968) "A theory of conditionals," in *Studies in Logical Theory, American Philosophical Quarterly,* Monograph 2, Oxford: Blackwell; also in E. Sosa (ed.) (1975) *Causation and Conditionals,* Oxford: Oxford University Press.

Stegmuller, W. et al. (eds) (1982) *Studies in Contemporary Economics,* vol. 2, *Philosophy of Economics.* Heidelberg and New York: Springer.

Stigum, Bernt and Wenstop, Fred (eds) (1983) *Foundations of Utility and Risk Theory With Applications.* Dordrecht: Reidel.

Strotz, R. H. (1955-6). "Myopia and inconsistency in dynamic utility maximization," *Review of Economic Studies* 23, 165-80.

Strotz, R. H. (1958) "How income ought to be distributed: a paradox in distributive ethics," *Journal of Political Economy* 66, 189-205.

Strotz, R. H. (1961) "How income ought to be distributed: paradox regained," *Journal of Political Economy* 69, 271-8.

Sugden, R. (1986) "New developments in the theory of choice under uncertainty," *Bulletin of Economic Research* 38, 1-24.

Tan, T. and Werlang, S. R. D. C. (1988) "A guide to knowledge and games," in M. Vardi (ed.), *Proceedings of the Second Conference on Theoretical Aspects of Reasoning about Knowledge,* Los Altos, CA: Morgan Kaufmann, 163-77.

Teller, P. (1973) "Conditionalization and observation," *Synthese* 26, 218-38.

Temkin, Larry S. (1987) "Intransitivity and the mere addition paradox," *Philosophy and Public Affairs* 16, 138-87.

Thaler, Richard (1987) "The psychology of choice and the assumptions of economics," in A. E. Roth (ed.), *Laboratory Experimentation in Economics,* Cambridge: Cambridge University Press.

Thomson, Judith Jarvis (1985) "Imposing risks," in M. Gibson (ed.), *To Breathe Freely,* Tokowa, NJ: Rowman & Allanheld.

Tomberlin, J. E. (ed.) (1988) *Epistemology,* Philosophical Perspectives, vol. 2. Northridge: Ridgeview.

Tversky, Amos (1967a) "Utility theory and additivity analysis of risky choices," *Journal of Experimental Psychology* 75, 27-36.

Tversky, Amos (1967b) "Additivity, utility and subjective probability," *Journal of Mathematical Psychology* 4, 175-201.

Tversky, Amos (1969) "Intransitivity of preferences," *Psychological Review* 76, 31-48.

Tversky, Amos (1975) "A critique of expected utility theory," *Erkenntnis* 9, 163-73.

Tversky, Amos and Kahneman, Daniel (1981) "The framing of decisions and the rationality of choice," *Science* 211, 453–8.

Tversky, Amos and Kahneman, Daniel (1986) "Rational choice and the framing of decisions," *Journal of Business* 59, 250–78.

Vardi, M. (ed.) (1988) *Proceedings of the Second Conference on Theoretical Aspects of Reasoning about Knowledge*. Los Altos, CA: Morgan Kaufmann.

Wakker, P. (1988) "Nonexpected utility as aversion to information," *Journal of Behavioral Decision Making* 1, 169–75.

Waldner, Ilmar (1978) "Prolegomena to a theory of rational motives," in C.A. Hooker, J.J. Leach and E.F. McClennen (eds), *Foundations and Applications of Decision Theory*, Dordrecht: Reidel.

Wallsten, T. (1971) "Subjective expected utility theory and subjects' probability estimates: use of measurement-free techniques," *Journal of Experimental Psychology* 88, 31–40.

Weber, Martin and Camerer, C. (1987) "Recent developments in modelling preferences under risk," *OR Spektrum* 9, 129–51.

Williams, Bernard (1973) "A critique of utilitarianism," in J.J.C. Smart and B. Williams, *Utilitarianism: For and Against*, Cambridge: Cambridge University Press; also in S. Scheffler (ed.) (1988) *Consequentialism and its Critics*, Oxford: Oxford University Press, 20–50.

Winter, Sidney (1964–5), "Economic 'natural selection' and the theory of the firm," *Yale Economic Essays* 4.

Yaari, Monahem (1985) "On the role of 'Dutch books' in the theory of choice under risk," Nancy L. Schwartz Memorial Lecture, J.L. Kellogg Graduate School of Management, Northwestern University.

Yaari, Monahem (1987) "The dual theory of choice under risk," *Econometrica* 55, 95–115.

Zabell, S.L. (1982) "W.E. Johnson's 'sufficientness' postulate," *Annals of Statistics* 10, 1091–9.

Zabell, S.L. (1989) "The rule of succession," Working Paper, Department of Mathematics, Northwestern University.

Index

act descriptions, 95-101
agent neutrality, 123-5, 128
agent relativity, 9, 123-7, 130
Allais, M., 49, 50, 115, 145
Allais Paradox, 52, 56-9, 72, 77, 86, 164
allocative mechanism design, 19
  see also decentralization of resource
    allocation
Anand, P., 54, 90
asymmetric information, 176-7, 176-93 passim
attitudes, structure of, 1-2
Aumann, R., 24-6, 28-30, 36, 225, 245, 250,
  251, 306-7, 315
availability of options, 97, 114, 116

Bacharach, M. O. L., 32, 38, 298, 301, 307
backward induction, 34, 281-90
Bales, R. E., 216
bargaining games, 35, 294-314
  axiomatic approach, 294-5
  and beliefs, justification of, 310-11
  existence of rational solution in, 294, 308
  focal point principle, 312-13
  Nash bargaining games, 308-13
  Nash solution to, 294-301
  Principle of Rational Determinacy, 36, 297,
    299, 300, 311
  prominent strategies in, 311-12
  and rationalizability, 308-11, 313
  Rubinstein's game, 313-14
  tacit bargaining (Schelling), 309-10
  and time, 295, 303-5
  trembling-hand equilibrium in, 301-8
Bayes, T., 226
Bayesian decision theory, 11, 25, 105, 110,
  147-9, 154, 220-1, 230-1,
  240
  see also decision theory, folk psychology
behavior norms, 106-9
beliefs, justification of, 211-15, 219, 310-11
Bell, D. E., 77
best-reply principle, 267, 268, 270-2, 279, 281,
  283-8, 292, 301
Bonjour, L., 219
Border, K., 89
Brandenburger, A., 292
Bratman, M., 216
Brennan, G., 174

Broome, J., 5, 9-10, 11, 14, 16, 89, 130, 133,
  138, 144, 145, 146, 165, 174
Brown, G. W., 240

Camerer, C., 88
Carnap, R., 226, 231, 239, 240
Carnapian deliberation, 229-31
causal decision theory, 4, 31, 266-7, 277, 290
causal dependencies, 270-1, 273-5, 277-9, 284,
  287
causality, 30-5, 115-16, 119, 121
Chew, S., 40, 49, 89
Chisholm, R., 219
coherentism, 213, 219, 233
commitment, 273
common knowledge
  and consequentialism, 101, 118
  and informational feedback, 221
  and inductive deliberation, 225-7
  and socialist planning, 176
  and traditional game theory, 2, 265, 298, 300
  and trembling-hand equilibrium, 306-7
common prior probability, 222
common ratio effect, 50
conditional preferences, 74-5
consequences
  admissible descriptions of, 11, 97, 116, 222,
    226, 231-8, 276, 288
  definition of, 83-7
  descriptions of, 95-101
consequentialism, 5-7, 37-8, 60-7, 75, 93-114
  and aversion to information argument, 63-4,
    72-3
  and Bayesianism, 105, 110
  in classical making-book argument, 63
  and causality, 115-16, 119, 121
  and context-dependence, 12-17
  and credal probabilities, 95-101, 118
  in dynamic inconsistency argument, 63
  in ethics, 9-10, 122, 124
  Hammond consequentialism, 7-8, 41, 92-4,
    103, 106-14
  and independence postulate, 7, 92, 113-15
  and non-expected utility models, 60-7
  and nonseparable preferences, 64-7
  and ordinality, 7-8, 94, 100-6, 111-14, 120-1
  proto-consequentialist assumption, 12-17,
    119-22